'A comprehensive synthesis of classic theory and cutting-edge research, *Visual and Motor Cognition in Infants and Children: What Develops and What Stays the Same* is a one-stop shop for novice and expert researchers alike. Lange-Küttner's clear and thorough descriptions are a boon to the field'.

Professor Stuart Marcovitch, *UNC Greensboro, North Carolina, USA*

'The book *Visual and Motor Cognition in Infants and Children: What Develops and What Stays the Same* ties together the development of visual, motor, and spatial cognition in the child: a very much needed endeavour, in the perspective of a unified science of cognitive development'.

Professor Sergio Morra, *Università di Genova, Italy*

VISUAL AND MOTOR COGNITION IN INFANTS AND CHILDREN

This insightful book offers an authoritative yet accessible introduction to the development of visual abilities and motor skills in infants and children. Based on theory and cutting-edge up-to-date research about the development of non-verbal intelligence, it provides readers with essential knowledge about the foundations of typical and atypical development.

Split into two parts, the book begins by describing the development of components of non-verbal intelligence in typical development. Several studies are presented that document the importance of a transition from an object-place to objects-region encoding for proper spatial categorisation. In the second part, the book discusses which of the visual, spatial, motor, imagery, categorisation, memory and planning processes may be affected in children with attention deficit hyperactivity disorder (ADHD), autism spectrum disorder (ASD) and developmental coordination disorder (DCD). Lange-Küttner introduces a *Spatial Model* that integrates object salience, speed and abstraction of spatial patterns of locations, re-occurring at different ages. She also develops a *Spatial Freedom Theory* that argues that spatial containment, constraints and exploration belong together.

The book encourages and stimulates new research ideas by discussing the most important research results to date and identifying new research questions. This text will be of interest to students and instructors as well as researchers in the fields of developmental, clinical, educational and cognitive psychology as well as neuroscience and physical education.

Christiane Lange-Küttner is a senior scientist who investigates spatial concepts and special needs of children. She currently works as Head of the BMBF research project 'INSIDE – Inclusion in and after lower secondary tier in Germany' at the Leibniz Institute for Educational Trajectories in Bamberg and as associate faculty at the University of Bremen, Germany. She is adjunct associate professor at the University of Nicosia, Cyprus. Chris was a post-doc research fellow in the Cognitive Science Lab at the Department of Experimental Psychology of the Free University of Berlin. She then became faculty at the Psychology Departments of the University of Aberdeen and London Metropolitan University, UK, and worked as professor of Developmental Psychology at the Universities of Konstanz and Greifswald, Germany.

International Texts in Developmental Psychology

Series editor: Peter K. Smith, Goldsmiths College, University of London, UK

This volume is one of a rapidly developing series in *International Texts in Developmental Psychology*, published by Routledge. The books in this series are selected to be state-of-the-art, high level introductions to major topic areas in developmental psychology. The series conceives of developmental psychology in broad terms and covers such areas as social development, cognitive development, developmental neuropsychology and neuroscience, language development, learning difficulties, developmental psychopathology and applied issues. Each volume is written by a specialist (or specialists), combining empirical data and a synthesis of recent global research to deliver cutting-edge science in a format accessible to students and researchers alike. The books may be used as textbooks that match on to upper level developmental psychology modules, but many will also have cross-disciplinary appeal.

Each volume in the series is published in hardback, paperback and eBook formats. More information about the series is available on the official website at: https://www.routledge.com/International-Texts-in-Developmental-Psychology/book-series/DEVP, including details of all the titles published to date.

Published Titles

Fathering Across Cultures: Pathways to Childhood Development
By Jaipaul L. Roopnarine and Elif Dede Yildirim

Emotional Development from Infancy to Adolescence: Pathways to Emotional Competence and Emotional Problems
By Dale Hay

Visual and Motor Cognition in Infants and Children: What Develops and What Stays the Same
By Christiane Lange-Küttner

VISUAL AND MOTOR COGNITION IN INFANTS AND CHILDREN

What Develops and What Stays the Same

Christiane Lange-Küttner

Routledge
Taylor & Francis Group
LONDON AND NEW YORK

Cover Image: © Getty Images

First published 2024
by Routledge
4 Park Square, Milton Park, Abingdon, Oxon OX14 4RN

and by Routledge
605 Third Avenue, New York, NY 10158

Routledge is an imprint of the Taylor & Francis Group, an informa business

British Library Cataloguing-in-Publication Data
A catalogue record for this book is available from the British Library

Library of Congress Cataloging-in-Publication Data
Names: Lange-Küttner, Christiane, 1957- author.
Title: Visual and motor cognition in infants and children: what develops and what stays the same/Christiane Lange-Küttner.
Description: Abingdon, Oxon; New York, NY: Routledge, 2024. |
Series: International texts in developmental psychology |
Includes bibliographical references and index.
Identifiers: LCCN 2023044432 (print) | LCCN 2023044433 (ebook) |
ISBN 9780367220686 (hbk) | ISBN 9780367220693 (pbk) |
ISBN 9780429270604 (ebk)
Subjects: LCSH: Motor ability in children. | Child development.
Classification: LCC BF723.M6 L33 2024 (print) |
LCC BF723.M6 (ebook) | DDC 155.4/123–dc23/eng/20231218
LC record available at https://lccn.loc.gov/2023044432
LC ebook record available at https://lccn.loc.gov/2023044433

ISBN: 978-0-367-22068-6 (hbk)
ISBN: 978-0-367-22069-3 (pbk)
ISBN: 978-0-429-27060-4 (ebk)

DOI: 10.4324/9780429270604

Typeset in Bembo
by Deanta Global Publishing Services, Chennai, India

This book is dedicated to Enno Küttner, who lets me do it my way most of the time.

CONTENTS

List of Figures *xii*
Preface *xiv*
Acknowledgements *xv*

PART 1: VISUAL AND MOTOR COGNITION IN TYPICALLY DEVELOPING INFANTS AND CHILDREN **1**

1 Historical Theories on Movement and Visual Abilities in Children 3
1.1 Stage and Field Theory 3
1.2 Subjective and Objective Groupings in the Spatial Field 5
1.3 The Field as a Psychological Construct 11

2 Recent Theories on Movement and Visual Abilities in Children 16
2.1 Neo-Piagetian Theory 16
2.2 Dynamic Systems Theory and Embodied Cognition 21
2.3 Developmental Neural Networks 24
2.4 Conclusions 27

3 The A-not-B Task 31
3.1 Infants Make Curious Mistakes 31
3.2 Object Conservation: The A-Error 32
3.3 Spatial Perseveration: The A-not-B Error 36
3.4 The Occipital Factor: Spatial Coding in the A-not-B Task 39
3.5 Learning in the A-not-B Task 42

3.6 Motor Development and the A-not-B Error 47
3.7 Conclusions 50

4 Motor Development 57
4.1 Motor Development 57
4.2 Spatial Constraints on Motor Development 58
4.3 Spatial Affordances and End-State Comfort 61
4.4 Spatial Objects and Fields in Sports Games 64
4.5 Conclusions 66

5 Drawing and Writing Development 72
5.1 Components of Drawing 72
5.2 Stages of Realism 73
5.3 The Construction of Pictorial Space 74
5.4 The Holistic Object 80
5.5 Fine Motor Skills in Drawing and Handwriting 82
5.6 Drawing, Flexibility and Creativity 86
5.7 Conclusions 89

6 Visual Search in Children 100
6.1 Development of Visual Attention 100
6.2 Principles of Visual Search 101
6.3 The Development of Visual Search 104
6.4 Learning in Visual Search 108
6.5 Applied Visual Search 108
6.6 Conclusions 112

7 Visual Memory Development in Children 118
7.1 Object and Place Memory 118
7.2 Concepts and Hebbian Learning in Object and Place Memory 141
7.3 Scene Memory 149
7.4 Conclusions 154

PART 2: VISUAL AND MOTOR SKILLS IN CHILDREN WITH DEVELOPMENTAL PROBLEMS 169

8 Motor and Visual Abilities in Attention Deficit Hyperactivity Disorder (ADHD) 171
8.1 Cognitive Functions in Children with ADHD 171
8.2 Fine and Gross Motor Skills in ADHD 172

8.3 Spatial Categories in Children with ADHD 173
8.4 Conclusions 176

9 Motor and Visual Abilities in Autism Spectrum Disorder (ASD) 180
9.1 Cognitive Functions in Children with ASD 180
9.2 Development of Spatial and Motor Abilities in ASD 181
9.3 Spatial Categories in Children with ASD 184
9.4 Mapping vs. Stages: Early Visual Realism in Children with ASD 186
9.5 Conclusions 188

10 Motor and Visual Abilities in Developmental Coordination Disorder (DCD) 196
10.1 Diagnosis of Children with DCD 196
10.2 Fine and Gross Motor Skills in Children with DCD 198
10.3 Motor Learning in Children with DCD 201
10.4 Conclusions 203

Index *209*

LIST OF FIGURES

Figure 1.1 The Surreal Spatial Field 12
Figure 2.1 Developmental Increase of the Neo-Piagetian M-Operator 17
Figure 2.2 Neo-Piagetian Models of Drawing Performance 19
Figure 2.3 Neo-Piagetian Model of Drawing Performance 20
Figure 2.4 The Change of the Spatial Field Due to Onset of Reaching 22
Figure 2.5 De-subjectification in Space 23
Figure 2.6 Acceleration of Reaction Times with Repetition 24
Figure 2.7 Neural Networks Learning to Read 26
Figure 3.1 The Increase of Delay Tolerance 34
Figure 3.2 The Switch in the Search Objective from Object to Place 36
Figure 3.3 The What-and-Where Distinction 37
Figure 3.4 The Spatial Field Model: The Emergence of Locations 39
Figure 3.5 Locations in the Spatial Field 40
Figure 3.6 In-the-Moment Success in the A-not-B Task 41
Figure 3.7 Object-Place Binding in the Two-Tables Experiment 42
Figure 3.8 Selective Optimisation with Compensation (SOC) 45
Figure 3.9 Selective Looking of Attenders (in milliseconds) 47
Figure 4.1 Self-selected Playpen 60
Figure 4.2 End-State-Comfort when Passing a Knife 62
Figure 4.3 Intermediate-State Comfort when Drinking from a Sippy Cup 63
Figure 4.4 Spatial Field Control 66
Figure 5.1 Imitation Score Predicts Representational Drawing 75
Figure 5.2 Drawing Object-Place and Objects-Region Binding 76

Figure 5.3 Unfolding of the Third Dimension in Pictorial Space 77
Figure 5.4 Built-in Perspective 3D Models 79
Figure 5.5 3D Earth Model with Three Cubes 80
Figure 5.6 Automated Analysis of Fine Motor Skills 86
Figure 5.7 Practice and Creativity in Drawing 88
Figure 6.1 Increase of Children's Letter Search Time 102
Figure 6.2 Increase of Search Time in Conjunction Search 103
Figure 6.3 Feature and Conjunction Search in Infants 104
Figure 6.4 Feature and Conjunction Search in Children and Adults 105
Figure 6.5 FIFA Rules: The Offside Position 109
Figure 6.6 The Offside Position Search Task 111
Figure 7.1 Visual Memory and Visual Similarity 120
Figure 7.2 Dwelling and Acceleration Strategies in Long Delays 124
Figure 7.3 What-and-Where Interference in the Delay 127
Figure 7.4 Rich and Sparse Retrieval Arrays for Location Memory 128
Figure 7.5 Individual Differences in Object and Place Memory 131
Figure 7.6 Topological and Metrical Spatial Array 134
Figure 7.7 Empty Space, Frame and Metrical Spatial Array 136
Figure 7.8 Object and Place Memory in Empty Space, Frame and Grid 137
Figure 7.9 Direct Visual Mapping of Common Region in Memory 138
Figure 7.10 Object Shape Priority in Spatial Memory of Children and Adults 143
Figure 7.11 Stimulus Sets for Testing Novelty and Repetition in Object and Place Memory 145
Figure 7.12 Object Shape Priority in Children's Spatial Memory of Novel vs. Repeated Memory Sets 146
Figure 7.13 The Structure of a Scene 150
Figure 7.14 Neural Substrates in Children's Scene Memory 153
Figure 8.1 Types of Unsystematic Coding of Spatial Categories 175
Figure 9.1 Unsystematic Common Region Allocation in Children with ASD 185
Figure 9.2 Visual Realism in 4-year-old Nadia's Drawing of a Horse 187
Figure 10.1 Increase of Trail-Making Time in Conjunction Search (Drawing/Walking) 199
Figure 10.2 Motor Learning in Children with DCD 201
Figure 10.3 Binding of the Motor Cortex into the What-and-Where System 203

PREFACE

This book began to take shape in Barcelona, Spain, on the Annual Conference of the Cognitive Section of the British Psychological Society. The then Routledge commissioner Ceri Griffith convinced me to write an English monograph about my research studies which had been published in *Brain and Cognition*, *Journal of Experimental Child Psychology*, *Developmental Psychology*, *Perceptual and Motor Skills*, the *International Journal of Developmental Science*, *Psychology of Aesthetics, Creativity and the Arts*, *Psychological Assessment* and many more. So what appeared to be rather diverse research interests are now brought together in the book *Visual and Motor Cognition in Infants and Children: What Develops and What Stays the Same* on non-verbal intelligence development. Fast microgenetic changes and slow macrogenetic changes of cognition in children are described. The microgenetic changes frequently involve repetition, which often does not enjoy a good reputation in education, but the results are compelling. The *Spatial Model* conceptualises how object salience, speed and abstraction of spatial patterns of locations are integrated in development. The *What-and-Where System* in the brain that controls attention to spatial fields and objects could be revealed to involve a mental transition from object-place to objects-region units in development that can be assessed with the freely available *Common Region Test (CRT)*. I have taken the liberty to let a *Spatial Freedom Theory* gradually develop out of the report of behavioural and neuroscience research which shows that some rules and response patterns in development do not change. The Spatial Freedom Theory explains the pros and cons of spatial constraints and confinement as well as those of spatial exploration. I have also included applied examples such as the utility of play pens and the identification of a player in an offside position in football. Maybe my next book should be about space and emotions.

ACKNOWLEDGEMENTS

I am grateful to Lynn S. Liben, Penn State U, US, for her encouragement and support over the years. She could have done so much more to help me if I would have let her. Sergio Morra, University of Genova, Italy, was the convenor of the poster workshop of my first international research presentation abroad in Stirling, Scotland, as a doctoral student. Amazingly, he discussed a first draft of this book with me over an Italian dinner in Madrid in June this year during the Annual Jean Piaget conference. For decades, Jörg Beringer has supported my research ideas and programming of experiments using Experimental Run Time System (ERTS), which has now transitioned into the *Cognition Lib and Lab* portals for writing and running online experiments. John Hucker at the London Metropolitan University, UK, was amazing and fun to discuss research designs with, being double-qualified as a psychologist and a Visual Basic programmer. I am also grateful to Nelson Cowan, U Missouri, US, for the comments driving improvements to my memory research and for our visit to the musical instrument museum in Brussels discussing research before a flight took each of us home from the European Society for Cognitive Psychology (ESCOP) in Lille, France. Bruno B. Averbeck, NIH/NIMH Betheshda, US, my doctoral student Maren Hentschel and our research on stochastic reasoning in children do not feature much in this book on visual and spatial cognition but I am lucky that we share the same range of research interests. The work as Associate Editor for *Cognitive Development* always gave me an impression of research endeavours that are currently interesting and the Editor-in-Chief Stuart Marcovitch, UNC Greenboro, US, lets me do the editing my way most of the time, too. I also thank my students Nikolay Lütke, Ridhi Kochhar, Lauren Fisher, Rahima Ahmed, Chenelle Beckles (now Collins), Hind Bechari-Martin, Alexandros Semertzi, Sophie Michalovic and Monika Markowska, to name just a few, who embarked on working with me in my research area and advanced it with their ideas and initiatives. The Leibniz Institute of Educational Trajectories, Bamberg, supported me to complete the book in the last months of its production. I thank my family and, on this occasion, especially my competition lawyer son Maximilian who was a young boy when he drew object-place units on the print-out of the paper of Stephen Palmer's Common Region study which I had left on a table in the living room. They all have inspired me in my work, but the mistakes in this book are all my responsibility. Please do let me know if you find them.

All presented studies are published journal articles. No unpublished data is included.

PART 1

Visual and Motor Cognition in Typically Developing Infants and Children

1

HISTORICAL THEORIES ON MOVEMENT AND VISUAL ABILITIES IN CHILDREN

1.1 Stage and Field Theory

Developmental psychologists at the beginning of the previous century often observed their own children, keeping diaries. This has often been objected to because observations are explorative but do not quantify the results. However, observations made in informal situations often lend themselves to new research questions and follow-ups by more systematic investigations. This chapter focusses on the development of the spatial concept in the first year as reported in the extensive observations by Jean Piaget (1954). Piaget was a contemporary of Arnold Gesell who also made qualitative observations but in addition computed quantitative frequencies of behaviours (Gesell, 1946). Gesell had added medical training to his psychology degree and developed a paediatric perspective on children. Hence, one could ask why the first chapter on historical research about spatial concept development does not start with Gesell. The reason is that Piaget was interested in the latest development in physics and mathematics at the time. He described cognitive processes in a way that was later used in cognitive and computational psychology, for instance, detailing the commands that are necessary for the seriation of objects (Johnson-Laird, 1988). This has still been further developed into a spatial layout theory where the arrangement and ordering of objects in a spatial field would determine abstract reasoning (Knauff, 2013). Piaget was not making claims about the brain, but he firmly believed that action was driving conceptual development, not perception (Piaget, 1977; see also Rochat, 2023).

Piaget's aim was to describe children's transition from egocentric perceptions and actions to allocentric cognitive processing: Egocentric cognitive functions relate the objects and their views to the own body, while allocentric representations involve conceptualising the relations between objects and views themselves.

DOI: 10.4324/9780429270604-2

Why would this be important? Allocentric spatial encoding resets causation and responsibilities within the field itself because it can be realised that dynamics are happening between other objects without oneself being involved. To use an example from the social world: The moment when one discovers that the rude language of bullying persecutors is the way they communicate with each other, allegations and threats lose their sting as their statements may only incidentally have something to do with one's own shortcomings. Thus, reckoning with interactions amongst external objects can lead to relief – as is also known from externalisation strategies. Moreover, allocentric encoding resets the stage from taking practical action towards mental planning and anticipation of interventions in the physical and social world. Yet another strand in development is children's increasingly stronger physical force (see Chapter 4) and mental speed that they have at their disposal to influence events towards their own aims and goals.

In the 1990s, relatively isolated theoretical and empirical strands were united into a 'new' discipline termed 'Developmental Science', an analogue to the emerging new discipline of 'Cognitive Science'. In this new area, the cognitive architecture and code of psychological processes were tested in neural network simulations involving fast and hundredfold repetitions (McLeod et al., 1998). At the same time, developmental psychologists became more interested in the real-time learning within one session (Siegler & Crowley, 1991). Thus, both neural networks and real-time learning of children tested what repetition could achieve. This new approach towards repetition also resulted in developmental psychologists taking a real interest in what training can achieve in children. This was and is likely to benefit children enormously.

Developmental Science not only investigates the synchrony of psychological and physiological processes in different age groups, but also claims that egocentric, embodied cognition is an important part of understanding children's development (Thelen & Smith, 1994). This approach relies heavily on technical innovation such as digital assessments as well as eye and motor trackers that can capture children's development on a micro level. Thus, given the ongoing research on the basic 'Piagetian' parameters in visual and motor development, in this first chapter, I am describing the groundbreaking work of Piaget in a selective way. I do not reiterate through the sensori-motor stages as these are well explained in infancy textbooks (e.g. Bremner, 1994), nor do I refer to the pre-operational to concrete and formal-operational stage transitions as they are well described in developmental psychology textbooks (e.g. Siegler et al., 2020). Instead, I focus on the development of spatial concepts for objects, places and arrays.

The development of the object concept is important in computing because machines have problems in identifying objects in pixelated images that do not have defined boundaries, except by contrast. Thus, field theory is an important complement to Piaget's stage concepts as it conceptualises the spatial context of objects. Moreover, it will be shown that conceptualisations of visuospatial fields and areas can occur independently of age, but show similarly in different tasks.

Hence, the reader will see that the problem of spatial conceptualisation repeats itself in the various chapters.

The idea of constant abilities is not new because some intelligence researchers have long assumed that a general intelligence G-factor is innate and unchangeable. However, this strand of research is not what is followed in this book. Instead, the surprise for a developmental psychologist, who is by definition interested in changes that occur with age, is that there are principles and rules in visuo-spatial tasks that do not change as such and that do not produce age differences in the performance pattern in studies with several age groups (Cowan et al., 2010) except for acceleration of mental speed. The notion of re-occurrence was conceptualized as a *representational redescription* (RR) into a different format that is more accessible and allows for children's verbal report of their problem-solving strategies (Karmiloff-Smith, 1992). While Karmiloff-Smith's RR theory did not focus on the process of automaticity that emerges with extended practice as in educational and cognitive psychology, like Piaget she described how automatic processes like reflexes in infancy and habits in childhood come under cognitive control and become multi-component flexible procedures.

Thus, this first chapter lays out the theoretical concept of subject, objects and space that was the basis for the many empirical experiments that were conducted thereafter with larger samples, testing the systematic observations of the improvised experiments that Piaget conducted hiding behind screens, lying on the floor, giving his infants the bottle the wrong way round, etc. For an extensive account of the empirical research, the reader is referred to the comprehensive introductions to infancy that are available (e.g., Bremner, 1994; Lamb et al., 2002).

1.2 Subjective and Objective Groupings in the Spatial Field

In infancy and childhood, the actual real space that a child can control expands, with the possible but counterintuitive consequence that the perceived size of the familiar space shrinks. Thus, we would expect that necessarily infants' concept of the visuo-spatial field would change, and the object concept along with this change. This is exactly how Piaget starts his chapter on the spatial field in his book on the construction of reality in the child: 'It can be said that the formation of the object concept is correlated to the organization of the spatial field' (Piaget, 1954, p. 97). He describes the generation of the spatial field as a developmental process from *practical to subjective to objective* and then to representational space concepts. In the following paragraphs, I focus on the relation between the self and the objects in the spatial field as discussed by Piaget in his chapter on the spatial field and the elaboration of groups of displacements.

For Piaget (1954), space has practical beginnings: Space is useful inasmuch as it serves the infant, who wholly depends on the often randomly occurring actions of others for its own survival. Piaget uses the term 'groups' to describe infants' observed behaviour, referring to the French mathematician Poincaré. A group describes that a constellation of instances remains invariant if, for instance, moved by two hours, or by two metres, amounting to spacetime isometry in the mind. This concept was also put forward by other mathematicians. An example from real life would be that you can move objects in their current arrangement if you move the space that contains them. For instance, if you move a cupboard by a metre, you move all the objects inside and they stay in the same arrangement. Thus, a reference to the totality of space is necessary if displacement of the objects in these groups is envisaged. In cognitive psychology, conceptualising instances in groups was later called 'grouping' or 'chunking', a process that facilitates memory also in adults.

Piaget uses the term groups to describe that in this early phase the infant can perform self-referenced practical action loops where an operation can return to the point of departure constituting close totalities which mathematically define 'a group'. His conclusion is that initially space consists of practical and heterogeneous action spaces and that no spatial field as such exists. In the next stage, such practical actions are combined into contingencies and thus are labelled subjective. Piaget defines this as a new stage of subjective space that is acquired but also limited by the reach of the hand. Thus, the action of the hand would guide the location of the self in space. Clearly, because space is tied to infants' reaching out, this makes a strong case for qualifying it as egocentric space.

However, one may ask whether the spatial field could also be defined by how far an infant is able to look. Most infancy research measures for how long infants are looking at an object close by. With respect to the visual field, it was measured how the width of the visuo-spatial field emerges and develops (Lange-Küttner & Crichton, 1999; Lewis & Maurer, 1992) rather than testing long-distance looking. Although we know from the attachment literature that infants have and need proximity, whether to parents or to relatives or to nursery caregivers (White & Redder, 2015), observations show that infants pay attention to their parents even if they are several metres away. It is currently unclear whether they do this only when they hear their voice, or if infants would also notice them when they could just see their parents at a long distance. Thus, while it is undoubtedly correct that the subjective action space extends at about an arm's length from the infant, their visual field may nevertheless be much larger and this should be highly relevant especially with regards to their perceptual judgements. One could also say that the action space is far more limited than the visual field.

To appreciate Piaget's dialectics of self, objects and space, the spatial field initially may have to be understood as narrowed down. While he states that reaching out towards an object is a first relationship between the child's own movement and the physical world, he persistently rejects that following objects with eyes in visual space could constitute a group. Infancy researchers agree that perceptual development is crucial in the first six months, and even a few weeks can make a large difference (Bremner et al., 2015). However, perceptual constraints were less of an issue for Piaget as he is trying to define when an infant conceptualises a spatial group.

When a young infant notices a parent at a distance, these are visual accommodations that for Piaget are different from groups because they are passive and unconscious; that is, they are following movements, finding positions and estimating distances and depth, but do not involve planned and reversible actions. Piaget uses the analogy of the flat earth theory, where for the medieval observer, stars in the sky were still images and not solid three-dimensional bodies that move in predetermined patterns. Thus, according to Piaget, at the beginning, space is divided up into near space and far space, with near space being the starting point for spatial control that an infant can exert itself compared to the distant, far space.

THE INFANT SELF

Mirror images appear to be culture-specific (Izard et al., 2022) as US children and adults could distinguish mirror images of visual shapes but Amazonian children did not. The Rouge test is the classic test of young children being able to distinguish between themselves and their own body and the reflection in the mirror. Infants are only able to recognise the rouge on their own nose between the ages of 1½ to 2 years (Amsterdam, 1972). However, it seems to be easier for infants to perceive another individual than the literal reflection of oneself. This goes some way to show how difficult it is to define the self. Piaget acknowledges that the child's space is already populated by figures and objects but claims that there is still some symbiotic relationship between the infant's self and the things. This was also confirmed by observational research on the concept of the 'transitional' object beginning at about four months (Winnicott, 1953). Like a parent, a transitional object can soothe and console. Winnicott conceptualises the transitional object as a first *not-me possession* that is under total (emotional) control of the child, also because the transitional object is of a handy size. Thus, the notion of *not-me* would also imply the notion of *just-me*. Beginning in infancy and lasting for several years, children feel great distress when objects that are important to them are withheld or taken away. According to the theory of the transitional object, this would constitute the loss of a dear possession. However, it could be claimed that the important part here would be that the transitional object completes an individual and thus the loss makes one feel incomplete as the object was *part-of-me*. Winnicott claims that when the symbiosis that dissolves between mother and child over the years, the symbolic transitional object is neither forgotten nor mourned nor repressed as it may only diffuse or move elsewhere. Piaget described this kind of object relation as being 'absorbed into things without knowing oneself' (Piaget, 1954, p. 105). Absorption is conceptualised in Psychology as flow experience (Csikszentmihalyi, 2008), or deep selective attention that occurs under perceptual load (Lavie, 1995).

Piaget's position on perceptual processes in the child is quite important to look at because initially infants could mainly use visual and vestibular information which only changes with the onset of locomotion (Bremner et al., 2011). There is a lot of face-to-face contact when infants are carried around in the first months, but measuring infant looking at various images showed that the onset of locomotion in the second year reduces looking at faces and increases looking at objects, for instance, edible ones, or those that are being looked at by others (Dalrymple et al., 2019).

Piaget claims that the self involves being aware that any action on an object also has an effect on oneself. This rather cryptic claim is then followed by a clearer explanation about the status of perception:

> There is nothing to prove that he has the impression of displacing himself as a function of the object; and when his glance, too slow or too fast, loses sight of the object and then recovers it, there is nothing to indicate that the subject is aware of a relationship between two displacements. He has no image of his own movements as trajectories in space and merely has the feeling of always recovering, through his own effort, a visual image that tends to disappear.
>
> *(Piaget, 1954, p. 110)*

It is likely that such a statement was a theoretical argument against research on the priority of perception by Gestalt theory, because, clearly, the words 'through his own effort' indicate an effortful action of the infant to create a more permanent perceptual input. This conclusion is backed up by another statement, where Piaget writes that if an infant directly relates to a moving object and re-adjusts the movement of the eyes and head in such a way as to stare at it (Piaget, 1954, p. 118), it would be impossible to accurately determine whether the group is subjective or objective, as there would be no indicator of awareness being absent or present.

However, Piaget states that if the perceived object is removed from its initial pathway, it is neither rediscovered nor even sought. Especially oblique pathways remain difficult until six months of age (Tham et al., 2020). This non-awareness of infants was also tested by behaviourist researchers. They found that indeed an infant does not have much of a mental representation in terms of memory, however, there are several factors that can help infants to develop awareness. For instance, if all sets of items are presented in the same serial order, this supports a mental representation at three and still at six months while different presentation orders do not yield a mental representation that could be memorised (Borovsky & Rovee-Collier, 1990; Fagen et al., 1984). However, reminders help tremendously, and the more, the better the mental representation (Hayne et al., 2000). Also showing the same set of stimuli in different contexts helps to strengthen its mental representation (Rovee-Collier & Dufault, 1991). For Piaget, however, such a memory that relies on the original percept constitutes a 'reproductive assimilation of sensori-motor memory' which would be neither perceptive nor representational. The child would experience a sort of internal *impression of return or rhythm*, with disappointment and dissatisfaction accompanying these sensations. Moreover, Piaget comments that the infant does in fact not remember a sequence, but has practical knowledge only of the original place. An inhibition of return to the original location and the move of attention to a new location indeed develops only between 3 and 6 months when infants focus on specific places further away than mid space in front of them (Clohessy et al., 1991; Valenza et al., 1994), along with the onset of reaching (Lange-Küttner & Crichton, 1999). The spontaneous development of a robust mental representation that gives rise to active search, memory and action will be explained in more detail in Chapter 3 on the A-not-B task.

Thereafter, objective space and conscious groupings emerge along with the recognition of objects in their own rights, accompanied by the acknowledgement that an object follows an independent trajectory. This new understanding completes the transition from practical space – that is divided up into heterogeneous spaces and varies according to modality (feeding, looking, touching, etc.) – to subjective space where the object is embedded in local eye-hand coordination processes. The condition under which objective space is supposed to become realised in the mind of the child is that children become more agile and the boundary between near and far space breaks down. Piaget (1954, pp. 120 and 155) described the process as the infant being 'displaced as an object among other objects': As the object becomes 'real', the infant also reveals concepts and action plans to an observer. For instance, Piaget describes that at about ten months, his infants repeatedly and deliberately hide objects themselves and retrieve them even when concealed by a screen, or they vary the distance or the angle at which they can view an object. In this way, they form reversible and objective groups of displacements. They also do not just act on things to obtain them, but develop an interest in the properties of the objects themselves as they vary circumstances and observe the different outcomes.

In a next step, infants devise such variations in a sequence of displacements. This ends perseverations to the original place and creates space as a homogeneous spatial field. At the time when infants are arranging objects in complex groups along various planes of depth, the well-known (and sometimes dreaded) constantly repeated successions of throwing away and picking up, balancing and letting fall, nesting and stacking, hiding and finding things emerge. All of these activities explore relations between the objects themselves and constitute an allocentric spatial field.

Finally, infants become able to imagine and envisage invisible displacements which were produced outside the perceptual field. This constitutes the final step which ends the journey from percept to concept in infancy. Anticipation is probably the most important aspect of conceptual thought because once events are foreseen, they can be prevented if dangerous, or welcomed if pleasant. Just in passing, Piaget states in brackets that foresight could also spring from habitual actions (p. 198), and not just from trial-and-error and experimentation. This statement will become important in Chapter 7 on rehearsal in visual memory. Now spatial relationships are not just tested and constructed, but mentally evoked before any action is taken, hence Piaget calls these mental spatial relationships 'representative groups'. This term was later generalised to the term 'mental representations'.

As a more detailed example of the absence of such spatial representation and imagery is needed, Piaget's observation 120 (p. 201) is described here. At the age of one year and three months, his son is able to put a number of objects such as pebbles and toys on a small board. He then wishes to look at the sight from underneath the board and turns it over. As if having no anticipation, he is surprised looking at the scattered toys and rearranges them on the board. Piaget concedes that he may have been distracted or simply unable to keep the board horizontal while looking underneath. However, he repeats the action without modification. Piaget concludes that he did not yet succeed in evoking the event in his mind that would have allowed him to think about a way to prevent the objects from falling down while looking underneath the board. It becomes clear that now much more complex and dynamic situations are at hand than spatial relationships within configurations and arrangements. There are other examples, like his daughter at one year and four months standing on a cushion and trying to lift it at the same time. Piaget claims that this absence of envisioning the spatial dynamics occurs because the child remains outside of the situation, and does not see itself as a part of the situation, that is, seeing herself as an object amongst objects.

Once mental spatial representations are available to the child, hesitations and delays occur that allow toddlers to account for obstacles and plan new itineraries that may be different from the object's pathway. Not only is invisible displacement now conceptualised, reconstructing what has happened, but also an immediate movement is *not* carried out until a reasonable anticipation of the future action can be made. It is certainly not coincidental that children at the age of one and a half years would have learned to walk and set their own itineraries in real life, which should also improve their sense of spatial orientation. Piaget concludes that these toddlers locate themselves in space and can track dynamic movements in a stable context across space and time. This mental spatial representation is then equivalent to a mathematical group insofar as global shifts can be imagined and conceptualised along a spatial or temporal continuum.

In summary, Piaget states that the development of the space concept in the first year of life progresses from an experience of incidental and uncoordinated visual phenomena while being carried around to more stable sensory images when being able to sit. This is followed by reaching out to objects in space, creating a practical space whereby the infant tries to achieve a hold of objects which constitutes a first possession. These are subjective groups in a practical space, equivalent to heterogeneous spatial fields of near and far space. Objective groups emerge once infants begin to experiment with objects and develop strategies to also obtain objects that are beyond reach in far space, breaking down this dichotomy which results in a homogeneous space concept. However, these objective groups are still constrained by what is visible. Another advance towards representative groups must be made in order to be able to imagine and conceptualise and deduce invisible object movements. Piaget (Piaget, 1954, p. 216) states that this gradual development towards a consolidated concept of space requires '*de-subjectification*', an important claim that I have never seen being discussed in the developmental literature, while the terms 'egocentric' and 'allocentric' spatial coding are established terms, especially in spatial cognition research (Burgess, 2006). De-subjectification, according to Piaget, implies that the infant sees and reflects on itself as an object in space. It means that the infant becomes able to interact with objects as an equal and, in this reciprocal way, becomes able to modify its own assumptions and behaviours.

In short, Piaget assumed that children need to conceptualise themselves as part of the world and use the eventual but inevitable resistance of the object and obstacles to modify and develop alternative problem-solving strategies. For instance, the mere act of perception can be problem-ridden:

> While the object does, of course, bring certain of its properties to the situation, various factors hinder its adequate attainment. For example, it may not be immediately perceptible as a whole because it is too big, too complex, or because its context is too complicated; or the duration of its exposure may be so short that it has to be represented by (...) a few encounters; or, if it does arouse several centrations, later ones may override the earlier ones, etc.
>
> *(Piaget, 1969, p. 365)*

Recent empirical research investigated infants' times when looking at natural scenes (Pomaranski et al., 2021): Infants between 4 and 12 months increasingly showed more selective attention and they became more similar in their looking behaviour as an age group, with age explaining 38% of looking behaviour. Moreover, they became relatively less dependent on visually salient regions in terms of colour contrast that nevertheless still explained an additional 18–27% of looking behaviour. Thus, the perceptual factor is not to be underestimated in the first year of life even if its impact on the spatial field conceptualisation is not constitutive.

1.3 The Field as a Psychological Construct

The resistance of the object was conceptualised by Lewin's topological field theory (Lewin, 1936). The main assumption of the field theory was that spatial fields have constraints that are created by internal and external barriers. Lewin (1936) describes that reality consists of such spatial fields and they have zones. A strong spatial field need not be a large one, as a small zone could shake up the entire spatial field. He holds that in spatial topology, what matters are distances, boundaries and obstacles. Size would not matter because in a spatial field, the proportional distance between drops of water and planets would be the same independently of the absolute size. Moreover, the zone could have any shape and contour. Action vectors are connecting destinations in different zones, giving rise to action plans.

If within the area of a spatial field a person experiences failures when trying to reach an aim, this results in frustration (Dembo, 1931). The frustration leads to unpleasant tension and the person tries to evade the situation by leaving the field (‘*aus-dem-Felde-gehen*’). For this consequence, having freedom of movement is essential. If leaving the spatial field is not possible and movement is constrained, there may be an experience of tiredness and a request to get a break, or an abrupt interruption of the time-on-task, or even permanent quitting. Moreover, there may also be also ‘infantile’ reactions such as crying or ranting, showing a lack of frustration tolerance when leaving the field is not an option.

Dembo (1931) suggested that another option is to react with the creation of a surreal spatial field that has some similarities with the real environment but is a mental fiction; see Figure 1.1. The more surreal the spatial field invention, the weaker the limitations, the barriers and its solidity, while the targeted aim would become fuzzy. An advantage of this template-like spatial field is that it would enable one to think about an action plan in more creative ways. A disadvantage of a surreal spatial field is that it could also lead to an avoidance of the constraints in the real field, especially if repeated trials do not lead to success (Dembo, 1931).

Lewin’s and Dembo’s spatial field theory may be seen as belonging to a psychodynamic social psychology research agenda, but there are similar theories in more recent cognitive psychology research even if Lewin’s field theory is not referred to. In computing science, there are symbolic arrays that are derived from spatial layout models (Knauff, 2013). In these models, the features of actual

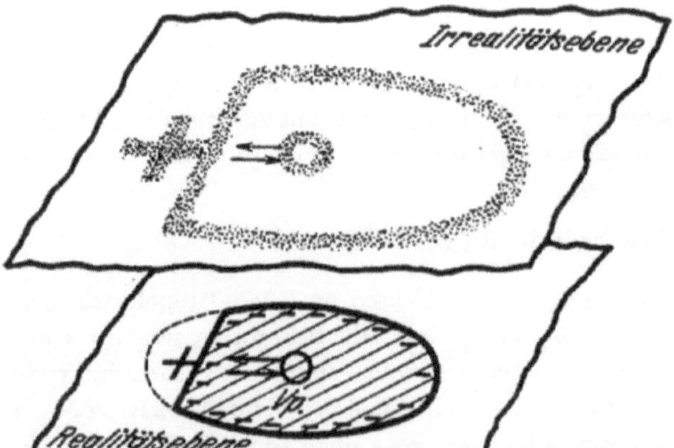

FIGURE 1.1 The Surreal Spatial Field (Dembo, 1931, p. 38). *Note*: Irrealitätsebene = surreal level, Realitätsebene = real level, Vp = participant

objects do not show, but are tagged with links to other virtual databases, while the spatial relations are sparse but allow for calculations or operations.

There are preferred layout models that are used by individuals, e.g. for transitive reasoning about sequences of objects, and they are never really discarded and only modified if failures are experienced. In such spatial layout models, images of objects would distract. Knauff (2013) does not offer visual material, though, but syllogisms that trigger mental processes, especially in the conclusions from the premises which are more likely to produce imagery. The preferred spatial layout model has the opposite starting point to the object files theory (Treisman, 2006) where the object representation is in the focus of the theory. The spatial field just serves as a context of the object's place specified in the object file. Within spatial cognition, there are object-based and space-based theories of attention (Logan, 1996). In this book on vision and motor development, it is important to keep these debates in mind while looking at the developmental sequence from rich objects in implicit space to such sparse spatial arrays (Lange-Küttner et al., 2022).

References

Amsterdam, B. (1972). Mirror self-image reactions before age two. *Developmental Psychobiology*, *5*(4), 297–305. https://doi.org/10.1002/dev.420050403

Borovsky, D., & Rovee-Collier, C. (1990). Contextual constraints on memory retrieval at six months. *Child Development*, *61*(5), 1569–1583. https://doi.org/10.1111/j.1467-8624.1990.tb02884.x

Bremner, J. G. (1994). *Infancy*. Blackwell.

Bremner, J. G., Hatton, F., Foster, K. A., & Mason, U. (2011). The contribution of visual and vestibular information to spatial orientation by 6 to 14-month-old infants and adults. *Developmental Science*, *14*(5), 1033–1045. https://doi.org/10.1111/j.1467-7687.2011.01051.x

Bremner, J. G., Slater, A. M., & Johnson, S. P. (2015). Perception of object persistence: The origins of object permanence in infancy. *Child Development Perspectives*, *9*(1), 7–13. https://doi.org/10.1111/cdep.12098

Burgess, N. (2006). Spatial memory: How egocentric and allocentric combine. *Trends in Cognitive Sciences*, *10*(12), 551–557. https://doi.org/10.1016/j.tics.2006.10.005

Clohessy, A. B., Posner, M. I., Rothbart, M. K., & Vecera, S. P. (1991). The development of inhibition of return in early infancy. *Journal of Cognitive Neuroscience*, *3*(4), 345–350. https://doi.org/10.1162/jocn.1991.3.4.345

Cowan, N., Morey, C. C., AuBuchon, A. M., Zwilling, C. E., & Gilchrist, A. L. (2010). Seven-year-olds allocate attention like adults unless working memory is overloaded. *Developmental Science*, *13*(1), 120–133. https://doi.org/10.1111/j.1467-7687.2009.00864.x

Csikszentmihalyi, M. (2008). *Flow: The psychology of optimal experience*. Harper Perennial Modern Classics.

Dalrymple, K. A., Jiang, M., Zhao, Q., & Elison, J. T. (2019). Machine learning accurately classifies age of toddlers based on eye tracking. *Scientific Reports*, *9*(1), article 6255. https://doi.org/10.1038/s41598-019-42764-z

Dembo, T. (1931). Untersuchungen zur Handlungs- und Affektpsychologie [Psychological studies of action and affect]. *Psychologische Forschung, 15*(1), 1–144. https://doi.org/10.1007/BF00406043

Fagen, J. W., Morrongiello, B. A., Rovee-Collier, C., & Gekoski, M. J. (1984). Expectancies and memory retrieval in three-month-old infants. *Child Development, 55*(3), 936–943. https://doi.org/1130145

Gesell, A. (1946). *Vision. Its development in infant and child.* Hoeber.

Hayne, H., Gross, J., Hildreth, K., & Rovee-Collier, C. (2000). Repeated reminders inrease the speed of memory retrieval by 3-month-old infants. *Developmental Science, 3*(3), 312–318. https://doi.org/10.1111/1467-7687.00125

Izard, V., Pica, P., & Spelke, E. S. (2022). Visual foundations of Euclidean geometry. *Cognitive Psychology, 136*, 1–24. https://doi.org/10.1016/j.cogpsych.2022.101494

Johnson-Laird, P. N. (1988). *The computer and the mind: An introduction to cognitive science.* Harvard University Press.

Karmiloff-Smith, A. (1992). *Beyond modularity. A developmental perspective on cognitive science.* MIT Press.

Knauff, M. (2013). *Space to reason.* MIT Press.

Lamb, M. E., Bornstein, M. H., & Teti, D. M. (2002). *Development in infancy* (4th ed.). Lawrence Erlbaum.

Lange-Küttner, C., Collins, C., Ahmed, R. K., & Fisher, L. E. (2022). Rich and sparse figurative information in children's memory for colorful places. *Developmental Psychology, 59*(2), 256–271. https://doi.org/10.1037/dev0001483

Lange-Küttner, C., & Crichton, M. T. (1999). Change of spatial field effects in 16- to 20-week-old infants. *Brain and Cognition, 39*(2), 75–92. https://doi.org/10.1006/brcg.1998.1059

Lavie, N. (1995). Perceptual load as a necessary condition for selective attention. *Journal of Experimental Psychology: Human Perception and Performance, 21*(3), 451–468. https://doi.org/10.1037/0096-1523.21.3.451

Lewin, K. (1936). *Principles of topological psychology.* Reprint 2013 by Read Books Ltd.

Lewis, T. L., & Maurer, D. (1992). The development of the temporal and nasal visual fields during infancy. *Vision Research, 32*(5), 903–911. https://doi.org/10.1016/0042-6989(92)90033-F

Logan, G. D. (1996). The CODE theory of visual attention. An integration of space-based and object-based attention. *Psychological Review, 103*, 603–649. https://doi.org/10.1037/0033-295X.103.4.603

McLeod, P., Plunkett, K., & Rolls, E. T. (1998). *Introduction to connectionist modelling of cognitive processes.* Oxford University Press.

Piaget, J. (1954). *The construction of reality in the child.* Routledge and Kegan Paul.

Piaget, J. (1969). *The mechanisms of perception.* Routledge and Kegan Paul.

Piaget, J. (1977). The role of action in the development of thinking. In F. W. Overton & J. MacCarthy Gallagher (Eds.), *Knowledge and development. Vol. 1, advances in research and theory* (pp. 17–42). Plenum Press.

Pomaranski, K. I., Hayes, T. R., Kwon, M.-K., Henderson, J. M., & Oakes, L. M. (2021). Developmental changes in natural scene viewing in infancy. *Developmental Psychology, 57*(7), 1025–1041. https://doi.org/10.1037/dev0001020

Rochat, P.(2023). The evolution of developmental theories since Piaget: A metaview. *Perspectives on Psychological Science.* https://doi.org/10.1177/17456916231186611

Rovee-Collier, C., & Dufault, D. (1991). Multiple contexts and memory retrieval at three months. *Developmental Psychobiology, 24*(1), 39–49. https://doi.org/10.1002/dev.420240104

Siegler, R. S., & Crowley, K. (1991). The microgenetic method: A direct means for studying cognitive development. *American Psychologist, 46*(6), 606–620. https://doi.org/10.1037/0003-066X.46.6.606

Siegler, R. S., Saffran, J., Gershoff, E., Eisenberg, N., & DeLoache, J. (2020). *How children develop*. Macmillan Learning.

Tham, D. S. Y., Rees, A., Bremner, J. G., Slater, A., & Johnson, S. P. (2020). Orientation effects in the development of linear object tracking in early infancy. *Child Development, 92*(1), 324–334 https://doi.org/10.1111/cdev.13419

Thelen, E., & Smith, L. B. (1994). *A dynamic systems approach to the development of cognition and action*. MIT Press.

Treisman, A. (2006). Object tokens, binding and visual memory. In H. D. Zimmer, A. Mecklinger, & U. Lindenberger (Eds.), *Handbook of binding and memory* (pp. 315–338). Oxford University Press.

Valenza, E., Simion, F., & Umiltà, C. (1994). Inhibition of return in newborn infants. *Infant Behavior and Development, 17*(3), 293–302. https://doi.org/10.1016/0163-6383(94)90009-4

White, E. J., & Redder, B. (2015). Proximity with under two-year-olds in early childhood education: A silent pedagogical encounter. *Early Child Development and Care, 185*(11–12), 1783–1800. https://doi.org/10.1080/03004430.2015.1028386

Winnicott, D. (1953). Transitional objects and transitional phenomena — A study of the first Not-Me possession. *International Journal of Psycho-Analysis, 34*, 89–97.

2

RECENT THEORIES ON MOVEMENT AND VISUAL ABILITIES IN CHILDREN

2.1 Neo-Piagetian Theory

The Neo-Piagetian approach operationalised Piaget's developmental model by separating several possible causes of development and identifying these factors with alphabetical letters (Morra et al., 2008). Pascual-Leone called his theory 'Theory of Constructive Operators' whereby the operators are not robots as the uninitiated may presume, but psychological and organismic factors that contribute to the development of pre-operational and operational thinking (Pascual-Leone & Goodman, 1979). An aspect that should not be underestimated is that the multitude of factors are often interacting in a complicated and non-obvious manner. In this way, Neo-Piagetian theory opened the door of Piaget's theory that used to be spelled out by qualitative observational methods and the clinical interview to the modern world of statistical analysis. Moreover, there are 'organismic' factors that were only mentioned *en passant* when describing individual children and that were not part of Piaget's theory (Pascual-Leone, 1976b). Whereas Piaget was interested in the meaning of the errors that children made as they allowed researchers to re-construct their belief system and task approach, Pascual-Leone requests a task analysis that shows which items are easy and which are difficult.

The Neo-Piagetian operational factors relate to Piaget's schematic and structural model of cognitive schemes (units). The constructive operators are the **C-operator** (*C*ontent learning), the **M-operator** (*M*ental attentional energy), the **I-operator** (*I*nterrupt), the **F-operator** (*F*ield), the **B-operator** (*B*ias and *B*elieve), and the **A-operator** (*A*ffect) (Pascual-Leone & Goodman, 1979). The **L-operator** (*L*earning, LC and LM) is a constructive operator that Pascual-Leone (1976a) mentions with respect to 'graded learning loops' in education. He assumes that if children fail already when easy items are used, for instance,

DOI: 10.4324/9780429270604-3

because they use figurative schemes that are not helpful, successive retesting of items can provide a basis from which the more difficult problems are solved automatically. This belief is based on the assumption that repeated presentations saturate perceptual learning and divert attention to a more advanced strategy.

Important for the focus of the present monograph on spatial context and spatial fields is that Pascual-Leone assumed an **F-operator** (*F*ield) that conceptualises field dependence or independence. The F-factor measures whether the child can override distracting perceptual impressions with its own conceptualisations (Pascual-Leone, 1989). Children's dominating reliance on cues from the environment is seen as a field-dependent attitude that prevents learning (Case & Pascual-Leone, 1975). The I-operator (*I*nhibition) denotes cognitive inhibition and interruption, and an **E-operator** (*E*xecutive) measures executive attention. However, the best known and most often measured one of all the neo-Piagetian factors is the M-operator, which assesses the increase in information processing capacity as the child matures.

There is a very clear schedule of the development of the attentional M-capacity in the sensori-motor period (Morra et al., 2008), see Figure 2.1, ranging from zero energetic units *e* which would be equivalent to not being able to do anything in the first four weeks, to a maximum capacity of 6 units at 36 months. The age scale is not equidistant but this should not concern us here. After these early years, increases in M-capacity occur at a slower pace every two years. This

	M Capacity	
Age	*e*	*e + k*
0–1 month	0	
1–4 months	1	
4–8 months	2	
8–12 months	3	
12–18 months	4	
18–26 months	5	
26 months–3 years	6	
3–5 years	7?	*e* + 1
5–7 years		*e* + 2
7–9 years		*e* + 3
9–11 years		*e* + 4
11–13 years		*e* + 5
13–15 years		*e* + 6
after 35–40 years		in decline

Note: The ages indicated are approximate values and relative to the population average. Certainly individual differences exist related to early or late maturation. The figure "7?" in the *e* column indicates that how *M* Capacity grows in terms of sesorimotor tasks after 3 years of age is not clearly determined.

FIGURE 2.1 Developmental Increase of the Neo-Piagetian M-Operator (Morra et al., 2008)

appears to be similarly arbitrary, as also in the fourth year of life important abilities such as inhibition develop (e.g. Gerstadt et al., 1994; Jones et al., 2003). M capacity is now denoted as $e + k$, where only k increases. The term k represents the number of operative and figurative schemes that can be activated simultaneously. Each unit is equivalent to one processing step in a task. Processing steps can be of a different quality in every task, yet they allow for dissecting a task into different components, which require the activation of a scheme. The important message here is that, while the operators describe the various qualitative types of processes that are going on when solving a task, they themselves are quantifiable. Because the factors are quantifiable, additional tasks are needed to measure them. For instance, when analysing a task such as the Piagetian water-level task, where children are drawing a tilted container but initially cannot depict the horizontal flow of imagined liquid in this tilted container, task components are the field operator *F* and the memory operator *M*, as well as physics knowledge (Morra, 2008). The M and F operators alone were responsible for drawing the flow in easy positions of the bottle (vertical and horizontal), while physics knowledge, in addition, predicted drawings of flow when the bottle was tilted into oblique positions. Thus, an impact of long-term knowledge occurred only in the more difficult versions of the task.

Interestingly, in a daring step across a theoretical abyss, Pascual-Leone revolutionised Piaget's theory by adopting a 'simple', quasi-behaviorist *S-R* subsystem, an abbreviation which could have meant stimulus-response system. However, *S* stands for 'simulation', while *R* would indeed denote the response behaviour. *S-R* repetition loops can establish habits as in the A-not-B search task (Chapter 3) but can also improve spatial memory as in what-and-where memory tasks (Chapter 7).

The many operators of Neo-Piagetian theory also allow for relatively large studies that analyse the pathways between components. As an example, Panesi and Morra (2018) were interested in the question of whether the development of drawing in children is determined by language or rather by planning and executive skills (see Chapter 6). The researchers outlined several possible models; see Figure 2.2. Memory constitutes the M-operator, inhibition, shifting and updating the E-operator, but language and drawing do not have an operator allocated.

In model a, drawing is influenced by language and simultaneously by the M and the E operators. In model b, drawing is not influenced by language but only by executive skills and working memory. In model c, language is a mediator of working memory and executive skills which do not have a direct impact on drawing. In model d, all factors correlate, while in model e this is also the case but without language having an impact on drawing. Model f is similar to model c but M and E operators are having a separate influence on language which then impacts on drawing. In model g, the M operator shows prior influence on the E operators which then impact on both language and drawing. Model h is the same as model g, but without language having an influence on drawing. Finally,

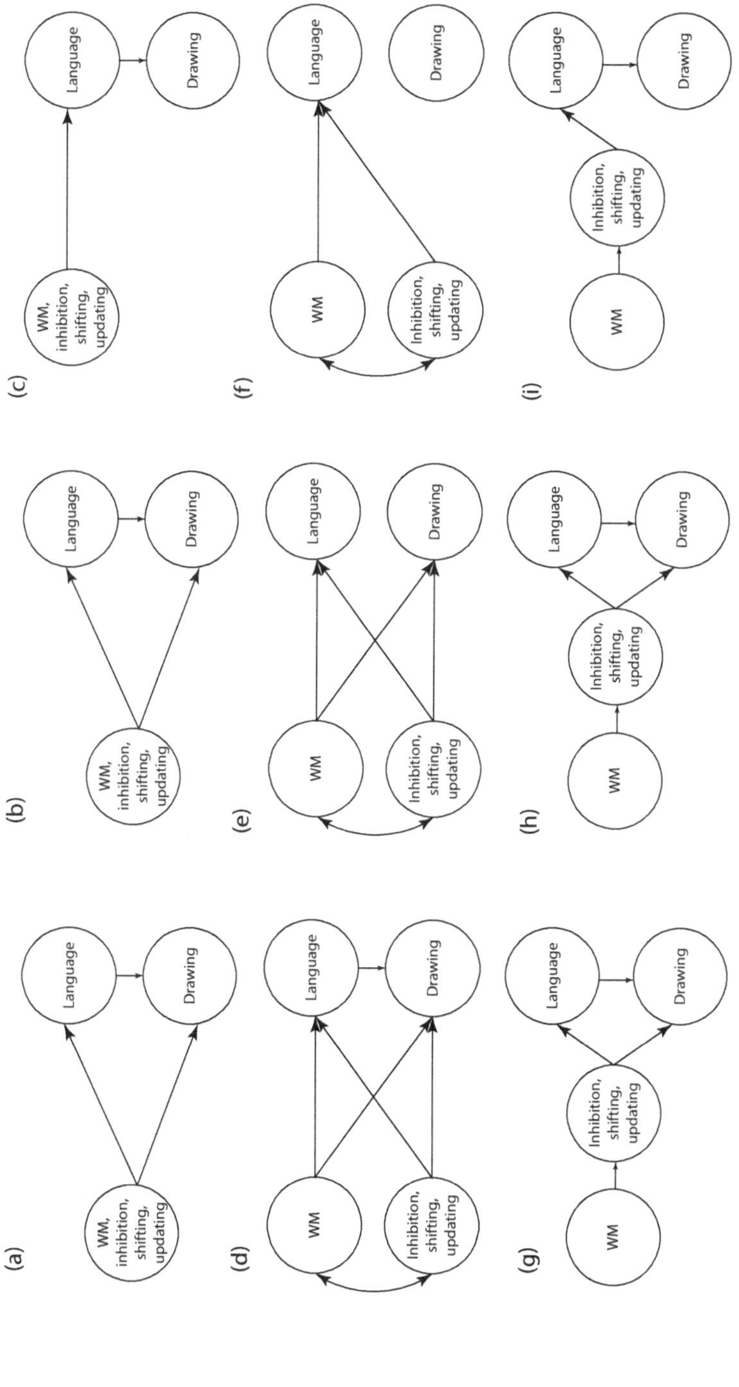

FIGURE 2.2 Neo-Piagetian Models of Drawing Performance (Panesi & Morra, 2018). WM = Working Memory

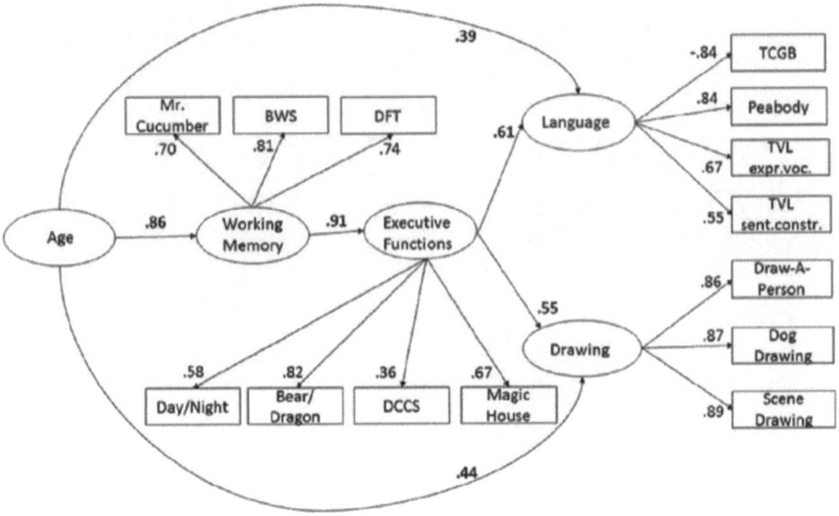

FIGURE 2.3 Neo-Piagetian Model of Drawing Performance (Panesi & Morra, 2022)

Note: BWS = Backward Word Span; DFT = Direction Following Task; DCCS = Dimensional Change Card Sorting; Peabody = Peabody Picture Vocabulary test; TCGB = Test of Grammar Comprehension for Children; TVL exp. voc. = Language Evaluation Test – Expressive Vocabulary; TVL sent. constr. = Language Evaluation Test – Spoken Sentences.

model i is also the same as model g, but without executive skills having a direct impact on drawing. Age is not included in any of the models.

These models were actually tested with an empirical sample of 3- to 6-year-old children (Panesi & Morra, 2022). Each factor was assessed with several tasks, for instance, drawing was assessed with established tests, the Goodenough's Draw-A-Person test, a Dog Drawing task and a Scene Drawing task that consists of a girl standing in a park near to a tree and another one of two boys shaking hands in a park with a fence just behind them. All in all, there were 14 tasks. After testing several of the pathway models, the final model resembles model h, without language having an impact on drawing; see Figure 2.3.

In addition, Panesi and Morra (2022) find that there is a direct influence of age on both language and drawing, respectively. It can be assumed here that other variables such as fine motor skills, which become more practiced with age, may play a role (Simpson et al., 2019). Thus, the conclusion would be that language ability does not play an important role for drawing at this age, even if, like drawing, the language faculty also depends on executive functions. But it is completely clear that memory for plans and categories does have an impact on drawing, which confirms the approach of Freeman that children have strategies (Freeman, 1980) and we need to distinguish between product and process (Freeman, 1972).

2.2 Dynamic Systems Theory and Embodied Cognition

That cognitive development consists of several components is also a theme of the dynamic systems theory. The dynamic systems theory measures and tests the integration of different domains and systems in the child. Especially in infancy and the first four years, multiple systems are developing at the same time, body size and weight, vision, language and so forth but they are not in complete synchrony. There are individual differences, for instance, in the onset of independent movement 'late walkers' (Chaplais & Macfarlane, 1984), or in the onset of articulation and speech 'late talkers' (Rescorla, 2011). While there may be neurological deficits which merit paediatricians' attention, very often apparently banal everyday reasons exist. For instance, about half of the sample of late walkers had 'idiopathic' reasons, to use a paediatric term for a psychological reason, and about half of these 'idiopathic' late walkers used a technique called 'bottom shuffle' to get ahead, which avoids the use of the legs for crawling or walking (Chaplais & Macfarlane, 1984). Late talkers often showed extensive use of gestures in communication at the expense of articulation and so became 'late bloomers' (Rescorla, 2011). One stunning difference between motor and mental development is that skills that support one way of moving do not necessarily support the next stage of getting ahead (Adolph, 2008).

The groundbreaking dynamic systems theory of Thelen and Smith (1994) introduced such physical factors into psychological studies, following a critical assessment of the work of Arnold Gesell (Thelen & Adolph, 1992, 1994). The dynamic systems theory also shifted the empirical focus from single main effects such as maturation to interactions. For instance, Piaget had assumed that infant behaviour develops as innate reflexes become gradually better controlled but would not completely disappear (Piaget, 1954; Thelen & Fisher, 1982). Thelen could demonstrate that the 'vanished' early stepping reflex could be elicited again when 7-month-old infants were placed on a treadmill (Thelen, 1986). She could also show that increasing body weight by adding iron weights suppressed the stepping reflex, while placing infants into waist-deep water relieved the body weight and released the stepping reflex (Thelen et al., 1984).

Infant reflexes can also re-emerge in adult neuropsychological conditions. For instance, the tonic neck reflex that turns the head right towards the mother who carries the baby close to the heart suppresses the scanning of the entire visual field but can also occur in stroke patients with visuo-spatial neglect (Lange-Küttner, 2018). The tonic neck reflex usually disappears between four and five months with the onset of reaching, at a time when binocular depth perception develops. The innate tonic neck reflex disappears in the same way as in the rehabilitation of adult stroke patients, namely by reaching into the neglected side of the spatial field, which is usually the left side (Lange-Küttner & Crichton, 1999).

The important aspect in such dynamic systems studies is that perceptual and motor systems interact rather than develop in isolation. While infants initially reach bimanually simultaneously with both outstretched and stiff arms for an object in the peripheries of the visual field, they week-by-week discover how to catch a toy in front of them; see Figure 2.4. For this reason, infants begin to prefer

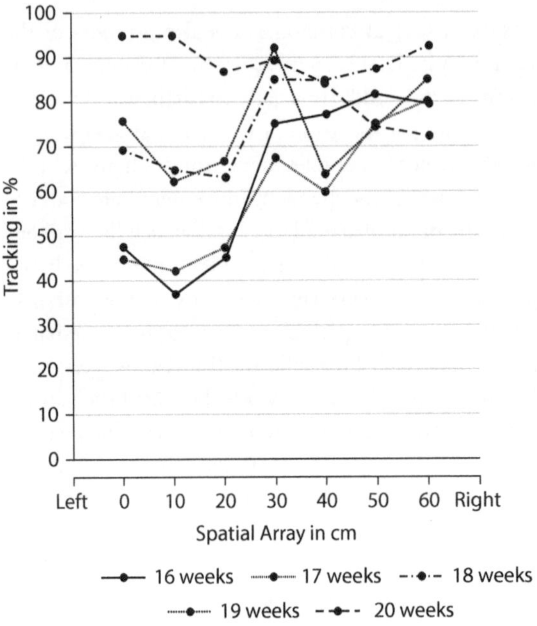

FIGURE 2.4 The Change of the Spatial Field Due to Onset of Reaching (Lange-Küttner & Crichton, 1999)

mechanical objects with a straight pathway over wayward real animals such as a hamster (Crichton & Lange-Küttner, 1999). The reaching for an object when it is close and in front of the infant requires (1) control of arousal due to proximity, (2) eye–hand coordination for reaching and (3) the control of the object's movement direction, that is, from where the object is coming and to where it is going. This segments the visual field into a left and a right spatial field which appears to support the emergence of binocular rivalry in the brain and the onset of depth perception.

While the Dynamic Systems Theory is quite clear insofar as, like in the Neo-Piagetian theory, there are multiple factors determining development, the Embodied Cognition theory is more far-reaching as it aims to revise Descartes' theorem (Descartes, 1644). It states that only because we think, do we exist. Descartes' priority of mind over body is disputed by Embodied Cognition theory. There are at least two reasons why Embodied Cognition became very successful and productive in re-evaluating existing psychological experiments (Goldinger et al., 2016; Wilson, 2002). One reason is the discovery of mirror neurons that become active over the implicit function of perceived objects, or allow to imagine a scene described in a sentence (Caramazza et al., 2014). This perception-action link in the brain without action taking place in the real world pointed to sensory origins of cognition rather than abstractions taking place. The second reason was that an Embodied Cognition theory became a necessary development as robotics came to its limits. It turned out that just knowing about brain systems would not suffice to build a robot that could be a counterpart to a human agent (Brooks et al., 2012) as human brain processes are much slower than those of a computer and neural networks. While in a car factory, an arm would suffice to build parts into an automobile, in many other fields such as an office, the robot needed a body (Brooks, 1991). Thus, at some point, research in psychology and cognitive science had to reflect the impact not just of ongoing motor control and eye-hand coordination, but of the central nervous system and the sensory interface of the whole body. In particular, the robot needed what Brooks made an especially contentious claim about, namely, that intelligence without representations and reason would be needed in embodied cognition because robots first needed to carefully map the world (Brooks, 1995). While a computer system could win against a human in games using small grids like in chess and Go by following clear rules of the game (Gobet et al., 2004), the world and its environment proved to be more challenging. For instance, when there were no rules on how to colour-in places of a grid when taking turns with the computer system, humans were intentionally building pathways and areas and not acting randomly like the computer, which could not behave otherwise (Lange-Küttner & Beringer, 2022). Instead, they immediately began to structure the grid in a way that made sense to them.

Embodied cognition theory was also set into reality in educational projects (Fugate et al., 2019). One especially relevant study in the current context is a space experiment in a virtual environment where 12- to 13-year-olds were briefed that they were asteroids in a solar system (Abrahamson & Lindgren, 2014); see Figure 2.5. In Chapter 1, it was described that Piaget assumed that a homogeneous space concept could be achieved through *de-subjectification whereby the child becomes an object amongst objects*. In the setup, a floor-projected image was linked to the movement of the asteroid and the task was to accurately predict

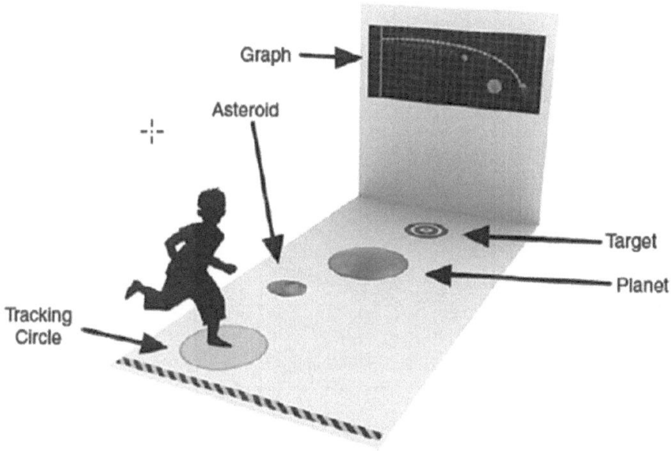

FIGURE 2.5 De-subjectification in Space (Abrahamson & Lindgren, 2014)

the movement of the asteroid by walking the correct path. The experimental parameters of position, speed and angle could be varied leading to differences in acceleration, velocity and gravitation force. When compared with a desktop version (Lindgren et al., 2016), teenagers in the embodied condition showed significantly better understanding of physics concepts. They also identified more with a science approach, with a medium effect size of .43, which is a good indicator of a change in attitude towards understanding space as a force field.

2.3 Developmental Neural Networks

It was mentioned that the blood flow in the human brain would be slower than information processing in a computer processor. One could also say that in children, reaction times are slower than in adults, while in adults, reaction times are slower than in a computer system. Robert Kail dedicated his entire career to prove that the slope of acceleration of reaction times would be similar across different tasks and hence the only relevant factor in development would be mental speed (Kail, 1993).

Kail found that he could train children up to adult levels; for instance, 11-year-old children were paid to get trained in 3,360 trials in 11 sessions to discriminate between correct and mirror images of rotated letters, that is, they were trained in a mental rotation task (Kail & Park, 1990). However, even in these experienced school children, about 2,000 trials were required to close the gap with adults; see Figure 2.6. It turned out that this training was item-specific and did not transfer to other shapes.

This sort of training is typical for neural networks run on computer systems. Neural networks can solve tasks in a few minutes that require several years until children have the capacity to solve them. But if children can redescribe and reformat their representations over the years (Karmiloff-Smith, 1992) on a macro-genetic level, would it not be possible for them to do the same on a micro-genetic level? After all, at some point in development, children also become convinced of the concept of rehearsal, which consists of internal repetition of words or visuals in order to remember more efficiently (Jarrold & Tam, 2010).

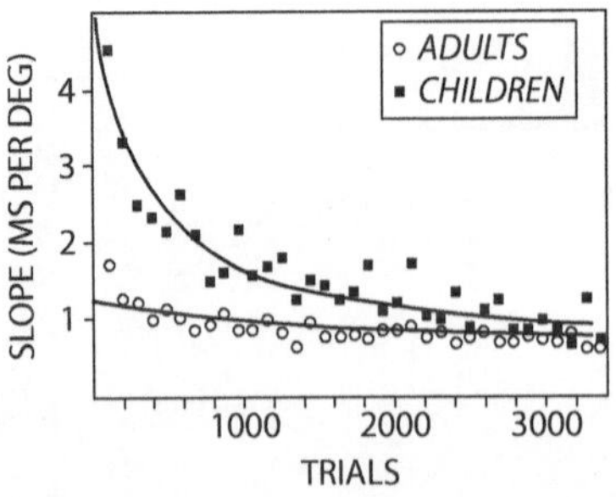

FIGURE 2.6 Acceleration of Reaction Times with Repetition (Kail & Park, 1990)

However, there is more to the idea of internal loops of information rehearsal since the technological development enabled to digitally simulate memory loops into their thousands (Plunkett & Elman, 1997). Encoded numerical values flow through a network of binary nodes from an input layer to an output layer with optional hidden layers in between that can transform the input. Recycling loops equivalent to working memory continue to adapt the content of the hidden transformational layers. It becomes clear at this point that Neo-Piagetian task analysis can be useful when building a neural network architecture that is supposed to produce a solution to a problem.

For instance, for perfect memory, there needed to be 200 swipes of direct mapping between input and output without any hidden transformational layers in between as they in fact drastically reduced memory performance (Lange-Küttner, 2011). In contrast, for other tasks such as learning the fingering of a tone on a flute as output (motor response) according to musical notes as input (visual perception), transformational layers were essential (Lange-Küttner & Finn, 2008) as they can categorise the input that needs to be changed from one system to another. In the flute example, the first hidden layer in the network processed the lower pitch tones and the semitones when learning to play an interval, while a second hidden layer transformed the notation into an appropriate fingering. After practising 5,000 swipes, the trained network could successfully play a song without further modification of its cognitive architecture. Thus, here is a principle that neural networks can reveal: Some inputs are better remembered as they are (mapping; rote learning), while others need more transformative processing steps (chunking; grouping), reducing the cognitive load of the material.

It is also extremely useful to have a look at the kind of neural network architectures that can solve a task with the least complex specifications. In a cross-cultural comparison of Scottish and German school beginners, it was investigated whether word memory would have an influence on learning to read (Lange-Küttner, 2005): British children showed a word structure effect with familiar words read best, rhymed words somewhat less well and novel scrambled words read the least well. This was not the case in the German children. Instead, they read familiar and novel words better than rhymed words. This question was not trivial, as there was a longstanding debate about the depth of English orthography and pronunciation in comparison to the transparency of other languages such as German (Ziegler & Goswami, 2006). Thus, in another study, it was tested whether children's word memory in the auditory or the visual modality was related to their reading (Lange-Küttner & Krappmann, 2011). Gathercole and Baddeley (1993) had assumed that the reason for good reading of novel words in German and Scandinavian children would be that they start school later at age six, while the Scottish children started school at age four. Hence, German children would be less exposed to written words and the visual modality, while they would have a larger auditory vocabulary that would benchmark what 'sounds right' (McKague et al., 2001). This turned out to be true, as visual word memory predicted reading in British children, while auditory word memory predicted reading in German children. Given that the working memory model has two sub-systems, the phonological loop and the visual-spatial sketchpad (Baddeley, 1986), neural networks were run in order to explore whether two memory systems would be needed to support learning to read number words, with truly surprising results.

Eight neural networks were run (Lange-Küttner & Krappmann, 2011). The first neural network was a feedforward network with an input layer, a small hidden layer and an output layer that matched the input layer in size, but without working memory. This basic model could not produce the number words. The second neural network was the same but with four nodes in the hidden layer which matched the number of letters, but without working memory it could not produce the words. The third neural network was now equipped with the two working memory sub-systems. Interestingly, this network now successfully produced a stagewise reduction of errors. The fourth network was the same but, because the children in the empirical sample had a bias towards one modality, one working memory sub-system was slashed. Surprisingly, this slimmed-down network also produced a stagewise reduction of errors when producing the words, see Figure 2.7, upper row. It was now tested whether reading could still be smoother without stages in error reduction. To achieve this, rather than having modality-specific working memory systems, the fifth network had a double input because this is what happens when we read to children: They look at the written words and we read aloud for them. To test whether this modification would make working memory redundant, it was completely removed. It

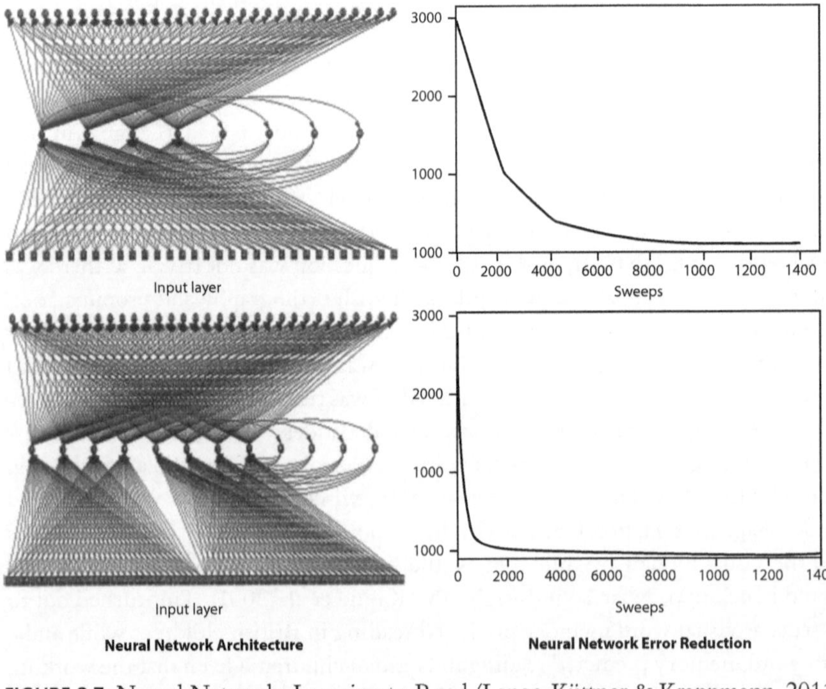

FIGURE 2.7 Neural Networks Learning to Read (Lange-Küttner & Krappmann, 2011)

turned out that the network could not read, so in the sixth network, one working memory sub-system was again added. The result was an immediate reduction of errors in word production, see Figure 2.7, bottom row. Finally, to test for transfer, instead of number words this network received the number words with a scrambled letter sequence as input which it could read just as well as the number words themselves.

Thus, the neural network simulations provided answers to several longstanding questions about reading. First, a stagewise development can occur but does not have to. Second, a working memory system is absolutely necessary for reading but it does not need to entail a modality-specific working memory. Third, double-modality input creates smooth and nearly errorless production of words and is portable to novel words.

Thus, we can see how neural networks offer to compress learning sessions of several years into a few minutes as the computer system just has superior computing power compared to real life practice. While psychophysiological measurements can give us insight about the brain anatomy and the real-time sequencing of attention, neural networks are in a different league as they draw on cognitive theories about development and require hypotheses in order to build the neural network architecture. Their potential lies in abbreviating macrogenetic development into microgenetic learning.

2.4 Conclusions

This chapter gives a short overview of new theories in developmental psychology. Studies with infants, children and adolescents in developmental psychology draw on research with adults and neuropsychological patients, and they also inspire robotics research. What became clear in this chapter is that the new theories are building on previous ones. They often use more sophisticated technological measurements. Also more often interactions between variables are predicted. More often repeated measurement within-subject designs are used that allow for testing longitudinal microgenetic changes. Researchers with such new theoretical approaches are now less sure about how development proceeds and what drives it because of the multiple domains, but we get to know more about learning. But because theoretical camps are less entrenched and also investigate tasks from other perspectives, we get to know more about the gaps that a just-one-theory approach cannot explain, and we can make very clear and compelling statements about the most important and the least important factors that can explain how development in children occurs.

References

Abrahamson, D., & Lindgren, R. (2014). Embodiment and embodied design. In R. K. Sawyer (Ed.), *The Cambridge handbook of the learning sciences* (2nd ed., pp. 358–376). Cambridge University Press.

Adolph, K. E. (2008). Learning to move. *Current Directions in Psychological Science, 17*(3), 213–218. https://doi.org/10.1111/j.1467-8721.2008.00577.x

Baddeley, A. D. (1986). *Working memory*. Clarendon Press.

Brooks, R. A. (1991). Intelligence without representation. *Artificial Intelligence, 47*(1), 139–159. https://doi.org/10.1016/0004-3702(91)90053-M

Brooks, R. A. (1995). Intelligence without reason. In L. Steels & R. A. Brooks (Eds.), *The artificial life route to artificial intelligence. Building embodied, situated agents* (pp. 25–81). Routledge. https://doi.org/10.4324/9781351001885

Brooks, R. A., Hassabis, D., Bray, D., & Shashua, A. (2012). Is the brain a good model for machine intelligence? *Nature, 482*(7386), 462–463. https://doi.org/10.1038/482462a

Caramazza, A., Anzellotti, S., Strnad, L., & Lingnau, A. (2014). Embodied cognition and mirror neurons: A critical assessment. *Annual Review of Neuroscience, 37*, 1–15. https://doi.org/10.1146/annurev-neuro-071013-013950

Case, R., & Pascual-Leone, J. (1975). Failure of conservation training of disadvantaged Black teenagers: A neo-Piagetian interpretation. *Perceptual and Motor Skills, 40*(2), 545–546. https://doi.org/10.2466/pms.1975.40.2.545

Chaplais, J. D., & Macfarlane, J. A. (1984). A review of 404 'late walkers'. *Archives of Disease in Childhood, 59*(6), 512. https://doi.org/10.1136/adc.59.6.512

Crichton, M. T., & Lange-Küttner, C. (1999). Animacy and propulsion in infancy: Tracking, waving and reaching to self-propelled and induced moving objects. *Developmental Science, 2*(3), 318–324. https://doi.org/10.1111/1467-7687.00077

Descartes, R. (1644). *Principia philosophiae [Principles of philosophy]*. Apud Ludovicum & Danielem Elzevirios.

Freeman, N. H. (1972). Process and product in children's drawings. *Perception, 1*(2), 123–140. https://doi.org/10.1068/p010123

Freeman, N. H. (1980). *Strategies of representation in young children*. Academic Press.

Fugate, J. M., Macrine, S. L., & Cipriano, C. (2019). The role of embodied cognition for transforming learning. *International Journal of School & Educational Psychology, 7*(4), 274–288. https://doi.org/10.1080/21683603.2018.1443856

Gathercole, S. E., & Baddeley, A. D. (1993). *Working memory and language*. Erlbaum.

Gerstadt, C. L., Hong, Y. J., & Diamond, A. (1994). The relationship between cognition and action: Performance of children 3 1/2-7 years old on a Stroop-like day-night test. *Cognition, 53*(2), 129–153. https://doi.org/10.1016/0010-0277(94)90068-X

Gobet, F., De Voogt, A., & Retschitzki, J. (2004). *Moves in mind. The psychology of board games*. Psychology Press.

Goldinger, S. D., Papesh, M. H., Barnhart, A. S., Hansen, W. A., & Hout, M. C. (2016). The poverty of embodied cognition. *Psychonomic Bulletin & Review, 23*(4), 959–978. https://doi.org/10.3758/s13423-015-0860-1

Jarrold, C., & Tam, H. (2010). Rehearsal and the development of working memory. In P. Barrouillet & V. Gaillard (Eds.), *Cognitive development and working memory* (pp. 177–200). Psychology Press.

Jones, L. B., Rothbart, M. K., & Posner, M. I. (2003). Development of executive attention in preschool children. *Developmental Science, 6*(5), 498–504. https://doi.org/10.1111/1467-7687.00307

Kail, R. V. (1993). Processing time decreases globally at an exponential rate during childhood and adolescence. *Journal of Experimental Child Psychology, 56*(2), 254–265. https://doi.org/10.1006/jecp.1993.1034

Kail, R. V., & Park, Y. S. (1990). Impact of practice on speed of mental rotation. *Journal of Experimental Child Psychology, 49*(2), 227–244. https://doi.org/10.1016/0022-0965(90)90056-E

Karmiloff-Smith, A. (1992). *Beyond modularity*. MIT Press.

Lange-Küttner, C. (2005). Word structure effects in German and British reading beginners. *Zeitschrift für Pädagogische Psychologie, 19*(4), 207–218. https://doi.org/10.1024/1010-0652.19.4.207

Lange-Küttner, C. (2011). Ebbinghaus simulated: Just do it 200 times. *IEEE XPlore, 2*, 1–6. https://doi.org/10.1109/DEVLRN.2011.6037363

Lange-Küttner, C. (2018). Disappearance of biased visual attention in infants: Remediated tonic neck reflex or maturating visual asymmetry? *Perceptual and Motor Skills, 125*(5), 839–865. https://doi.org/10.1177/0031512518786131

Lange-Küttner, C., & Beringer, J. (2022). How to create an area when playing against a machine. *International Journal of Human–Computer Interaction*, 1–13. https://doi.org/10.1080/10447318.2022.2096737

Lange-Küttner, C., & Crichton, M. T. (1999). Change of spatial field effects in 16- to 20-week-old infants. *Brain and Cognition, 39*(2), 75–92. https://doi.org/10.1006/brcg.1998.1059

Lange-Küttner, C., & Finn, C. (2008). Musical notation and fine motor skills when playing the Soprano recorder: Making a neural network lift a finger. In M. Schlesinger, L. Berthouze, & C. Balkenius (Eds.), *Proceedings of the eighth international conference on epigenetic robotics: Modeling cognitive development in robotic systems* (p. article 139). Lund University Cognitive Studies.

Lange-Küttner, C., & Krappmann, L. (2011). Ein modalitätsspezifisches Wortgedächtnis ist ausreichend: Wortgedächtnismodalität bei Leseanfängern und Neuronalen Netzen [One modality-specific word memory is sufficient – Word memory modality in reading beginners and neural networks]. *Zeitschrift für Pädagogische Psychologie, 25*(1), 19–37. https://doi.org/10.1024/1010-0652/a000027

Lindgren, R., Tscholl, M., Wang, S., & Johnson, E. (2016). Enhancing learning and engagement through embodied interaction within a mixed reality simulation. *Computers & Education, 95*, 174–187. https://doi.org/10.1016/j.compedu.2016.01.001

McKague, M., Pratt, C., & Johnston, M. B. (2001). The effect of oral vocabulary on reading visually novel words: A comparison of the dual-route-cascaded and triangle frameworks. *Cognition, 80*(3), 231–262. https://doi.org/10.1016/S0010-0277(00)00150-5

Morra, S. (2008). A test of a neo-Piagetian model of the water-level task. *European Journal of Developmental Psychology, 5*(3), 369–400. https://dx.doi.org/10.1080/17405620600902928

Morra, S., Gobbo, C., Marini, Z., & Sheese, R. (2008). *Cognitive development: Neo-Piagetian perspectives*. Erlbaum.

Panesi, S., & Morra, S. (2018). Relationships between the early development of drawing and language: The role of executive functions and working memory. *The Open Psychology Journal, 11*, 15–24. https://dx.doi.org/10.2174/1874350101811010015

Panesi, S., & Morra, S. (2022). The relation between drawing and language in preschoolers: The role of working memory and executive functions. *Cognitive Development, 61*, 1–20. https://doi.org/10.1016/j.cogdev.2021.101142

Pascual-Leone, J. (1976a). On learning and development, Piagetian style: I. A reply to Lefebvre-Pinard. *Canadian Psychological Review / Psychologie Canadienne, 17*(4), 270–288. https://doi.org/10.1037/h0081845

Pascual-Leone, J. (1976b). On learning and development, Piagetian style: II. A critical historical analysis of Geneva's research programme. *Canadian Psychological Review / Psychologie Canadienne, 17*(4), 289–297. https://dx.doi.org/10.1037/h0081846

Pascual-Leone, J. (1989). An organismic process model of Witkin's field-dependence-independence. In T. Globerson & T. Zelniker (Eds.), *Cognitive style and cognitive development* (pp. 36–70). Ablex.

Pascual-Leone, J., & Goodman, D. (1979). Intelligence and experience: A neoPiagetian approach. *Instructional Science, 8*(4), 301–367. https://doi.org/10.1007/BF00117011

Piaget, J. (1954). *The construction of reality in the child* (digital edition 2007 ed.). Routledge.

Plunkett, K., & Elman, J. L. (1997). *Exercises in rethinking innateness. A handbook for connectionist simulations.* The MIT Press.

Rescorla, L. (2011). Late talkers: Do good predictors of outcome exist? *Developmental Disabilities Research Reviews, 17*(2), 141–150. https://doi.org/10.1002/ddrr.1108

Simpson, A., Al Ruwaili, R., Jolley, R., Leonard, H., Geeraert, N., & Riggs, K. J. (2019). Fine motor control underlies the association between response inhibition and drawing skill in early development. *Child Development, 90*(3), 911–923. https://doi.org/10.1111/cdev.12949

Thelen, E. (1986). Treadmill-elicited stepping in seven-month-old infants. *Child Development, 57*(6), 1498–1506. https://doi.org/10.2307/1130427

Thelen, E., & Adolph, K. E. (1992). Arnold L. Gesell: The paradox of nature and nurture. *Developmental Psychology, 28*(3), 368–380. https://doi.org/10.1037/0012-1649.28.3.368

Thelen, E., & Adolph, K. E. (1994). Arnold L. Gesell: The paradox of nature and nurture. In R. D. Parke, P. A. Ornstein, J. J. Rieser, & C. Zahn-Waxler (Eds.), *A century of developmental psychology* (pp. 357–387). American Psychological Association. https://doi.org/https://doi.org/10.1037/10155-027

Thelen, E., & Fisher, D. M. (1982). Newborn stepping: An explanation for a "disappearing" reflex. *Developmental Psychology, 18*, 760–775. https://doi.org/10.1037/0012-1649.18.5.760

Thelen, E., Fisher, D. M., & Ridley-Johnson, R. (1984). The relationship between physical growth and a newborn reflex. *Infant Behavior and Development,* 7(4), 479–493. https://doi.org/10.1016/S0163-6383(84)80007-7

Thelen, E., & Smith, L. B. (1994). *A dynamic systems approach to the development of cognition and action*. MIT Press.

Wilson, M. (2002). Six views of embodied cognition. *Psychonomic Bulletin & Review, 9*(4), 625–636. https://doi.org/10.3758/BF03196322

Ziegler, J. C., & Goswami, U. (2006). Becoming literate in different languages: Similar problems, different solutions. *Developmental Science, 9*(5), 429–436. https://doi.org/10.1111/j.1467-7687.2006.00509.x

3

THE A-NOT-B TASK

3.1 Infants Make Curious Mistakes

The A-not-B search task is probably the most researched infancy task so far and was named a 'marker task' by cognitive neuroscientists (Posner & Raichle, 1997). The important lesson that we can learn from the many studies about this task is not only that infants at the end of their first year search in a systematic fashion, but also that this task shows that many theories are needed to explain the curious errors they make on the way.

The A-not-B task is one of the best examples not only of how an observation is developed into quantitative empirical studies, but an example that errors in some tasks are best explained by testing from different theoretical perspectives. In the first chapter of this book, it was described that Piaget (1954) specifies several conceptual changes in sensory-motor cognition that are needed in order to arrive at a stable memory representation (object concept) and how the child discovers groupings of objects and places in the spatial field (space concept). Piaget claims nothing less than that in the first year or so, an infant becomes able to change from subjective practical actions to objective mental anticipations based on internal representations.

The classic form of the A-not-B search task consists of the infant searching for an object that has been hidden in one place, and then gets hidden in a second place, from where it needs to be retrieved again. There are two errors which infants can make, one is not to hunt for the object after it was hidden, as if it was forgotten in an out-of-sight-out-of-mind way. This first, and developmentally earlier error was the actual reason which caused Piaget (1954) to ascertain that infants would need a concept of *object permanence* to solve the task, and this concept would not exist before the age of about six months. The second error in this task occurs after the infant is already able to search and find the object. This error

DOI: 10.4324/9780429270604-4

has been called the *A-not-B error* because of the perseverative search at the first place A, when the infant in fact should have searched in the second place B where the experimenter had hidden the object in full view in front of the infant. In the literature, *object permanence* is also often used as an explanation for the *A-not-B error* because both mistakes would have the same underlying deficit (Munakata et al., 2001) but this may not be the case. In addition to the mere phenomenon of perseveration to the initial place of the object, it is especially curious that infants were more likely to search in the dark for a toy than when it was hidden in full view underneath or behind an occluder (Shinskey & Munakata, 2003). Would the perceptual event of an object's disappearance hinder infants for some reason to search?

3.2 Object Conservation: The A-Error

Until about six months of age when infants have acquired stable seating, they do not look for the object in location A (J. G. Bremner, 1993). We have seen in Chapter 1 that the infant does not have environmental control over a stable image because a lot of the time a baby lies supine or is rotated in space when it is carried about. Piaget describes egocentric space as linked to the infant's body insofar as an object must be within reach so that the infant can control the object in action. If more objects are involved, he speaks of subjective groupings. Also J. G. Bremner (1993) suggested that by counteracting gravity through their own effort, babies would develop an understanding of external objects.

The 'Out of sight, out of mind' argument claims that the infant does not search because visual working memory capacity is insufficient and it has forgotten about the now invisible object. This means that the internal representation of the object is still very short-lived. However, some scientists claimed that this hypothesis would imply that the infant believes that the object dissolves as a physical entity (Baillargeon, 1986, 1987). As a result, many follow-up studies were conducted about whether infants have a concept of 'solidity' of objects (Spelke et al., 1992). In what was a formidable challenge, their experiments rejected the claim of Piaget's theory that cognition develops based on an experiential foundation of their own perceptual and motor experience. In contrast, their assumption was that infants have an innate, unchanging core knowledge of gravity and inertia and that these early concepts would just become enriched during the course of development. This hypothesis was tested with displays of objects disappearing in containers, behind screens and hidden beneath covers, and unexpectedly not reappearing when the obstruction was removed (Baillargeon, 2004). However, in such experiments, gravity and inertia were not an infant experience, but concerned the objects that they were watching while sitting.

Nevertheless, we will see in Chapter 5 on drawing and handwriting in children that even drawing overlapping objects is still difficult for older children because they have to apply specific drawing strategies, but not because they believe that the occluded object is truly morphed into only a partial object.

Clearly, the assumption that core concepts are present in infants without perceptual or motor experience could have been immediately refuted by the classical visual cliff studies on depth perception: The visual cliff experiment involved a table with a glass surface where the second half of the surface had a real and visible cliff underneath. Yet the glass surface made it safe to crawl to the other end of the table. Infants' indicated awareness of depth when they began to hesitate to crawl over the apparent visual cliff (Gibson & Walk, 1960). This reaction only began to show at seven months. The earlier the crawling onset, but not the more extensive the crawling experience, the more likely it was that babies dared to cross the cliff (Richards & Rader, 1981). J. G. Bremner (1993) suggests that this was the case because these babies would have used the tactile rather than the visual channel of experience. However, even at a young age, there are important temperamental differences and some babies are more daring and less anxious than others (Moller, Majdandzic & Bogels, 2014). They also pay attention to adults' feedback, both in the visual cliff task (Moller et al., 2014) and in the A-not-B task (Dunn & J. G. Bremner, 2020) as well as to the presence of a puppet (Marcovitch et al., 2016) and changing experimenters (Werchan & Amso, 2020). The A-not-B error is also reliable in a real-life context: The retrieval of the person of the mother from two rooms functioned in a similar manner as object retrieval in the two-choice A–B task (Corter et al., 1980). Corter et al. (1980, p. 67) found that successful retrievers showed selective looking towards the mother's exit, i.e. they first localised where the mother had disappeared, and then looked more at her exit. Unsuccessful infants gave both doorways the same attention and were subsequently confused in their active search.

Importantly, when crossing a real cliff where they would be caught if they fell, those starting from a stable sitting position showed more avoidance trials than when they were in a crawling position (Adolph, 2000). They could better oversee the gap while sitting than when having their eyes at a lower level while crawling. Here infants' knowledge of their own gravity was tested. A stable upright posture led to a realistic risk awareness in babies. Thus, there seems to be indeed a direction of a developmental causality from mobility to cognition as Piaget (1954) and J. G. Bremner (1993) suggested – rather than an impact of core physical notions of solidity and gravity.

It must be said that the Piagetian A-not-B task was about mental object representations (Shinskey & Munakata, 2005). The surprise reaction following the violation-of-expectation that occurs when seeing an impossible event such as an object disappearing without a trace (Baillargeon, 1986, 1987) was a new methodology that appeared within a scientific context. Other researchers at the time used this paradigm to find that unusual word pairs improved adults' memory (Hirshman, 1988), or that infant crying following expectation-of-violation novel events would diminish long-term memory (Fagen & Ohr, 1985; Fagen et al., 1985). In fact, recent research found that 17-month-old infants react with surprise towards mislabelled objects, and this did predict pupil dilation in a memory test, but not better memory (Csink et al., 2021). These studies do not suggest that the violation-of expectation is relevant for object retrieval (Zmyj et al., 2015). Accordingly, infants who react with surprise if an object is retrieved in front of their eyes from an 'impossible location', and thus had perceived a model action, still failed to retrieve it in the same setup if their own action was required (Ahmed & Ruffman, 1998).

Without an active mental object representation in memory, an infant would have no reason to actually search for an object. One of the earliest behavioural studies that investigated whether a lack of working memory would explain the failure to search was the work of Diamond (1985, 1988).

Diamond (1985) tested 25 infants longitudinally with the A-not-B task; see Figure 3.1. Girls tolerated longer delays than boys but otherwise showed similar success rates. Individual differences did not change as the standard error stayed about the same in the course from 7½ months to 12 months. If a training effect due to the repeated measurement had been involved, one would have expected that individual differences between infants would have decreased (Diamond, 1985, p. 876), but this was not the case.

We remember from Chapter 1 that the main change that occurs in the transition from subjective to objective space would be that the infant places itself as an object amongst objects and '*de-subjectifies*'. How Piaget backs up this claim is not well known. The increase in delay tolerance certainly suggests a more gradual change than the Piagetian sensori-motor stages suggested. However, there

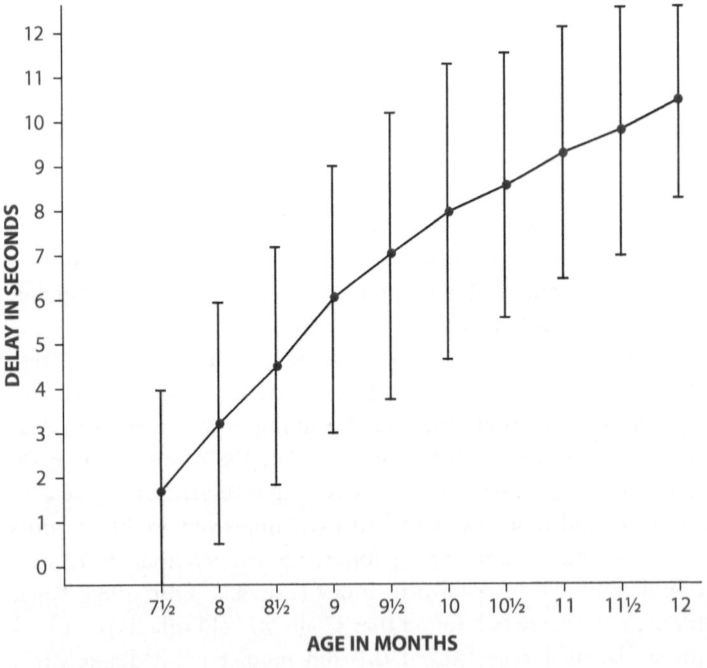

FIGURE 3.1 The Increase of Delay Tolerance (Diamond, 1985)

is always the possibility that both are true, a qualitative change from a focus on body-related spatial relations to inter-object relations accompanied by an increase in information processing resources. In fact, there are quite some visual search studies in cognitive psychology on the question of whether we remember features of one object better (selective attention) than features distributed on several objects (distributed attention) that consistently show that distributed attention towards several objects (set size) is an important factor that changes the slope of search times (see Chapter 6). Current research also investigated whether 6-month-old infants can identify one object from another in multi-object arrays. This would to some degree correspond to Piaget's concept of an objective group in a spatial field. Cantrell et al. (2019) found that in an array with just two similar objects, colour changes were difficult for 6-month-old infants to detect unless items were individuated and differed in shape and colour, had separate onsets, would move independently, or were visible for a relatively long time.

Piaget (1954) observed that infants at about 5 or 6 months would be able to find parts of an object that they want to suck, such as a rattle, and labelled this as a 'simple motor accommodation to the object' (p. 125) or practical aim as they would search for one that fits into the mouth. Moreover, babies would bring an object very close to their face and then hold it further away. In the same vein, they bring their face close to the object and then retreat again. This gives the observer the impression that infants believed that their close inspection would reveal object properties that are not visible from a distance. It could also be that the moment the eyes converge gives infants a sensation of an altogether different, alien object. Thus, here the infant is exploring an object at different distances and angles in order to experience a changed visual object appearance. Piaget takes this observation as an indication that the 10-month-old infant now explores geometric relations between itself and the object without attention to its utility for sucking (p. 161). Thus, the infant changes from instrumental intelligence to rational intelligence. However, if it could be confirmed that the object really changes from something that can be used to one's own advantage to an object in its own right, infants should become more relaxed in their idiosyncratic desires and also become more tolerant of a delay. An object that potentially satisfies their urgent needs and interests changes to an object that may have some informational value. Thus, from a Piagetian perspective it is not the ability to inhibit a response (Diamond, 1990) but their decrease of oral fixation that allows for a more detached interest.

According to Piaget (1954, p. 177), this developmental change also involves a transition from an object being an image to an object becoming 'real'. He observes that although an infant would be able to reach out for an object, the infant entirely relies on the perceptual image until a *spatial field* is discovered that represents a zone of action (p. 117). Piaget did not refer to Kurt Lewin, who had published a monograph on field theory (Lewin, 1951) that a spatial field would be divided into zones. Like Piaget, Lewin also referred to topological spatial theory, as he claimed that only the location and the distance of the zones would be important, but neither the size nor the shape of the zones. Instead, distance, boundaries and obstacles would cause tensions and action plans, so that even small zones could shake up the entire spatial field. In comparison, Piaget squarely puts the human back into the spatial field. Initially, Piaget holds, actions are subjective and practical, but in the older infant, actions become objective and account for spatial interrelations between objects within the field independently of the own position.

3.3 Spatial Perseveration: The A-not-B Error

Also the second error in the A-not-B task is curious. While infants are now searching successfully in location A, they do not look for the object in the second, new location B. Instead, until about nine months, infants search again in location A, hence this error was labelled the A-not-B error. This repeated search is called *perseverative search*, an important psychological term that applies whenever there is a failure to switch from one goal to another, at any age (Kirkham & Diamond, 2003).

According to Piaget (1954), this second error is important because it proves the difference between egocentric 'subjective' space and allocentric 'objective' space (see Chapter 1). This hypothesis puts some weight on the spatial overview that infants gain along with sitting, crawling and walking. In short, Piaget claimed that infants' change in the type of spatial coding was responsible for the A-not-B error because the coordination of the arm movement would now need to occur between two locations, rather than between one object in relation to the self. This implies a switch in the search objective from object to place; see Figure 3.2.

Because initially, the infant would be after the object to satisfy oral needs, and successfully so even when it was hidden, the question when searching in the

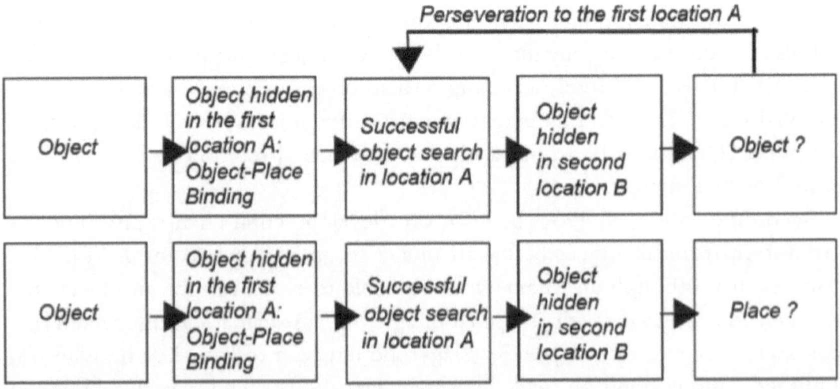

FIGURE 3.2 The Switch in the Search Objective from Object to Place (Lange-Küttner, 2008)

first place was *where is the object*. However, search in a second place would require coordination between two places in a spatial field, hence the question is now *where is the new place* where the object is located. The path diagram in Figure 3.2 shows what would happen if the infant kept hunting for the object throughout the A-not-B task, without changing the primary search objective from object to place. When object and place are encoded into one unit, and if the infant continues to use this first cognitive processing unit, the perseveration to location A is so-to-say a logical necessity, as the object is just returning to 'its place'. Because in the second half of the task the place is new, while the object is known, the infants must dissociate this previously formed object-and-place unit in order to bind the object to a second place. Hence, in the mind of the child the initial search objective 'where is the object' would need to be changed midway through the task to something like 'I have the object, but where is the (new) place', that is, in this sense the infant would 'have' object permanence, but this object priority would need to be changed to a place priority.

In conclusion, the change of the search objective from object to place requires an executive task-switching process. The A-not-B task dynamic is well explained using a *binding* approach: The first step is an object-place *association*, the second step an object-place *dissociation*, and the third step an object-new-place *association*, thus the processes could be conceptualised in an Association-Dissociation-Association (ADA) model. In short, the A-not-B error occurs if the infant does not switch the search objective.

The distinction between egocentric and allocentric space is well established in neuropsychological research, where clearly separated brain regions could be identified for spatial coding in relation to object shape versus a spatial field (Burgess, 2006; Mishkin et al., 1983; Ungerleider & Mishkin, 1982); see Figure 3.3.

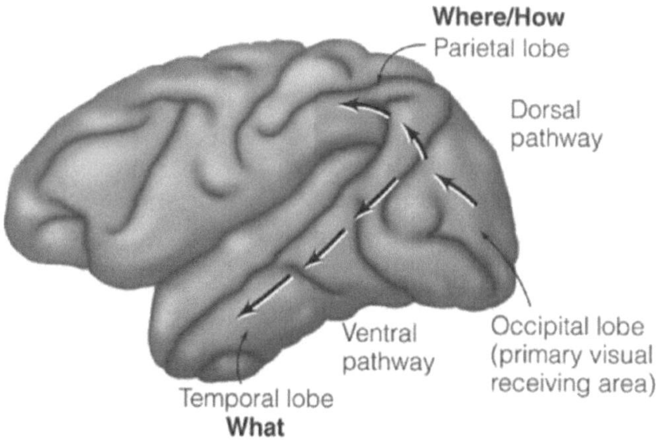

FIGURE 3.3 The What-and-Where Distinction (Goldstein, 2010, after Mishkin, Ungerleider & Macko, 1983)

Ungerleider and Mishkin (1982) found that the parietal lobe processes monitoring of the entire *spatial field* as well as object movement across the spatial field. In contrast, activations in the temporal lobe process static object features such as color, size or typical contour. Note that reaching towards an object would be controlled elsewhere, namely in the motor cortex, which is located more anteriorly in the neocortex and in the sub-cortical basal ganglia. However, the actual brain networks that control the coordination between object and place encoding and planning motor acts such as object retrieval are still not well known (Battaglia-Mayer & Caminiti, 2019).

Hence, while in these areas object and place are encoded separately, these percepts would need binding in the frontal lobes in working memory, and probably also unbinding, or de-correlation (Murre et al., 2006). This where-system is initially poorly integrated with the what-system (Mareschal & Bremner, 2006), develops later than the what-system and is the first to be delayed in developmental disorders such as autism (Atkinson, 2002; Braddick et al., 2003). Neither the perceptual field processed in the parietal cortex, nor long-term memory for spatial fields processed in the subcortical hippocampus, contributed to the failure to retrieve an object or the A-not-B error when these areas were lesioned in monkeys (Diamond, 1991). Instead, the prefrontal lobe was responsible for the A-not-B error (see also Chapter 10 on motor coordination disorders). Accordingly, in a large recent study with near-infrared spectroscopy (NIRS) with 10-month-old human infants, inhibition did require activation of the right prefrontal and parietal cortices (Fiske et al., 2022).

Figure 3.4 shows the theoretical *Spatial Field Model* that conceptualises the emergence of locations. The top layer of Figure 3.4 visualises how initially only appearances of objects may enter the what-processing stream, with the where-system not yet involved.

With an increase of processing speed – as represented in more density in the what-and-where processing stream in the middle graph of Figure 3.4. – also places are entered one-by-one because they are still linked to the object and do not exist in their own right. This corresponds to the notion of object files where input from the what-and-where system is entered into an object representation such that the place belongs to an object (Treisman, 2006) (object-place binding).[1] Finally, another layer of just locations would be entered, which corresponds to the spatial field. In this layer (in the bottom graph of Figure 3.4) places do not need salient features of object placeholders in order to constitute an array or field of locations that enters the where-system. In this *Spatial Field Model*, the important factor is not a perceptual or memory function that would be located in a certain brain area but the more general acceleration of information processing speed in the nervous system (see also Chapter 10). Also in infants, speed of

1 Note that here a 'place' is mentioned when an object-location binding is denoted, but a 'location' denotes when it is a flexible option within an 'objective' spatial field without objects indicating places.

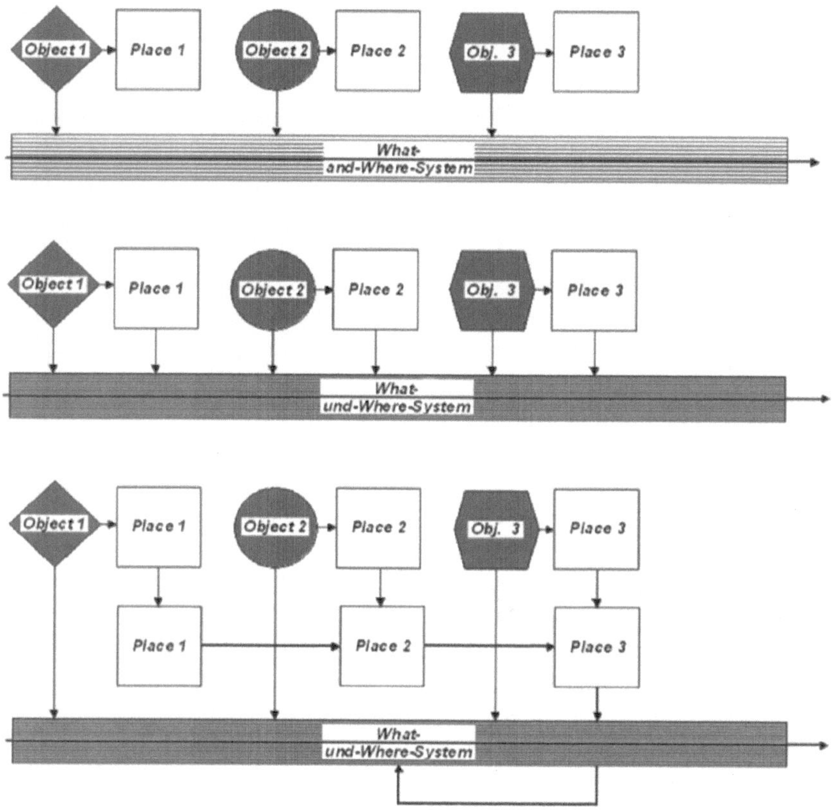

FIGURE 3.4 The Spatial Field Model:The Emergence of Locations

processing is a factor that underlies many cognitive operations, such as fixation duration (Colombo, 1993).

3.4 The Occipital Factor: Spatial Coding in the A-not-B Task

Interestingly and rarely mentioned, there is EEG research that measured timing of infant brain processes directly, for instance, when watching a spin ball in a bingo wheel, followed by the A-not-B task (MacNeill et al., 2018). Like in the Diamond research with infants and monkeys (1991), this study did not find that individual differences in the A-not-B task were occurring because of differences in parietal cortex processes, and not even in the frontal cortex activations, but because of a difference in bilateral occipital processing which controls looking (MacNeill et al., 2018). Those infants performing well in the A-not-B task at six months showed a lower bilateral occipital baseline and thus less reliance on seeing, but more occipital activation in the months thereafter. When EEG was actually measured during the task, good A-not-B problem solvers showed greater parietal and occipital activations at 8 months of age, while frontal activations occurred in all infants (Bell, 2001).

Occipital activations are very early basic visual processes that relate to a raw visual structure of the input before these are further elaborated in the what-and-where system. Hence, this result could explain why (1) seeing may need to be of lower value and relevance for object retrieval (A error) than a mental representation and (2) strong colour cues in the visual field of the A-not-B task are efficient at least in the moment of the task. To have an overview of the situation within the spatial field from a bird's eye perspective does help infants to solve the A-not-B task (Lew et al., 2007; Smith et al., 1999). But what are the cues in the spatial field that infants pick up in order to solve this task? An early, important study systematically investigated the effectiveness of visual structure cues, as well as the question of a learning transfer from highly pre-structured arrays to the classic, unstructured version of the A-not-B search task (Butterworth et al., 1982), see Figure 3.5.

Figure 3.5 shows that Butterworth et al. created several types of set-up with highly pre-structured visual fields. In the classic version, the background and the covers were in a neutral colour. In the background condition, one half of the visual field was in a different colour than the other half visual field. In the place condition, only the hiding containers in the two places were visually enhanced with a colour contrast. In the rotation condition, both the two visual fields and the places were colour-contrasted. In the repeated condition, this combined visual field-place array was just repeated instead of rotated.

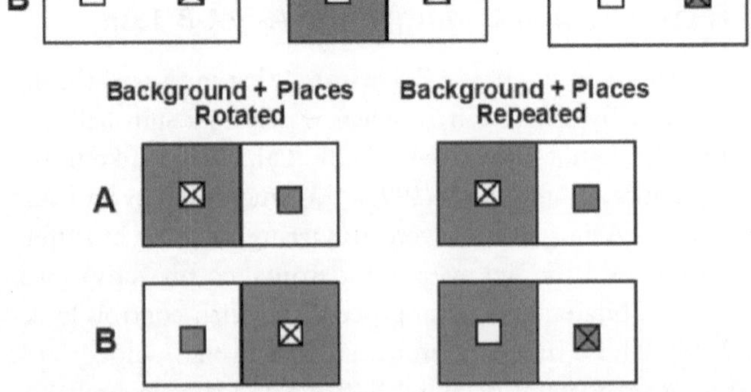

FIGURE 3.5 Locations in the Spatial Field (Lange-Küttner, 2008)

Butterworth et al. thus had the places and the spatial field schema systematically varied. The question was which visual cues would prevent the perseveration to the initial place A, and whether the combined visual cues of place and visual field would further add to a reduction of perseverative A-not-B errors. The results were clear; the dark columns in Figure 3.6 show that every additional visual cue reduced perseverative errors, background more than the places, and background plus places more than background alone. Especially interesting is that the simple repetition of the super-structured place-field combination was more efficient than its entire rotation, an early finding of a practice effect in this task. Thus, instead of cues competing with one another for attention in the visual field and overshadowing each other (Mackintosh, 1976), the cues of colouring the spatial field and the locations supported each other, which may be reflected in the simultaneous activation of frontal and occipital lobes (Bell, 2012; Cuevas & Bell, 2011; Cuevas et al., 2012).

However, the grey columns in Figure 3.6 show that there was no transfer from any of these pre-structured spatial arrays to the simple, classic, non-structured array. This would imply that the visual structure would have guided the reaches insofar as the colour contrasts enabled the infant to reach for the ready-made salient spatial segment in a nearly reflex-like fashion. The colour contrast of the visual field would have facilitated the left-right orientation, the colour contrast of the places facilitated precision reaching, while the repetition would have increased the familiarity with the spatial array. However, the lack of transfer

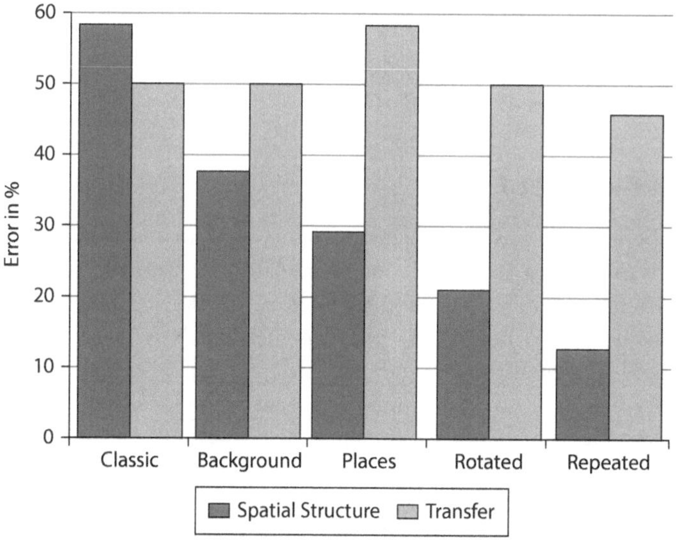

FIGURE 3.6 In-the-Moment Success in the A-not-B Task (Data from Butterworth et al., 1982; Lange-Küttner, 2008)

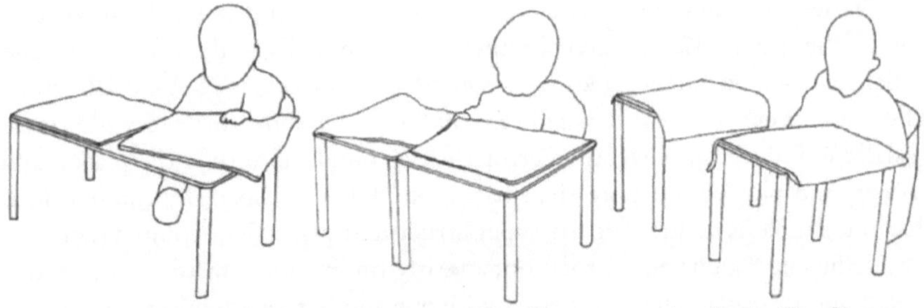

FIGURE 3.7 Object-Place Binding in the Two-Tables Experiment (after Lange-Küttner, 2008)

implies that the infant could not remember a *spatial structure* to discriminate between the two places when again confronted with one homogenous region.

If one were to refrain from using colour as a cue and instead present the object on two separate tables, would this intervention promote a transfer of learning? The idea was that real infant-sized individual tables, shown to infants before the task and merged in front of them into one surface should enhance their awareness of the separateness of the places where the toy was to be hidden, see Figure 3.7. The toy was hidden up to three times in location A until the infant responded, and then hidden in location B.

The knowledge that there were two tables with places did not reduce the A-not-B error. However, a clearly visible air gap between the two tables enabled infants to see two *places as such* did reduce the A-not-B error and lifted search performance above chance, but again only for the moment, without any transfer to the homogeneous spatial field (Lange-Küttner, 2008). Nevertheless, the experiment clearly proved that the ability for flexible object-place binding was necessary to prevent the A-not-B error.

3.5 Learning in the A-not-B Task

Surely there must be a reason why this learning support only survived the actual trial and did not transfer to a setup without cues. After all, learning support should achieve permanent improvement. There are two ways to identify the factors that prevent deep learning. One method is meta-analysis that reviews and analyses multiple studies of the A-not-B task (Marcovitch & Zelazo, 1999; Wellman, Cross and Bartsch, 1987) and another approach is to look at microgenetic changes and practice effects during an experimental session with different training groups (Siegler, 2004).

The meta-analyses of the A-not-B error revealed several factors that were important, not just one. Both Wellman et al. (1987) and Marcovitch and Zelazo (1999) found that age and the number of locations as well as delay duration reliably predicted the A-not-B error. Moreover, they confirmed that the number of trials at the A location was a significant predictor which indicated that a hiding place for an object (object-place unit) could be conditioned (Smith et al., 1999). Also Harris (1986) and Zelazo et al. (1998) had suggested that infants would build up a motor response memory from searches at one place, which would be so strong that it would interfere with the search in the next place. It could be demonstrated that the more A trials were given, the higher the A-not-B error, both in 9-month-old infants (Marcovitch et al., 2002) and in 2-year-olds (Marcovitch & Zelazo, 2006). This pointed to a very different theory as an explanation of the A-not-B error than the Piagetian theory, namely the stimulus-response theory (Wickens, 1954) whereby (1) perceptual responses are primary, (2) they mediate overt responses and (3) are predictable from prior experiences of the organism.

Although Smith et al. (1999) were also critical of the fact that in most of the literature, the A-not-B error was still conceptualised as indicative of object permanence, their conclusion was even more radical. They preferred a *space-centred* over an *object-centred* explanation because both the places A and B could be arbitrarily reinforced with repetition and training. Thus, they argued against Diamond's notion that the A-not-B error would reflect a lack of inhibition of a pre-potent response. Their theoretical conclusion was even stronger than the one of Marcovitch and Zelazo:

> Infants reach correctly to B not when a prepotent habit to reach to A is inhibited but when the immediate perceptual input biasing the system in the B direction is stronger than the biasing internal activity from the previous reaches to A.
>
> *(Smith et al., 1999, p. 257)*

This notion of forces in the spatial field is very close to Lewin's theory (1951) introduced in Chapter 1, but lacks the more wilful and reflective dimension of human action.

In contrast, Marcovitch and Zelazo did not favour the one theory over the other but claimed that there are two *hierarchically competing systems* (Marcovitch & Zelazo, 2006): One would be a response-based system that corresponds to motor memory and learns implicitly and incrementally according to associative principles, while the other would be a conscious and reflective representational system that, if developed accordingly, potentially has the ability to control the response-based system. Proof was that while the amount of A trials did predict perseveration, after a higher number of trials, perseveration disappeared. Thus, an important aspect of the hierarchical competing system theory is that the representational system is capable of reflecting on (or reprocessing) its own representations to control response biases.

Hence, is the concept of *object permanence* exaggerated and in fact truly misleading? With the onset of reaching, infants begin to appreciate predictable object trajectories (Crichton & Lange-Küttner, 1999). If success in location A is higher than in location B, is the main difficulty for the human infant to keep the two locations apart, or to track the object on its pathway from one location to another? Furthermore, the fact that infants still search even if just lids are used (A. Bremner & Bryant, 2001) is further evidence against an object permanence account for perseverative search. One explanation of the search for a non-existent object was indeed that the object would only be a more or less distinctive placeholder in a specific situation where the action is more important than the object itself. Thus, is spatial search in two consecutive places object-based or space-based? The question of an object-based or space-based visual search mechanism is also discussed in research with adults (e.g. Driver, 2001; Humphreys et al., 1999; Logan, 1996), see Chapter 6.

The assumption that there is a dynamic object and place *binding* (Treisman, 2006) taking place in the A-not-B task which occurs on a perceptual level and does not necessarily involve motor responses was tested with a neural network (Thelen et al., 2001). Not only an A-not-B error, but also a B-not-A error could be simulated. While this was further proof for the role of reinforcement in this task, a B-not-A error occurs very rarely in real data sets. This allows one to conclude that the frequently occurring A-not-B error may be indeed an involuntary, but not an arbitrary mistake, which distinguishes human from machine error.

What could be the specifically human error in this task? A re-analysis of an A-not-B task repeated five times (J. G. Bremner, 1978; J. G. Bremner & Bryant, 1977) showed clear learning effects in human infants for location B. The more often infants repeated the task, the fewer perseverative errors occurred in location A, and the more success was achieved in location B. However, in these two studies, success in trials 2 and 3 was nearly identical, but in the following trials 4 and 5 it seemed as if the sample of the 1977 study decided to increase success in location A, while success in location B dropped and was back to the initial starting level. In contrast, the sample of the 1978 study further closed the performance gap between the two hiding locations (Lange-Küttner, 1998, Figure 1).

This result showed that the A-not-B task requires considerable resources in terms of sustained attention and seems to be a touchstone for selective attention towards two places. Infants who were improving their success in location B seemed to deploy selective attention in a compensatory fashion, i.e. the stronger performance in one location was achieved at the expense of success in the other location. Infants either optimised what they were already good at (retrieving the toy in location A) and forgot about what they were not so good at (retrieving the toy in location B), or bravely improved success rates in what they were not so good at (location B), but at the expense of what they were already good at (location A). To obtain such a result with 10-month-old infants is rather remarkable, and is known as *selective optimisation with compensation* (SOC) in research on older people's management of limited cognitive and sensorimotor resources (Baltes & Baltes, 1990; Lindenberger & Baltes, 1994; Lindenberger et al., 2000). In infancy research, this was conceptualised as a capacity account where an action strand is taxed only when a task is more challenging than can be comfortably managed (Berger, 2004, 2010).

If capacity is the human problem, there should also be individual differences due to infant fitness. In fact, infants living in poverty show significantly more A-not-B and other errors on this task (Lipina et al., 2005). Moreover, nutritional factors (Willatts & Forsyth, 1998) such as the amount of arachidonic (AA) and docosahexaenoic (DHA) fatty acids have an impact on neural and vascular development of infants (Cunnane & Crawford, 2003; Hieu et al., 2006; Thomas et al., 2005). In a one-site search task (Willatts et al., 1998) breast-fed infants performed better than infants who had been bottle-fed with a conventional formula. Infants whose bottle milk was enriched with more fatty acids performed in between these two groups.

The impact of breastfeeding on learning in the A-not-B task was also directly compared (Lange-Küttner, 1998). Both breast-fed and bottle-fed infants showed comparable overall performance on the A-not-B task, but spatial learning during the task interacted with both age and feeding type. Breast-fed babies at both under and over 8 months of age showed selective improvement during repetition, and closed the gap between success rates in locations A and B, while bottle-fed infants did not; see Figure 3.8. SOC occurred independently of whether performance was below or above chance.

Interestingly, the difference between breast-fed and bottle-fed infants was categorical and occurred independently of the duration (in months) of breast-feeding. Thus, there may have been some social-sensory experience that infants made during breast-feeding that bottle-fed infants did not make. In a one-site search task used by Munakata et al. (1997) as well as in neural network simulations, on-line learning during trials showed an earlier success in location A,

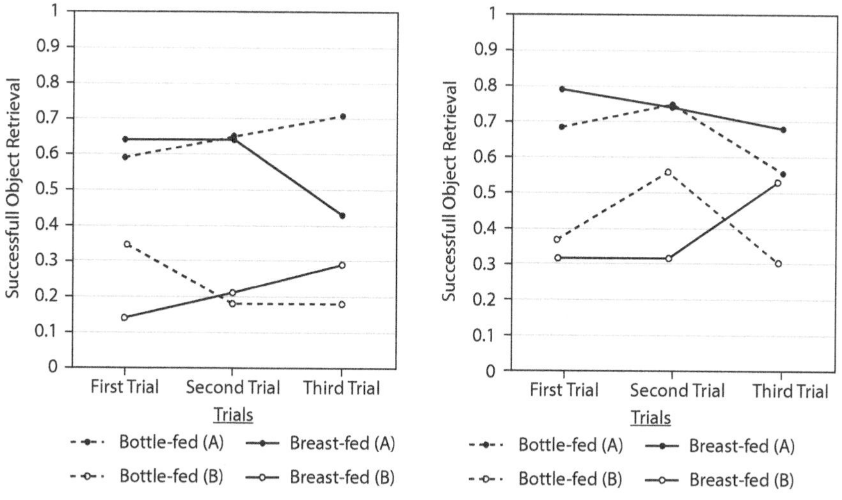

FIGURE 3.8 Selective Optimisation with Compensation (SOC) (Lange-Küttner, 1998)

with success in location B increasing with practice/sweeps (see also Mareschal et al., 1999; Munakata, 1998a, 1998b). However, a SOC trade-off between the two locations as in the study of Lange-Küttner (1998), which was controlled for nutrition, was not found in the computer simulation.

If SOC would have been merely a matter of nutritional value, duration should have been a relevant factor. Harlow (1958) demonstrated that nutrition in mother-infant interactions plays only a minor role compared to using her as a safe base for spatial exploration. Dawson (1994) compared brain processing of 12- to 15-month-old and 21-month-old infants in a separation episode. She found that the younger infants generally showed more frontal lobe activation, while the older infants showed no change in frontal lobe processing, but a marked change in posterior parietal processing demonstrating some reckoning and overview of the spatial field.

An effect of familiarity also becomes prominent at this age as infants show increased stranger anxiety around nine months of age when they develop a conscious preference for their mother and reject approaches from a stranger, e.g. by refusing to be carried. Stranger anxiety peaks between eight to ten months at exactly the same age when infants begin to successfully solve the A-not-B task. Moreover, there are other tasks which require discrimination that are sensitive to familiarity at this age. Diamond et al. (1994) compared a speech task, a classification task and the A-not-B task. The speech task involved recognition of a familiar speech contrast, as opposed to a non-familiar non-native speech contrast. Diamond et al. found that every single infant who passed the A-not-B task had also passed the speech task. Thus, it may be the case that the more general ability for perceptual discrimination enters infants' awareness faster at this age than in the months before.

The individual differences in selective improvement in repeated trials in the A-not-B task are particularly illuminating when one is interested in the underlying learning mechanism. From a logical perspective, when selectivity occurs in constrained cognitive systems, there is the implicit possibility that a trade-off occurs, producing a disadvantage for the non-selected instance. However, when the information processing capacity of the system increases, the trade-off is likely to be smaller or absent because of increased resources. One explanation of the less successful learning mechanism of the bottle-fed infants would be that following the complete pathway of the object from the experimenter to location A back to the experimenter and on to location B got out of focus and, as a consequence, either a spatial primacy effect occurred (improvement in location A with deteriorating performance in location B), or places were regulated as if without an object, i.e. as if in a void (non-selective processing of locations A and B) (Lange-Küttner, 2008).

Two groups of infants were also found in an eye-tracking study investigating selective looking to locations A and B by 9-month-old infants (Popick et al., 2011). They found that 17 (53% 'attenders') were actually looking at place A, while 15 infants (47% 'non-attenders') were not. During repetitions, attenders

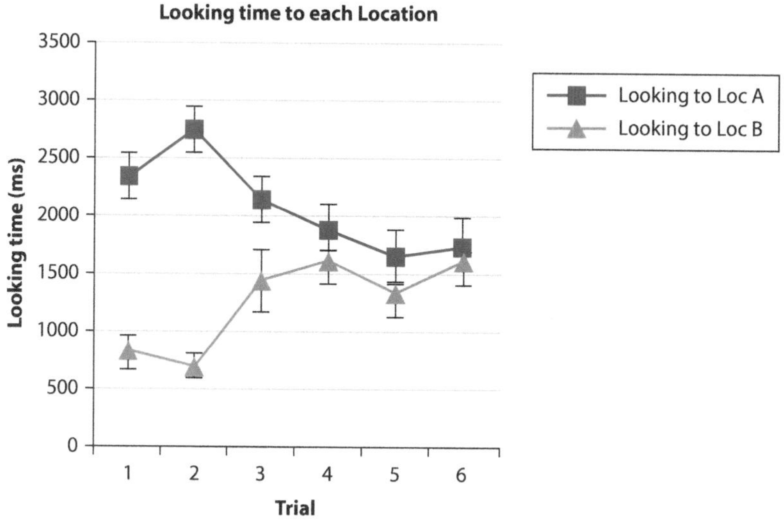

FIGURE 3.9 Selective Looking of Attenders (in milliseconds) (Popick et al., 2011)

gradually looked less at location A, and increasingly more at the location B, with selective looking ceasing after the third trial; see Figure 3.9. Non-attenders showed a bias to the right side, which reflects the innate infant visual neglect (see also Lange-Küttner, 2018).

Interestingly, Popick et al. also ran computer simulation studies that successfully predicted selective looking to location B should supersede selective looking to location A, but in the real sample this was dependent on paying attention to locations. Thus, the conclusion here would be that infants were actively counteracting the selective bias towards location A and they were not just subjected to field forces. This confirms the *hierarchically competing systems theory* of Marcovitch and Zelazo (2006), where the aim is to control these field forces by representing the spatial context in the mind. In 7.5-month-old infants, a strong object representation of always the same familiar object is needed to stimulate search through the repetitions (Shinskey & Munakata, 2005). Thus, a strong object representation may be necessary for finding a hidden object in the first place, but a switch towards a strong place representation should be necessary to turn to a new place and initiate a spatial rather than an object search.

3.6 Motor Development and the A-not-B Error

One factor that is especially obvious in the first year of life is infants' physical development. Even though Piaget's sensori-motor stages would have implied follow-up studies on fine and gross motor development, this did not happen (Adolph & Robinson, 2015). This was most likely the case because in his work he tried to keep motor abilities as a constant factor that could be excluded in favour of a psychological explanation. For instance, Piaget described that infants explore various kinds of objects with their hands, only with the aim to find which is the 'good part' to insert into their mouths. Extensive observations were made on object rotation by using a bottle with a nipple mouthpiece (Piaget, 1954, p. 126). Piaget varied the sight of the nipple by showing the infant the bottle upside down, letting the infant see only the nipple, or varying the distance of the object with both ends in the visual field of the infant. When the bottle was upside down, the infant either looked away at once and started to howl, or started to suck the glass (the bottom) and, finding no food, also started to howl. When only shown a glimpse of the rubber nipple, the infant managed to rotate the bottle. Piaget also described that at a distance the infant would visually explore both ends of the bottle indicating intellectual interest, but when the bottom end was moved towards the infant, the same sucking of the bottom end of the bottle occurred. Piaget therefore concluded that, although the infant was technically and motorically able to rotate the bottle, as well as perceptually interested in the bottle as such, the infant understood nothing as soon as the bottle was spatially close (Piaget, 1954, p. 127). However, at eight months – when the A-not-B error is also less likely to occur – the whole object was appreciated even when close to the body. The infant no longer sucked the wrong end nor abandoned all retrieval attempts, cried or struggled, but immediately explored the whole object by displacing the wrong end, anticipating the nipple visually and leaning the body sideways to obtain the right end (Piaget, 1954, p. 163).

Reaching in the A-not-B task clearly has a gross motor component when orienting the arm towards the goal, rather than just a fine motor component when grasping the object by opening and closing the hand (Lange-Küttner, 2018). In the classic version of the A-not-B task, the arm had to be turned either to the right or the left, but lateralised reaching develops only gradually over months because initially infants reach bimanually, especially when an object passes the midline in front of them which excites them (Lange-Küttner & Crichton, 1999). While 6- and 8-month old infants had significantly less success in reaching when an object moved from right to left than when it moved from left to right, this was not the case in 10-month-old infants anymore (Fagard et al., 2009).

A setup with multiple search sites (Bjork & Cummings, 1984; Cummings & Bjork, 1981, 1983a, 1983b) tested whether a centration of the arm towards the goal location occurred in repeated trials. In a five-location hiding site with locations A and B at the periphery of the spatial field, 9-month-old infants had no difficulty reaching towards location A, but the second search in location B was distributed across the intermediate places on the side of the correct place B. The most erroneous searches were at the neighbour site of location B (Bjork & Cummings, 1984). Moreover, infants' search increasingly centred on the targeted location within three practice trials showing the practice effect as described above. This would be a very practical explanation that would not need to involve mental object representations but just motor control of the spatial field. However, in another study by the same authors, in three-location and five-location setups also with locations A and B at the periphery, infants were more likely to erroneously search at midpoint but in these experiments location C was also a valid hiding site whose impact was unclear (Cummings & Bjork, 1983b).

Hence, it was tested to what effect infants would search if the object was hidden at the midpoint location C itself (Cummings & Bjork, 1983a) in a five-location setup. The middle location always had a very high success retrieval rate whether devised at the beginning, the middle or at the end of the experiment. Perseverative search occurred more rarely, as searches clustered around hiding sites. Thus, if one accepts that the error at location B occurred because the arm could not be calibrated towards the exact location but landed just short, the conclusion would be that infants would find it difficult to adjust the tempo and velocity of their arm movement. If a third location is added at midline, this facilitates the A-not-B task, first, because the midline point gets elevated attention due to proximity, especially when searched first (Cummings & Bjork, 1983a), and second, because distances between places would be shorter and arm movements easier to calibrate. Also, sitting in a stable way facilitates attention to a location change, as the arms would not be needed for balancing the body (Berger et al., 2019).

Another strand of research followed up the finding that the A-not-B task also worked when a person was leaving a room consecutively through two exit doors (Corter et al., 1980). In such a task, not just the arm movement is relevant, but the infants crawl to find their mothers who had left. The same A-not-B error was observed insofar as infants could find their mothers in the first exit, but not after she left via the second exit. But would the A-not-B error also occur in infants who are even more motorically advanced? Walking 13-month-old infants could accommodate their pathway to a visible parent a metre away after six trials if the parent had moved 90 degrees to a different location B. However, if this pathway involved walking down four steps of a staircase, a sizeable proportion of infants walked first to location A before turning to location B, and this was even more pronounced when they had to turn around in order to walk to location B (Berger, 2004). In a variation, the pathway was indirect, or covered as a tunnel (Berger, 2010). The indirect pathway did not cause any perseveration, but the tunnel was negotiated better by crawlers than by walkers, who showed A-not-B errors significantly more often. This may have occurred because crawlers look down at the floor (Kretch et al., 2014) and thus would have had less difficulty adjusting to the tunnel, which was just about an infant body height. A comparison of the tunnel with the stairs demonstrated comparable levels of spatial perseveration caused by the spatial obstacles. Because the A-not-B error could be generalised to different set-ups, Berger came to the same conclusion that limited motor capacity in infants would make spatial perseveration more likely (Berger et al., 2018). The conclusion of Berger is that 'infants sacrifice their weakest skills' to carry out the task (Berger, 2010, p. 335), which is the very opposite to what was found in the analysis of the learning curve of younger infants, who sacrificed their stronger achievement in location A in order to improve upon their weaker skill of retrieval in location B (Lange-Küttner, 1998). Such divergent conclusions may occur when outcome is compared with learning – two different psychological processes.

3.7 Conclusions

This chapter on the A-not-B task shows that spatial perseveration already occurs in the second half of the first year of life as a quasi-natural occurrence in every infant, and not only in school children with attentional difficulties (Wilding, 2003) (see Chapter 8). Decades of research about this task have shown that it has generated, but also taxed, multiple theories that in turn each have explained some aspect of spatial perseveration. The most important remaining research question is of course how infants can replace the scaffolding of visual cues that helped in the moment and commit it to long-term memory. Could it be the transition from object-place coding to common region coding of objects, and is common region the equivalent for the generation of a mental representation of a layout of locations that does not need placeholders at all? We will see in the next chapters how spatial categorisation and location maps develop in older children.

References

Adolph, K. E. (2000). Specificity of learning: Why infants fall over a veritable cliff. *Psychological Science, 11*(4), 290–295. https://doi.org/10.1111/1467-9280.00258

Adolph, K. E., & Robinson, S. R. (2015). Motor development. In L. S. Liben, U. E. Müller, & R. M. Lerner (Eds.), *Handbook of child psychology and developmental science: Cognitive processes* (Vol. 2, 7th ed., pp. 113–157). John Wiley & Sons, Inc.

Ahmed, A., & Ruffman, T. (1998). Why do infants make A not B errors in a search task, yet show memory for the location of hidden objects in a nonsearch task? *Developmental Psychology, 34*(3), 441–453. https://doi.org/10.1037/0012-1649.34.3.441

Atkinson, J. (2002). *The developing visual brain*. Oxford University Press.

Baillargeon, R. (1986). Representing the existence and the location of hidden objects: Object permanence in 6- and 8-month-old infants. *Cognition, 23*(1), 21–41. https://doi.org/10.1016/0010-0277%2886%2990052-1

Baillargeon, R. (1987). Object permanence in 3 1/2- and 4 1/2-month-old infants. *Developmental Psychology, 23*(5), 655–664. https://doi.org/10.1037/0012-1649.23.5.655

Baillargeon, R. (2004). Infants' reasoning about hidden objects: Evidence for event-general and event-specific expectations. *Developmental Science*, 7(4), 391–424. https://doi.org/10.1111/j.1467-7687.2004.00357.x

Baltes, P. B., & Baltes, M. M. (1990). Psychological perspectives on successful aging: A model of selective optimization with compensation. In P. B. Baltes & M. M. Baltes (Eds.), *Successful aging: Perspectives from the behavioral sciences* (pp. 1–33). Cambridge University Press.

Battaglia-Mayer, A., & Caminiti, R. (2019). Corticocortical systems underlying high-order motor control. *The Journal of Neuroscience, 39*(23), 4404. https://doi.org/10.1523/JNEUROSCI.2094-18.2019

Bell, M. A. (2001). Brain electrical activity associated with cognitive processing during a looking version of the A-Not-B task. *Infancy, 2*(3), 311–330. https://doi.org/10.1207/S15327078IN0203_2

Bell, M. A. (2012). A psychobiological perspective on working memory performance at 8 months of age. *Child Development, 83*(1), 251–265. https://doi.org/10.1111/j.1467-8624.2011.01684.x

Berger, S. E. (2004). Demands on finite cognitive capacity cause infants' perseverative errors. *Infancy, 5*(2), 217–238. https://doi.org/10.1207/s15327078in0502_7

Berger, S. E. (2010). Locomotor expertise predicts infants' perseverative errors. *Developmental Psychology, 46*(2), 326–336. https://doi.org/10.1037/a0018285

Berger, S. E., Harbourne, R. T., Arman, F., & Sonsini, J. (2019). Balancing act(ion): Attentional and postural control strategies predict extent of infants' perseveration in a sitting and reaching task. *Cognitive Development, 50*, 13–21. https://doi.org/10.1016/j.cogdev.2018.12.001

Berger, S. E., Harbourne, R. T., & Horger, M. N. (2018). Cognition–action trade-offs reflect organization of attention in infancy. In J. B. Benson (Ed.), *Advances in child development and behavior* (Vol. 54, pp. 45–86). JAI. https://doi.org/10.1016/bs.acdb.2017.11.001

Bjork, E. L., & Cummings, E. M. (1984). Infant search errors: Stage of concept development or stage of memory development. *Memory & Cognition, 12*(1), 1–19. https://doi.org/10.3758/BF03196993

Braddick, O., Atkinson, J., & Wattam-Bell, J. (2003). Normal and anomalous development of visual motion processing: Motion coherence and 'dorsal-stream vulnerability'. *Neuropsychologia, 41*(13), 1769–1784. https://doi.org/10.1016/S0028-3932(03)00178-7

Bremner, A., & Bryant, P. (2001). The effect of spatial cues on infants' responses in the AB task, with and without a hidden object. *Developmental Science, 4*(4), 408–415. https://doi.org/10.1111/1467-7687.00182

Bremner, J. G., & Bryant, P. E. (1977). Place versus response as the basis of spatial errors made by young infants. *Journal of Experimental Child Psychology, 23*(1), 162–171. https://doi.org/10.1016/0022-0965(77)90082-0

Bremner, J. G. (1978). Spatial errors made by infants: Inadequate spatial cues or evidence of egocentrism? *British Journal of Psychology, 69*(1), 77–84. https://doi.org/10.1111/j.2044-8295.1978.tb01634.x

Bremner, J. G. (1993). Motor abilities as causal agents in infant cognitive development. In G. J. P. Savelsbergh (Ed.), *The development of coordination in infancy* (pp. 47–77). North-Holland/Elsevier Science Publishers. https://doi.org/10.1016/S0166-4115(08)60949-8

Burgess, N. (2006). Spatial memory: How egocentric and allocentric combine. *Trends in Cognitive Sciences, 10*(12), 551–557. https://doi.org/10.1016/j.tics.2006.10.005

Butterworth, G., Jarrett, N., & Hicks, L. (1982). Spatiotemporal identity in infancy: Perceptual competence or conceptual deficit? *Developmental Psychology, 18*(3), 435–449. https://doi.org/10.1037/0012-1649.18.3.435

Cantrell, L. M., Kanjlia, S., Harrison, M., Luck, S. J., & Oakes, L. M. (2019). Cues to individuation facilitate 6-month-old infants' visual short-term memory. *Developmental Psychology, 55*(5), 905–919. https://doi.org/10.1037/dev0000683

Colombo, J. (1993). *Infant cognition: Predicting later intellectual functioning.* Sage Publications, Inc. https://doi.org/10.4135/9781483326481

Corter, C. M., Zucker, K. J., & Galligan, R. F. (1980). Patterns of infant's search for mother during brief separation. *Developmental Psychology, 16*, 62–69. https://doi.org/10.1037/0012-1649.16.1.62

Crichton, M., & Lange-Küttner, C. (1999). Tracking, waving and reaching in 16- to 20-weeks old infants to self-propelled and passive objects. *Developmental Science*, *2*(3), 318–324. https://doi.org/10.1111/1467-7687.00077

Csink, V., Mareschal, D., & Gliga, T. (2021). Does surprise enhance infant memory? Assessing the impact of the encoding context on subsequent object recognition. *Infancy*, *26*(2), 303–318. https://doi.org/10.1111/infa.12383

Cuevas, K., & Bell, M. A. (2011). EEG and ECG from 5 to 10 months of age: Developmental changes in baseline activation and cognitive processing during a working memory task. *International Journal of Psychophysiology*, *80*(2), 119–128. https://doi.org/10.1016/j.ijpsycho.2011.02.009

Cuevas, K., Bell, M. A., Marcovitch, S., & Calkins, S. D. (2012). Electroencephalogram and heart rate measures of working memory at 5 and 10 months of age. *Developmental Psychology*, *48*(4), 907–917. https://doi.org/10.1037/a0026448

Cummings, E. M., & Bjork, E. L. (1981). The search behavior of 12 to 14 month-old infants on a five-choice invisible displacement hiding task. *Infant Behavior and Development*, *4*, 47–60. https://doi.org/10.1016/S0163-6383(81)80007-0

Cummings, E. M., & Bjork, E. L. (1983a). Perseveration and search on a five-choice visible displacement hiding task. *Journal of Genetic Psychology*, *142*, 283–291. https://doi.org/10.1080/00221325.1983.10533519

Cummings, E. M., & Bjork, E. L. (1983b). Search behavior on multi-choice hiding tasks: Evidence for an objective conception of space in infancy. *International Journal of Behavioral Development*, *6*, 71–87. https://doi.org/10.1177/016502548300600105

Cunnane, S. C., & Crawford, M. A. (2003). Survival of the fattest: Fat babies were the key to evolution of the large human brain *Comparative Biochemistry and Physiology. Part A, Molecular & Integrative Physiology*, *136*, 17–26. https://doi.org/10.1016/S1095-6433(03)00048-5

Dawson, G. (1994). Development of emotional expression and emotion regulation in infancy. In G. Dawson & K. W. Fischer (Eds.), *Human behavior and the developing brain* (pp. 346–379). The Guildford Press.

Diamond, A. (1985). Development of the ability to use recall to guide action, as indicated by infants' performance on AB. *Child Development*, *56*(4), 868–883. https://doi.org/10.2307/1130099

Diamond, A. (1988). Abilities and neural mechanisms underlying AB performance. *Child Development*, *59*(2), 523–527. https://doi.org/10.2307/1130330

Diamond, A. (1990). Developmental time course in human infants and infant monkeys, and the neural bases of inhibitory control in reaching. *Annals of the New York Academy of Sciences*, *608*, 637–676. https://doi.org/10.1111/j.1749-6632.1990.tb48913.x

Diamond, A. (1991). Neuropsychological insights into the meaning of object concept development. In S. Carey & R. Gelman (Eds.), *The epigenesis of mind: Essays on biology and cognition* (pp. 67–110). Erlbaum.

Diamond, A., Cruttenden, L., & Neiderman, D. (1994). AB with multiple wells: I. Why are multiple wells sometimes easier than two wells? II. Memory or memory + inhibition? *Developmental Psychology*, *30*(2), 192–205. https://dx.doi.org/10.1037/0012-1649.30.2.192

Driver, J. (2001). A selective review of selective attention research from the past century. *British Journal of Psychology*, *92*(1), 53–78. https://doi.org/10.1348/000712601162103

Dunn, K., & Bremner, J. G. (2020). Investigating the social environment of the A-not-B search task. *Developmental Science*, *23*(3), ArtID e12921. https://doi.org/10.1111/desc.12921

Fagard, J. W., Spelke, E., & von Hofsten, C. (2009). Reaching and grasping a moving object in 6-, 8-, and 10-month-old infants: Laterality and performance. *Infant Behavior & Development, 32*(2), 137–146. https://doi.org/10.1016/j.infbeh.2008.12.002

Fagen, J. W., & Ohr, P. S. (1985). Temperament and crying in response to the violation of a learned expectancy in early infancy. *Infant Behavior & Development, 8*(2), 157–166. https://doi.org/10.1016/S0163-6383%2885%2980003-5

Fagen, J. W., Ohr, P. S., Fleckenstein, L. K., & Ribner, D. R. (1985). The effect of crying on long-term memory in infancy. *Child Development, 56*(6), 1584–1592. https://doi.org/10.2307/1130477

Fiske, A., de Klerk, C., Lui, K. Y. K., Collins-Jones, L., Hendry, A., Greenhalgh, I., Hall, A., Scerif, G., Dvergsdal, H., & Holmboe, K. (2022). The neural correlates of inhibitory control in 10-month-old infants: A functional near-infrared spectroscopy study. *NeuroImage, 257*, 119241. https://doi.org/10.1016/j.neuroimage.2022.119241

Gibson, E. J., & Walk, R. D. (1960). The "visual cliff". *Scientific American, 202*(4), 64–71. https://doi.org/10.1038/scientificamerican0460-64

Harlow, H. F. (1958). The nature of love. *American Psychologist, 13*(12), 673–685. https://doi.org/10.1037/h0047884

Harris, P. (1986). Bringing order to the A-not-B error. *Monographs of the Society in Child Development, 51*, 52–61.

Hieu, N. T., Gainsborough, M., Simpson, J. A., Thuy, N. T., Hang, N. N., Taylor, A. M., Ghebremeskel, K., Crawford, M., Golfetto, I., Dubowitz, L., & Farrar, J. (2006). Neurological status of low-risk Vietnamese newborns: A comparison with a British newborn cohort. *Journal of Health, Population and Nutrition, 24*(1), 57–63. https://www.jstor.org/stable/23499267

Hirshman, E. (1988). The expectation-violation effect: Paradoxical effects of semantic relatedness. *Journal of Memory and Language, 27*(1), 40–58. https://doi.org/10.1016/0749-596X(88)90047-2

Humphreys, G. W., Duncan, J., & Treisman, A. (1999). *Attention, space, and action: Studies in cognitive neuroscience*. Oxford University Press.

Kirkham, N. Z., & Diamond, A. (2003). Sorting between theories of perseveration: Performance in conflict tasks requires memory, attention and inhibition. *Developmental Science, 6*(5), 474–476. https://doi.org/10.1111/1467-7687.00303

Kretch, K. S., Franchak, J. M., & Adolph, K. E. (2014). Crawling and walking infants see the world differently. *Child Development, 85*(4), 1503–1518. https://doi.org/10.1111/cdev.12206

Lange-Küttner, C. (1998). Which babies are closing the AB gap? Learning effects in object retrieval. *Archives de Psychologie, 66*, 85–103. INIST-CNRS ID 2306188

Lange-Küttner, C. (2008). When one is really two: Switching from object to place memory in the A-not-B search task. *European Journal of Developmental Science, 2*(4), 370–386. https://doi.org/10.3233/DEV-2008-2403

Lange-Küttner, C. (2018). Disappearance of biased visual attention in infants: Remediated tonic neck reflex or maturating visual asymmetry? *Perceptual and Motor Skills, 125*(5), 839–865. https://doi.org/10.1177/0031512518786131

Lange-Küttner, C., & Crichton, M. T. (1999). Change of spatial field effects in 16- to 20- week-old infants. *Brain and Cognition, 39*, 75–92. https://doi.org/10.1006/brcg.1998.1059

Lew, D., Hopkins, B., Owen, L. H., & Green, M. (2007). Postural change effects on infants' AB task performance: Visual, postural or spatial? *Journal of Experimental Child Psychology, 97*, 1–13. https://doi.org/10.1016/j.jecp.2006.12.009

Lewin, K. (1951). *Field theory in social science*. Harper Brothers.

Lindenberger, U., & Baltes, P. B. (1994). Sensory functioning and intelligence in old age: A strong connection. *Psychology and Aging*, *9*, 339–355. https://doi.org/10.1037/0882-7974.9.3.339

Lindenberger, U., Marsiske, M., & Baltes, P. B. (2000). Memorizing while walking: Increase in dual-task costs from young adulthood to old age. *Psychology and Aging*, *15*, 417–436. https://doi.org/10.1037/0882-7974.15.3.417

Lipina, S. J., Martelli, M. I., Vuelta, B., & Colombo, J. A. (2005). Performance on the A-not-B task of Argentinean infants from unsatisfied and satisfied basic needs homes. *Revista Interamericana de Psicología*, *39*(1), 49–60. https://dialnet.unirioja.es/servlet/articulo?codigo=2987875

Logan, G. D. (1996). The CODE theory of visual attention. An integration of space-based and object-based attention. *Psychological Review*, *103*, 603–649. https://doi.org/10.1037/0033-295X.103.4.603

Mackintosh, N. J. (1976). Overshadowing and stimulus intensity. *Animal Learning & Behavior*, *4*(2), 186–192. https://doi.org/10.3758/bf03214033

MacNeill, L. A., Ram, N., Bell, M. A., Fox, N. A., & Perez-Edgar, K. (2018). Trajectories of infants' biobehavioral development: Timing and rate of A-not-B performance gains and EEG maturation. *Child Development*, *89*(3), 711–724. https://doi.org/10.1111/cdev.13022

Marcovitch, S., Clearfield, M. W., Swingler, M., Calkins, S. D., & Bell, M. A. (2016). Attentional predictors of 5-month-olds' performance on a looking A-not-B task. *Infant and Child Development*, *25*(4), 233–246. https://doi.org/10.1002/icd.1931

Marcovitch, S., & Zelazo, P. D. (1999). The A-not-B error: Results from a logistic meta-analysis. *Child Development*, *70*(6), 1297–1313. https://doi.org/10.1111/1467-8624.00095

Marcovitch, S., & Zelazo, P. D. (2006). The influence of number of A trials on 2-year-olds' behavior in two A-not-B-type search tasks: A test of hierarchical competing systems model. *Journal of Cognition and Development*, *7*, 477–501.

Marcovitch, S., Zelazo, P. D., & Schmuckler, M. A. (2002). The effect of the number of A trials on performance on the A-not-B task. *Infancy*, *3*(4), 519–529. https://doi.org/10.1207/S15327078IN0304_06

Mareschal, D., & Bremner, A. J. (2006). When do 4-months-olds remember the 'what' and'where' of hidden objects? In Y. Munakata & M. H. Johnson (Eds.), *Processes of change in brain and cognitive development. Attention and performance XXI* (pp. 427–447). Oxford University Press.

Mareschal, D., Plunkett, K., & Harris, P. (1999). A computational and neuropsychological account of object-oriented behaviours in infancy. *Developmental Science*, *2*(3), 306–317. https://doi.org/10.1111/1467-7687.00076

Mishkin, M., Ungerleider, L. G., & Macko, K. A. (1983). Object vision and spatial vision: Two cortical pathways. *Trends in Neurosciences*, *6*, 414–417.

Moller, E. L., Majdandzic, M., & Bogels, S. M. (2014). Fathers' versus mothers' social referencing signals in relation to infant anxiety and avoidance: A visual cliff experiment. *Developmental Science*, *17*(6), 1012–1028. https://doi.org/10.1111/desc.12194

Munakata, Y. (1998a). Infant perseveration and implications for object permanence theories: A PDP model of the AB task. *Developmental Science*, *1*(2), 161–184. https://doi.org/10.1111/1467-7687.00021

Munakata, Y. (1998b). Infant perseveration: Rethinking data, theory, and the role of modelling. *Developmental Science*, *1*(2), 205–211. https://doi.org/10.1111/1467-7687.00031

Munakata, Y., Lacerda, F., von Hofsten, C., & Heimann, M. (2001). Task dependency in infant behavior: Toward an understanding of the processes underlying cognitive development. In *Emerging cognitive abilities in early infancy* (pp. 29–52). Lawrence Erlbaum Associates Publishers.

Munakata, Y., McClelland, J. L., Johnson, M. H., & Siegler, R. S. (1997). Rethinking infant knowledge: Toward an adaptive process account of successes and failures in object permanence tasks. *Psychological Review, 104*(4), 686–713. https://doi.org/10.1111/1467-7687.00021

Murre, J. M. J., Wolters, G., & Raffone, A. (2006). Binding in working memory and long-term memory: Towards an integrated model. In H. D. Zimmer, A. Mecklinger, & U. Lindenberger (Eds.), *Handbook of binding and memory* (pp. 221–250). Oxford University Press.

Piaget, J. (1954). *The child's construction of reality*. Routledge and Kegan Paul.

Popick, H., Dye, M., Kirkham, N., & Ramscar, M. (2011). Investigating how infants learn to search in the A-not-B task. *Proceedings of the Annual Meeting of the Cognitive Science Society, 33*. https://escholarship.org/uc/item/5fd1b3v5

Posner, M. I., & Raichle, M. E. (1997). *Images of mind*. Scientific American Library.

Richards, J. E., & Rader, N. (1981). Crawling-onset age predicts visual cliff avoidance in infants. *Journal of Experimental Psychology: Human Perception and Performance*, 7(2), 382–387. https://doi.org/10.1037/0096-1523.7.2.382

Shinskey, J. L., & Munakata, Y. (2003). Are infants in the dark about hidden objects? *Developmental Science, 6*(3), 273–282. https://doi.org/10.1111/1467-7687.00283

Shinskey, J. L., & Munakata, Y. (2005). Familiarity breeds searching: Infants reverse their novelty preferences when reaching for hidden objects. *Psychological Science, 16*(8), 596–600. https://doi.org/10.1111/j.1467-9280.2005.01581.x

Siegler, R. S. (2004). Learning about learning. *Merrill-Palmer Quarterly, 50*(3), 353–368. https://doi.org/10.1353/mpq.2004.ßß25

Smith, L. B., Thelen, E., Titzer, R., & McLin, D. (1999). Knowing in the context of acting: The task dynamics of the A-not-B error. *Psychological Review, 106*, 235–260. https://doi.org/0033-295X/99/S3.00

Spelke, E. S., Breinlinger, K., Macomber, J., & Jacobson, K. (1992). Origins of knowledge. *Psychological Review, 99*, 605–632. https://doi.org/10.1037/0033-295X.99.4.605

Thelen, E., Schöner, G., Scheier, C., & Smith, L. B. (2001). The dynamics of embodiment: A field theory of infant perseverative reaching. *Behavioral and Brain Sciences, 24*, 1–34. https://doi.org/10.1017/S0140525X01003910

Thomas, B. A., Ghebremeskel, K., Lowy, C., Offley-Shore, B., & Crawford, M. A. (2005). Plasma fatty acids of neonates born to mothers with and without gestational diabetes. *Prostaglandins Leukotocins Essential Fatty Acids, 72*, 335–341. https://doi.org/10.1016/j.plefa.2005.01.001

Treisman, A. (2006). Object tokens, binding and visual memory. In H. D. Zimmer, A. Mecklinger, & U. Lindenberger (Eds.), *Handbook of binding and memory* (pp. 315–338). Oxford University Press.

Ungerleider, L. G., & Mishkin, M. (1982). Two cortical visual systems. In D. J. Ingle, M. A. Goodale, & R. J. W. Mansfield (Eds.), *Analysis of visual behavior* (pp. 549–586). MIT Press.

Wellman, H. M., Cross, D., & Bartsch, K. (1987). Infant search and object permanence: A meta-analysis of the A-not-B error. *Monographs of the Society for Research in child Development, 51*(3), 1–51.

Werchan, D. M., & Amso, D. (2020). Adaptive rule learning of event sequences during the A-not-B task in 9-month-old infants. *Developmental Psychobiology, 62*(8), 1021–1034. https://doi.org/10.1002/dev.21999

Wickens, D. D. (1954). Stimulus-response theory as applied to perception. In *Learning theory, personality theory, and clinical research: The Kentucky symposium* (pp. 22–35). John Wiley & Sons Inc. https://doi.org/10.1037/11280-002

Wilding, J. M. (2003). Attentional difficulties in children: Weakness in executive function or problems in coping with difficult tasks? *British Journal of Psychology, 94*(4), 427–436. https://doi.org/10.1348/000712603322503015

Willatts, P., & Forsyth, J. S. (1998). Long-chain polyunsaturated fatty acids, infant formula, and breastfeeding. Author's reply. *Lancet, 352*, article 1703. https://doi.org/10.1016/S0140-6736(05)61476-6

Willatts, P., Forsyth, J. S., DiModugno, M. K., Varma, S., & Colvin, M. (1998). Effect of long-chain polyunsaturated fatty acids in infant formula on problem solving at 10 months of age. *The Lancet, 352*, 688–692. https://doi.org/10.1016/S0140-6736(97)11374-5

Zelazo, P. D., Reznick, J. S., & Spinazzola, J. (1998). Representational flexibility and response control in a multistep multilocation search task. *Developmental Psychology, 34*(2), 203–214. https://doi.org/10.1037/0012-1649.34.2.203

Zmyj, N., Prinz, W., & Daum, M. M. (2015). Eighteen-month-olds' memory interference and distraction in a modified A-not-B task is not associated with their anticipatory looking in a false-belief task. *Frontiers in Psychology, 6*, article 857. https://doi.org/10.3389/fpsyg.2015.00857

4

MOTOR DEVELOPMENT

4.1 Motor Development

As has already been made clear in the first chapter, the sensori-motor development of the infant in the first year is a major contributor to the development of intelligence in the absence of language. It is also the period when the human lags behind the animal world where motor development in general is much more rapid. It was, for instance, noted by Porter (1914) that Rhesus monkeys are superior to human infants in sensori-motor development, imitation and even some rational actions. Thus, monitoring motor development was important even at the beginning of the last century because it was seen as the main indicator for intellectual development (Heller, 1925), and not only in the Piagetian theory of sensori-motor stages. As early as 1916, an inclusive sample of over 4,000 children was tested for psycho-motor capacity, and age norms were developed (Wallin, 1916).

There are groups where pronounced motor development problems occur in children showing typical intellectual development (Heller, 1925; Oseretzky, 1925). Common reasons for motor development problems are premature birth before gestation age and asphyxia during birth (Siegel et al., 1982). Moreover, motor development problems can have biochemical reasons, for instance, because of substance abuse during pregnancy. It is important to monitor whether they cause short- to medium-term effects (Singer et al., 2012; Smith et al., 2011), or whether there are long-lasting effects (Hendricks et al., 2020), or if there are no effects at all when controlled for socio-economic status (Soepnel et al., 2022). In the latter case, the social situation may need support or intervention and not the motor development as such. Thus, understandably, especially in the paediatric literature there appear to be more studies on motor development problems in special populations than developmental studies of neurotypical groups.

DOI: 10.4324/9780429270604-5

Motor development in the early years concerns basic motor skills – *posture* (from head lifting to sitting and standing), supporting the body against gravitational and inertial forces; *manual skills* for interacting with objects and surfaces; and *locomotion* for moving the body through the environment (Rachwani et al., 2020). The classic developmental psychology textbook concept for motor development consists of the six sensori-motor stages of Piaget (1954) specifying different levels of 'circular reactions' (Bremner, 1994, see Table 4.1, p. 124). For Piaget, though, motor development was only the vehicle for the development of strong-willed infants who are actively engaged yet still only more or less successful in interactions. Piaget carried out error analyses as errors would give cues about thinking in the wrong direction, see Chapters 1 and 3. Thus, Piaget was not interested in posture, manual skills and locomotion as such, or in developmental milestones. Indeed, there is much variability when children, for instance, begin to walk, and there are no clear developmental sequences, with some children crawling before walking, while others would only draw themselves up and begin to walk (Adolph & Robinson, 2015). We remember from Chapter 1 that the infant is initially passively exposed to perceptions and has perceptions imposed when being carried around or placed somewhere. But along with increasing motoric agility and mobility, the spatial field widens and can be actively controlled by toddlers as far as their feet can carry them. This sense of agency is currently a central research question in robotics (Hafner et al., 2020; Schillaci et al., 2016). Hafner et al. (2020) holds that three main behavioural and computational components can enable autonomous acquisition of motor skills in a robot and the implementation of basic cognitive capabilities: (1) Exploration behaviours; (2) internal body representations and (3) sensori-motor simulations. The latter are the equivalent to using memory in action sequences that make infants more independent from visual impressions (see also Chapter 10). However, the three components still provide only a simplified idea of motor development. A central component of Piaget's sensori-motor stages is the transition from reflex-like automatic behaviour to the infants' will to control and to say no. In this first emergence of defiance, infants would reject adults' offers and contingencies. Defiance is not identical to inhibition. In inhibition, one's own thinking and behaviour is controlled, while in defiance, others' action sequences are countered. Thus, this chapter gives some examples of motor development that are also important for a theory of spatial freedom and the effects of spatial constraints imposed by a playpen. Moreover, the development of eye–hand and eye–mouth coordination in relation to object affordances by drinking from a cup, tool use when hammering, and motor development in sports are covered. The development of fine motor skills is discussed in Chapter 5 on drawing and handwriting.

4.2 Spatial Constraints on Motor Development

We are now aware that adults initially have complete spatial control over their infant, but when it begins to move independently, there are at least two options.

One option is to allow *free movement* and make the environment infant-safe, for instance by inserting child safety plugs into sockets or by following wherever a toddler is moving along. Another option is to get an infant used to *spatial constraints*, for instance a playpen where activities are contained and limited to play activities with toys. Conversations are still possible, but movement is constrained.

Playpens now occupy many young families' reception rooms (Cieraad, 2013). On the one hand, they are a spatial constraint for toddlers' movements that have the potential to limit motor development (Abbott & Bartlett, 2001). On the other hand, children in extended day care who are placed in a pen in pairs show an increase of positive and sustained social interactions from the second to the third year (Sarafino, 1985). Playpens can also be dangerous places if toys are not suitable; for instance, semi-rigid toys can suffocate an infant if they cover the mouth and nose at the same time (Nakamura et al., 2003).

A playpen imposes an explicit boundary that provides containment. In a cross-cultural comparison, 92% of Dutch parents placed their infants in a playpen, while only 16% of Israeli parents did (Oudgenoeg-Paz et al., 2020). Dutch children were also in the playpen for longer than they were in a baby bouncer. Dutch parents used sleeping bags more often (73%) than Israeli parents (4%), which drastically limits leg but not arm movements. This did not mean that Dutch parents would not place their infants into 'unlimited space' such as on a mat, carpet or floor where infants could engage in spatial exploration and would need more constant and close supervision: 74% of the Dutch parents also used this setting, while 90.7% of Israeli parents did. Because only first-born infants were assessed, this result was independent of the number of children in the family. The parent preferences also occurred independently of the age of their children, although Israeli families used a playpen somewhat more once their children reached the age of 2½ months (27%). Both the time in the sleeping bag (−.30) and in the playpen (−.15) had a negative correlation with an alert prone position (lying on the stomach), while playing on the floor surface had a positive correlation of .22. Prone position prevents the infants' heads from becoming deformed (positional plagiocephaly; see Boere-Boonekamp & van der Linden-Kuiper, 2001). Nevertheless, despite these differences in rearing, there were no effects of cultural parental belief and practice on outcome variables at 10 months such as crawling or pulling to stand.

Another study compared motor development and communication skills longitudinally in two cultures (Lohaus et al., 2011), in a countryside setting in Cameroon compared with an urban setting in Germany. The result was that countryside babies were better at gross-motor skills, while urban babies were adept in social communication, both at 3 and 6 months. At 3 months, 94.5% of the countryside infants were sitting with support, but only 6.8% of the urban children did. Moreover, at 6 months, 65.8% of the countryside infants made stepping movements and 91.8% supported their weight, but only 13.5% of urban children did and just 6.3% supported their weight. These were significant differences even though standard deviations were high due to the normal variability in motor development.

In the urban babies, the Bayley Scales cognition score was correlated with fine and gross motor development at 3 and 6 months, while in the countryside group, it was only correlated with fine motor skills at both points of measurement. Interestingly, receptive and expressive communication skills were hardly correlated at all with cognition, and even less so in 6-month-old infants, but only with each other. Thus, although the built environment and the presence of children's rooms were not assessed in this study, it seems that the relatively unlimited and unconstrained space of farming communities is more conducive to motor development.

In another study, an introduction of playpens in rural Ethiopian communities led to higher perceived safety due to a reduction of wandering about, to separation from animals, and to developmental and hygiene benefits such as protection from *E. coli* bacteria as well as relief from physical stress and worry for caregivers (J. Rosenbaum et al., 2021). Thus, imposing spatial constraints on infants enabled a more productive and safe life so much so that all parents opted to keep the playpen rather than taking a relatively large amount of cash. Often older siblings or parents joined infants in the playpen. Similar playpen advantages are reported by US mothers (Pierce, 2000).

FIGURE 4.1 Self-selected Playpen (Courtesy L.A. and K.M. Küttner). *Note:* A 22-month-old girl playing with animal toys whom she tells to sit properly in her self-selected cardboard box. The girl had never played in a playpen because her parents rejected the notion of spatial constraints.

We still do not know whether playpens would delay motor development apart from skilfully holding a prone position (Oudgenoeg-Paz et al., 2020). In a study with rats, those with access to a playpen showed more walking, running, climbing, and digging, while those without access showed more social activities such as grooming, resting, hiding in a shelter, eating and drinking (Ratuski et al., 2021). In another study with the same aim of making lab rats more comfortable, a playpen could even successfully attenuate the negative affective effects of the drug FG7142, which has anorectic, anxiogenic and pro-convulsant consequences, increases the release of stress-related noradrenaline, but also acetylcholine which improves memory retention (Hinchcliffe et al., 2022). However, while for the rats, the playpen was larger and more richly endowed than their normal 'home' cage, playpens of human infants are usually smaller and more constrained places within the home.

Spatial exploration behaviour rather than onset of walking is predictive for spatial memory even years later in pre-school children (Oudgenoeg-Paz et al., 2014). Gross motor but not object exploration was found to be especially predictive for spatial memory and spatial language in 2- to 3-year-olds (Oudgenoeg-Paz et al., 2015). So far, not one study covers all aspects, but one could draw the hypothetical conclusion that imposing spatial constraints by limiting infants' spatial field with a playpen is likely to limit gross motor development if not complemented by outdoor roaming, but may favour sustained attention and fine motor skills.

4.3 Spatial Affordances and End-State Comfort

Gibson's ecological perceptual theory was very different from the traditional Gestalt theory approach insofar as its impetus was on extraction of invariants from an ongoing visual flow during observer movement (Gibson, 1979). Initially, Gibson's concept of *affordances* was given less attention as it referred to the meaning of objects. He claimed that affordances are objects' functional features and that they are directly perceptible without further thought or explanation. Handles, for instance, are such a feature. A container with a handle is not a vase, but it could be a mug. 'Intellectually realistic' children would not omit a handle when drawing mugs even if the handle is turned away from sight (Lange-Küttner, 2011, see Chapter 5) because the handle is defining the object as a mug. Likewise, a hammer has a handle. If the hammer were just a heavy piece its function for banging would not be that obvious, but the handle defines the heavy piece of iron as an object for hammering.

Another important concept is that of *end-state comfort* (D. A. Rosenbaum, 2010). The concept implies that we initially accept some discomfort in order to reach a comfortable state in the end. Moreover, when politely passing a knife to a person sitting opposite us, the end-state comfort has to be not considered for only oneself, but also with respect to the person receiving it; see Figure 4.2.

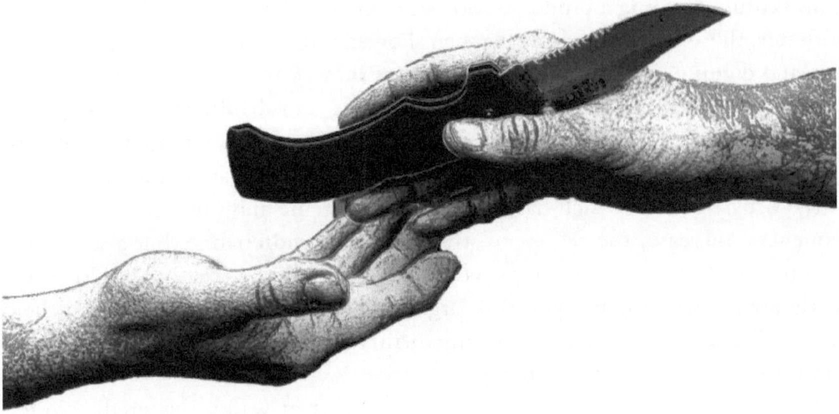

FIGURE 4.2 End-State-Comfort when Passing a Knife (adapted from www.qph.cf2.quoracdn.net)

The drawing in Figure 4.2 illustrates that one cannot just take the knife by the handle and pass it on to a partner who would then need to grasp the knife by the blade and could get cuts in the fingers when clasping the sharp edge of the blade. Instead, one needs to turn around the knife so that the blade comes to rest with the blunt side in one's own hand so that the other person can then grasp the handle of the knife and neither of the two gets hurt. There are many research studies on children's ability to rotate objects in their mind (e.g. Lütke & Lange-Küttner, 2015, 2021). However, motor control studies investigate whether, given the normal affordances (grasp the handle), children would really rotate an object in a relatively awkward way in order to reach a comfortable end-state. In studies with children, usually safer objects than knives are used; however, passing a knife the right way does belong to table manners, which may be decisive for an offspring's future success in business dinners.

One of the earliest and very necessary achievements is drinking from an open cup (Scarborough et al., 2018). The multiple necessary motor coordinations are hand and jaw, stabilisation of head and trunk, lip closure and volitional control of the tongue. However, how the sucking reflex transforms into drinking is not described, nor are the different types of cups described that are on offer to ease this transition.

We go to great lengths to make this transition from sucking to drinking more comfortable for children and parents. Scarborough et al. (2018) describe that infants have immature fine motor skills and do not grasp a cup with one hand. This is to be expected as they also do not cup the breast or the bottle with just one hand. Figure 4.3 shows a 'sippy' cup that is designed to ease the transition from sucking to drinking as the straw still allows for sucking and there are two

FIGURE 4.3 Intermediate-State Comfort when Drinking from a Sippy Cup (www.nakedbaby.co.nz)

handles for holding the cup bi-manually as handedness still develops at this age. One could see the sippy cup as allowing an intermediate state of comfort because some features facilitate the transition, while training babies straightaway on adult cups with open tops and one handle could create real discomfort (Fournier et al., 2019). The infant may close the lips around the upper rim rather than the lower rim and all drink would be spilled. Still at two years of age, only 57% of a large sample were drinking from a regular cup without help (Carruth et al., 2004). Those who managed were more likely to have had higher intakes of energy and fat.

All developmental studies with older children show that they take years to spontaneously use an awkward grasp in order to reach a comfortable end-state. For instance, 3- to 5-year-olds were asked to grasp hammers with a non-dominant hand (Ossmy et al., 2022). Ossmy et al. distinguished between an overhand grip, where palms are facing towards the body, and an underhand grip, with palms facing away from the body. Younger children ('nonadaptive planners') used a habitual overhand grip, where an arm lift would have been needed for hammering, whereas adults and older children ('adaptive planners') used an adaptive underhand grip, where the hand could easily be turned into the right position for hammering. Nonadaptive children used a habitual overhand grip immediately before any gathering of visual information, leaving insufficient time to form a plan before acting. Likewise, when shape sorting by inserting them into matching slots, adults adjusted object orientation during transport, whereas children adjusted object orientation only after arriving at the box (Ossmy et al., 2020).

When comparing different age groups on the end-state comfort grip on a rotated cylinder, most 9- to 14-year-old children could apply an initially less comfortable grip, but only half of the 5- to 8-year-old children did (Van Swieten et al., 2010). One reason is that children until at least four years are still increasing the precision required for simple grasping, which in turn decreases the variability of the grasping patterns and increases the frequency of right-handed strategies (Fagard & Lockman, 2005). Another reason is that the actual reach trajectory, when measured with motor tracking, becomes less variable and more efficient with clear age trends (Jung et al., 2015) and trajectories become also shorter.

Moreover, 3- to 5-year-old children do not really focus on the actual grip when watching clips with efficient versus awkward end-states (Ossmy et al., 2021). When they watched a video of an adult hammering in a peg, they would look at everything: The face of the adult, the non-dominant passive hand, and the dominant hand, the hammer and the peg. Adults would only watch the link between the active hand and the hammer, and the hammer and the peg. Pupil size differences clearly indicated that adults differentiated between an efficient grip vs. a non-efficient grip. Brain activations showed that brain responses were above chance in adults, but not in one single child. These and several other studies show a steadily increasing but very protracted development of end-state comfort anticipation in the vast majority of 10-year-old children, but even at this age, still not by as many as in adults (D. A. Rosenbaum et al., 2012).

4.4 Spatial Objects and Fields in Sports Games

With the onset of school, both fine and gross motor skills develop further, first, because of the onset of handwriting, and second, because children are taught various sports disciplines, some up to Olympic standards (Bondi et al., 2022). This new and systematic motor development tuition also introduces sports competition as a new factor to children (Tofler & Butterbaugh, 2005), although some may have participated in sports clubs before being schooled. Moreover, several research studies found that sports and physical exercise substantially, but indirectly, improved cognitive performance, especially executive attention (Oberer et al., 2018; Schmidt et al., 2017). Also other factors such as physical fitness and nutrition play a role (Ishihara et al., 2018; Ishihara et al., 2020).

However, it works also the other way round insofar as intellectual and perceptual abilities as well as coordinative skills discriminate elite from non-elite junior athletes (Faber et al., 2016). Object control skills are seen as the foundation for further sports skill development (Butterfield et al., 2012), but intelligence (IQ) also has an impact as children with lower IQ scored significantly lower on almost all specific motor skill items than typically developing children (Westendorp et al., 2011). In contrast, a lower socio-economic status (SES) of the parents does not need to be an obstacle as girls from schools in a low SES area in Ireland had better object control proficiency than girls in schools located in the better-off districts in the same town (Neville et al., 2019). In general, girls' skill in throwing and striking a ball is lower than in boys (Angell et al., 2018; Butterfield et al., 2012). However, another large Irish study showed that self-perceived movement skill was more important than the actual sports competence (Peers et al., 2020). Hence low SES may have been an advantage because there may have been permission to roam and play, while high SES parents would have probably insisted on more motorically and spatially constrained activities like sitting at desks doing homework.

Interestingly, in football games in their own time, children more often show competitive than cooperative behaviour than in teacher-instructed lessons, for instance when tackling in 1:1 situations, ball touches and finishing a goal (Nybakken & Falco, 2022). This is most likely the case because in sports lessons, children are taught the correct motor sequences, along with the aim of getting children to play together and to teach the rules of the different games (Newell & Rovegno, 2021). Spatial constraints are set by boundaries and violation is regulated by lines(wo)men. Also, parents need to stay behind the sidelines and avoid interference (Seccareccia-DeClerico, 2020).

In a game like football, the boundaries and lines are probably less important than the actual interactions between attackers and defenders of spatial regions (Caetano et al., 2021; Narizuka et al., 2021; Vilar et al., 2014) because the decisive area for winning is only the small region within the goal. If a football lands outside the spatial field, the other team gets to throw in the ball into the field without any consequence. However, in a game like tennis, a winning point for the opponent is scored as soon as a serve or return lands the ball outside the field. Thus, the field boundaries in tennis are much more important and user-driven sorting, clustering and layout techniques to exactly analyse whether a ball lands on or besides the line have been developed (Polk et al., 2020) but have not been used yet in developmental studies.

While both ballgames and aerobic exercise can improve children's executive attention, team games are especially important to improve the ability to shift attention (Schmidt et al., 2015). In ballgames, children learn to distribute themselves in the spatial field that can vary in size. For instance, a tennis field is smaller than a football field and only has two players. A table tennis field is still smaller. Larger fields require and activate more physiological resources, but this also depends on the number of players, as fewer players even in a small field need to show more effort (Dellal et al., 2012). Hence, field size can be set to smaller measurements for younger players (Gimenez-Egido et al., 2019; Larson & Guggenheimer, 2013). Also, the shape and size of sub-fields may vary according to the game; for instance, there is a box in front of the goal in football but a semi-circle in basketball. Moreover, there is a difference between novice and experienced football players in the field (Williams et al., 1999): While expert players monitor a large area within the field and survey other players with or without a ball, novice players were more likely to show a tunnel vision towards the player

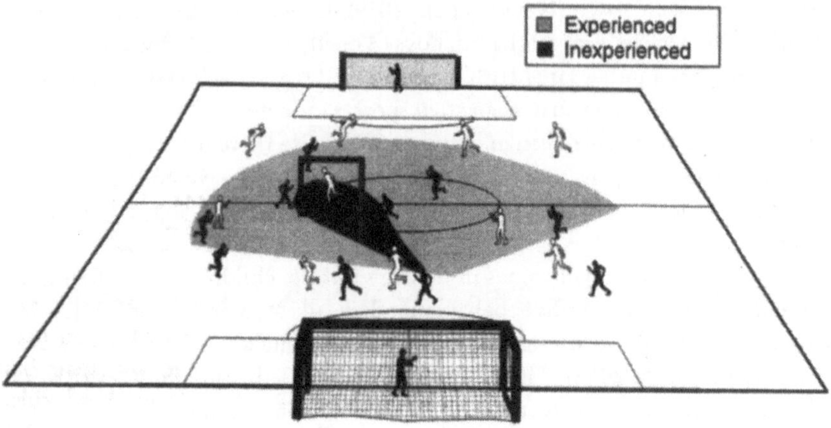

FIGURE 4.4 Spatial Field Control (Williams et al., 1999, p. 160)

in possession of the ball (see Figure 4.4). This shows that expert players are considering an area with several players (common region or objects-region binding) rather than just the location of an individual player (object-place binding).

4.5 Conclusions

This chapter on motor development might at first sight look more applied than theoretical. However, the impact of spatial constraints and spatial freedom on development are important ingredients for a spatial theory. While in the next chapters the spatial constraints occur on paper, on the screen, or just in visual memory and the imagination, the current chapter has laid the basis using examples from a time in life when infants do not yet draw recognisable pictures or solve tasks on a screen. Moreover, it was described in this chapter that motor development branches out into engagements with various sports, with many of them involving spatial fields and different types of spatial boundaries. We will see in the following chapters that such boundaries gradually emerge in development as a concept. We will also see in the chapter on visual memory that spatial boundaries can determine whether objects or places are remembered. The current chapter on motor development is also complemented by the last chapter of this book on developmental coordination disorders, which draws together all the factors that contribute to the development of smooth motor functioning.

References

Abbott, A. L., & Bartlett, D. J. (2001). Infant motor development and equipment use in the home. *Child: Care, Health and Development*, (3), 295–306. https://doi.org/10.1046/j.1365-2214.2001.00186.x

Adolph, K. E., & Robinson, S. R. (2015). Motor development. In R. M. Lerner, L. S. Liben, & U. Mueller (Eds.), *Handbook of child psychology and developmental science: Cognitive processes* (Vol. 2, 7th ed., pp. 113–157). Wiley.

Angell, R. M., Butterfield, S. A., Tu, S., Loovis, E., Mason, C. A., & Nightingale, C. J. (2018). Children's throwing and striking: A longitudinal study. *Journal of Motor Learning and Development*, *6*(2), 315–332. https://doi.org/10.1123/jmld.2017-0026

Boere-Boonekamp, M. M., & van der Linden-Kuiper, L. T. (2001). Positional preference: Prevalence in infants and follow-up after two years. *Pediatrics*, *107*(2), 339–343. https://doi.org/10.1542/peds.107.2.339

Bondi, D., Robazza, C., Lange-Küttner, C., & Pietrangelo, T. (2022). Fine motor skills and motor control networking in developmental age. *American Journal of Human Biology*, *34*(8), e23758. https://doi.org/10.1002/ajhb.23758

Bremner, J. G. (1994). *Infancy*. Blackwell.

Butterfield, S. A., Angell, R. M., & Mason, C. A. (2012). Age and sex differences in object control skills by children ages 5 to 14. *Perceptual and Motor Skills*, *114*(1), 261–274. https://doi.org/10.2466/10.11.25.PMS.114.1.261-274

Caetano, F. G., Barbon Jr., S., Torres, R. D. S., Cunha, S. A., Ruffino, P. R. C., Martins, L. E. B., & Moura, F. A. (2021). Football player dominant region determined by a novel model based on instantaneous kinematics variables. *Scientific Reports*, *11*(1), article 18209. https://doi.org/10.1038/s41598-021-97537-4

Carruth, B. R., Ziegler, P. J., Gordon, A., & Hendricks, K. (2004). Developmental milestones and self-feeding behaviors in infants and toddlers. *Journal of the American Dietetic Association*, *104*, 51–56. https://doi.org/10.1016/j.jada.2003.10.019

Cieraad, I. (2013). The family living room: A child's playpen? *Home Cultures*, *10*(3), 287–314. https://doi.org/10.2752/175174213X13712175825557

Dellal, A., Owen, A., Wong, D. P., Krustrup, P., van Exsel, M., & Mallo, J. (2012). Technical and physical demands of small vs. large sided games in relation to playing position in elite soccer. *Human Movement Science*, *31*(4), 957–969. https://doi.org/10.1016/j.humov.2011.08.013

Faber, I. R., Bustin, P. M., Oosterveld, F. G., Elferink-Gemser, M. T., & Nijhuis-Van der Sanden, M. W. (2016). Assessing personal talent determinants in young racquet sport players: A systematic review. *Journal of Sports Sciences*, *34*(5), 395–410. https://doi.org/10.1080/02640414.2015.1061201

Fagard, J., & Lockman, J. J. (2005). The effect of task constraints on infants' (bi)manual strategy for grasping and exploring objects. *Infant Behavior and Development*, *28*(3), 305–315. https://doi.org/10.1016/j.infbeh.2005.05.005

Fournier, L. R., Coder, E., Kogan, C., Raghunath, N., Taddese, E., & Rosenbaum, D. A. (2019). Which task will we choose first? Precrastination and cognitive load in task ordering. *Attention, Perception & Psychophysics*, *81*(2), 489–503. https://doi.org/10.3758/s13414-018-1633-5

Gibson, J. J. (1979). *The ecological approach to visual perception*. Houghton Mifflin.

Gimenez-Egido, J. M., Ortega-Toro, E., Palao, J. M., Verdú-Conesa, I., & Torres-Luque, G. (2019). Effect of modification rules in competition on technical-tactical action in young tennis players (Under-10). *Frontiers in Psychology*, *10*, article 2789. https://doi.org/10.3389/fpsyg.2019.02789

Hafner, V. V., Loviken, P., Pico Villalpando, A., & Schillaci, G. (2020). Prerequisites for an artificial self. *Frontiers in Neurorobotics*, *14*, article 5. https://doi.org/10.3389/fnbot.2020.00005

Heller, T. (1925). On motor retardations in children. *Zeitschrift für Kinderforschung*, *30*, 1–10.

Hendricks, G., Malcolm-Smith, S., Stein, D. J., Zar, H. J., Wedderburn, C. J., Nhapi, R. T., Chivese, T., Adnams, C. M., & Donald, K. A. (2020). Prenatal alcohol exposure is associated with early motor, but not language development in a South African cohort. *Acta Neuropsychiatrica, 32*(3), 145–152. https://doi.org/10.1017/neu.2019.51

Hinchcliffe, J. K., Jackson, M. G., & Robinson, E. S. (2022). The use of ball pits and playpens in laboratory Lister Hooded male rats induces ultrasonic vocalisations indicating a more positive affective state and can reduce the welfare impacts of aversive procedures. *Laboratory Animals, 56*(4), 370–379. https://doi.org/10.1177/00236772211065920

Ishihara, T., Sugasawa, S., Matsuda, Y., & Mizuno, M. (2018). Relationship between sports experience and executive function in 6–12-year-old children: Independence from physical fitness and moderation by gender. *Developmental Science, 21*(3), 1–13. https://doi.org/10.1111/desc.12555

Ishihara, T., Yuta, K., & Mizuno, M. (2020). Relationships between tennis experience, executive function, and self-regulation of dietary behaviour in children. *International Journal of Sport and Exercise Psychology, 18*(2), 143–155. https://doi.org/10.1080/1612197X.2018.1511625

Jung, W. P., Kahrs, B. A., & Lockman, J. J. (2015). Manual action, fitting, and spatial planning: Relating objects by young children. *Cognition, 134*, 128–139. https://doi.org/10.1016/j.cognition.2014.09.004

Lange-Küttner, C. (2011). Sex differences in visual realism in drawings of animate and inanimate objects. *Perceptual and Motor Skills, 113*(2), 439–453. https://doi.org/10.2466/04.10.24.PMS.113.5.439-453

Larson, E. J., & Guggenheimer, J. D. (2013). The effects of scaling tennis equipment on the forehand groundstroke performance of children. *Journal of Sports Science & Medicine, 12*(2), 323–331. https://www.ncbi.nlm.nih.gov/pmc/articles/PMC3761839/

Lohaus, A., Keller, H., Lamm, B., Teubert, M., Fassbender, I., Freitag, C., Goertz, C., Graf, F., Kolling, T., Spangler, S., Vierhaus, M., Knopf, M., & Schwarzer, G. (2011). Infant development in two cultural contexts: Cameroonian Nso farmer and German middle-class infants. *Journal of Reproductive and Infant Psychology, 29*(2), 148–161. https://doi.org/10.1080/02646838.2011.558074

Lütke, N., & Lange-Küttner, C. (2015). Keeping it in three dimensions: Measuring the development of mental rotation in children with the Rotated Colour Cube Test (RCCT). *International Journal of Developmental Science, 9*(2), 95–114. https://doi.org/10.3233/dev-14154

Lütke, N., & Lange-Küttner, C. (2021). The magical number four in children's mental rotation of cube aggregates. *Developmental Psychology, 57*(2), 211–226. https://doi.org/10.1037/dev0001139

Nakamura, S. W., Pollack-Nelson, C., & Chidekel, A. S. (2003). Suction-type suffocation incidents in infants and toddlers. *Pediatrics, 111*(1), e12–e16. https://doi.org/10.1542/peds.111.1.e12

Narizuka, T., Yamazaki, Y., & Takizawa, K. (2021). Space evaluation in football games via field weighting based on tracking data. *Scientific Reports, 11*(1), article 5509. https://doi.org/10.1038/s41598-021-84939-7

Neville, R. D., Lyons, F., Doyle, B., & Lakes, K. D. (2019). Girls from socioeconomically disadvantaged schools exhibit greater object control skills than girls from schools on the upper levels of socioeconomic development. *Journal of Motor Learning and Development*, 7(3), 320–335. https://doi.org/10.1123/jmld.2019-0014

Newell, K. M., & Rovegno, I. (2021). Teaching children's motor skills for team games through guided discovery: How constraints enhance learning. *Frontiers in Psychology, 12*, article 724848. https://doi.org/10.3389/fpsyg.2021.724848

Nybakken, T., & Falco, C. (2022). Activity Level and nature of practice and play in children's football. *International Journal of Environmental Research and Public Health, 19*(8). https://doi.org/10.3390/ijerph19084598

Oberer, N., Gashaj, V., & Roebers, C. M. (2018). Executive functions, visual-motor coordination, physical fitness and academic achievement: Longitudinal relations in typically developing children. *Human Movement Science, 58*, 69–79. https://doi.org/10.1016/j.humov.2018.01.003

Oseretzky, N. (1925). A metric scale for the study of the motor ability of children. *Zeitschrift für Kinderforschung, 30*, 300–314.

Ossmy, O., Han, D., Cheng, M., Kaplan, B. E., & Adolph, K. E. (2020). Look before you fit: The real-time planning cascade in children and adults. *Journal of Experimental Child Psychology, 189*, 104696. https://doi.org/10.1016/j.jecp.2019.104696

Ossmy, O., Han, D., Kaplan, B. E., Xu, M., Bianco, C., Mukamel, R., & Adolph, K. E. (2021). Children do not distinguish efficient from inefficient actions during observation. *Scientific Reports, 11*(1), 18106. https://doi.org/10.1038/s41598-021-97354-9

Ossmy, O., Kaplan, B. E., Han, D., Xu, M., Bianco, C., Mukamel, R., & Adolph, K. E. (2022). Real-time processes in the development of action planning. *Current Biology, 32*(1), 190–199. https://doi.org/10.1016/j.cub.2021.11.018

Oudgenoeg-Paz, O., Atun-Einy, O., & van Schaik, S. D. M. (2020). Two cultural models on infant motor development: Middle class parents in Israel and the Netherlands. *Frontiers in Psychology, 11*, article 119. https://doi.org/10.3389/fpsyg.2020.00119

Oudgenoeg-Paz, O., Leseman, P. P. M., & Volman, M. J. M. (2014). Can infant self-locomotion and spatial exploration predict spatial memory at school age? *European Journal of Developmental Psychology, 11*(1), 36–48. https://doi.org/10.1080/17405629.2013.803470

Oudgenoeg-Paz, O., Leseman, P. P. M., & Volman, M. J. M. (2015). Exploration as a mediator of the relation between the attainment of motor milestones and the development of spatial cognition and spatial language. *Developmental Psychology, 51*, 1241–1253. https://doi.org/10.1037/a0039572

Peers, C., Issartel, J., Behan, S., O'Connor, N., & Belton, S. (2020). Movement competence: Association with physical self-efficacy and physical activity. *Human Movement Science, 70*, article 102582. https://doi.org/10.1016/j.humov.2020.102582

Piaget, J. (1954). *The construction of reality in the child*. Routledge and Kegan Paul.

Pierce, D. (2000). Maternal management of the home as a developmental play space for infants and toddlers. *The American Journal of Occupational Therapy, 54*(3), 290–299. https://doi.org/10.5014/ajot.54.3.290

Polk, T., Jackle, D., Haussler, J., & Yang, J. (2020). CourtTime: Generating actionable insights into tennis matches using visual analytics. *IEEE Transactions on Visualization and Computer Graphics, 26*(1), 397–406. https://doi.org/10.1109/tvcg.2019.2934243

Porter, J. P. (1914). Habit formation, imitation and higher mental processes of animals. *Psychological Bulletin, 11*(8), 294–303. https://doi.org/10.1037/h0070382

Rachwani, J., Hoch, J., & Adolph, K. E. (2020). Action in development: Plasticity, variability, and flexibility. In J. J. Lockman & C. S. Tamis-LeMonda (Eds.), *The Cambridge handbook of infant development: Brain, behavior, and cultural context* (pp. 469–494). Cambridge University Press.

Ratuski, A. S., Makowska, I. J., Dvorack, K. R., & Weary, D. M. (2021). Using approach latency and anticipatory behaviour to assess whether voluntary playpen access is rewarding to laboratory mice. *Scientific Reports, 11*(1), article 18683. https://doi.org/10.1038/s41598-021-98356-3

Rosenbaum, D. A. (2010). *Motor control*. Academic Press.

Rosenbaum, D. A., Chapman, K. M., Weigelt, M., Weiss, D. J., & van der Wel, R. (2012). Cognition, action, and object manipulation. *Psychological Bulletin, 138*(5), 924–946. https://doi.org/10.1037/a0027839

Rosenbaum, J., Tenaw, E., Clemmer, R., Israel, M., & Albert, J. (2021). Exploring the use and appeal of playpens to protect infants from exposure to animals, animal feces, and dirt in rural Ethiopia. *American Journal of Tropical Medicine and Hygiene, 104*(1), 346–356. https://doi.org/10.4269/ajtmh.20-0445

Sarafino, E. P. (1985). Peer-peer interaction among infants and toddlers with extensive daycare experience. *Journal of Applied Developmental Psychology, 6*(1), 17–29. https://doi.org/10.1016/0193-3973(85)90013-9

Scarborough, D., Brink, K. E., & Bailey-Van Kuren, M. (2018). Open-cup drinking development: A review of the literature. *Dysphagia, 33*(3), 293–302. https://doi.org/10.1007/s00455-017-9871-6

Schillaci, G., Hafner, V. V., & Lara, B. (2016). Exploration behaviors, body representations, and simulation processes for the development of cognition in artificial agents. *Frontiers in Robotics and AI, 3*, article 39. https://doi.org/10.3389/frobt.2016.00039

Schmidt, M., Egger, F., Benzing, V., Jäger, K., Conzelmann, A., Roebers, C. M., & Pesce, C. (2017). Disentangling the relationship between children's motor ability, executive function and academic achievement. *PLoS One, 12*(8), article e0182845. https://doi.org/10.1371/journal.pone.0182845

Schmidt, M., Jäger, K., Egger, F., Roebers, C. M., & Conzelmann, A. (2015). Cognitively engaging chronic physical activity, but not aerobic exercise, affects executive functions in primary school children: A group-randomized controlled trial. *Journal of Sport and Exercise Psychology, 37*(6), 575–591. https://doi.org/10.1123/jsep.2015-0069

Seccareccia-DeClerico, S. (2020). *Sideline parents in youth sport: A serious game that warrants the attention of clinical psychology* (Publication Number 8-B) (Dissertation). Capella University, Minneapolis, MN, USA.

Siegel, L. S., Saigal, S., Rosenbaum, P. L., Morton, R. A., Young, A., Berenbaum, S., & Stoskopf, B. (1982). Predictors of development in preterm and full-term infants: A model for detecting the at risk child. *Journal of Pediatric Psychology, 7*(2), 135–148. https://doi.org/10.1093/jpepsy/7.2.135

Singer, L. T., Moore, D. G., Fulton, S., Goodwin, J., Turner, J. J., Min, M. O., & Parrott, A. C. (2012). Neurobehavioral outcomes of infants exposed to MDMA (Ecstasy) and other recreational drugs during pregnancy. *Neurotoxicology and Teratology, 34*(3), 303–310. https://doi.org/10.1016/j.ntt.2012.02.001

Smith, L. M., LaGasse, L. L., Derauf, C., Newman, E., Shah, R., Haning, W., Arria, A., Huestis, M., Strauss, A., Della Grotta, S., Dansereau, L. M., Lin, H., & Lester, B. M. (2011). Motor and cognitive outcomes through three years of age in children exposed to prenatal methamphetamine. *Neurotoxicology and Teratology, 33*(1), 176–184. https://doi.org/10.1016/j.ntt.2010.10.004

Soepnel, L., Nicolaou, V., Draper, C., Levitt, N., Klipstein-Grobusch, K., & Norris, S. (2022). Cognitive and motor development in 3- to 6-year-old children born to mothers with hyperglycaemia first detected in pregnancy in an urban African population. *Maternal and Child Health Journal, 26*, 1328–1338. https://doi.org/10.1007/s10995-021-03331-z

Tofler, I. R., & Butterbaugh, G. J. (2005). Developmental overview of child and youth sports for the twenty-first century. *Clinics in Sports Medicine*, *24*(4), 783–804. https://doi.org/10.1016/j.csm.2005.05.006

Van Swieten, L. M., Van Bergen, E., Williams, J. H., Wilson, A. D., Plumb, M. S., Kent, S. W., & Mon-Williams, M. A. (2010). A test of motor (not executive) planning in developmental coordination disorder and autism. *Journal of Experimental Psychology: Human Perception and Performance*, *36*(2), 493–499. https://doi.org/10.1037/a0017177

Vilar, L., Araújo, D., Travassos, B., & Davids, K. (2014). Coordination tendencies are shaped by attacker and defender interactions with the goal and the ball in futsal. *Human Movement Science*, *33*, 14–24. https://doi.org/10.1016/j.humov.2013.08.012

Wallin, J. (1916). Age norms of psycho-motor capacity. *Journal of Educational Psychology*, 7(1), 17–24. https://doi.org/10.1037/h0073948

Westendorp, M., Houwen, S., Hartman, E., & Visscher, C. (2011). Are gross motor skills and sports participation related in children with intellectual disabilities? *Research in Developmental Disabilities*, *32*(3), 1147–1153. https://doi.org/10.1016/j.ridd.2011.01.009

Williams, A. M., Davids, K., & Williams, J. G. (1999). *Visual perception and action in sport*. Taylor & Francis.

5

DRAWING AND WRITING DEVELOPMENT

5.1 Components of Drawing

As long ago as 1895, a chapter on children's drawings was included in an encyclopaedia on child development (Sully, 1895) but in today's handbooks, drawing is not included. Drawing was of special interest in teacher education (e.g. Burk, 1902; Clark, 1897; Kerschensteiner, 1905) because it was, and still is, the preferred medium of pre-schoolers and school beginners to express their ideas in the absence of the ability to write. Thorndike began to measure children's intellectual ability from drawings using a scale (Starch, 1916). The characteristics, peculiarities, errors and idiosyncrasies were classified and conceptualised into a stage theory of realism (Luquet, 1927/2001). Drawings of the human figure were investigated as a measure of, and in correlation with established IQ intelligence tests (Goodenough, 1926). Longitudinal observations of children's drawings were carried out (Eng, 1931). Children's drawings of figures from Gestalt psychology were used as a window into their neuropsychological functioning (Bender, 1938). Rare emotional indicators could be identified (Koppitz, 1966). Piaget and others used children's drawings to demonstrate the unfolding of a Euclidean three-dimensional space concept on a two-dimensional surface when learning to draw in perspective (Piaget & Inhelder, 1956; Piaget et al., 1960; Volkelt, 1931/1968).

Because drawing involves many component skills (Lange-Küttner & Thomas, 1995; Lange-Küttner & Vinter, 2008; Lange-Küttner, 2020), theoretical models for drawing often reflect one aspect, for instance, the theory of a sensory core which would be repressed by iconic and symbolic drawings (Costall, 1995), an information-processing account that differentiates between different spatial projection systems (Willats, 2005), a neuropsychological account which reports case studies showing systematic distortions and errors in patients' drawings who

DOI: 10.4324/9780429270604-6

have lost imagery or suffer from form agnosia (Van Sommers, 1989) and blind patients who refer to the tactile properties of objects in their drawings (Vinter et al., 2012). There is, of course, the Piagetian (Lange-Küttner & Reith, 1995) and Neo-Piagetian approach (Morra, 2008) to the creation of three-dimensional pictorial space on paper but also approaches that put special weight on executive problems in the sequencing of graphic schemata (Freeman, 1975). Another approach was to investigate whether children could evaluate their drawings as creations in their own right or whether they believed that a change in the picture would also cause a change in the real object (Thomas et al., 1994). Finally, there is the Vygotskian theory claiming that drawings are part of a semiotic system determined by language (Stetsenko, 1995). Thus, as in other domains of development such as in research on perseveration in the A-not-B task, there are also multiple theoretical approaches to explain the curious errors that young children make when they are drawing.

5.2 Stages of Realism

For a long time, Luquet's stage theory of realism (1927/2001) was the dominant theoretical approach to children's drawings: The first stage is the *incidental realism* (fortuitous realism) where no realistic depiction is intended but instead the pen is used as an action tool. For instance, instead of drawing a hopping rabbit, the pen would hop across the page leaving a trace. The second stage is the *failed realism*, where an intention to draw a recognisable object is present but the graphic form is not recognisable. The third stage is *intellectual realism* when children selectively draw what they know about objects and efficiently use schemata to depict familiar, canonical object views. Finally, the fourth stage is *visual realism*, where recognisable renditions are produced which agree with the optical impression and potentially can depict any view of an object.

The stage theory was challenged by a case study about an autistic girl, Nadia, who could draw visually realistically like an adult artist at the age of 3½, and skipped all drawing stages (Selfe, 1977). This was noted by the art psychologist Arnheim (1980), but it took a few years until developmental psychologists realised the implications for the stage theory. Empirical studies did not find autistic child geniuses who skipped stages (e.g. Charman & Baron-Cohen, 1993), but instead they found children on the autistic spectrum who showed drawing fragmentation and transparent layering of silhouettes (Fein et al., 1990). However, this new research question yielded more studies and finally commonalities between talented typically developing children (Drake et al., 2010), adults (Drake & Winner, 2011) and individuals with autism spectrum disorder (ASD) were revealed with respect to their selective attention to detail (local processing bias). Likewise, when typically developing children were presented with 3D drawing models that had trapezoid spatial floorplans indicating perspective as a built-in property, thus appealing to their intellectual realism, already 7-year-olds showed the type of perspective sketching that talented and some autistic children demonstrate (Lange-Küttner, 2014).

The method of using drawings produced to a theme changed into experimental studies where production factors were systematically varied and included control groups. Freeman's (1980) monograph on children's drawing strategies was akin to a scientific manifesto. Three years before, Kosslyn et al. (1977) had commented that drawings would not be a reliable source of children's internal representations because of the gap between their ability to perceive how things should look like compared to what they were actually able to create in their drawings (Kosslyn et al., 1977; but see Moore, 1986a). Freeman (1980) argued that drawings could not be taken as windows into a child's mind unless their graphic abilities underwent more rigorous experimental scrutiny. Freeman introduced the difference between competence and performance into the drawing literature by telling his readers that children use strategies. He argued that many oddities in the early drawings of children resulted from a lack of planning in children, a precursor to current research on the development of executive function and mental flexibility. Thus, he argued that psychologists should set up cues that could help children to better plan their drawings and then test whether these cues were efficient to enable children to achieve a higher level of drawing, or even to accelerate their development.

5.3 The Construction of Pictorial Space

When you are told that you see something out of context, this is usually not meant as a compliment. It means that you are either exaggerating the size of the problem, or that you are underestimating it. Young children usually do not draw the spatial context of the objects (Dillon, 2022). The 'what' of the drawing seems more important than the 'where'. Figures are drawn very large by young children and fill the page, so large that sometimes not even the trunk can be fitted onto the page after the head has been drawn (Freeman, 1975), showing their lack of awareness of spatial constraints. Sensitivity to the spatial context was already investigated by Löwenfeld (1939), who could show that indeed the amount of spatial context in drawings increases with age: For the topic 'pick an apple from a tree', the tree became much larger in relation to the human figure.

This lack of spatial context may also occur because young children still struggle to depict a recognisable object and do not have the mental capacity to depict the context too. It was hypothesised that scribbles are more alike to gestures than to drawing (Longobardi et al., 2015). Scribbling progresses from uncontrolled scribbling to controlled scribbling to closed shapes and then to aggregates of shapes (Morra & Panesi, 2017). In a sample of 1½- to 3-year-olds, progress towards representative and recognisable drawings was best predicted by the imitation sorting task (Alp, 1994), $r_s > .69$, and even when age was controlled, residual correlations still were $r_s > .52$ (Morra & Panesi, 2017), see Figure 5.1.

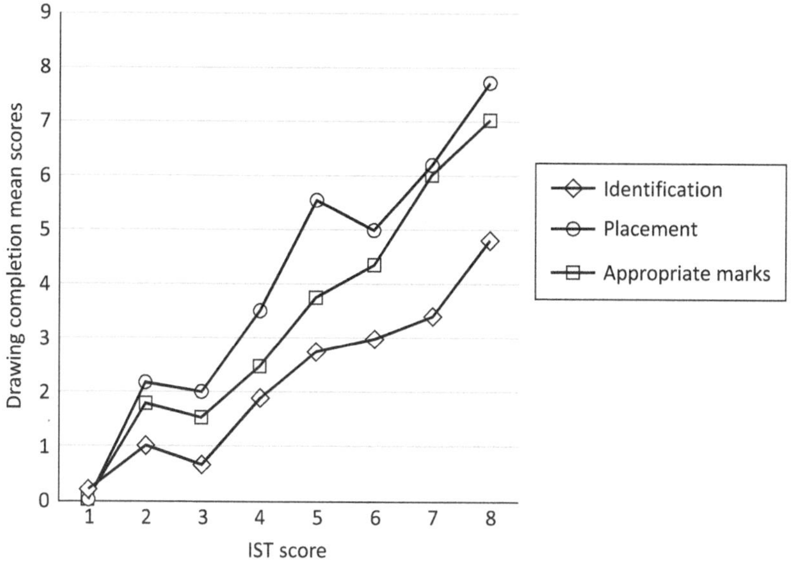

FIGURE 5.1 Imitation Score Predicts Representational Drawing (Morra & Panesi, 2017)

Gradually in development, objects become depicted in three dimensions, and so does their space. There are three aspects of space depiction in children's drawings: First, the distinction between implicit and explicit space; second, the problem of drawing in perspective; and third, the impact of the spatial context on objects. Although young children draw objects without a spatial context, they do differentiate between locations. For instance, when copying a spatial arrangement where one object is further away than the other, this is represented in the drawing with the one that is further away being at the top on the page and above the object in the foreground (Light & MacIntosh, 1980). Light and MacIntosh suggested that children would show orientation towards the visual *world* rather than the visual *field*.

There is a drawing test that measures this transition from space defined by objects, to space defined as common area. The Common Region Test (CRT) is a drawing test that measures object-place binding and objects-region binding (Lange-Küttner, 2006). Palmer (1992) referred to Wertheimer (1923) and claimed that common region constitutes a new kind of Gestalt principle. Common region consists of an extrinsic grouping effect created by explicit spatial boundaries while most of the other Gestalt principles would be intrinsic effects. In Chapter 10 on visual memory, it will be described that this test also reliably predicts object and place memory: Object-place encoding in the CRT predicted better object memory, while objects-regions encoding predicted better place memory. The test is very easy to administer by asking children to draw a circle around those dots which they believe belong together (Lange-Küttner, 2021); see Figure 5.2. They are presented with three rows of dots, one equidistant, one with pairs of dots closer together, and one with pairs of dots identical in color, as seen in Figure 5.2 upper left.

In a first study using the CRT, Lange-Küttner (2006) asked 4- to 10-year-old children to draw a circle around those dots which they thought would belong together. The CRT drawings clearly showed a transition from object-place associations (see Figure 5.2 upper right), to objects-region associations that consider objects' equality, proximity and colour when allocating common region (see Figure 5.2, lower right). In a transition phase, children showed unsystematic allocations; see Figure 5.2, lower left. In children with developmental problems, unsystematic coding is the most frequent response, see Chapter 8 on ADHD and Chapter 9 on ASD.

In short, 4- to 5-year-old children allocate a place to each object by drawing a boundary around each shape, but with increasing age, they allocate a region to those shapes which have something in common. Interestingly, children were not able to explain why they were drawing the boundaries in the way they did. The object-place spatial bindings in the CRT seem to occur without awareness. In Chapter 9 on autism spectrum disorder (ASD), we will see that this early way to allocate space to objects persists much longer in children with ASD than in neurotypically developing children: In unsystematic spatial binding, there is not only an early objects-region binding response, but also immature object-place binding. Object-based versus space-based encoding is also a topic in the adult literature. Both Duncan (1984) and Logan (1996) state that a central question

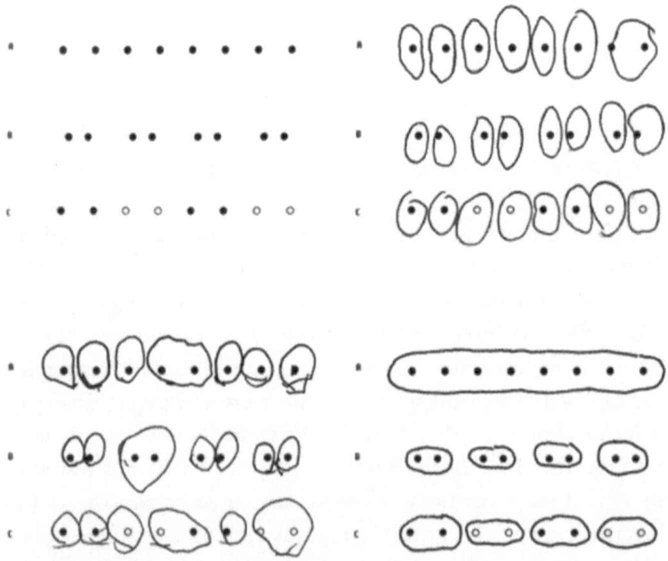

FIGURE 5.2 Drawing Object-Place and Objects-Region Binding (Lange-Küttner, 2006)

in visual attention research is whether it is focused on objects (Baylis & Driver, 1992, 1993), or on a region (Eriksen & Yeh, 1985). Unfortunately, while the CRT has been investigated as a predictor for visual memory (see Chapter 7), it was never tested as a predictor for the unfolding of the explicit spatial concepts in children's drawings.

The explicit spatial context quite predictably emerges with age in drawings in a sequence of drawing systems (Lange-Küttner, 2009); see Figure 5.3. Initially, children draw objects in empty space (space system 1). Thereafter, children draw ground lines or use the lower edge of the page to align figures (Cox & Chapman, 1995; Lewis, 1990) (space system 2). A major change is the drawing of spatial fields or regions that are created with explicit boundaries (space system 3) and finally, a viewpoint perspective is constructed with converging diagonal spatial axes (space systems 4 and 5). However, only a small minority of about 10% of children draw in perspective on their own accord (Lange-Küttner, 1989, 1994, 1997). Even in adults, drawing in perspective is so rare that Margaret Hagen claimed that there was no development (Hagen, 1985).

Thus, 7- to 17-year-old children were presented with a series of the ready-made pre-drawn 2D spatial systems in Figure 5.3 and asked to draw themselves with either one or four friends (Lange-Küttner, 2009). Therefore, they only

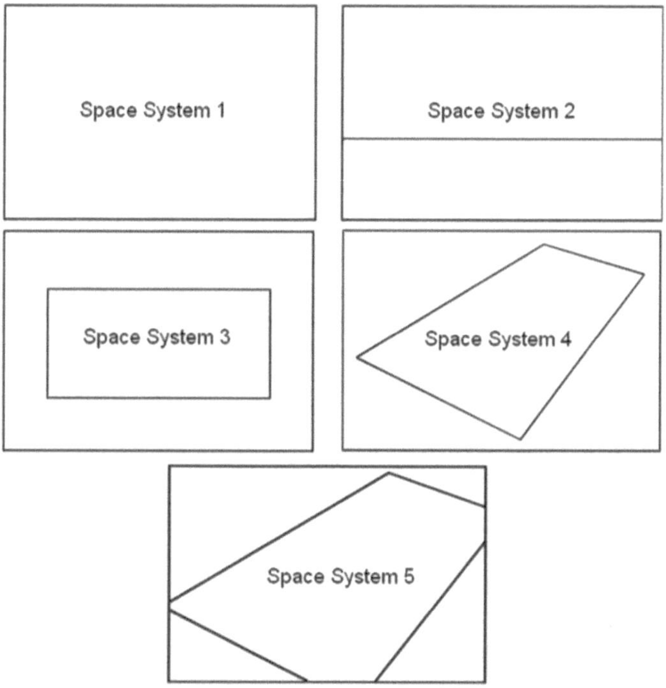

FIGURE 5.3 Unfolding of the Third Dimension in Pictorial Space (Lange-Küttner, 2009)

needed to draw the figures themselves and were relieved of drawing the spatial context.

When, in previous research, children were asked to draw themselves with their friends at play, it could be shown that up to the age of about nine years, the size of the human figure drawing depended on the number of persons that were drawn on the page, but thereafter, figure size was regulated by orthogonal and diagonal spatial axes systems (Lange-Küttner, 1997, 2004). Thus, the hypothesis for the study using the ready-made spatial systems was that a larger group of friends would need to be drawn smaller as several figures had to share the common region of limited pictorial space. Another hypothesis was that the constraints of the spatial axes systems would only have an impact on figure size as drawn by the older children. Finally, the spatial axes systems were given in either a logical or in a random sequence, and there was a control condition with empty pages resembling implicit space. Already 7-year-olds gradually reduced the average figure size, but only if they encountered the unfolding spatial axes systems in a logical sequence. The size reduction was so subtle that it was not smaller or larger than in the other two conditions. This was called 'habitual size' drawing. Size reduction was more pronounced in the 9- and 11-year-old children, who were drawing significantly larger in the implicit space control condition. Seventeen-year-old teenagers would reduce figure size only in the orthogonal playing field because in their perspective drawings, they were drawing large foreground figures and small background figures, showing that not just size reduction, but size modification develops.

In another study, the spatial systems were built as small three-dimensional models like those used in architecture. Children from 7 to 11 years were presented with playing fields which embodied the stages of the spatial concepts for drawings (Lange-Küttner, 2014). The spatial models always contained five figures as more objects on a page cue smaller size. The perspective models were constructed in such a way that the floor plan of the playing field – rather than being rectangular – had a trapezoid shape, that is, the sides converged in a diagonal fashion, see Figure 5.4. Thus, some of the drawing models had a built-in perspective just like the Ames room (Ittelson, 1952) which produces size distortions.

Surprisingly, more 7-year-old than 11-year-old children would draw in perspective. They would not laboriously and methodically construct perspective, but instead they would sketch like the autistic girl Nadia or talented children, demonstrating that they can draw visually realistically if the model appeals to their intellectual realism. Thus, the problem of typically developing children when drawing in perspective seems to be the fact that perspective is a property of the visual system and not a property of the outside world.

This was the first and only study so far that shows that 7-year-old children would draw in perspective. The theory of a sensory core assumes that children's sensory impressions are suppressed by learning to draw symbolic icons of objects (Costall, 1995). The use of an icon template with its typical 'canonical' contours is seen as an indicator of a lack of creativity and awareness of changes in viewpoint

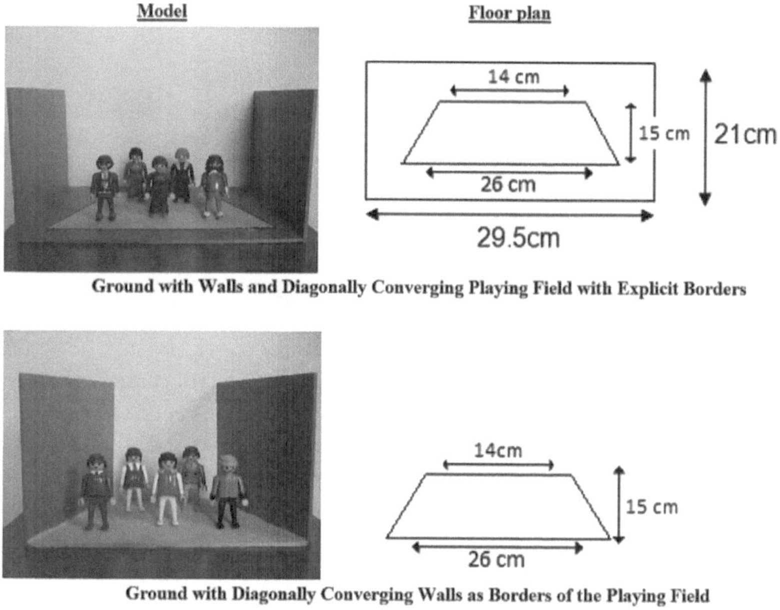

FIGURE 5.4 Built-in Perspective 3D Models (Lange-Küttner, 2014). *Note*: Only the floor plans show the difference between the orthogonal and the trapezoid base, but not the camera shots.

(Deregowski & Dziurawiec, 1994; Deręgowski & Dziurawiec, 1996). Especially object naming fostered icon drawing (Bremner & Moore, 1984; Walker et al., 2008). Still, such icons are also in use in the adult world wherever fast communication is of the essence that does not depend on language, for instance, at international airports.

Nevertheless, a logical conclusion would be that if drawing templates of objects prevent the drawing of advanced spatial systems, the explicitly instructed omission of such objects may foster drawing in perspective. Such is the negative space drawing technique which requires drawing the transparent space around and between the objects, rather than drawing the objects themselves (Edwards, 1987, 1992). However, spatial context is often ignored being just the intermedium between objects, and only spatial axes systems could make air visible even when it was coloured (Jaensch, 1911). In a recent study, a space-based instruction to draw the intermedium was expected to attenuate object-specific visual attention and to enhance perception of a spatial expanse (Lange-Küttner & Vinueza Chavez, 2022). Children from 5 to 12 years of age and adults were asked to copy a three-dimensional wooden, colourfully painted spacebox with three cubes placed inside; see Figure 5.5. The sky of the earth model space box was symbolised with a blue lid alluding to the stripey air gap pictures that children

FIGURE 5.5 3D Earth Model with Three Cubes (Lange-Küttner & Vinueza Chavez, 2022)

draw until they are about 11 to 12 years of age when they begin to draw the sky down to the horizon (Lewis, 1990). Children followed two instructions, a *Visual Realism Instruction* ('Please draw the three cubes and the box as you can see them') and a *Negative Space Instruction* ('Please draw the space around the objects').

Outline drawings began to show only from nine years onwards. A positive effect of the negative space technique occurred for the drawing of the occluded cubes inside the spacebox: The depiction of common contour of objects could create a cohesive scene feature such as a horizon. In contrast, the visual realism instruction focused visual attention towards the optical impression of the space box and enhanced 3D drawing of both the spacebox and the cubes. Such visually realistic progressive structuring rather than simple mapping was seen as essential to the epistemology of perception (Piaget, 1969). It indicated that children aimed to draw the entire scene in three dimensions. It suggests that the instruction to focus on the optical impression unifies objects and surroundings on one picture plane (Lange-Küttner & Reith, 1995; Reith & Dominin, 1997). Thus, the transition from implicit to explicit space creates a new layer of a *holistic scene* that developmentally follows on from the early *holistic objects* that children draw. This conclusion is in stark contrast to the theory that there is a holistic-to-analytic shift in development (Kemler, 1983).

5.4 The Holistic Object

Like the three dimensions in space, so do the dimensions and details of single objects unfold in the development of drawing. Because young children evaluate their drawing as good or bad (Quaglia et al., 2015), sketching may be evaluated by young children as not adequate to their aim of drawing an unambiguously recognisable object. The intellectually realistic drawings of objects show symbolic icons which are abstractions insofar as they point to a generalised prototype rather than to a concrete object (Uttal et al., 1999). In most cases, the human figure is the first object that an infant would draw and it often fills the page (Cox, 1993). This large size may occur because children at all ages tend to draw figures they like larger and negatively connotated figures smaller (Burkitt et al., 2003), but it also could just be the desire to fill the entire page with one shape as in the earliest tadpole drawings which consist of just a face (head), with legs where usually the trunk would be, and arms attached where usually the ears would be. On the one hand, this shows the enormous significance that the human face has for the young child; on the other hand, Freeman (1975) showed that even drawing beginners do not create figures with arms and legs coming out of the head when they start from a pre-drawn trunk. They gradually aggregate the shapes in the proper order when they add more detail. Because these shapes are usually round without a visually realistic contour, they were called geometric primitives (Willats, 1997, see also Biederman, 1987). Humanlike shapes of animate and inanimate objects coexist based on the same template of aggregated circles with extensions (Silk & Thomas, 1986).

School-age children gradually integrate such geometric shapes parts into a smooth silhouette with a natural contour (Lange-Küttner, 2011; Lange-Küttner et al., 2002), and are able to depict the human figure in profile (Goodnow & Friedman, 1972) and in motion (Goodnow, 1977; Morra, 2005). This development is so reliable that it was used as an estimate of intelligence (IQ) from early on (Goodenough, 1926; Goodenough & Harris, 1950), and was later validated with thousands of children (Arden et al., 2014; Naglieri, 1988; Naglieri & Ronning, 2000).[1] Yet, potentially even young children can use detail to define an object. They draw, for instance, just one characteristic semantic feature such as arm rings depicting swimming aids when asked to draw a human figure in a swimsuit which allows identificating of a specific context despite not being depicted in a visually realistic fashion (Lange-Küttner et al., 2002).

Individual differences when drawing inanimate spatial objects are rarely reported (Lange-Küttner, 2011). Typical drawing models are, for instance, a mug (e.g. Davis, 1983; Freeman & Janikoun, 1972), a table (Willats, 1995; Willats, 1997) or a cube (e.g. Bremner & Batten, 1991; Cox, 1986; Freeman, 1986; Lange-Küttner & Ebersbach, 2013; Mitchelmore, 1978). The holistic object representation is the most obvious in the experiments using cubes: Young children would copy a cube with six differently coloured sides as a square shape with the colours of all the six sides drawn into this one shape (Moore, 1986b). In development, then gradually the sides of the cube are unfolded until all six are visible in a diagrammatic layout – which may be drawn more often by girls than boys (Lange-Küttner & Ebersbach, 2013). The final stage is achieved when the diagonal appears and the sides are integrated into viewpoint perspective, with omission of those sides that are not visible.

1 For a critique of the Draw-A-Person test, please see Willcock, E., Imuta, K., & Hayne, H. (2011). Children's human figure drawings do not measure intellectual ability. *Journal of Experimental Child Psychology*, *110*(3), 444–452. https://doi.org/10.1016/j.jecp.2011.04.013 and Lange-Küttner, C., Küttner, E., & Chromekova, M. (2014). Deterioration and recovery of DAP IQ scores in the repeated assessment of the Naglieri Draw-A-Person (DAP) test in 6- to 12-year-old children. *Psychological Assessment*, *26*(1), 297-306. https://doi.org/10.1037/a0034581

Creating 3D depth on a picture plane without the use of spatial axes but just by using objects can be produced by techniques such as drawing occlusion or minimising size with distance (Lange-Küttner & Green, 2007). The depiction of overlapping objects clearly increases with age also when tested on a longitudinal basis (Chen & Holman, 1989; Lange-Küttner, 1994). However, the preference to draw holistic and complete figures with minimal yet characteristic defining details creates a challenge when starting to draw overlap because the occluded figure needs to have an incomplete outline (Lange-Küttner, 2000, 2008; Lange-Küttner & Vinueza Chavez, 2022). The early graphic forms of closed shapes rather than scribbles involve an effort where the aim is to have the beginning and the end of the drawing movement meet in one point (Meulenbroek et al., 1993). Once this achievement is mastered, the drawing of an open contour involves inhibition of the drawing movement (Berti & Freeman, 1997; Karmiloff-Smith, 1990). Inhibition depends on the development of executive attention which children develop from four years onwards (Gerstadt et al., 1994; Jones et al., 2003). Thus, drawings produced earlier may show 'transparency' or 'interposition' where objects drawn intended to show that they are placed behind one another are just drawn over one another, producing a rather noisy picture (Andersson, 1995; Crook, 1984). An alternative and more common strategy of young children than interposition or transparency for drawing overlapping objects is instead to just depict the two objects individually side by side (Crook, 1984; Freeman et al., 1977; Ingram & Butterworth, 1989; Lange-Küttner & Ebersbach, 2013). Freeman (1980, p. 217) introduced the term hidden line elimination (HLE) for the omission of the contour lines that are not visible behind the object in the foreground. The HLE concept is also used in computing (Nurmi, 1985). This algorithm works on the simple assumption that in a 3D space with spatial axes (x, y, z), if the contour of a shape is not visible, it is hidden. It is indeed possible to automatise the analysis of children's drawings using a computer algorithm (Jensen et al., 2023; Tabatabaey-Mashadi et al., 2015).

5.5 Fine Motor Skills in Drawing and Handwriting

There are basically two time-windows when fine motor skills become especially important. The first time-window is the actual onset of drawing recognisable shapes instead of scribbles, while the second time-window is the onset of handwriting in school, which also changes the way in which children draw. There are neuropsychological studies with children and adults involving assessment of fine motor control parameters in drawing, which are included in Chapters 8 and 9 in this book. In this current chapter, only studies with typically developing children will be presented, laying a foundation to understand research that tested drawing ability in children with developmental challenges.

5.5.1 The Recognisable Object Shape

Probably the largest and earliest study of scribbles was carried out by Rhoda Kellogg (1959) who collected over 100,000 drawings and paintings by 2- to 4-year-old kindergarten children. She differentiated between 20 types of basic scribbles and six basic diagrams and aggregates. Her classification based on this large collection showed that young children's drawings can consist of more than mainly circles and extensions (Willats, 1985).

The scribbles of young children and those of older adults with Alzheimer (Bonoti et al., 2015) or severe semantic dementia (Patterson & Erzinclioglu, 2009) are distinct in kind yet both fairly unrecognisable. Yet, when these older adults were given the opportunity to train on five consecutive days to recognise the same limited number of ten objects in spatial contexts, to label these objects and to draw them, recognisable graphic objects could be observed on the last day (Bechari-Martin & Lange-Küttner, 2022). Object-in-Scene recognition predicted this rehabilitation of the graphic shape, but even more so the daily practice of the fine motor skills. How could young children improve their graphic production?

Drawing beginners cannot recognise their own scribbled drawings (Campbell et al., 2008). They would rather post-hoc invent a label of what they have been drawing (Freeman & Adi-Japha, 2008). However, when re-drawing the contours of a shape, this sensori-motor exercise helps transition to draw a recognisable object also in young children (Ross, 2008). Variability of drawing material for tracing exercises can enhance training effects in children (Desmottes et al., 2017). Especially inhibition (Riggs et al., 2013) and working memory (Morra & Panesi, 2017) – both components of executive function – play an important role for fine motor control when drawing. Inhibition controls when to stop drawing a line as this is required to draw an open form rather than the fast loops that mimic actions (Lange-Küttner, 1998). Working memory allows to monitor inclusion of specific detail that differs between drawing templates, for instance, of a dog and a human figure when drawing the number of legs (Panesi & Morra, 2016). Crucial aspects of drawings such as the spontaneous identification of missing elements, correct placement and use of adequate shapes for denotation of objects were nearly completely explained by such early working memory capacity (Morra & Panesi, 2017).

When do children recognise that a drawing is a referent that stands for another object, and is not in itself the object that it depicts? Evidence is mixed, with some studies finding that 2-year-old children already understand that a drawing or photo represents an object, but a small-scale model does not have the same effect (DeLoache, 1991). When a change is made to a real model, children until the age of four assume an automatic correspondence between the real object and its depiction (Jolley, 2008). However, these studies did not involve children themselves drawing. A more relevant research question would be to ask about their meta-knowledge, that is, whether children can recognise that they themselves are drawing in an increasingly visually realistic fashion. While 5-year-olds could rank drawings only of their own age group, this ability increases with age (Trautner et al., 1989). When children were asked to produce multiple drawings in the way that children would draw at different ages, this ability emerged only at 10 years of age when they were able to look back in time (Tryphon & Montangero, 1992). In short, while young children draw the way they typically would do, older children may have a whole repertoire of styles from which they can choose.

5.5.2 Change in Fine Motor Skills and Drawing with the Onset of Handwriting

Fine motor skills predict reasoning in children as young as five years of age (Martzog et al., 2019). However, fine motor skills in drawing seem to become especially relevant once children need to modify visually realistic contours. Toomela (2002) tested two age clusters, 2- to 7-year-olds and 8- to 11-year-old children, who were drawing a cube and a doll from a model. These age groups were selected as it was assumed that the younger age group would produce iconic, intellectually realistic drawings, while the older age group would engage in visually realistic drawing. A sample of 300 children (30 children in each year) was tested with a large battery of tests. Age, block construction and mental rotation, but not fine motor skills, were correlated with the averaged drawing score in the younger group. In contrast, for the 8- to 11-year-olds, while block construction and mental rotation were still significantly correlated with drawing, age was no longer predictive and instead fine motor skills predicted drawing performance.

While preschool children's strategies for drawing and writing initially differ (Brenneman et al., 1996), with the onset of handwriting, drawing also changes. In particular, *movement fluency* rather than stroke-by-stroke movements in drawing is a new achievement probably determined by learning to write in Western Latin script (Palmis et al., 2017). While children writing Latin script connect about 26 letters (with loops) in their handwriting (Vinter & Chartrel, 2010), Asian children learn, and Asian adults use, thousands of unique pictograms. For instance, it takes Hong Kong children until age six just to become able to write their own name correctly (Tse et al., 2019). Copying word icons of Vietnamese, Korean and Hebrew scripture could predict a dyslexia diagnosis in Chinese readers, with an effect size of .67 to .80 (McBride-Chang et al., 2011). Thus, while the following section focusses on studies of handwriting that is fluently connected (Latin, Arabic) rather than composed stroke-by-stroke, this does not imply that fluent handwriting is more challenging than other scripts. A comparison between Latin and Chinese script shows that the simple short word 'car' requires two highly differentiated icons 汽 車 (simplified 汽车) (Microsoft Word translator). Presumably, even a single one of these icons would command both higher fine motor skills to create than writing 'car' in Latin script, and require higher visual resolution to read.

Kinematic analysis of hand movements showed that speed, efficiency and pressure increase with age, whereas variability decreases (Lange-Küttner, 1998; Rückriegel et al., 2008; Vinter & Mounoud, 1991). While young children draw picture primitives of circles with extensions all the time, with the onset of handwriting, drawing circles gains a new quality and recruits much more attention in terms of time (Lange-Küttner, 1998). One would have expected angular forms to be more difficult to draw if understanding of advanced geometry would simultaneously raise the drawing difficulty level (Piaget et al., 1960). However, in terms of kinematics, this was not the case as changes in stroke direction of angular forms were found to be easier than drawing spaced-out loops (Lange-Küttner, 1998; Lin et al., 2015).

Using an automated analysis (Tabatabaey-Mashadi et al., 2015), 6- to 7-year-old children with normal and poor handwriting were compared on two Beery Visual Motor Integration Test (BVMI) figures. Boys with poor handwriting showed less left-to-right sequences in drawing and more directional diversity. They were also less likely to start at the touching point of circle and diamond, see Figure 5.6, and more likely to start somewhere at the top right. Starting at the touching point makes it easier to draw the diamond counterclockwise, but boys with poor handwriting instead showed idiosyncratic strategies and attached the diamond just somewhere rather than at the pre-defined point as if intending to draw spatially isolated shapes. The conclusion was that in children with poor handwriting, drawing still dominated handwriting. Moreover, handwriting parameters guided drawing sequences in those with good handwriting.

An interesting test is 'Drawing between the lines' which improves with repetition and was predicted by executive function (EF) measured with independent tasks (Maurer & Roebers, 2020). EF did not predict performance on other tasks requiring fine motor skills such as threading beads or posting coins. The same drawing test as well as age also predicted chopstick-using skills (Beilei et al., 2002) in 4- to 8-year-old children, demonstrating that drawing a line within a constrained space is a task that also challenges EF required in daily life. In another study, an aggregate score that consisted of drawing between lines and pointing towards the centre of circles showed about 30% of shared variance with age, processing speed, attention, knowledge and reasoning, while fine motor speed (repeated button presses) shared about half, and dexterity (finger agility) about two thirds of variance (Martzog et al., 2019). Making right-handed children draw with the left hand changed their movement direction when drawing a cross (Braswell & Rosengren, 2002). Brain activations of executive function are mainly involved when learning new drawing and writing tasks and subside once mastery has been achieved (Lindenberger & Lövdén, 2019; Wenger et al., 2017).

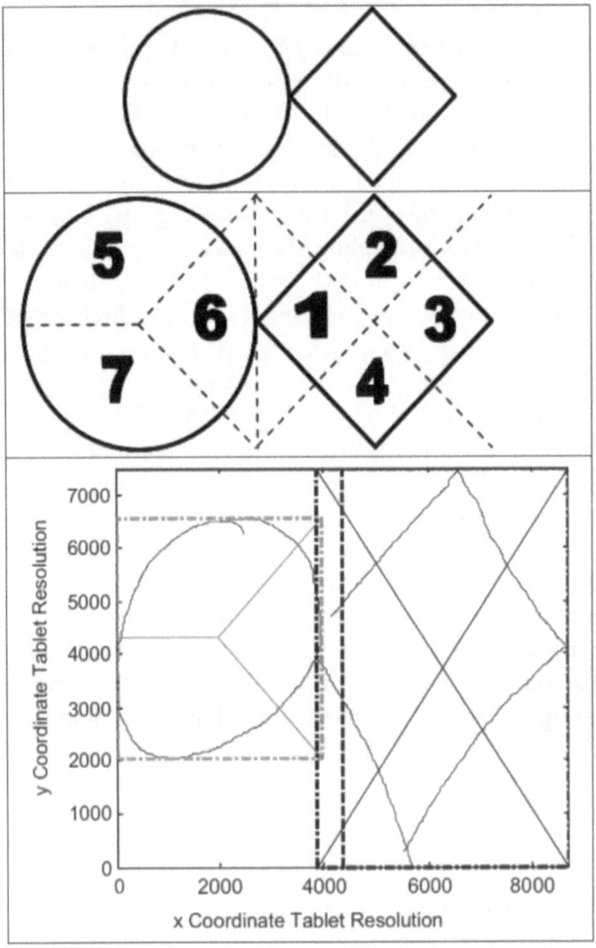

FIGURE 5.6 Automated Analysis of Fine Motor Skills (Tabatabaey-Mashadi et al., 2015)

5.6 Drawing, Flexibility and Creativity

In drawing development research, cognitive flexibility is expected to emerge in the progression towards visually realistic drawing (e.g. Allen et al., 2016; Ebersbach & Hagedorn, 2011; Karmiloff-Smith, 1990; Picard & Vinter, 1999, 2007). Staying flexible even if tasks are already mastered at a routine level became especially important because established drawing templates appeared to stunt children's creativity. Thus, here creativity refers not to the creation of ingenious drawings or paintings, but as a counterweight to rigid problem-solving strategies. Drawing abilities can also show regression to earlier levels in clinical samples, but in typically developing children, this is very rare. It is more likely that they would show sparsity in the number and type of objects that are depicted

(Lange-Küttner, 1989), or stagnation, which could involve drawing the same type of picture when encountering the same drawing topic even after years have passed (Lange-Küttner, 1994). Van Sommers attributed these repeat drawings to the conservatism of children (Van Sommers, 1984). The creativity researcher Margaret Hagen (1985) concluded that there would be no development even in adults' abilities to represent objects in a visually realistic fashion.

In Chapter 9 about visual and motor skills in children with autism spectrum disorder (ASD), it is described that they often obsessively practice certain skills, including drawing. Also talented children show an intense interest and deliberately persevere in drawing practice for longer durations and at a much earlier age (Milbrath, 1998; Winner, 1996; Winner & Drake, 2013). Thus, a microgenetic study was run with repeated drawings of typically developing children in order to test whether practice improves drawing. The human figure drawing was chosen because the Draw-A-Person (DAP) test has psychometric norms available which highly correlate with IQ (Naglieri, 1988). The DAP test seems fairly robust as norms return to a personal average after an instruction boost due to anatomy lessons (Cronin et al., 2017). However, here the DAP test was not used to classify or diagnose children as 'impaired' or 'superior', but to assess the role of repetition and practice when creating a graphic representation.

Lange-Küttner, Küttner and Chromekova (2014) asked children between 6 and 12 years to draw a person three times and then switched the topic to drawing a police (wo)man three times, with the sequence counterbalanced. Like in Bartlett's descriptions of adults' condensed and fading recall of narratives (Bartlett, 1932), there was loss of detail in children's repeat drawings. Moreover, some real-time regressions occurred that were never reported before, as a young child resorted to tadpole drawings and an older child began to draw figures with infantile proportions; see Figure 5.7. Thus, repetition of drawings, which are so common in artists, was stressful for children. Only 12-year-old children would spontaneously create new content on each drawing occasion, which prevented the DAP-IQ score from deteriorating during repetition.

The loss of detail was equivalent to several DAP-IQ points. For most of the children, new content (police man/woman) could temporarily halt the deterioration, but only if the new content made the drawing more challenging and required adding more specific features such as a uniform and insignia of the police to an ordinary human figure drawing. In the developmental memory literature, this has been labelled as 'attentional refreshing' of memory (Camos et al., 2018). However, in the Lange-Küttner et al. drawing experiment, mental refreshing did not appear to occur via memory rehearsal, that is by repetition, but by changing the content of the task. Mental refreshing can also be necessary for mathematics when children continue to use the same strategy even though the format of the task changed (Luchins, 1950; Luchins & Luchins, 1959). They had formed a ‚mental set‘ and the process which occurred during the repetition was termed the '*mechanization of intelligence*'. Various help, such as writing and taking notes, increased instead of decreasing the impact of the mental set. A successful

FIGURE 5.7 Practice and Creativity in Drawing (Lange-Küttner et al., 2014)

intervention, however, was a changed visual appearance during the repetition which improved participants' perception and appreciation of each single maths problem.

The formation of a mental set is also known from infant research. Interest wanes during stimulus repetition, which is taken as a measure of habituation, that is, as a consolidation of a memory template which would be more impoverished than an exact copy of the visual impression (see Chapter 7). Sutton and Rose (1998) found that visually realistic drawing required more divided visual attention between the drawing and the model itself. They showed that during development, increasingly less attention would be paid to the actual drawing, and more attention to comparison processes that would match and adjust discrepancies between percept and the graphic product.

The impact of children's mental flexibility on drawing was also measured with additional assessments of executive function (Ebersbach & Hagedorn, 2011). Drawing a visual scene from a model was not predicted by the Wisconsin Card Sorting Test (WCST) as there was no switch in the drawing task, but drawing a scene was predicted by the ability to create new patterns and knowing what to omit (Ebersbach et al., 2011). Already 4- to 6-year-old children are able to change or delete a shape, but older children can insert parts from different categories, e.g., human eyes as windows of a house (that does not exist) (Karmiloff-Smith, 1990). In this task, children become able to interrupt and inhibit their drawing routine to insert shapes from different categories rather than modify the usual shape sequence (Picard & Vinter, 2007). However, in studies involving drawing the Rey-Osterrieth Complex Figure, which is often used in neuropsychological assessments, digit span and the WCST predicted between 20–30% of the variance between children's drawings, but it must be kept in mind that this sample had a mean IQ of 93 and suffered from various developmental disorders (Ogino et al., 2009; Watanabe et al., 2005). Moreover, the age of this sample was also heterogeneous, ranging from 5 to 14 years. They showed fragmented drawings that lacked cohesion and organisation showing that executive function was a most important parameter. However, a lack of executive attention would have been more of an issue in this sample than in neurotypical populations.

5.7 Conclusions

Research on drawing development is gradually including and assessing the major components of the process that are involved in creating a graphic representation. Scribbles become recognizable graphic objects. Iconic graphic templates become more refined and visually realistic with the onset of handwriting. Spatial concepts become increasingly explicit and complex and have an impact on the graphic object concept. In this chapter, the impetus was on drawing figures that are small yet accurate, down to points in mathematic space. But it should be remembered that it is size modification that develops and not just size reduction. Portraits that fill a page show that enlargement of features also belongs to the graphic repertoire. Moreover, the contribution of cognitive parameters such as long-term memory, memory capacity, fine motor skills and executive function were considered. An important innovation in the last decades was the integration of familiarity and novelty into experimental designs for drawing research, which enabled researchers to demonstrate when learning occurs and whether this leads to robust developmental progress.

References

Allen, M. L., Nurmsoo, E., & Freeman, N. (2016). Young children show representational flexibility when interpreting drawings. *Cognition*, *147*, 21–28. https://doi.org/10.1016/j.cognition.2015.11.003

Alp, I. E. (1994). Measuring the size of working memory in very young children: The imitation sorting task. *International Journal of Behavioral Development, 17*(1), 125–141. https://doi.org/10.1177/016502549401700108

Andersson, S. (1995). Projection systems and X-ray strategies in children's drawings: A comparative study in three cultures. *British Journal of Educational Psychology, 65*(4), 455–464. https://doi.org/10.1111/j.2044-8279.1995.tb01165.x

Arden, R., Trzaskowski, M., Garfield, V., & Plomin, R. (2014). Genes influence young children's human figure drawings and their association with intelligence a decade later. *Psychological Science, 25*(10), 1843–1850. https://doi.org/10.1177/0956797614540686

Arnheim, R. (1980). The puzzle of Nadia's drawings. *The Arts in Psychotherapy,* 7(2), 79–85. https://doi.org/10.1016/0197-4556(80)90013-1

Bartlett, F. C. (1932). *Remembering.* Cambridge University Press.

Baylis, G. C., & Driver, J. (1992). Visual parsing and response competition: The effect of grouping factors. *Perception & Psychophysics, 51*(2), 145–162. https://doi.org/10.3758/BF03212239

Baylis, G. C., & Driver, J. (1993). Visual attention and objects: Evidence for hierarchical coding of location. *Journal of Experimental Psychology: Human Perception and Performance, 19*(3), 451–470. https://doi.org/10.1037/0096-1523.19.3.451

Bechari-Martin, H. S., & Lange-Küttner, C. (2022). Object-based practice effects recover the graphic object concept in Alzheimer's dementia. *Psychology of Aesthetics, Creativity, and the Arts,* article 452. https://doi.org/10.1037/aca0000452

Beilei, L., Lei, L., Qi, D., & von Hofsten, C. (2002). The development of fine motors and their relations to children's academic achievement. *Acta Psychologica Sinica, 34*(5), 494–499. https://journal.psych.ac.cn/acps/EN/Y2002/V34/I05/52

Bender, L. (1938). *A visual motor Gestalt test and its clinical use.* American Orthopsychiatric Association.

Berti, A. E., & Freeman, N. H. (1997). Representational change in resources for pictorial innovation: A three-component analysis. *Cognitive Development, 12,* 501–522. https://doi.org/10.1016/S0885-2014(97)90020-4

Biederman, I. (1987). Recognition-by-Components: A theory of human image understanding. *Psychological Review, 94*(2), 115-147. https://doi.org/10.1037/0033-295X.94.2.115

Bonoti, F., Tzouvaleka, E., Bonotis, K., & Vlachos, F. (2015). Do patients with Alzheimer's disease draw like young children? An exploratory study. *Journal of Alzheimer's Disease, 43*(4), 1285–1292. https://doi.org/10.3233/JAD-140528

Braswell, G. S., & Rosengren, K. S. (2002). The role of handedness in graphic production: Interactions between biomechanical and cognitive factors in drawing development. *British Journal of Developmental Psychology, 20*(4), 581–599. https://doi.org/10.1348/026151002760390963

Bremner, J. G., & Batten, A. (1991). Sensitivity to viewpoint in children's drawings of objects and relations between objects. *Journal of Experimental Child Psychology, 52*(3), 375–394. https://doi.org/10.1016/0022-0965(91)90070-9

Bremner, J. G., & Moore, S. (1984). Prior visual inspection and object naming: Two factors that enhance hidden feature inclusion in young children's drawings. *British Journal of Developmental Psychology, 2*(4), 371–376. https://doi.org/10.1111/j.2044-835X.1984.tb00944.x

Brenneman, K., Massey, C., Machado, S. F., & Gelman, R. (1996). Young children's plans differ for writing and drawing. *Cognitive Development, 11*(3), 397–419. https://doi.org/10.1016/S0885-2014(96)90011-8

Burk, F. (1902). The genetic versus the logical order in drawing. *The Pedagogical Seminary, 9*(3), 296–323. https://doi.org/10.1080/08919402.1902.10534187

Burkitt, E., Barrett, M., & Davis, A. (2003). The effect of affective characterizations on the size of children's drawings. *British Journal of Developmental Psychology, 21*(4), 565–584. https://doi.org/10.1348/026151003322535228

Camos, V., Johnson, M., Loaiza, V., Portrat, S., Souza, A., & Vergauwe, E. (2018). What is attentional refreshing in working memory? *Annals of the New York Academy of Sciences, 1424*(1), 19–32. https://doi.org/10.1111/nyas.13616

Campbell, R. N., Duncan, P. A., Harrison, A. L., & Mathewson, L. C. (2008). Style and other factors affecting children's recognition of their own drawings. In C. Lange-Küttner & A. Vinter (Eds.), *Drawing and the non-verbal mind: A life-span perspective* (pp. 63–85). Cambridge University Press.

Charman, T., & Baron-Cohen, S. (1993). Drawing development in autism: The intellectual to visual realism shift. *British Journal of Developmental Psychology, 11*(2), 171–185. http://dx.doi.org/10.1111/j.2044-835X.1993.tb00596.x

Chen, M. J., & Holman, J. (1989). Emergence of drawing devices for total and partial occlusion: A longitudinal study. *Perception, 18*(4), 445–455. https://doi.org/10.1068/p180445

Clark, A. B. (1897). The child's attitude towards perspective problems. *Studies in Education, 1*(18), 283–294.

Costall, A. (1995). The myth of the sensory core: The traditional versus the ecological approach to children's drawings. In C. Lange-Küttner & G. V. Thomas (Eds.), *Drawing and looking: Theoretical approaches to pictorial representation in children* (pp. 16–26). Harvester Wheatsheaf/Pearson.

Cox, M. V. (1986). Cubes are difficult things to draw. *British Journal of Developmental Psychology, 4*(4), 341–345. https://doi.org/10.1111/j.2044-835X.1986.tb01029.x

Cox, M. V. (1993). *Children's drawings of the human figure.* Lawrence Erlbaum Associates, Inc.

Cox, M. V., & Chapman, L. (1995). The air-gap phenomenon in young children's pictures. *Educational Psychology, 15*(3), 313–322. https://doi.org/10.1080/0144341950150306

Cronin, A., Gross, J., & Hayne, H. (2017). The effect of instruction on children's human figure drawing (HFD) tests: Implications for measurement. *Psychology of Aesthetics, Creativity, and the Arts, 11*(2), 179–186. https://doi.org/10.1037/aca0000097

Crook, C. (1984). Factors influencing the use of transparency in children's drawing. *British Journal of Developmental Psychology, 2*(3), 213–221. https://doi.org/10.1111/j.2044-835X.1984.tb00927.x

Davis, A. (1983). Contextual sensitivity in young children's drawings. *Journal of Experimental Child Psychology, 35*(3), 478–486. https://doi.org/10.1016/0022-0965(83)90022-X

DeLoache, J. S. (1991). Symbolic functioning in very young children: Understanding of pictures and models. *Child Development, 62*(4), 736–752. https://doi.org/10.1111/j.1467-8624.1991.tb01566.x

Deregowski, J. B., & Dziurawiec, S. (1994). Perceptual impulsions and unfamiliar solids: Evidence from a drawing task. *British Journal of Psychology, 85*(1), 1–15. https://doi.org/10.1111/j.2044-8295.1994.tb02504.x

Deręgowski, J. B., & Dziurawiec, S. (1996). The puissance of typical contours and children's drawings. *Australian Journal of Psychology, 48*(2), 98–103. https://doi.org/10.1080/00049539608259512

Desmottes, L., Maillart, C., & Meulemans, T. (2017). Mirror-drawing skill in children with specific language impairment: Improving generalization by incorporating variability into the practice session. *Child Neuropsychology*, *23*(4), 463–482. https://doi.org/10.1080/09297049.2016.1170797

Dillon, M. R. (2022). Rooms without walls: Young children draw objects but not layouts. *Journal of Experimental Psychology: General*. https://doi.org/10.1037/xge0000984

Drake, J. E., Redash, A., Coleman, K., Haimson, J., & Winner, E. (2010). 'Autistic' local processing bias also found in children gifted in realistic drawing. *Journal of Autism and Developmental Disorders*, *40*(6), 762–773. https://doi.org/10.1007/s10803-009-0923-0

Drake, J. E., & Winner, E. (2011). Realistic drawing talent in typical adults is associated with the same kind of local processing bias found in individuals with ASD. *Journal of Autism and Developmental Disorders*, *41*(9), 1192–1201. https://doi.org/10.1007/s10803-010-1143-3

Duncan, J. (1984). Selective attention and the organization of visual information. *Journal of Experimental Psychology: General*, *113*(4), 501–517. https://doi.org/10.1037/0096-3445.113.4.501

Ebersbach, M., & Hagedorn, H. (2011). The role of cognitive flexibility in the spatial representation of children's drawings. *Journal of Cognition and Development*, *12*(1), 32–55. https://doi.org/10.1080/15248372.2011.539526

Ebersbach, M., Stiehler, S., & Asmus, P. (2011). On the relationship between children's perspective taking in complex scenes and their spatial drawing ability. *British Journal of Developmental Psychology*, *29*(3), 455–474. https://doi.org/10.1348/026151010X504942

Edwards, B. (1987). *Drawing on the artist within*. Collins.

Edwards, B. (1992). *Drawing on the right side of the brain*. Souvenir Press.

Eng, H. (1931). *The psychology of children's drawings*. Harcourt, Brace.

Eriksen, C. W., & Yeh, Y.-Y. (1985). Allocation of attention in the visual field. *Journal of Experimental Psychology: Human Perception and Performance*, *11*(5), 583–597. https://doi.org/10.1037//0096-1523.11.5.583

Fein, D., Lucci, D., & Waterhouse, L. (1990). Brief report: Fragmented drawings in autistic children. *Journal of Autism and Developmental Disorders*, *20*(2), 263–269. https://doi.org/10.1007/bf02284723

Freeman, N. H. (1975). Do children draw men with arms coming out of the head? *Nature*, *254*(5499), 416–417. https://doi.org/10.1038/254416a0

Freeman, N. H. (1980). *Strategies of representation in young children*. Academic Press.

Freeman, N. H. (1986). How should a cube be drawn? *British Journal of Developmental Psychology*, *4*(4), 317–322. https://doi.org/10.1111/j.2044-835X.1986.tb01025.x

Freeman, N. H., & Adi-Japha, E. (2008). Pictorial intention, action and interpretation. In C. Lange-Küttner & A. Vinter (Eds.), *Drawing and the non-verbal mind: A life-span perspective* (pp. 104–120). Cambridge University Press.

Freeman, N. H., Eiser, C., & Sayers, J. (1977). Children's strategies in producing three-dimensional relationships on a two-dimensional surface. *Journal of Experimental Child Psychology*, *23*(2), 305–314. https://doi.org/10.1016/0022-0965(77)90107-2

Freeman, N. H., & Janikoun, R. (1972). Intellectual realism in children's drawings of a familiar object with distinctive features. *Child Development*, *43*(3), 1116–1121. https://doi.org/10.2307/1127668

Gerstadt, C. L., Hong, Y. J., & Diamond, A. (1994). The relationship between cognition and action: Performance of children 3 1/2–7 years old on a Stroop-like day-night test. *Cognition*, *53*(2), 129–153. https://doi.org/10.1016/0010-0277(94)90068-X

Goodenough, F. L. (1926). *Measurement of intelligence by drawings*. World Book Co.

Goodenough, F. L., & Harris, D. B. (1950). Studies in the psychology of children's drawings: II 1928–1949. *Psychological Bulletin*, *47*(5), 369–433. https://doi.org/10.1037/h0058368

Goodnow, J. J. (1977). *Children's drawings*. Fontana.

Goodnow, J. J., & Friedman, S. (1972). Orientation in children's human figure drawings: An aspect of graphic language. *Developmental Psychology*, 7(1), 10–16. https://doi.org/10.1037/h0032697

Hagen, M. A. (1985). There is no development in art. In N. Freeman & M. V. Cox (Eds.), *Visual order* (pp. 78–100). Cambridge University Press.

Ingram, N., & Butterworth, G. (1989). The young child's representation of depth in drawing: Process and product. *Journal of Experimental Child Psychology*, *47*(3), 356–369. https://doi.org/10.1016/0022-0965(89)90019-2

Ittelson, W. H. (1952). *The Ames demonstrations in perception; a guide to their construction and use*. Princeton University Press.

Jaensch, E. R. (1911). *Über die Wahrnehmung des Raumes. Eine experimentell-psychologische Untersuchung nebst Anwendung auf Ästhetik und Erkenntnislehre [On perception of space. An experimental study including application in aesthetics and epistemology]*. Barth.

Jensen, C. A., Sumanthiran, D., Kirkorian, H. L., Travers, B. G., Rosengren, K. S., & Rogers, T. T. (2023). Human perception and machine vision reveal rich latent structure in human figure drawings. *Frontiers in Psychology*, *14*, article 1029808. https://doi.org/10.3389/fpsyg.2023.1029808

Jolley, R. (2008). Children's understanding of the dual nature of pictures. In C. Lange-Küttner & A. Vinter (Eds.), *Drawing and the non-verbal mind: A life-span perspective* (pp. 86–103). Cambridge University Press.

Jones, L. B., Rothbart, M. K., & Posner, M. I. (2003). Development of executive attention in preschool children. *Developmental Science*, *6*(5), 498–504. https://doi.org/10.1111/1467-7687.00307

Karmiloff-Smith, A. (1990). Constraints on representational change: Evidence from children's drawing. *Cognition*, *34*(1), 57–83. https://doi.org/10.1016/0010-0277(90)90031-E

Kellogg, R. (1959). *What children scribble and why*. National Press.

Kemler, D. G. (1983). Holistic and analytic modes in perceptual and cognitive development. In T. Tighe & B. E. Shepp (Eds.), *Perception, cognition, and development: Interactional analyses* (pp. 77–102). Erlbaum.

Kerschensteiner, G. (1905). *Die Entwicklung der zeichnerischen Begabung [The development of graphic talent]*. Gerber.

Koppitz, E. M. (1966). Emotional indicators on human figure drawings of children: A validation study. *Journal of Clinical Psychology*, *22*(3), 313–315. https://doi.org/10.1002/1097-4679(196607)22:3<313::AID-JCLP2270220321>3.0.CO;2-Z

Kosslyn, S. M., Heldmeyer, K. H., & Locklear, E. P. (1977). Children's drawings as data about internal representations. *Journal of Experimental Child Psychology*, *23*(2), 191–211. https://doi.org/10.1016/0022-0965(77)90099-6

Lange-Küttner, C. (1989). *Raumbegriff und Objektbeziehungen beim Kind. Die Entstehung des perspektivischen Zeichnens bei verhaltensgestörten und normalen Kindern. Eine empirische Untersuchung [Space concept and object relations in the child. The development of perspective drawing in children with and without behavioural difficulties. An empirical investigation]*. Lang.

Lange-Küttner, C. (1994). *Gestalt und Konstruktion. Die Entwicklung der grafischen Kompetenz beim Kind. [Gestalt and construction. The development of graphic competence in the child]*. Huber.

Lange-Küttner, C. (1997). Development of size modification of human figure drawings in spatial axes systems of varying complexity. *Journal of Experimental Child Psychology*, *66*(2), 264–278. https://doi.org/10.1006/jecp.1997.2386

Lange-Küttner, C. (1998). Pressure, velocity and time in speeded drawing of basic graphic pattern by young children. *Perceptual and Motor Skills, 86*, 1299–1310. https://doi.org/10.2466/pms.1998.86.3c.1299

Lange-Küttner, C. (2000). The role of object violation in the development of visual analysis. *Perceptual and Motor Skills, 90*(1), 3–24. https://doi.org/10.2466/PMS.90.1.3-24

Lange-Küttner, C. (2004). More evidence on size modification in spatial axes systems of varying complexity. *Journal of Experimental Child Psychology, 88*(2), 171–192. https://doi.org/10.1016/j.jecp.2004.02.003

Lange-Küttner, C. (2006). Drawing boundaries: From individual to common region - The development of spatial region attribution in children. *British Journal of Developmental Psychology, 24*(2), 419–427. https://doi.org/10.1348/026151005X50753

Lange-Küttner, C. (2008). Figures in and out of context: Absent, simple, complex and halved spatial fields. In C. Lange-Küttner & A. Vinter (Eds.), *Drawing and the non-verbal mind: A life-span perspective* (pp. 195–216). Cambridge University Press.

Lange-Küttner, C. (2009). Habitual size and projective size: The logic of spatial systems in children's drawings. *Developmental Psychology, 45*(4), 913–927. https://doi.org/10.1037/a0016133

Lange-Küttner, C. (2011). Sex differences in visual realism in drawings of animate and inanimate objects. *Perceptual and Motor Skills, 113*(2), 439–453. https://doi.org/10.2466/04.10.24.PMS.113.5.439-453

Lange-Küttner, C. (2014). Do drawing stages really exist? Children's early mapping of perspective. *Psychology of Aesthetics, Creativity, and the Arts, 8*(2), 168–182. https://doi.org/10.1037/a0036199

Lange-Küttner, C. (2020). Drawing. In M. Harris & G. Westermann (Eds.), *The Encyclopedia of Child and Adolescent Development* (Vol. III Cognition, pp. 1277–1291). Wiley-Blackwell. https://onlinelibrary.wiley.com/doi/book/10.1002/9781119171492

Lange-Küttner, C. (2021). Common Region Test (CRT). A drawing test for assessment of the development of spatial organization in children. APA PsycTESTS control number 9999-79011-000.

Lange-Küttner, C., & Ebersbach, M. (2013). Girls in detail, boys in shape: Gender differences when drawing cubes in depth. *British Journal of Psychology, 104*(3), 413–437. https://doi.org/10.1111/bjop.12010

Lange-Küttner, C., & Green, H. (2007). What is the age of mental rotation ? In *Proceedings of the 6th IEEE international conference on development and learning* (pp. 259–263). IEEE Press. https://doi.org/10.1109/DEVLRN.2007.4354043

Lange-Küttner, C., Kerzmann, A., & Heckhausen, J. (2002). The emergence of visually realistic contour in the drawing of the human figure. *British Journal of Developmental Psychology, 20*(3), 439–463. https://doi.org/10.1348/026151002320620415

Lange-Küttner, C., Küttner, E., & Chromekova, M. (2014). Deterioration and recovery of DAP IQ scores in the repeated assessment of the Naglieri Draw-A-Person (DAP) test in 6- to 12-year-old children. *Psychological Assessment, 26*(1), 297–306. https://doi.org/10.1037/a0034581

Lange-Küttner, C., & Reith, E. (1995). The transformation of figurative thought: Implications of Piaget and Inhelder's developmental theory for children's drawings. In C. Lange-Küttner & G. V. Thomas (Eds.), *Drawing and looking* (pp. 75–92). Harvester Wheatsheaf/Pearson.

Lange-Küttner, C., & Thomas, G. V. (Eds.). (1995). *Drawing and looking. Theoretical approaches to pictorial representation in children*. Harvester Wheatsheaf/Pearson.

Lange-Küttner, C., & Vinter, A. (Eds.). (2008). *Drawing and the non-verbal mind. A life-span perspective.* Cambridge University Press.

Lange-Küttner, C., & Vinueza Chavez, X. (2022). The space paradox in graphic representation. *Frontiers in Developmental Psychology, 13,* article 968918. https://doi.org/10.3389/fpsyg.2022.968918

Lewis, V. (1990). Young children's painting of the sky and the ground. *International Journal of Behavioral Development, 13,* 49–65. https://doi.org/10.1177/016502549001300104

Light, P. H., & MacIntosh, E. (1980). Depth relationships in young children's drawings. *Journal of Experimental Child Psychology, 30*(1), 79–87. https://doi.org/10.1016/0022-0965(80)90076-4

Lin, Q., Luo, J., Wu, Z., Shen, F., & Sun, Z. (2015). Characterization of fine motor development: Dynamic analysis of children's drawing movements. *Human Movement Science, 40,* 163–175. https://doi.org/10.1016/j.humov.2014.12.010

Lindenberger, U., & Lövdén, M. (2019). Brain plasticity in human lifespan development: The exploration–selection–refinement model. *Annual Review of Developmental Psychology, 1*(1), 197–222. https://doi.org/10.1146/annurev-devpsych-121318-085229

Logan, G. D. (1996). The CODE theory of visual attention. An integration of space-based and object-based attention. *Psychological Review, 103*(4), 603–649. https://doi.org/10.1037/0033-295x.103.4.603

Longobardi, C., Quaglia, R., & Iotti, N. O. (2015). Reconsidering the scribbling stage of drawing: A new perspective on toddlers' representational processes. *Frontiers in Developmental Psychology, 6,* article 1227. https://doi.org/doi/10.3389/fpsyg.2015.01227

Löwenfeld, V. (1939). *The nature of creative activity* (O. A. Oeser, Trans.). Harcourt Brace.

Luchins, A. S. (1950). New experimental attempts at preventing mechanization in problem solving. *The Journal of General Psychology, 42,* 279–297.

Luchins, A. S., & Luchins, E. H. (1959). *Rigidity of behaviour.* University of Oregon Press.

Luquet, G.-H. (1927/2001). *Children's drawings (Le dessin enfantin)* (A. Costall, Trans.). International Specialized Book Services.

Martzog, P., Stoeger, H., & Suggate, S. (2019). Relations between preschool children's fine motor skills and general cognitive abilities. *Journal of Cognition and Development, 20*(4), 443–465. https://doi.org/10.1080/15248372.2019.1607862

Maurer, M. N., & Roebers, C. M. (2020). Is the fine motor-executive functions link stronger for new compared to repeated fine motor tasks? *PLoS One, 15*(11). http://dx.doi.org/10.1371/journal.pone.0241308

McBride-Chang, C., Chung, K. H. K., & Tong, X. (2011). Copying skills in relation to word reading and writing in Chinese children with and without dyslexia. *Journal of Experimental Child Psychology, 110*(3), 422–433. https://doi.org/10.1016/j.jecp.2011.04.014

Meulenbroek, R. G. W., Vinter, A., & Mounoud, P. (1993). Development of the start-rotation principle in circle production. *British Journal of Developmental Psychology, 11*(3), 307–320. https://doi.org/10.1111/j.2044-835X.1993.tb00605.x

Milbrath, C. (1998). *Patterns of artistic development in children: Comparative studies of talent.* Cambridge University Press.

Mitchelmore, M. C. (1978). Developmental stages in children's representation of regular solid figures. *The Journal of Genetic Psychology: Research and Theory on Human Development, 133*(2), 229–239. https://doi.org/10.1080/00221325.1978.10533380

Moore, V. R. (1986a). The relationship between children's drawings and preferences for alternative depictions of a familiar object. *Journal of Experimental Child Psychology, 42*(2), 187–198. https://doi.org/10.1016/0022-0965(86)90022-6

Moore, V. R. (1986b). The use of a colouring task to elucidate children's drawings of a solid cube. *British Journal of Developmental Psychology, 4*(4), 335–340. https://doi.org/10.1111/j.2044-835X.1986.tb01028.x

Morra, S. (2005). Cognitive aspects of change in drawings: A neo-Piagetian theoretical account. *British Journal of Developmental Psychology, 23*(3), 317–341. https://doi.org/10.1348/026151005X27182

Morra, S. (2008). Spatial structures in children's drawings: How do they develop? In C. Lange-Küttner & A. Vinter (Eds.), *Drawing and the non-verbal mind: A life-span perspective* (pp. 159–194). Cambridge University Press.

Morra, S., & Panesi, S. (2017). From scribbling to drawing: The role of working memory. *Cognitive Development, 43*, 142–158. https://dx.doi.org/10.1016/j.cogdev.2017.03.001

Naglieri, J. A. (1988). *Draw a person: A quantitative scoring system*. Psychological Corporation.

Naglieri, J. A., & Ronning, M. E. (2000). Comparison of White, African American, Hispanic, and Asian children on the Naglieri nonverbal ability test. *Psychological Assessment, 12*(3), 328–334. https://doi.org/10.1037/1040-3590.12.3.328

Nurmi, O. (1985). A fast line-sweep algorithm for hidden line elimination. *BIT Numerical Mathematics, 25*(3), 466–472. https://doi.org/10.1007/bf01935366

Ogino, T., Watanabe, K., Nakano, K., Kado, Y., Morooka, T., Takeuchi, A., Oka, M., Sanada, S., & Ohtuska, Y. (2009). Predicting executive function task scores with the Rey-Osterrieth complex figure. *Brain & Development, 31*(1), 52–57. https://doi.org/10.1016/j.braindev.2008.07.003

Palmer, S. E. (1992). Common region: A new principle of perceptual grouping. *Cognitive Psychology, 24*, 436–447. https://doi.org/10.1016/0010-0285(92)90014-S

Palmis, S. E., Danna, J., Velay, J.-L., & Longcamp, M. (2017). Motor control of handwriting in the developing brain: A review. *Cognitive Neuropsychology, 34*(3–4), 187–204. http://dx.doi.org/10.1080/02643294.2017.1367654

Panesi, S., & Morra, S. (2016). Drawing a dog: The role of working memory and executive function. *Journal of Experimental Child Psychology, 152*, 1–11. http://dx.doi.org/10.1016/j.jecp.2016.06.015

Patterson, K., & Erzinclioglu, S. (2009). Drawing as a "window" on deteriorating conceptual knowledge in neurodegenerative disease. In C. Lange-Küttner & A. Vinter (Eds.), *Drawing and the non-verbal mind. A life-span perspective* (pp. 285–316). Cambridge University Press.

Piaget, J. (1969). *The mechanisms of perception*. Routledge and Kegan Paul.

Piaget, J., & Inhelder, B. (1956). *The child's conception of space*. Routledge and Kegan Paul.

Piaget, J., Inhelder, B., & Szeminska, A. (1960). *The child's conception of geometry*. Routledge and Kegan Paul.

Picard, D., & Vinter, A. (1999). Representational flexibility in children's drawings: Effects of age and verbal instructions. *British Journal of Developmental Psychology, 17*(4), 605–622. https://doi.org/10.1348/026151099165500

Picard, D., & Vinter, A. (2007). Relationships between procedural rigidity and interrepresentational change in children's drawing behavior. *Child Development, 78*(2), 522–541. https://doi.org/10.1111/j.1467-8624.2007.01013.x

Pridmore, P., & Lansdown, R. (1997). Exploring children's perceptions of health: Does drawing really break down barriers? *Health Education Journal, 56*(3), 219–230. https://doi.org/10.1177/001789699705600302

Quaglia, R., Longobardi, C., Iotti, N. O., & Prino, L. E. (2015). A new theory on children's drawings: Analyzing the role of emotion and movement in graphical development. *Infant Behavior and Development, 39*, 81–91. https://doi.org/10.1016/j.infbeh.2015.02.009

Reith, E., & Dominin, D. (1997). The development of children's ability to attend to the visual projection of objects. *British Journal of Developmental Psychology, 15*(2), 177–196. https://doi.org/10.1111/j.2044-835X.1997.tb00733.x

Riggs, K. R., Jolley, R. P., & Simpson, A. (2013). The role of inhibitory control in the development of human figure drawing in young children. *Journal of Experimental Child Psychology, 114*(4), 537–542. https://doi.org/10.1016/j.jecp.2012.10.003

Ross, J. (2008). Drawing production, drawing re-experience and drawing re-cognition. In C. Lange-Küttner & A. Vinter (Eds.), *Drawing and the non-verbal mind: A life-span perspective* (pp. 42–62). Cambridge University Press.

Rückriegel, S. M., Blankenburg, F., Burghardt, R., Ehrlich, S., Henze, G., Mergl, R., & Hernáiz Driever, P. (2008). Influence of age and movement complexity on kinematic hand movement parameters in childhood and adolescence. *International Journal of Developmental Neuroscience, 26*(7), 655–663. https://doi.org/10.1016/j.ijdevneu.2008.07.015

Schwamborn, A., Mayer, R. E., Thillmann, H., Leopold, C., & Leutner, D. (2010). Drawing as a generative activity and drawing as a prognostic activity. *Journal of Educational Psychology, 102*(4), 872–879. https://doi.org/10.1037/a0019640

Selfe, L. (1977). *Nadia - A case of extraordinary drawing ability in an autistic child.* Academic Press.

Silk, A. M., & Thomas, G. V. (1986). Development and differentiation in children's figure drawings. *British Journal of Psychology, 77*, 399–410. https://doi.org/10.1111/j.2044-8295.1986.tb02206.x

Starch, D. (1916). *Educational measurements.* MacMillan.

Stetsenko, A. (1995). The psychological function of children's drawing: A Vygotskian perspective. In C. Lange-Küttner & G. V. Thomas (Eds.), *Drawing and looking: Theoretical approaches to pictorial representation in children* (pp. 147–158). Harvester Wheatsheaf.

Sully, J. (1895). The young draughtsman. In J. Sully (Ed.), *Studies of childhood* (pp. 331–398). Longmans, Green and Co.

Sutton, P. J., & Rose, D. H. (1998). The role of strategic visual attention in children's drawing development. *Journal of Experimental Child Psychology, 68*(2), 87–107. https://doi.org/10.1006/jecp.1997.2419

Tabatabaey-Mashadi, N., Sudirman, R., Khalid, P. I., & Lange-Küttner, C. (2015). Automated syntax analyses of drawing two tangent patterns in children with low and average handwriting ability. *Perceptual and Motor Skills, 120*(3), 865–894. https://doi.org/10.2466/24.10.PMS.120v15x1

Thomas, G. V., Nye, R., & Robinson, E. J. (1994). How children view pictures: Children's responses to pictures as things in themselves and as representations of something else. *Cognitive Development, 9*(2), 141–164. https://doi.org/10.1016/0885-2014(94)90001-9

Toomela, A. (2002). Drawing as a verbally mediated activity: A study of relationships between verbal, motor, and visuospatial skills and drawing in children. *International Journal of Behavioral Development, 26*(3), 234–247. https://doi.org/10.1080/01650250143000021

Trautner, H. M., Lohaus, A., Sahm, W. B., & Helbing, N. (1989). Age-graded judgements of children's drawings by children and adults. *International Journal of Behavioral Development, 12*(4), 421–431. https://doi.org/10.1177/016502548901200401

Tryphon, A., & Montangero, J. (1992). The development of diachronic thinking in children: Children's ideas about changes in drawing skills. *International Journal of Behavioral Development, 15*(3), 411–424. https://doi.org/10.1177/016502549201500308

Tse, L. F. L., Siu, A. M. H., & Li-Tsang, C. W. P. (2019). Assessment of early handwriting skill in kindergarten children using a Chinese name writing test. *Reading and Writing: An Interdisciplinary Journal, 32*(2), 265–284. http://dx.doi.org/10.1007/s11145-018-9861-6

Uttal, D. H., Liu, L. L., & DeLoache, J. S. (1999). Taking a hard look at concreteness: Do concrete objects help young children learn symbolic relations? In Balter, L., & Tamis-LeMonda, C. S. (Eds.), *Child psychology: A handbook of contemporary issues* (pp. 177–192). Psychology Press.

Van Sommers, P. (1984). *Drawing and cognition. Descriptive and experimental studies of graphic production processes.* Cambridge University Press.

Van Sommers, P. (1989). A system for drawing and drawing-related neuropsychology. *Cognitive Neuropsychology, 6*(2), 117–164. https://doi.org/10.1080/02643298908253416

Vinter, A., & Chartrel, E. (2010). Effects of different types of learning on handwriting movements in young children. *Learning and Instruction, 20*(6), 476–486. https://doi.org/10.1016/j.learninstruc.2009.07.001

Vinter, A., Fernandes, V., Orlandi, O., & Morgan, P. (2012). Exploratory procedures of tactile images in visually impaired and blindfolded sighted children: How they relate to their consequent performance in drawing. *Research in Developmental Disabilities, 33*(6), 1819–1831. https://doi.org/10.1016/j.ridd.2012.05.001

Vinter, A., & Mounoud, P. (1991). Isochrony and accuracy of drawing movements in children: Effects of age and context. In J. Wann, A. M. Wing, & N. Sõvik (Eds.), *Development of graphic skills: Research perspectives and educational implications* (pp. 113–134). Academic Press.

Volkelt, H. (1931/1968). *Die Prinzipien der Raumdarstellung des Kindes [Principles of spatial depictions in the child].* Selbstverlag.

Walker, P., Bremner, J. G., Smart, L., Pitt, T., & Apsey, D. (2008). Object categorisation, object naming, and viewpoint independence in visual remembering: Evidence from young children's drawings of a novel object. *Memory, 16*(6), 626–636. https://doi.org/10.1080/09658210802135369

Watanabe, K., Ogino, T., Nakano, K., Hattori, J., Kado, Y., Sanada, S., & Ohtsuka, Y. (2005). The Rey-Osterrieth complex figure as a measure of executive function in childhood. *Brain & Development, 27*(8), 564–569. https://doi.org/10.1016/j.braindev.2005.02.007

Wenger, E., Kühn, S., Verrel, J., Mårtensson, J., Bodammer, N. C., Lindenberger, U., & Lövdén, M. (2017). Repeated structural imaging reveals nonlinear progression of experience-dependent volume changes in human motor cortex. *Cerebral Cortex, 27*(5), 2911–2925. https://doi.org/10.1093/cercor/bhw141

Wertheimer, M. (1923). Untersuchungen zur Lehre von der Gestalt [Studies on gestalt theory]. *Psychologische Forschung, 4*, 301–350.

Willats, J. (1985). Drawing systems revisited: The role of denotation systems in children's figure drawings. In N. H. Freeman & M. V. Cox (Eds.), *Visual order* (pp. 78–100). Cambridge University Press.

Willats, J. (1995). An information-processing approach to drawing development. In C. Lange-Küttner & G. V. Thomas (Eds.), *Drawing and looking: Theoretical approaches to pictorial representation in children* (pp. 27–43). Harvester Wheatsheaf/Pearson.

Willats, J. (1997). *Art and representation: New principles in the analysis of pictures.* Princeton University Press.

Willats, J. (2005). *Making sense of children's drawings.* Lawrence Erlbaum Associates Publishers.

Willcock, E., Imuta, K., & Hayne, H. (2011). Children's human figure drawings do not measure intellectual ability. *Journal of Experimental Child Psychology, 110*(3), 444–452. https://doi.org/10.1016/j.jecp.2011.04.013

Winner, E. (1996). The rage to master: The decisive role of talent in the visual arts. In K. A. Ericsson & K. A. Ericsson (Eds.), *The road to excellence: The acquisition of expert performance in the arts and sciences, sports, and games* (pp. 271–301). Lawrence Erlbaum Associates, Inc.

Winner, E., & Drake, J. E. (2013). The rage to master: The decisive role of talent in the visual arts. In S. B. Kaufman (Ed.), *The complexity of greatness: Beyond talent or practice* (pp. 333–365). Oxford University Press.

6

VISUAL SEARCH IN CHILDREN

6.1 Development of Visual Attention

Experimental psychology has been investigating for a long time how attention helps to obtain an alert state, to orient to sensory events, and to control output from competing response tendencies (Posner, 2019). Attention is a cognitive process that mediates between perception and memory. The way this mediation process works when transforming impressions into memory has been a topic of many undergraduate psychology essays (Eysenck & Keane, 1995). Is attention focused only on selected aspects of perception using a filter (Broadbent, 1958), or is attention taking in all perceived information, with and without awareness, and only capacity constraints account for attentional limitations (Treisman, 1964)? Moreover, a well-known differentiation of the types of attention are the concepts of selective, divided, sustained and orienting attention (Gray et al., 2016). Although short-term memory and modality-specific working memory are often conceptualised in similar ways as attention (Nobre & Stokes, 2011), these processes are more likely to be allocated to working memory rather than to attention research (Cowan, 2008).

In developmental psychology, the development of attention was seen as closely linked to the temperament of children, as it is of course a main aim of parents and teachers that children learn to pay attention and stay on task (Rothbart et al., 2014, 2020). The concept that Rothbart and Posner are most well-known for is the Attention Network Test (ANT). It assumes that attention has three functions: Alerting, orienting and executing. They could identify the brain sources and biochemical substrates controlling these processes. Especially interesting is their research on spatial conflict. This paradigm exploits the finding that eye-hand coordination is lateralised, that is, if a stimulus is on the left side, a child will be faster to respond with the hand on the left than on the right side. Between 2

DOI: 10.4324/9780429270604-7

and 3 years of age, children still show perseverative responding in such a task, and only at around 4 years old do children show the expected added-on reaction time when contralaterally responding to a task with spatial conflict (Gerardi-Caulton, 2000). The spatial conflict task score was correlated with eye movement measures (Rothbart et al., 2003). Also, in another version of a spatial conflict task, using distracter fish swimming in the same or in a different direction, children showed left–right confusion when handling two response buttons, which was reflected in more strongly separated anterior-posterior brain activation than in adults, who were less challenged by the distracters (Rueda et al., 2004). This display of the row of fish, with one swimming in the opposite direction than the other fish, resembles many of the visual search displays which involve finding a target in noise. Visual search tasks can be carried out already with 4- and 6-month-old infants who would look first and were faster to look at singletons, and were also looking for longer depending on a graded score computed from the physical salience measures colour, edge orientation, and intensity (DeBolt et al., 2022).

6.2 Principles of Visual Search

The first visual search studies were rather applied as participants were tested to see if their blinking rate increased during prolonged visual search (Carpenter, 1948), or investigated the duration of effective selective visual attention and vigilance (Mackworth, 1948). However, this changed to a more specific research question where the main aim was to find a target in visual noise. One of the earliest findings was that the speed to find a prescribed detail was dependent on the presentation rate and the display load (Mackworth & Mackworth, 1958). It has also been known for decades that the size of the display itself adds to the load (Enoch, 1959). Neisser (1964) claimed that many comparisons can be carried out in parallel during visual search, for instance finding a famous face in a crowd. Finding a target would involve looking for less than the full meaning but also for more than components and details. Neither peripheral acuity, foveal acuity, nor eye dominance scores correlated significantly with search time, but decision making was required (Erickson, 1966). For instance, neurotic traits facilitate decision-making about whether a target is absent, while conscientiousness prolongs search time for a non-existing target (Lange-Küttner & Puiu, 2021). In infants, identifying the target depended on optimal arousal (Kleberg et al., 2019).

In the same year as Erickson's study, the first visual search study with children was published by Gibson and Yonas (1966). It closely followed the experimental design of Neisser's (1964) word lists where a certain letter amongst others needed to be identified. In addition to error rates, Eleanor Gibson also measured reaction times (see Figure 6.1), and cleanly and closely matched the letters in three experimental conditions. In one condition, the search letter G had no visual similarity in terms of *curvature* with the distracters L, K, V, M, X and A that all involved straight lines only (see also Wolfe et al., 1992). In another condition, two targets

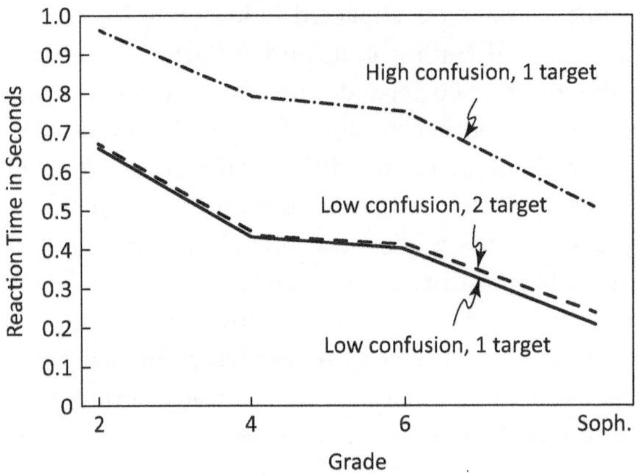

Effect of Target Number and Low and High - Confusion Context on Scanning Rate.

FIGURE 6.1 Increase of Children's Letter Search Time (Gibson & Jonas, 1966)

were to be found, G and R, both involving curvature. In the third condition, the distracter letters B, Q, C, J, S and R shared the feature curvature with the target G. A visual search task with shared features between target and distracters is called conjunctive search. As already E. Gibson presumed, serial search through the distracters is required in conjunctive search (Treisman & Gelade, 1980).

Gibson and Yonas (1966) tested 7-year-old second graders, 9-year-old fourth graders and 11-year-old sixth graders as well as older students (sophomores). While younger children were slower than the older age groups and needed more time, there was absolutely no interaction with task condition: All participants needed the same time whether one or two distinct targets were involved (low confusion), and they all clearly needed longer when target and distracters shared curvature features (high confusion), so this appeared to stay the same.

Wickens (1974) concluded that because no interactions could be found, the difference between children's and adults' visual search would only be due to the difference in experience and learning the stimulus features. However, a short look at Figure 6.1 suffices to conclude that this conclusion cannot be valid because children showed the same sensitivity to the letter feature curvature as adults. The only question that appears to be left in the Gibson and Yonas study (1966) is why it takes children longer than adults, but then young children take longer in almost every task (which can tax adults' patience) (Kail, 1991). The stimulus combinations of target and distracters that Gibson and Yonas labelled as low and high confusion were later conceptualised as disjunction or feature search versus conjunction search by Treisman and Gelade (1980); see Figure 6.2.

Treisman and Gelade (1980) also used letters, but randomly dispersed on the display. Rather than just varying the curvature of the letters, they also varied the

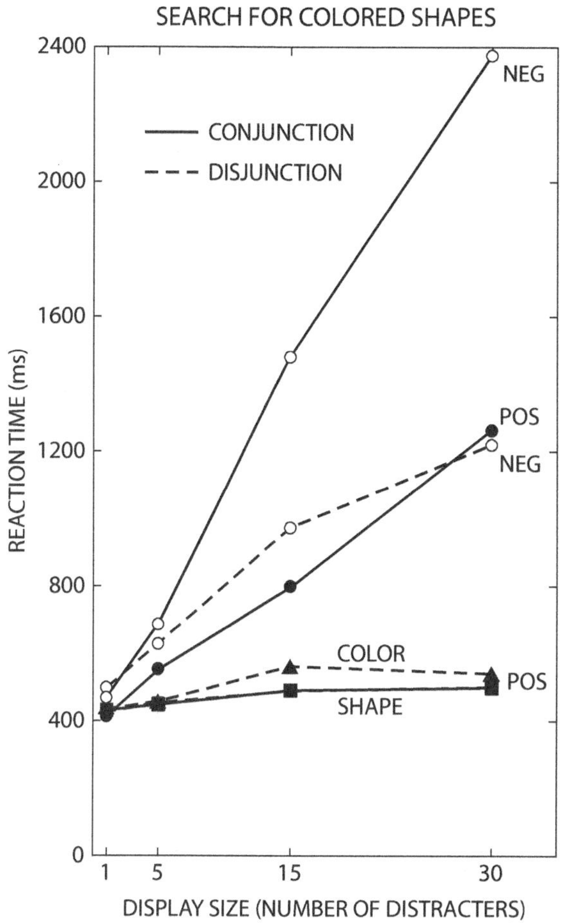

FIGURE 6.2 Increase of Search Time in Conjunction Search (Treisman & Gelade, 1980)

colour. Distracters were always brown Ts and green Xs. In the feature condition, the targets were a blue letter (colour) or an S (shape), while in the conjunction search, the target letter was a green T, that is, the same letter as the T distracters but in the colour of X. They found that in feature search, the number of distracters (set size) did not matter, but in conjunction search, latencies became longer as more distracters were present. This effect was strongly enlarged in target-absent compared to target-present trials. The authors thus suggested that search is serial and self-terminating with a scanning rate of about 60 ms per item.

Hence, while feature search is automatic (A.-S. Li et al., 2022), serial search is guided by attention strategies of various sources, e.g., (1) top-down and (2) bottom-up feature guidance, (3) prior history (e.g., priming), (4) reward and (5) scene syntax and semantics (Wolfe, 2021) as well as personality traits (Lange-Küttner & Puiu, 2021).

6.3 The Development of Visual Search

The research of Gibson and Yonas was extended to younger children and even infants at one year of age. Gerhardstein and Rovée-Collier (2002) tested infants from 1 to 3 years. They used drawings of two different types of dinosaur shapes in two colours to set up the feature and conjunction search on a computer touch screen. One-year-old infants did not manage conjunction search, but otherwise, astonishingly, from 1½ years of age, the principles of adult visual search were revealed also in the results of young infants.

The plotted means in Figure 6.3 clearly show that from 18 months onwards, infant conjunction search was sensitive to the number of distracters while feature search was not (Gerhardstein & Rovee-Collier, 2002). When comparing Figures 6.2 and 6.3 with respect to conjunction search time, the y-axes show that the maximum search time in adults could go up to 2,400 ms. The maximum search time was 6,000 ms in 1½-year-olds, but the average conjunction search time had about halved in 3-year-olds. The differences in slopes did not reach significance and stayed the same in this age range.

This kind of result was also found in 7- to 12-year-old children (Lobaugh et al., 1998). In the feature search, distracters varied on only one dimension, colour or orientation, while these features were shared between target and distracters in the conjunction search. Only in the hardest condition of conjunction search of a display with 36 distracters did an age difference show: The youngest children in this sample, the 7-year-old children, were less likely to detect the target. In

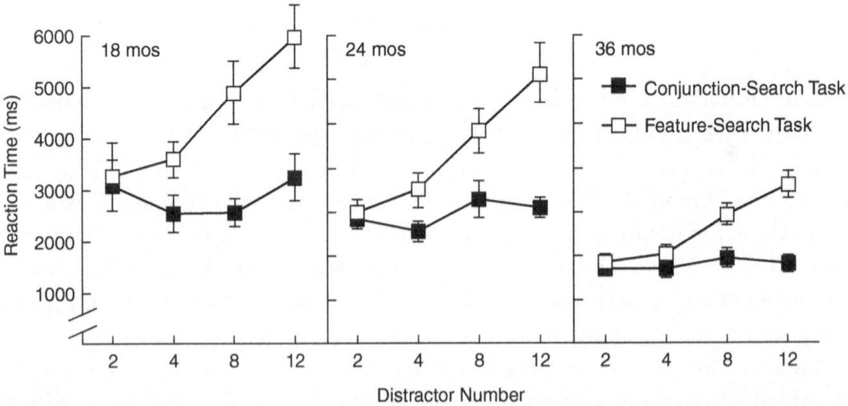

FIGURE 6.3 Feature and Conjunction Search in Infants (Gerhardstein & Rovee-Collier, 2002)

target-absent trials, differences in spatial orientation led to steeper serial search than colour differences, in all age groups of children and adults, see Figure 6.4.

Figure 6.4 shows that Lobaugh et al. (1998) used set sizes of 4, 16, and 36 distracters and that the search time more steeply increased when the target was absent than when it was present. The curves for orientation and colour feature search are different, though. If the search target differed by orientation, search time steeply increased when the target was absent. However, if the target differed by colour, search time stayed flat even when the target was absent. Thus, while a colour difference predictably generated pop-out search, the search for a differently orientated unique target was more similar to conjunction search. This principle was the same in all children's and adults' age groups and thus stayed the same between 7 and 12 years.

Colour is an important visual cue in children, for instance, in mental rotation of objects (Lütke & Lange-Küttner, 2015, 2021). Also, the Raven Progressive

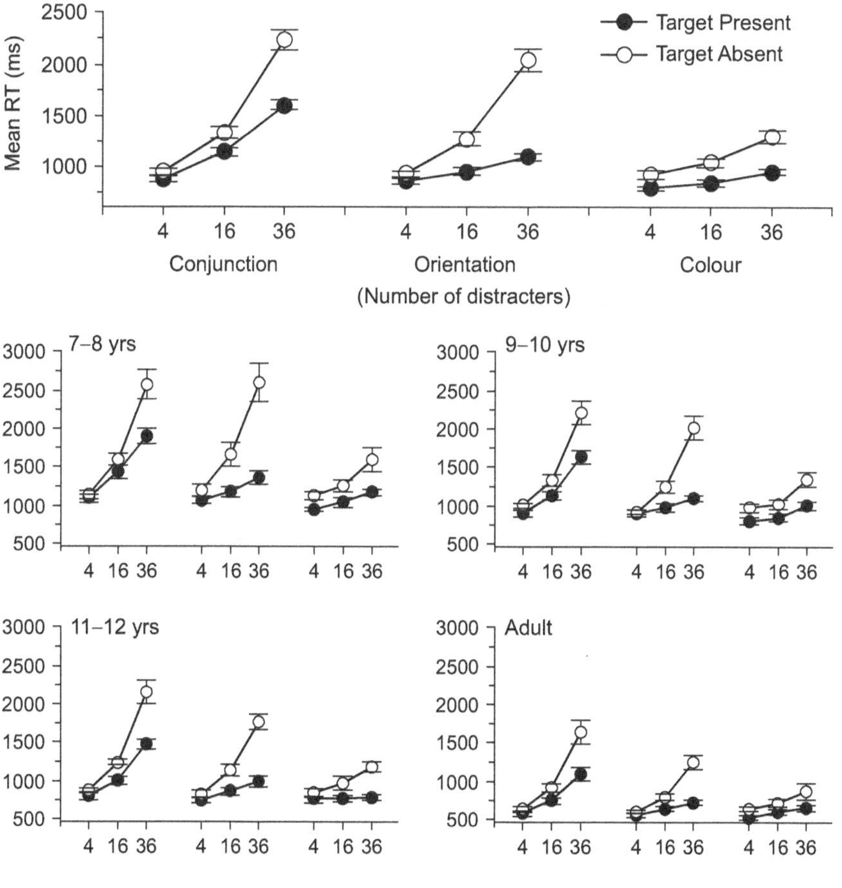

FIGURE 6.4 Feature and Conjunction Search in Children and Adults (Lobaugh et al., 1998)

Matrices Test is available in colour for children and in black-and-white for adults (Raven & Raven, 2003). Moreover, other studies also revealed that a different orientation made visual search targets hard to find, from infancy to school age and in adults (Amso & Johnson, 2006; Donnelly et al., 2007). Thus, the sequence of dominant features even in adults is assumed to be colour, followed by object size, and lastly orientation (Rutishauser & Koch, 2007). Because colour can turn a conjunction search into a pop-out search in adults as well, it is suggested that there is a flexible visual priority map (A.-S. Li et al., 2022).

The fact that orientation is a feature that is hard to detect for children seems to suggest that a visual search task has a predominantly spatial dimension and probably requires path finding amongst items. The hypothesis was explicitly tested by Woods et al. (2013) with a sample of 2- to 17-year-olds. They devised a visual search task only after a cancellation test of 16 apples in a display cluttered with 16 panda bears and 16 gift-wrapped boxes as distracters, which is also used in neuropsychological research. Cancellations could follow a smooth pathway or cross-over distracters. The cancellations test showed a significant and steep developmental improvement in systematic pathways and fewer pathway cross-overs of distracters until age 12, when gains became less pronounced. Reaction times were not analysed. As could be expected, feature search was near ceiling in all age groups, while conjunction search showed improvements with age. Interestingly, covariate regressions showed that systematic pathways in the series of cancellations were related to conjunction search, which is proof for the expected serial processing in children's visual search. In another study, backward memory span was correlated with distance and intersections in visual search (Guilbert et al., 2020). For adults, such systematic pathways were directly measured and shown to be relevant using eyetracking (Rutishauser & Koch, 2007). In children, these could also be measured, for instance with the well-known Corsi blocks (Arce & McMullen, 2021), but this has not been carried out so far.

FMRI analyses of conjunction search in adults (Kamienkowski et al., 2012) showed that distracters yielded more (late) activation in the left frontal lobe (inhibition), while the target activated the right frontal lobe (identification). Moreover, distracters continuously activated the central parietal lobe most likely because distracters were distributed in the spatial field while a target only occupied one location. In contrast, the target showed more late bilateral activation in the occipital lobes than the distracters as if vision of the target had sharpened and selective attention achieved an optimal spotlight size (Anton-Erxleben & Carrasco, 2013). With regard to brain processing in children, an event-related (ERP) EEG study with children from 7 to 12 years concluded that item features would be more important than serial processing as developmental changes were significant only for late parietal processes of size vs. colour, but not for feature vs. conjunction search (Taylor et al., 1999). Thus, an aspect that needs to be investigated more fully in children are the items of visual search. For instance, in typically developing children, the Embedded Figures Test (EFT) that involves the detection of the contour of a shape in visual noise predicted their conjunction search (Jarrold et al., 2005).

It is also of interest whether Gestalt features in the spatial field impact on visual search. Burack et al. (2000) created a visual search task with three compound figures with Gestalt features: (1) Four identically coloured dots forming a chain, (2) a chain of dots with alternating colours, and (3) a chain with grouped colours. If a figure consisted of two pairs of differently coloured dots,  one could also perceive two figures instead of four, each in a different colour. In this way, such Gestalt synthesis could have halved the perceived number of distracters contributing to set size. In the visual display, the target had a different *orientation*. There were right-left decisions about the target to be made from a fixation point at the centre display as a starting point. The target could be close or further away from the fixation point. While the colour contrasts did not have any effect on reaction times, 6-year-olds showed larger amounts of errors when the target was further away from the fixation point and had the highest number of 18 distracters and had pairs of dots within a figure grouped by colour. Thus, 6-year-olds were less sensitive to a perceptual Gestalt factor, namely, grouping by similarity (see also the CRT test in Chapter 5). In another study (Zupan et al., 2018), 6-year-olds were slower and less correct than 8- and 12-year-olds, and this was not related to the executive functions of attention switching and working memory. They found that 6-year-olds had more difficulty ignoring long-duration distracters. Thus, as is often the case in visual search tasks, a combination of the 'hard factors' such as large set size, target absent trials, and strengthening the spatial and temporal features of the distracters are likely to produce slower search times in the younger age groups.

Another study used complex figures as targets and distracters (Krakowski et al., 2016) that were similar to the Navon Figure (Navon, 1977). Part–whole integration in the Navon Figure is necessary because the overall Gestalt (global level) is a letter that is different from the smaller letters that the overall letter is composed of (local level). In young children, drawing of such a figure can be biased towards the whole and omitting the parts (Lange-Küttner, 2000), or towards focussing on the parts and disregarding the whole (Vinter et al., 2010). Krakowski et al. (2016) devised complex items where *curvature* was the main factor: Round figures could be made up from round parts or square parts. Five-year-old preschoolers, 6-year-old first graders, 9-year-old children, and young adults had to decide whether a square was present in the display. Children often miss out on very small detail in figures at ages 5 and 6 (Lange-Küttner, 2000) and accordingly Krakowski et al. found that the target-absent condition was the hardest for these age groups as they made more errors, but not for 9-year-olds and young adults. Nevertheless, all age groups needed more time in target-absent trials, where they needed to scrutinise not only distracters but also their small detail.

6.4 Learning in Visual Search

Given that age differences in reaction times occur across tasks and the principles of visual search do not change much with age except under cognitive load, one wonders why training would be necessary except for speeding up reaction times. The reason is that training studies can reveal differences in efficiency, especially in the more difficult conjunction search.

A training study with a comparison of 11- and 19-year-olds (Hale et al., 1993) showed that they both could improve in visual search in 18 repetitions of each experimental condition (6 vs. 18 set size × target present/absent) in both reaction times and error rates. Because the younger group started off slower, they improved even more. Moreover, the 11-year-olds showed the same significant effect of longer reaction times in target-absent trials as the young adults, demonstrating self-terminating search and a comparable capacity to make decisions in this task. Hale et al. found a global reaction time function across different tasks; that is, reaction time measurements of a visual search, a choice reaction time task, and matching tasks could all be plotted with a linear function, which explained more than 90 per cent of the variance between children. When comparing the impact of age, speed, working memory and intelligence on children's acceleration of speed in another study on visual search (Fry & Hale, 2000), the factor age was the most important with a correlation of −.86, working memory was the second most important factor with −.51 while intelligence made no direct contribution, with −.02.

In a study using animal silhouettes, with the target striking a different pose (cats, dogs) or birds showing a sleeker silhouette, all children from age 6 to age 12 became relatively faster in responding with repeated trials when the target was always in the same location (Yang & Merrill, 2015). Learning from repeated object-location bindings is also conducive for visual memory (Lange-Küttner & Küttner, 2015); see the following Chapter 7. However, in the study of Yang and Merrill, without explicit instruction to memorise, an unexpected memory test of the target location after the visual search task proved that children's memory was significantly below chance level, suggesting that visual search is an implicit learning task. This result demonstrated that visual search experiments may tap into a baseline competence that implicitly reacts rather than reflects on the target and that training can improve identification efficiency. Yet visual scenes as a background to a visual search task help adults to remember search items (Draschkow et al., 2014) and this may also be the case in children.

6.5 Applied Visual Search

As we have seen, visual search is a very robust task paradigm where performance follows clear principles that appear to be age-independent. Only the mental speed and the ability to cope with a larger cognitive load (type of target feature, target absent, set size) develops with age (Gil-Gomez de Liano et al., 2020).

Mindfulness training, which involves mental imagery and breathing exercises, has been found to help 10-year-olds to cope with cognitive load (Tarrasch, 2018). Also natural likeness objects such as 3D bricks (Gerhardstein et al., 2002) or crayons (Darby et al., 2014) make easier visual search items.

Thus, visual search tasks using applied contexts appear to be ideally suited for children. Sports would be such an applied context. Lange-Küttner and Bosco (2016) asked 7- and 9-year-old children to identify whether the target is in an offside position, which would be against the rules of football. Football is a favourite outdoors rule-based game (Christidou et al., 2013) and becoming a professional footballer is a top choice (Looft, 1971). The offside rule is special as it forbids a player to take an unfair advantage by scoring a goal from a place behind the 'enemy' line, where the defence of the opposing team is circumvented; see Figure 6.5.

The offside rule task is a visual search paradigm where a social rule (you should not take an unfair advantage) is applied to a complex spatial configuration of players in the football field. On the one hand, the offside rule of football forbids sending a spy behind the defence line who then carries out an operation

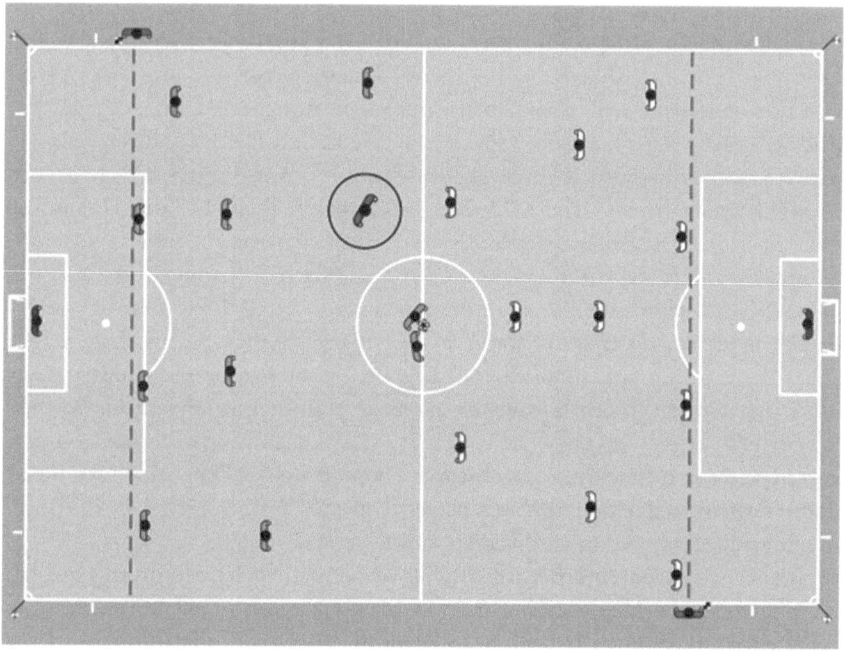

FIGURE 6.5 FIFA Rules: The Offside Position (Lange-Küttner & Bosco, 2016) *Note:* The drawing (FIFA, 2014, p.85) shows vertical broken lines which are not part of the playing field boundaries. Instead, they are imaginary projective lines that need to be made *ad hoc* by the lines(wo)men in order to be able to judge whether a player is before, on, or behind the implicit defence line of the opposing players.

where the success is only the result of circumventing the opposing team who is trying to defend the goal in their half of the spatial field. But on the other hand, there is the offside trap where defence players isolate a striker and build up a defence line behind this attacker (from the view of the goalie) so that the striker finds himself in a wrong and illegitimate position without actually having had the intention to short-cut the defence. This strategic move of the offside trap was already spontaneously mentioned by a 9-year-old boy in the sample.

If a footballer scores from such a wrong offside place, the resulting goal would be disallowed and would not count. Studies of real football games found that refereeing decisions in FIFA games showed more false positive (86.6%) than false negative errors (13.4%) (Helsen et al., 2006). That is, few offside situations escaped the attention of the referees, but they did blow the whistle more often than necessary.

Contrary to current belief, spectators are not the only group who may move in crowds and who can be so noisy that they disturb the referee's judgment (Nevill et al., 2002). Primary school-aged players also often move together across the pitch as if in a swarm, which means that they cannot pass the ball towards different points on the pitch. To understand strategic positioning in the field, children need a cognitive understanding of projective space to grasp that playing in a team does not mean that you stay physically close – in talking distance – to other team members. Instead, players can occupy a point in space to pass the ball across the field into an area where there is another free-standing team player with few opponents who then can score from an unexpected angle. Piaget and Inhelder (1956) regarded empty space as a core notion for the understanding of spatial expanses because it involves 'decentration' from figures which occupy space (Lange-Küttner et al., 2023; Lange-Küttner & Reith, 1995). This is also reflected in their increasingly spatially distributed drawings of games, with top-down views on arrays with increasingly small figures (Lange-Küttner, 1997, 2004, 2009), see Chapter 5. A top-down view (Ogilvie, 2000) is more conducive for offside judgments than the natural view of a referee (Oudejans et al., 2000). Thus, in a training task about the offside rule, 7- and 9-year-old children drew two teams with one football player in an offside position until the offside position was correctly depicted. They had to achieve this as a learning criterion for being admitted to the offside-rule visual search computer task. The visual search task required them to decide whether a player preparing to shoot the football (indicated by an arrow) was in an offside position; see Figure 6.6.

Children showed significantly higher accuracy when recognising an offside position than when judging that the player was not in an offside position. Experience of playing a ballgame on a nearly daily basis in real life was more conducive than the prior offside rule training with a Subbuteo football game. Seven-year-olds were slower to decide than 9-year-olds by a margin of nearly 200%. This increase in efficiency in 9-year-olds in decision-making occurred independently of experience; on the contrary, there was a trend that football-experienced children made slower and presumably more careful decisions. In

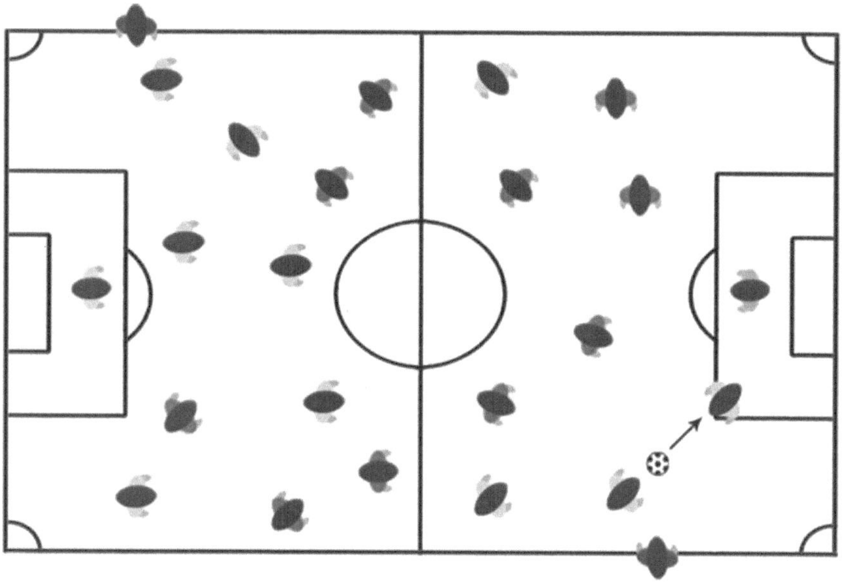

FIGURE 6.6 The Offside Position Search Task (Lange-Küttner & Bosco, 2016)

both age groups, reaction times were comparably slow (Lange-Küttner, 2012): With reaction times between 4,000 and 9,000 ms, they were longer than in classic visual search tasks, where children between 6 and 12 years do not have reaction times above 3,000 ms (Darby et al., 2014; Merrill & Conners, 2013). This may have been the case because, in order to make a decision, first the particular figure needed to be identified, then it had to be considered whether the positions of other players formed a line-up, and only then the position of the target player could be considered. In a classic version of a visual search task, decision-making is much easier, as the target is just one figure with just slightly different features at any place in a display.

The impact of experience on the offside visual search task was in accordance with a study showing that football training on the ground not only improved physical scores such as sprinting and jumping, but also a visual discrimination score which measured figure-ground perception, perceptual grouping, and discrimination of detail in 7- to 11-year-old children (Alesi et al., 2015), see also Chapter 4. Hence, visual tracking of the ball in the real-life game improves visual search, but also action video games can improve visual search efficiency (Castel et al., 2005; J. Li et al., 2022; Wu & Spence, 2013). However, these latter studies usually involve adolescents because of legal limitations on action gaming in children. It may be the case that younger children – who often do not appreciate competitive games (Priewasser et al., 2013) – first need to learn about the fierce competition and rule violations that occur to gain possession of the ball. A meta-analysis showed that indeed competitive games lead to more cognitive enhancement than collaborative games (Sailer & Homner, 2020).

6.6 Conclusions

This chapter on the development of visual search showed surprising consistency of the principles of visual search in children across age. While the overall speed and efficiency of visual search increases from year one to adulthood (Trick & Enns, 1998), research studies to date have identified that the factors set size, shared features between target and distracters and target-absent trials contribute to cognitive load in visual search for both children and adults. Thus, here we find a task where the principles of cognitive processing stay the same in development. Of further interest are not only the target features but also the role of locations in the different types of visual search tasks. The identity of the location – that is, the control whether it is still the same or has changed, or whether it is the right or wrong place – makes decisions easier or harder and thus can produce extended search times and considerable difficulty in both children and adult populations.

References

Alesi, M., Bianco, A., Padulo, J., Luppina, G., Petrucci, M., Paoli, A., Palma, A., & Pepi, A. (2015). Motor and cognitive growth following a football training program. *Frontiers in Psychology, 6*, article 1627. https://doi.org/10.3389/fpsyg.2015.01627

Amso, D., & Johnson, S. P. (2006). Learning by selection: Visual search and object perception in young infants. *Developmental Psychology, 42*(6), 1236–1245. https://doi.org/10.1037/0012-1649.42.6.1236

Anton-Erxleben, K., & Carrasco, M. (2013). Attentional enhancement of spatial resolution: Linking behavioural and neurophysiological evidence. *Nature Reviews Neuroscience, 14*(3), 188–200. https://doi.org/10.1038/nrn3443

Arce, T., & McMullen, K. (2021). The Corsi Block-tapping test: Evaluating methodological practices with an eye towards modern digital frameworks. *Computers in Human Behavior Reports, 4*, 100099. https://doi.org/10.1016/j.chbr.2021.100099

Broadbent, D. E. (1958). The selective nature of learning. In *Perception and communication* (pp. 244–267). Pergamon Press. https://doi.org/10.1037/10037-010

Burack, J. A., Enns, J. T., Iarocci, G., & Randolph, B. (2000). Age differences in visual search for compound patterns: Long- versus short-range grouping. *Developmental Psychology, 36*(6), 731–740. https://doi.org/10.1037/0012-1649.36.6.731

Carpenter, A. (1948). The rate of blinking during prolonged visual search. *Journal of Experimental Psychology, 38*(5), 587–591. https://doi.org/10.1037/h0053628

Castel, A. D., Pratt, J., & Drummond, E. (2005). The effects of action video game experience on the time course of inhibition of return and the efficiency of visual search. *Acta Psychologica, 119*(2), 217–230. https://doi.org/10.1016/j.actpsy.2005.02.004

Christidou, V., Tsevreni, I., Epitropou, M., & Kittas, C. (2013). Exploring primary children's views and experiences of the school ground: The case of a Greek school. *International Journal of Environmental and Science Education, 8*(1), 59–83. http://eric.ed.gov/?id=EJ1008595

Cowan, N. (2008). What are the differences between long-term, short-term, and working memory? In W. S. Sossin, J.-C. Lacaille, V. F. Castellucci, & S. Belleville (Eds.), *Progress in Brain Research* (Vol. 169, pp. 323–338). Elsevier.

Darby, K. P., Burling, J. M., & Yoshida, H. (2014). The role of search speed in the contextual cueing of children's attention. *Cognitive Development, 29*, 17–29. https://doi.org/10.1016/j.cogdev.2013.10.001

DeBolt, M. C., Mitsven, S. G., Pomaranski, K. I., Cantrell, L. M., Luck, S. J., & Oakes, L. M. (2022). A new perspective on the role of physical salience in visual search: Graded effect of salience on infants' attention. *Developmental Psychology, 59*(2), 326–343. https://doi.org/10.1037/dev0001460

Donnelly, N., Cave, K., Greenway, R., Hadwin, J. A., Stevenson, J., & Sonuga-Barke, E. (2007). Visual search in children and adults: Top-down and bottom-up mechanisms. *The Quarterly Journal of Experimental Psychology, 60*(1), 120–136. https://doi.org/10.1080/17470210600625362

Draschkow, D., Wolfe, J. M., & Vo, M. L. (2014). Seek and you shall remember: Scene semantics interact with visual search to build better memories. *Journal of Vision 14*(8), article 10. https://doi.org/10.1167/14.8.10

Enoch, J. M. (1959). Effect of the size of a complex display upon visual search. *Journal of the Optical Society of America, 49*, 280–286. https://doi.org/10.1364/JOSA.49.000280

Erickson, R. A. (1966). Visual search experiment: Noise persistence, acuity, response time. *Journal of the Optical Society of America, 56*(4), 491–498. https://doi.org/10.1364/JOSA.56.000491

Eysenck, M. W., & Keane, M. T. (1995). *Cognitive psychology*. Psychology Press.

FIFA. (2014). *The laws of the game*. Fédération Internationale de Football Association.

Fry, A. F., & Hale, S. (2000). Relationships among processing speed, working memory, and fluid intelligence in children. *Biological Psychology, 54*(1), 1–34. https://doi.org/10.1016/S0301-0511(00)00051-X

Gerardi-Caulton, G. (2000). Sensitivity to spatial conflict and the development of self-regulation in children 24–36 months of age. *Developmental Science, 3*(4), 397–404. https://doi.org/10.1111/1467-7687.00134

Gerhardstein, P., Kraebel, K. S., Gillis, J., & Lassiter, S. (2002). Visual search for high-level configural differences as well as low-level critical features is highly efficient early in childhood. *Developmental Psychobiology, 41*(3), 241–252. https://doi.org/10.1002/dev.10074

Gerhardstein, P., & Rovee-Collier, C. (2002). The development of visual search in infants and very young children. *Journal of Experimental Child Psychology, 81*(2), 194–215. https://doi.org/10.1006/jecp.2001.2649

Gibson, E. J., & Yonas, A. (1966). A developmental study of visual search behavior. *Perception & Psychophysics, 1*(6), 169–171. https://doi.org/10.3758/BF03215778

Gil-Gomez de Liano, B., Quiros-Godoy, M., Perez-Hernandez, E., & Wolfe, J. M. (2020). Efficiency and accuracy of visual search develop at different rates from early childhood through early adulthood. *Psychonomic Bulletin & Review, 27*(3), 504–511. https://doi.org/10.3758/s13423-020-01712-z

Gray, R., Gaska, J., & Winterbottom, M. (2016). Relationship between sustained, orientated, divided, and selective attention and simulated aviation performance: Training & pressure effects. *Journal of Applied Research in Memory and Cognition, 5*(1), 34–42. https://doi.org/10.1016/j.jarmac.2015.11.005

Guilbert, A., Perguilhem, S., & Guiraud-Vinatea, H. (2020). Visual search strategies in children: A reflection of working memory processes? *Journal of Clinical and Experimental Neuropsychology, 42*(10), 975–981. https://doi.org/10.1080/13803395.2020.1830033

Hale, S., Fry, A. F., & Jessie, K. A. (1993). Effects of practice on speed of information processing in children and adults: Age sensitivity and age invariance. *Developmental Psychology, 29*(5), 880–892. https://doi.org/10.1037/0012-1649.29.5.880

Helsen, W. F., Gilis, B., & Weston, M. (2006). Errors in judging 'offside' in association football: Test of the optical error versus the perceptual flash-lag hypothesis. *Journal of Sports Sciences, 24*(5), 521–528. https://doi.org/10.1080/02640410500298065

Jarrold, C., Gilchrist, I. D., & Bender, A. (2005). Embedded figures detection in autism and typical development: Preliminary evidence of a double dissociation in relationships with visual search. *Developmental Science, 8*(4), 344–351. https://doi.org/10.1111/j.1467-7687.2005.00422.x

Kail, R. (1991). Developmental change in speed of processing during childhood and adolescence. *Psychological Bulletin, 109*(3), 490–501. https://doi.org/10.1037/0033-2909.109.3.490

Kamienkowski, J. E., Ison, M. J., Quiroga, R. Q., & Sigman, M. (2012). Fixation-related potentials in visual search: A combined EEG and eye tracking study. *Journal of Vision 12*(7), article 4. https://doi.org/10.1167/12.7.4

Kleberg, J. L., del Bianco, T., & Falck-Ytter, T. (2019). How infants' arousal influences their visual search. *Child Development, 90*(4), 1413–1423. https://doi.org/10.1111/cdev.13198

Krakowski, C.-S., Poirel, N., Vidal, J., Roell, M., Pineau, A., Borst, G., & Houde, O. (2016). The forest, the trees, and the leaves: Differences of processing across development. *Developmental Psychology, 52*(8), 1262–1272. https://doi.org/10.1037/dev0000138

Lange-Küttner, C. (1997). Development of size modification of human figure drawings in spatial axes systems of varying complexity. *Journal of Experimental Child Psychology, 66*(2), 264–278. https://doi.org/10.1006/jecp.1997.2386

Lange-Küttner, C. (2000). The role of object violation in the development of visual analysis. *Perceptual and Motor Skills, 90*(1), 3–24. https://doi.org/10.2466/pms.2000.90.1.3

Lange-Küttner, C. (2004). More evidence on size modification in spatial axes systems of varying complexity. *Journal of Experimental Child Psychology, 88*(2), 171–192. https://doi.org/10.1016/j.jecp.2004.02.003

Lange-Küttner, C. (2009). Habitual size and projective size: The logic of spatial systems in children's drawings. *Developmental Psychology, 45*(4), 913–927. https://doi.org/10.1037/a0016133

Lange-Küttner, C. (2012). The importance of reaction times for developmental science: What a difference milliseconds make. *International Journal of Developmental Science, 6*(1–2), 51–55. https://doi.org/10.3233/DEV-2012-11089

Lange-Küttner, C., Beckles, C. F., Ahmed, R. K., & Fisher, L. E. (2023). Rich and sparse figurative information in children's memory for colorful places. *Developmental Psychology, 59*(2), 256–271. https://doi.org/10.1037/dev0001483

Lange-Küttner, C., & Bosco, G. (2016). On being in the wrong place: The role of children's conceptual understanding and ballgame experience when judging a football player's offside position. *International Journal of Developmental Science, 10*(1–2), 73–84. https://doi.org/10.3233/DEV-160185

Lange-Küttner, C., & Küttner, E. (2015). How to learn places without spatial concepts: Does the what-and-where reaction time system in children regulate learning during stimulus repetition? *Brain and Cognition, 97*, 59–73. https://doi.org/0.1016/j.bandc.2015.04.008

Lange-Küttner, C., & Puiu, A.-A. (2021). Perceptual load and sex-specific personality traits: The impact of the big five personality dimensions and the autism quotient on visual search. *Experimental Psychology, 68*(3), 149–164. https://doi.org/10.1027/1618-3169/a000520

Lange-Küttner, C., & Reith, E. (1995). The transformation of figurative thought: Implications of Piaget and Inhelder's developmental theory for children's drawings. In C. Lange-Küttner & G. V. Thomas (Eds.), *Drawing and looking* (pp. 75–92). Harvester Wheatheaf/Pearson.

Li, A.-S., Bogaerts, L., & Theeuwes, J. (2022). Statistical learning of across-trial regularities during serial search. *Journal of Experimental Psychology: Human Perception and Performance, 48*(3), 262–274. https://doi.org/10.1037/xhp0000987

Li, J., Zhou, Y., & Gao, X. (2022). The advantage for action video game players in eye movement behavior during visual search tasks. *Current Psychology: A Journal for Diverse Perspectives on Diverse Psychological Issues*, Online first publication. https://doi.org/10.1007/s12144-022-03017-x

Lobaugh, N. J., Cole, S., & Rovet, J. F. (1998). Visual search for features and conjunctions in development. *Canadian Journal of Experimental Psychology/Revue Canadienne de Psychologie Experimentale, 52*(4), 201–212. https://doi.org/10.1037/h0087293

Looft, W. R. (1971). Sex differences in the expression of vocational aspirations by elementary school children. *Developmental Psychology, 5*(2), 366–366. https://doi.org/10.1037/h0031432

Lütke, N., & Lange-Küttner, C. (2015). Keeping it in three dimensions: Measuring the development of mental rotation in children with the Rotated Colour Cube Test (RCCT). *International Journal of Developmental Science, 9*, 95–114. https://doi.org/10.3233/DEV-14154

Lütke, N., & Lange-Küttner, C. (2021). The magical number four in children's mental rotation of cube aggregates. *Developmental Psychology, 57*(2), 211–226. https://doi.org/10.1037/dev0001139

Mackworth, N. H. (1948). The breakdown of vigilance during prolonged visual search. *The Quarterly Journal of Experimental Psychology, 1*, 6–21. https://doi.org/10.1080/17470214808416738

Mackworth, N. H., & Mackworth, J. F. (1958). Visual search for successive decisions. *British Journal of Psychology, 49*, 210–221. https://doi.org/10.1111/j.2044-8295.1958.tb00659.x

Merrill, E. C., & Conners, F. A. (2013). Age-related interference from irrelevant distracters in visual feature search among heterogeneous distracters. *Journal of Experimental Child Psychology, 115*(4), 640–654. https://doi.org/10.1016/j.jecp.2013.03.013

Navon, D. (1977). Forest before trees: The precedence of global features in visual perception. *Cognitive Psychology, 9*(3), 353–383. https://doi.org/10.1016/0010-0285(77)90012-3

Neisser, U. (1964). Visual search. *Scientific American, 210*(6), 94–102. https://doi.org/10.1038/scientificamerican0664-94

Nevill, A. M., Balmer, N. J., & Williams, A. M. (2002). The influence of crowd noise and experience upon refereeing decisions in football. *Psychology of Sport and Exercise, 3*(4), 261–272. https://doi.org/10.1016/S1469-0292(01)00033-4

Nobre, A. C., & Stokes, M. G. (2011). Attention and short-term memory: Crossroads. *Neuropsychologia, 49*(6), 1391–1392. https://doi.org/10.1016/j.neuropsychologia.2011.04.014

Ogilvie, J. (2000). Inside, outside, offside? *Trends in Cognitive Sciences, 4*(4), 130. https://doi.org/10.1016/S1364-6613(00)01480-7

Oudejans, R. R., Verheijen, R., Bakker, F. C., Gerrits, J. C., Steinbrückner, M., & Beek, P. J. (2000). Errors in judging 'offside' in football. *Nature, 404*(6773), 33. https://doi.org/10.1038/35003639

Piaget, J., & Inhelder, B. (1956). *The child's conception of space*. Routledge and Kegan Paul.

Posner, M. I. (2019). Attention: Awareness and control. In R. J. Sternberg & W. E. Pickren (Eds.), *The Cambridge handbook of the intellectual history of psychology* (pp. 111–134). Cambridge University Press.

Priewasser, B., Roessler, J., & Perner, J. (2013). Competition as rational action: Why young children cannot appreciate competitive games. *Journal of Experimental Child Psychology, 116*(2), 545–559. https://doi.org/10.1016/j.jecp.2012.10.008

Raven, J., & Raven, J. (2003). Raven progressive matrices. In R. S. McCallum (Ed.), *Handbook of nonverbal assessment* (pp. 223–237). Springer. https://doi.org/10.1007/978-1-4615-0153-4_11

Rothbart, M. K., Ellis, L. K., Rueda, M., & Posner, M. I. (2003). Developing mechanisms of temperamental effortful control. *Journal of Personality, 71*(6), 1113–1143. https://doi.org/10.1111/1467-6494.7106009

Rothbart, M. K., Posner, M. I., & Sheese, B. E. (2020). Temperament and brain networks of attention. In P. J. Corr & G. Matthews (Eds.), *The Cambridge handbook of personality psychology* (pp. 155–168). Cambridge University Press.

Rothbart, M. K., Sheese, B. E., & Posner, M. I. (2014). Temperament and emotion regulation. In J. J. Gross (Ed.), *Handbook of emotion regulation* (pp. 305–320). The Guilford Press.

Rueda, M., Posner, M. I., Rothbart, M. K., & Davis-Stober, C. P. (2004). Development of the time course for processing conflict: An event-related potentials study with 4 year olds and adults. *BMC Neuroscience, 5*, article 39. https://doi.org/10.1186/1471-2202-5-39

Rutishauser, U., & Koch, C. (2007). Probabilistic modeling of eye movement data during conjunction search via feature-based attention. *Journal of Vision,* 7(6), 5–5. https://doi.org/10.1167/7.6.5

Sailer, M., & Homner, L. (2020). The gamification of learning: A meta-analysis. *Educational Psychology Review, 32*(1), 77–112. https://doi.org/10.1007/s10648-019-09498-w

Tarrasch, R. (2018). The effects of mindfulness practice on attentional functions among primary school children. *Journal of Child and Family Studies, 27*(8), 2632–2642. https://doi.org/10.1007/s10826-018-1073-9

Taylor, M. J., Shakeela, C. K., & Malone, M. A. (1999). Parallel and serial attentional processes: A developmental ERP study. *Developmental Neuropsychology, 15*(3), 351–358. https://doi.org/10.1080/87565649909540754

Treisman, A. M. (1964). Verbal Cues, language, and meaning in selective attention. *The American Journal of Psychology,* 77(2), 206–219. https://doi.org/10.2307/1420127

Treisman, A. M., & Gelade, G. (1980). A feature-integration theory of attention. *Cognitive Psychology, 12*(1), 97–136. https://doi.org/10.1016/0010-0285(80)90005-5

Trick, L. M., & Enns, J. T. (1998). Lifespan changes in attention: The visual search task. *Cognitive Development, 13*(3), 369–386. https://doi.org/10.1016/S0885-2014(98)90016-8

Vinter, A., Puspitawati, I., & Witt, A. (2010). Children's spatial analysis of hierarchical patterns: Construction and perception. *Developmental Psychology, 46*(6), 1621–1631. https://doi.org/10.1037/a0020615

Wickens, C. D. (1974). Temporal limits of human information processing: A developmental study. *Psychological Bulletin, 81*(11), 739–755. https://doi.org/10.1037/h0037250

Wolfe, J. M. (2021). Guided Search 6.0: An updated model of visual search. *Psychonomic Bulletin & Review, 28*(4), 1060–1092. https://doi.org/10.3758/s13423-020-01859-9

Wolfe, J. M., Yee, A., & Friedman-Hill, S. R. (1992). Curvature is a basic feature for visual search tasks. *Perception, 21*(4), 465–480. https://doi.org/10.1068/p210465

Woods, A. J., Goksun, T., Chatterjee, A., Zelonis, S., Mehta, A., & Smith, S. E. (2013). The development of organized visual search. *Acta Psychologica, 143*(2), 191–199. https://doi.org/10.1016/j.actpsy.2013.03.008

Wu, S., & Spence, I. (2013). Playing shooter and driving videogames improves top-down guidance in visual search. *Attention, Perception, & Psychophysics, 75*(4), 673–686. https://doi.org/10.3758/s13414-013-0440-2

Yang, Y., & Merrill, E. C. (2015). The impact of signal-to-noise ratio on contextual cueing in children and adults. *Journal of Experimental Child Psychology, 132*, 65–83. https://doi.org/10.1016/j.jecp.2014.12.005

Zupan, Z., Blagrove, E., & Watson, D. G. (2018). Learning to ignore: The development of time-based visual attention in children. *Developmental Psychology, 54*(12), 2248–2264. https://doi.org/10.1037/dev0000582

7

VISUAL MEMORY DEVELOPMENT IN CHILDREN

As in the previous chapters, the topic of this chapter on visual memory concerns objects and their places versus objects in regions and areas and spatial fields. Piaget and Inhelder mostly worked on conceptual reasoning, but they also published a book on memory development (e.g. Piaget & Inhelder, 1968/2015). Their studies are all based on the premise that memory does not only consist of encoding the visual input, but that memory development in children is a process of refinement and elaboration of memory representations themselves which is dependent on the development of intelligence (Liben, 1981). Thus, children's memory of the experiments they had taken part in would become better with time along with the onset of operational thinking bringing order to stored impressions and memories.

Thus, in the following sections, studies on children's developing memory of objects and places, arrays and fields and entire scenes are presented. It is expected that tasks which can be solved with mapping and rote learning would not show age differences, while memory that requires transformations of the input will show increasingly efficient memory accuracy with age. For instance, there is memory research showing that a scene is more than an aggregate of objects: Hundreds of scenes can be remembered with very high precision (Konkle et al., 2010). Already 7-year-olds remember their own snapshots with an accuracy of 77%, while adults' memory was only 10% better (Pathman et al., 2011). This episodic scene memory appears to stay the same rather than develop.

7.1 Object and Place Memory

7.1.1 Presentation and Encoding

Memory by definition involves assessing events that happened in the past. This slice of the past can be milliseconds, seconds, minutes, hours, days, months and

DOI: 10.4324/9780429270604-8

years ago. Researchers in cognitive psychology have worked very hard to categorise types of time-limited memory storage. The most common definition is the multi-store model, with a sensory register of about 500 ms, a short-term store (STS) which is subject to decay within 30 seconds and a time-unlimited, permanent long-term store (LTS) (Shiffrin & Atkinson, 1969). This model has been modified to introduce two modality-specific working memory systems instead of a STS with a capacity of just a few seconds, controlled by a central executive (Baddeley & Hitch, 1974) and with an episodic buffer instead of the sensory register that can directly store cohesive scenes into long-term memory (Baddeley, 2000). STS is still in usage as a term but abbreviated STM (short-term memory), and LTS is used accordingly as LTM (long-term memory).

In working memory research, the presentation phase is usually seen as the most important phase in the memory process because this is the time when the initial percept is encoded and thus would become reduced in complexity. One question is whether a visual percept is encoded in a visual format, or whether it is encoded in words. Children aged 5 to 11 can encode objects holistically (Towse & Hitch, 1995), while this is more difficult for places or the spatial context due to the apparent lack of a semantic dimension.

For the encoding phase during the presentation, the working memory model provided a suitable approach with modality-specific sub-systems to test whether the visuo-spatial sketchpad would capture the image of the visual percept, or whether the phonological loop would be providing a linguistic system that would allow for verbal encoding and rehearsal. It is unclear whether visual images can be rehearsed, but repeated presentations and trials generate familiarity of visual objects (Bechari-Martin & Lange-Küttner, 2022; Kail, 1986; Kail & Park, 1990). Theoretically, rehearsal of images could generate an internal film like in dreams. In fact, comparisons of watching film clips generated from scenes between and within films in an FMRI scanner showed that adults' hippocampal brain areas were more active while watching clips of film scenes from different films (Benear et al., 2022). This was also the case in 7-year-old children but only if they had seen the films before, relying more on prior knowledge. If they had not seen the film clip before, the hippocampus was highly active both for the short episodes from between and within film clips.

One of the most compelling studies on modality encoding in children's visual working memory was carried out by Hitch et al. (1988). They presented children with printed pictures of either unique dissimilar visual objects (control, top), similar visual objects (centre) or objects with long names (bottom), see the examples in Figure 7.1. It turned out that during recall, 5-year-olds, but not 10-year-olds, were more confused by visually similar objects. The older children were more confused by objects with long names. This indicated a change from a preference of visually encoding objects to verbally encoding objects. Moreover, in word memory, there is a change from better memory of spoken words to better remembering of written words (Lange-Küttner & Martin, 1999). Thus, in

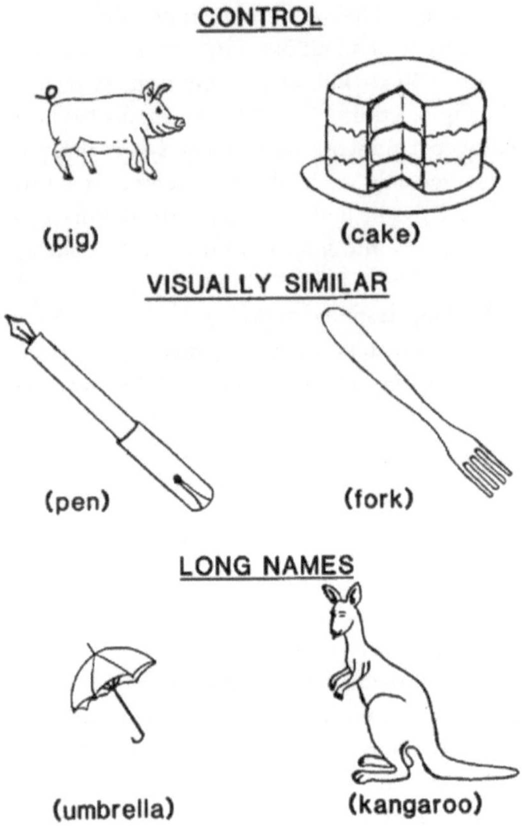

FIGURE 7.1 Visual Memory and Visual Similarity (Hitch et al., 1988)

short, with the onset of reading and writing, there is a developmental change from encoding objects visually and auditorily to mentally naming them.

In Chapter 5 on drawing development, there was another change described with the onset of schooling, namely the change from drawing iconic objects to drawing visually realistic impressions. Thus, the onset of literacy can change the encoding of visual information (Dellatolas et al., 2003) but it is not known whether visual memory templates themselves also change in children's minds. It appears that adults have the capacity to refer to either iconic objects or to their visual features in their visual memory (Hardman & Cowan, 2015; Vergauwe & Cowan, 2015).

Visual memory was further explored in memory experiments that used a dual task load during encoding. Matrices with black-and-white places in various patterns had to be recalled either in a simultaneous way or a serial pattern (Pickering et al., 2001). The presentation was computerised, but children's reaction times were not measured when they pointed to the black places. Two types of secondary tasks were given during the encoding phase of the memory experiment while children just watched. A tapping task on a pegboard was expected to interfere with visual pattern memory more than a repetitive non-sense articulation task that was devised to suppress spontaneous naming. It became clear that the purely visual memory task without a secondary task yielded the best memory; the articulation task lowered memory, but the tapping task lowered performance the most. This interference was the same whether a simultaneous or serial pattern was shown and whether children were 6 or 10 years old. Thus, visual memory was modality-specific and effortful. This was also shown in a more technologically sophisticated study testing 6- to 10-year-old children's pathway learning in virtual reality, along with a number of other, separate spatial and verbal memory tasks (Merrill et al., 2016). While this study did not involve a dual-task load, it turned out unequivocally that the use of verbal memory was detrimental to spatial pathway learning.

7.1.2 The Delay between Seeing and Remembering

7.1.2.1 Delay Time

The terms 'operating efficiency' and 'storage capacity' both try to explain that children's developmental increase of operations makes them also more efficient in storing memories (Cowan et al., 2011). Cowan et al. suggested that storage capacity should be corrected for task difficulty because tasks become easier when children's efficiency increases, with the danger of ceiling effects. However, giving them increasingly difficult tasks would not demonstrate their increasing efficiency because older children may perform at the same level as younger ones, and this result would give the impression that nothing really changes.

One way to assess visual working memory (VWM) capacity was to take array size (set size) divided by D Prime (probabilities of the hit rate minus the false positives) resulting in the memory measure Cowan's *k*. This measures children's capacity; that is, the increasing memory performance with age independently of task difficulty (Cowan, 2022). For instance, an event-related potential (ERP) study showed that when individuals memorise a set of coloured squares, the brain activation that a set of squares elicits does increase, the larger the set size. This makes sense because also the size of the area that a larger set of items covers would be increased (array size) (Luria et al., 2016). When brain activation due to the increase of the set size was divided by the number of items, there was a cap on the activation at three or four items, thereafter activation reached a plateau. This was taken as proof for a basic memory capacity of four items as claimed by Cowan (2010). However, there was not just one brain area, but a contralateral activated brain area mirrored the activation of the original input. The contralateral activity was generated in the left brain on right presentation trials and in the right brain during left presentation trials thus generating bilateral activation.

Moreover, this activation persisted from the presentation long into the memory delay period (contra-lateral delay activity) (Luria et al., 2016).

The existence of a memory after-image has been known for a very long time (Allport, 1928; Daniels, 1895), following observations by Fechner (1860). Daniels showed that the memory after-image during a delay would not last longer than 15 seconds. However, if it was refreshed by conscious attention, it could outlast 20 seconds (Daniels, 1895). Daniels also found that a larger group of items could not be maintained for as long as a single item, thus supporting the link between array set size and brain activation. The stereoscopic effect of a memory after-image is also known (Brückner, 1956), as well as the luminance degradation with time (Pannevis, 1947). Moreover, it was already suspected that the after-image is not just a retinal phenomenon but requires cortical activation because of the possibility of attention refreshment and maintenance (Tse et al., 2010). Thus, previous behavioural research supports the neuroscience findings. However, how would the memory after-image materialise in children? Allport (1928) assumed that children would experience a purer eidetic image that is situated between a perceptual after-image and an actively imagined memory image. Such visual memory capture or buffer is indeed different from a memory representation that results from a strategy like rehearsal that younger children are not convinced to use (utilisation deficit) (Bjorklund et al., 1997).

What needs to be considered here when testing children's memory development is that the speed of the nervous system accelerates with age. Adults have on average (depending on task complexity) reaction times between 500 and 1,200 ms., but children can show reaction times between 1,000 and 10,000 ms. depending on age and task (Lange-Küttner, 2012). For instance, Kosslyn et al. (1990) found that five-year-old children needed about 9,500 ms. for imagery processes, but adults only needed 1,500 ms. For image maintenance, children needed 4,000 ms but adults required 1,000 ms. For perceptual processing, children needed 2,000 ms, but adults needed 500 ms. Hence, when an external stimulus is involved, reaction times had accelerated fourfold in adults compared to children.

Kail demonstrated that the acceleration of children's reaction times occurs in an exponential fashion across different tasks, but at a more pronounced rate in verbal than in non-verbal tasks (Kail & Miller, 2006). Kail could train 11-year-old children to become faster with extended training in mental rotation of objects, but only for learning of specific object features (*item-specific learning*) that did not transfer to other objects (Kail & Park, 1990). Age differences between 9- to 13-year-old children and adults were eliminated after 1,500 trials (Kail, 1986).

In computerised experiments with children, the control of timing needs to be considered for (1) stimulus onset and stimulus offset (*stimulus duration*) in presentation and test, (2) interstimulus interval (ISI) (*duration between stimuli*) in presentation and test, and (3) delay duration *between* presentation and test. Barrouillet and Camos (2012) endorse a time-based account of visual memory development. They describe an increasing ability of children for sustained attention in order to maintain the memory trace. In one of their studies with 8- to 14-year-old children, Barrouillet et al. (2009) varied stimulus duration times from 375 to 1875 ms and the pace created by interstimulus intervals (ISI) varied from 125 to 625 ms ISI in the presentation and in the delay. The faster the pace, the lower the memory span, and the slower the pace, the longer the memory span. They showed that surprisingly the older children – with faster information processing ability – benefited even more from the spaced-out presentation times than the younger children. Why would spaced-out presentation times become beneficial? The decay theory would predict that the memory trace would become degraded during a delay, but this was not the case.

For instance, during critical developmental periods in infancy, longer looking times can be beneficial: At 6 months, infants who take longer to scrutinise a face are better at face recognition (Orlian & Rose, 1997), but at 7 and 10 months, looks of shorter duration and more shifts of gaze predicted face recognition (Rose et al., 2002). It is likely that memory encoding initially needs longer time, but once memory templates are acquired, faster processing is possible.

A longer duration of the ISI would also give useful time to the older children because the extended time could allow them to consolidate an after-image into a memory trace, or to apply memory strategies to mentally organise the material, while younger children may just sit during pauses and delays and wait for the memory test. Thus, a longer delay would challenge younger children more because their memory trace is not maintained or refreshed over longer intervals. The question of whether memory functions in an item-based (span) or time-based (decay) fashion (Portrat et al., 2008; Shimi & Scerif, 2017) is important and unresolved.

Lange-Küttner (2012) in a short, topical, invited report systematically compared an *age-constant* and an *age-adapted* filled delay condition in 5- to 6-, 7- to 8- and 10- to 11-year-old children. In the age-constant delay condition, all age groups encountered six perceptual judgment trials during the delay, while in the age-adapted delay, 5- to 6-year-olds had a delay of five trials, 7- to 8-year-olds of seven trials and 10- to 11-year-olds experienced a delay of nine trials. The hypothesis was that an identical number of delay items for all age groups should selectively benefit the older children because they would have increased processing speed available. In contrast, in an age-adapted delay with increasingly more items in the delay, gains of older children should be comparably more modest because any maturational increase in cognitive resources may be offset by the greater challenge of a prolonged memory delay. Figure 7.2 shows the number of delay items in grey and the real-time delay that considers the actual time children took for the perceptual judgments during the delay in black. The comparison showed that in the age-constant delay (6-6-6), children of all age groups showed comparable memory response latencies (see Figure 7.2, left), with only very subtle acceleration in the 10- to 11-year-olds. However, the age-adapted delay (5-7-9) had accelerated the older children and especially the 10- to 11-year-olds had

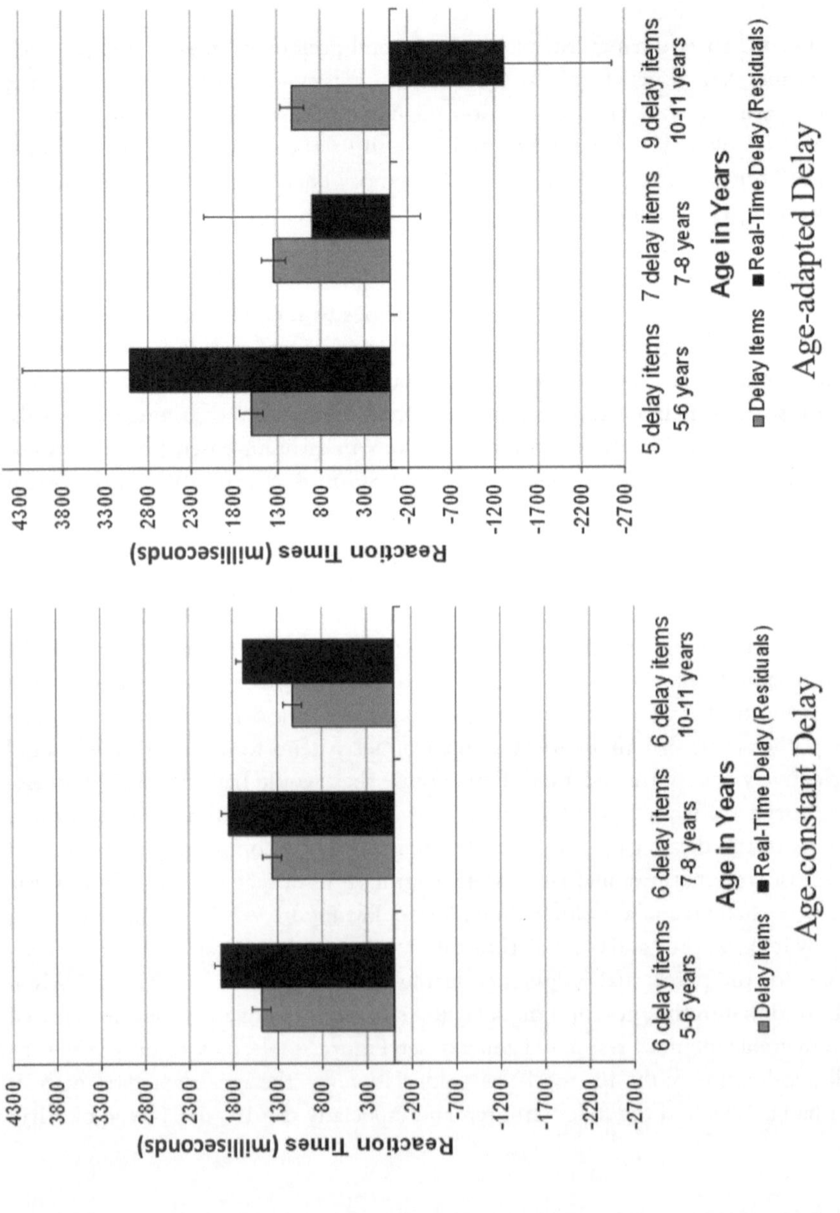

FIGURE 7.2 Dwelling and Acceleration Strategies in Long Delays (Lange-Küttner, 2012)

become much faster than in the age-constant delay; see Figure 7.2 right (Lange-Küttner, 2012).

Another study on mental rotation showed that the most challenging condition yielded the best results in a group of 11-year-old children, but more liberal conditions were more conducive for younger children (Lange-Küttner & Green, 2007). Some children already are 'at speed' when they enter school, while others appear to be relatively laid back (Kail & Ferrer, 2007). Individual differences between young children (and thus standard deviations) can be large, especially due to post-error slowing (Richardson et al., 2011; Dubravak et al., 2022).

7.1.2.2 Delay Time Filled with What-and-Where Tasks

Studies on the development of visuo-spatial memory used time-based age-adapted delays of 5 and 10 seconds for 6-year-olds and 10 and 15 seconds for 11-year-olds (Spencer & Hund, 2003), or a constant delay of half-a-second (Pickering et al., 2001), or no delay (Schumann-Hengsteler et al., 2004). Not surprisingly, they come to different conclusions when visual memory is up to adult standards, with those using shorter delays assuming an earlier onset of efficient visuo-spatial memory in children. A delay can also be filled with tasks that selectively interfere more or less with the memory test thereafter. For instance, Towse et al. (2002) used addition and multiplication tasks during the delay before testing memory for three digits in 8- to 17-year-olds. Addition performance was correlated with memory, but multiplication performance was not. When delimited delay durations were considered, there was no effect of the type of the two types of math delay tasks. Also a delay task difficulty variation involving word categorisation did not selectively interfere with memory; just delay duration mattered. It was a reasonable assumption to presume that because addition is learned earlier than multiplication in school, the latter should provide a higher 'dosage' of interference with the memory material. However, the brain basis for development of mathematics is still unclear (Peters & De Smedt, 2018). Especially the role of language in addition versus multiplication is unresolved (Suárez-Pellicioni et al., 2023). It is suggested here that in mathematical addition, $5 + 5 + 5 + 5 + 5 = 25$ is a long verbal expression, in multiplication $5 \times 5 = 25$ is shorter, and in potentiation $5^2 = 25$ is the shortest expression, all for the same result. Given that the word length effect becomes more prominent in children's memory (Hitch et al., 1988), an effect of mathematical notation length may need to be considered.

In contrast, in visual cognition, the what-and-where system (see Figure 3.3.) has a firmly established psychophysiological basis in the brain (Rao et al., 1997) that allows for a neuroscientifically plausible interference design. The what-system matures earlier than the where-system, which stays more vulnerable in developmental disorders (Atkinson & Braddick, 2003). The vulnerability of the where-system also shows in behavioural studies with older children; for instance, under stress, boys with ADHD ignored the left side of the spatial field in a line cancellation test (Manly et al., 2005) as if the where-system in the parietal lobe had been affected by a stroke (Robertson et al., 1998). Brain systems have a limited processing capacity, so a secondary delay task that draws on the same brain substrate as the primary memory task should cause more interference than a secondary task that draws on another brain region. The prediction was that memory for objects' shapes would be interfered by tasks activating the what-system that processes static information such as colour, while memory for objects' locations would be interfered with by tasks activating the where-system which processes dynamic information. From the dual-task research on encoding during presentation, we know that tapping interferes with memory for location. However, the what-and-where system can theoretically interfere at any stage of the perception -encoding-consolidation/delay-retrieval stage in the memory process (Klauer & Zhao, 2004). Thus, experiments were designed – instead of with a dual-task paradigm that investigates encoding during presentation – using what-and-where tasks during the delay that were expected to selectively interfere with memory retrieval thereafter.

For adults, a reliable selective what-and-where interference during the delay could be found (e.g. Klauer & Zhao, 2004; Mecklinger & Meinshausen, 1998; Mecklinger & Müller, 1996; Mecklinger & Pfeifer, 1996; Tresch et al., 1993). Would this interference also occur in children? An object and place reaction-time/accuracy task with selective what-and-where interference was programmed with timing and content adapted for children. In this first and the following studies, always five objects' shapes or objects' places had to be remembered and distinguished from four distracters. The what-and-where interference in the delay used two types of perceptual judgment delay tasks, a what-system task that was supposed to interfere with object memory and a where-system task that was predicted to interfere with place memory (Lange-Küttner, 2010a, 2010b, 2013; Lange-Küttner & Friederici, 2000; Lange-Küttner & Küttner, 2015), see Figure 7.3. In all these studies, the what-system interference involved children making a static perceptual size estimation of animal stimuli that were the same size on the screen but in real life they were either very large or very small (Figure 7.3, upper row). In the dynamic where-system interference, children were asked to judge whether the animal was flying at the top or at the bottom of the screen (Figure 7.3, lower row). The where-system interference would involve children's visual attention to wander across the screen in a similar manner to when they would be scrutinising locations in the array. Thus, the size judgment delay task was supposed to interfere with object memory, while the direction judgment delay task was expected to interfere with place memory.

The initial research using this selective interference paradigm showed that only 5-year-olds but not 7- to 8-year olds and 9- to 10-year-olds, experienced the predicted where-delay interference effect for place memory in the grid and the predicted what-delay interference effect for object memory in the landmarked array (Lange-Küttner & Friederici, 2000). In another study using this paradigm (Lange-Küttner, 2013), the what-and-where delay tasks yielded only

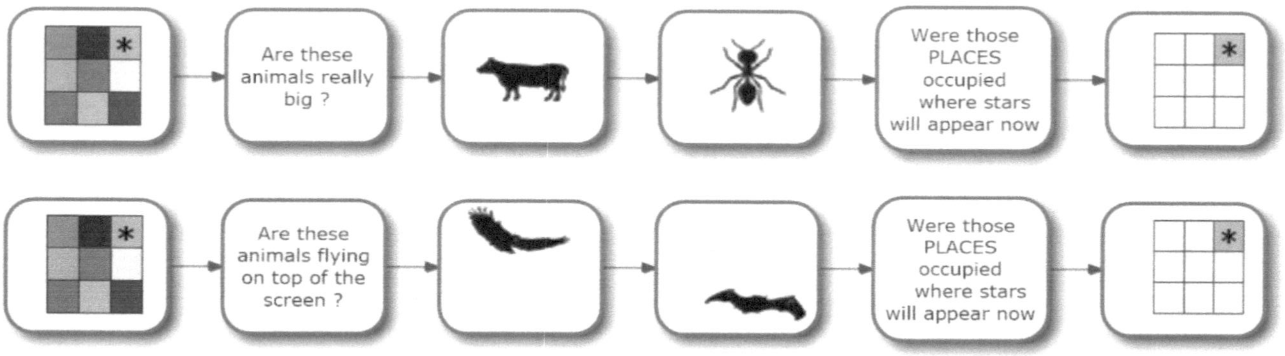

FIGURE 7.3 What-and-Where Interference in the Delay (Lange-Küttner et al., 2023). *Note:* The delay involved two types of perceptual judgment. The upper row shows the what-interference (small or large animal?), the lower row shows the where-interference task (flying on top or at the bottom?)

an unspecific interference effect and again only in the youngest age group of 6- to 7-year-old children.

In these studies, the retrieval array assessing spatial memory was always the same as the presentation array, consisting of unique shapes for object memory and black stars as uniform placeholders for place memory. However, the selective interference of the where-delay went in the predicted direction for all age groups of 5- to 10-year-old children when the amount of information in the retrieval arrays was controlled (Lange-Küttner et al., 2023). Instead of using only uniform black stars as placeholders (see the last trial in Figure 7.3), memory for objects' location was expected to be supported by places with a unique colour, thereby increasing the salience and visibility of places (see Figure 7.4). The amount of information during retrieval could be rich, consisting of the entire array from the presentation (Figure 7.4a), or poor, consisting of one coloured place with a placeholder (Figure 7.4b), or sparse, consisting of just one unique colourful place (Figure 7.4c), or it could be a control condition consisting of unique shapes in the same colour as the places, like in the previous experiments using this paradigm (Figure 7.4d). It turned out that the sparser the retrieval array, the lower was children's place memory, and the more it was interfered by the where-system delay task in the first block. In other words, the less there was to see in the retrieval array, the more spatial imagery would have been needed to remember whether the place was occupied during presentation and the more the where-delay task could interfere.

There used to be a debate about whether imagery really exists and why it should be used (Kosslyn, 1996; Pylyshyn, 2001). It turned out that school-age children can maintain images relatively well but find scanning, rotating, and generating objects as mental images more challenging (Kosslyn et al., 1990). In children, these different types of image processing abilities appear to be unrelated to each other (Bates & Farran, 2021). In 7-year-old children, the reliability of mental rotation of cube aggregates was found to be as low as .56 (Carr et al., 2008). In the classical mental rotation task of ten-cube aggregates, many younger children at this age perform at floor level and below chance, but mental rotation would not be at random as significant correlations with other tasks showed in

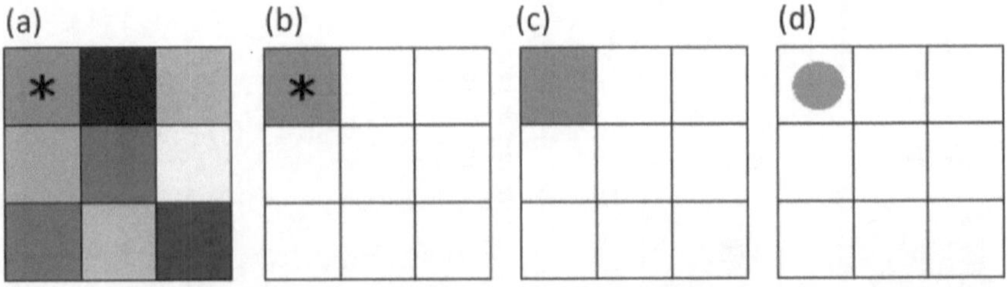

FIGURE 7.4 Rich and Sparse Retrieval Arrays for Location Memory (after Lange-Küttner et al., 2023)

another study (Hawes et al., 2015). In any case, when the number of cubes was adapted to children's capacity of four (cubes), mental rotation was reliable in 5- to 10-year-old children and significantly correlated with general non-verbal intelligence (Lütke & Lange-Küttner, 2021). Thus, as this is the same age range as in the Lange-Küttner et al. 2023 study, it seems justified to conclude that the fewer visual support is offered in a sparse retrieval array, the more visual imagery would be necessary, and the larger the where-delay interference.

Sometimes children would draw a figure consisting of the configuration of places on the table during the delay. While these are anecdotal observations, spatial grouping can be directly tested with the Common Region Test (CRT), which is a drawing task that assesses spatial binding and was introduced in Chapter 5 on drawing.

7.1.3 Spatial Binding Predicts Object and Place Memory

In the above section, the what-and-where system was tested with selective delay interference tasks. The aim of dual-task and selective interference research is to prove, at least, that there are abilities that are necessary and shared across a number of tasks, and at most, to provide behavioural neuroscience evidence that there are brain areas specialised in processing objects' shapes (what-system) versus their locations (where-system).

However, when assessing children's object and place memory, there is a way to test children's spatial binding with a second task. In Chapter 5 on drawing, the Common Region Test was described as a drawing task that clearly shows that the development of spatial binding in children progresses from object-place binding to objects-region binding. Drawing has been used as an aid to explore children's memory before, yet often a more free-format style of drawing is used (Barlow et al., 2011). Drawings can facilitate event recall more than verbal descriptions even after long delays of up to one year (Bruck et al., 2000). Drawing of events makes 5- to 6-year-old children, whose verbal accounts of events normally tend to be very sparse, more productive and more accurate in their recall (even though it did not change suggestibility). Drawing scenes has also been demonstrated to be a valid instrument to assess visual memory in adults (Bainbridge et al., 2019, 2021).

Therefore, the CRT (Lange-Küttner, 2021) – see Figure 5.2 in Chapter 5 – was used as a measure of spatial binding in a separate task to predict spatial memory in children. The hypothesis is that older children bind objects' shapes into a common region during a randomised presentation. Spatial regions narrow down and delineate the actual retrieval space for places. That larger regions of space come to children's attention is also apparent in the strong development of visual pattern memory in children from age seven (Logie & Pearson, 1997). Long-term memory for spatial patterns was even more robust in 7- and 11-year-olds than in adults (Hund & Plumert, 2002, 2005).

A spatial field can have a regular structure of occupied places, as for instance in a chess configuration that organises places, while an irregular and random structure of a chessboard would not (Schneider, 1986). Such spatial configurations can represent a good Gestalt [*Gute Gestalt*] that increases the probability of better remembering an exact location (Cowan et al., 2015; Uttal & Chiong, 2004). Thus, here the hypothesis is that object-place binding should predict better object than place memory, while objects-region binding would predict better place than object memory.

This was the case as children with an object-place binding strategy in the CRT showed better memory for object shapes, while participants with an objects-region binding strategy in the CRT showed better memory for the places of these objects (e.g. Lange-Küttner, 2010b). Why would this be the case? According to the binding theory (Treisman, 2006; Zimmer et al., 2006), the location as an object feature would not have privileged access to memory in its own right as it belongs to an object file. The place would need to become dissociated from the object and thus would require one more processing step than the object itself. So why would objects-region binding improve place memory to become as good, or even better than object memory? The *Spatial Freedom Theory* involves thinking space-based in terms of region/area and allows to build a zone within an array, in the current task a zone of occupied space vs. empty space. This is an especially important skill when places are tested one at a time in a constantly randomised order. The intention to gradually create a region, an area, or a zone in the mind where places are occupied over time would greatly facilitate place memory as in the occupied zone a place can be located by default.

Place Versus Location in the Spatial Freedom Theory

A reliable finding is that object-place attribution in the CRT predicted better object memory, while objects-region coding predicted better place memory (Lange-Küttner, 2010b, 2013). This result is quite intriguing because the object-place binding confirmed the object file theory (e.g. Treisman & Zhang, 2006) as well as the one-place predicate of an object (Pylyshyn, 2007). But collectively binding matching items into a common region allows more spatial degrees of freedom. Even collectively cancelling out objects in a spatial test predicted success in children's visual search (Guilbert et al., 2020). In essence, the place of an object no longer needs to be a feature of this object, but an object can be located in several potential locations within a delimited region. It is very likely that this awareness of freedom and spatial possibilities as well as of constraints is the motor that drives improved place memory.

The relevance of a *Spatial Freedom* theory was further elaborated in a study with another sample of 5- to 11-year-old children from diverse cultural contexts (Lange-Küttner, 2010a). Only girls showed the predicted transition from object-place to objects-region binding in the CRT, but the boys' age groups showed a U-shaped trend for objects-region binding with some 6-year-old boys already

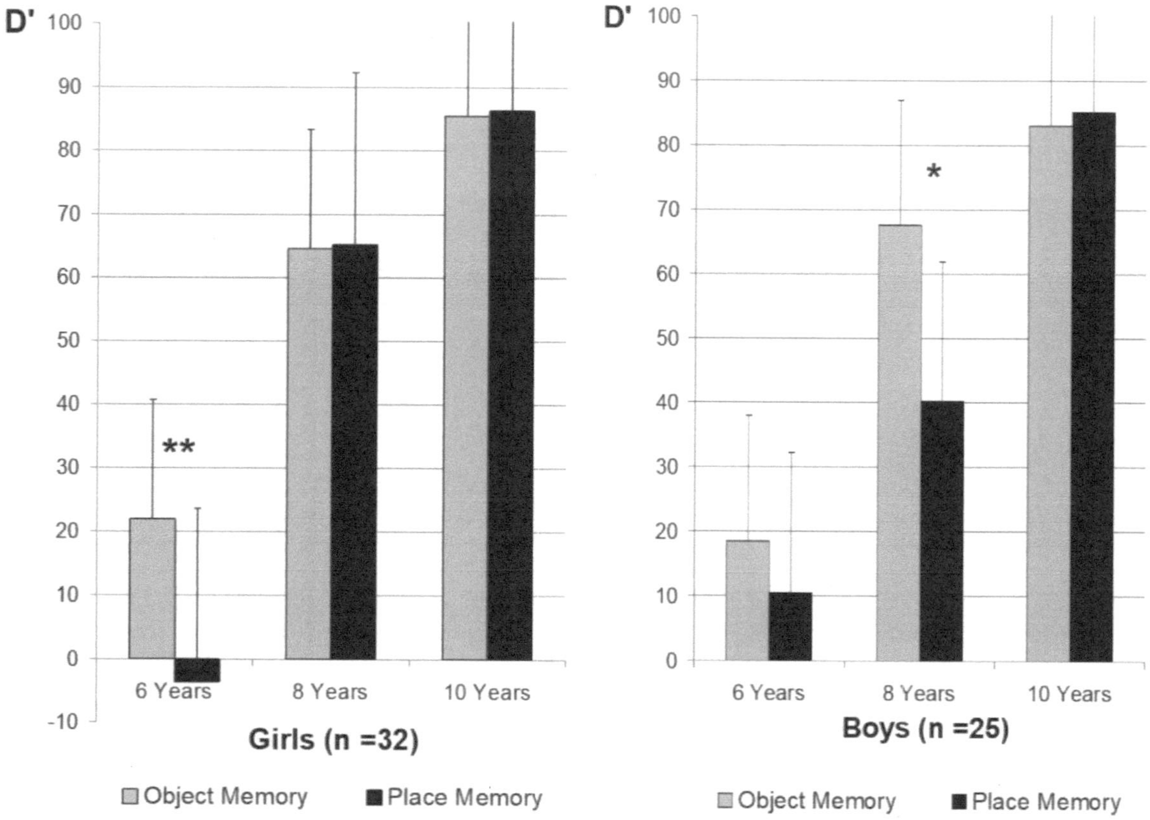

FIGURE 7.5 Individual Differences in Object and Place Memory (Lange-Küttner, 2010a)

creating common regions. As this result was unexpected, it was controlled for ethnic and socio-economic status (SES) because such differences can affect spatial skills in children and adults (Dehaene et al., 2006; Goh et al., 2007; Levine et al., 2005). There were no ethnic differences. There was no SES difference in the CRT for girls. However, the more immature object-place binding occurred more often in boys from socio-economically disadvantaged backgrounds.

Accordingly, in this study of object and place memory development, SES explained 63% of the variance in boys, but in girls, it was age that explained 58% of the variance in a multiple regression. Figure 7.5 demonstrates that 6-year-old boys already showed some correct place memory while the 6-year-old girls remembered no places at all, but both genders showed some accurate object memory. Yet in the group of 8-year-olds this had changed, as girls as a group had remarkably improved with such a large developmental increase that it could be called a 'stage': Place memory was increased from below zero to more than 60% correct, while in boys the increase was more moderate. When the CRT was added to the model, in boys, it absorbed some variance from the predictor SES, reducing it to 49% of the variance, but in girls, adding the CRT boosted the predictive power of age explaining to now 30% more, i.e. together age and the CRT explained 88% of the variance. Thus, the conclusion is that in this particular sample, girls' conceptualisation of common region massively helped to improve their place memory.

Evolution and the Spatial Freedom Theory

Levine et al. (2005) found that boys from a lower socio-economic background performed more similarly to girls than boys from families with middle or upper class SES. Gender differences in favour of females' language-related skills and in favour of males in spatial cognition have been known for a long time, not only in adults (Halpern, 2000; Kimura, 1999) but also in children (Owen Blakemore et al., 2009). However, it seems that modern education has worked insofar as this gender gap is closing in Western societies (Guiso et al., 2008), or is limited to gender differences in specific skills within one domain (Spelke, 2005). One common speculation for enhanced spatial skills in males stems from an evolutionary perspective, where males are characterised as more active and roaming in the environment than females (Halpern, 2000; Silverman et al., 2007). The advantage of a *Spatial Freedom Theory* is that one does not need to recur to past societies of hunters and gatherers. The *Spatial Freedom Theory* can explain the role of spatial exploration and young boys' awareness of their spatial degrees of freedom in a more modern way. Punishment of severe misdeeds tends to no longer be death, but spatial confinement. It may not be a coincidence that the most highly constrained spaces in modern society are prisons where the male sex is represented at a younger age than the female sex and with a clear majority (Tyler et al., 2019; van Koppen, 2018). Spatial confinement in prisons has been used since medieval times (Geltner, 2008), but the church used also cloister cells to foster sustained attention and studying (Brooke, 2003). Libraries and departments still use cubicles for study. Thus, evolutionary male spatial freedom of roaming needs a theoretical counterpart of spatial constraints and these two strands are integrated in the *Spatial Freedom Theory*.

The memory studies that combined the CRT with a computerised memory task confirmed the hypothesis that the type of spatial binding would predict visual memory in primary school-aged children. They consistently showed, for the first time, cross-domain links between spatial encoding in drawing and visual memory performance, and contributed to an integration of object- and space-based accounts of visual cognition.

7.1.4 Visual Arrays and Visual Fields

One of Piaget and Inhelder's (1956) most intriguing experiments to prove the absence of a projective space concept in young children was a task where children were asked to line up figures diagonally on a rectangular table connecting two points A and B. Children until the age of 4 (stage 1) were not able to line up the figures between points A and B, but instead clustered their figures in close proximity to each other. Between 4 and 7 years, children used the edge of the table corner as an external cue to line up the figures, but this obviously did not result in a diagonal line-up across the table (stage 2). Instead, the boundaries of the table acted as an orthogonal interference distracting from the diagonal. Only from age 7 did children increasingly try to free themselves from the external support of the table edges and construct the correct diagonal figure line-up between points A and B (stage 3). Follow-up research confirmed that the conceptualisation of the diagonal emerges late not only in drawings, but in general (Olson, 1996).

Vectors are spatial axes that we construct in our minds, while spatial boundaries can be directly perceived. However, this distinction may be on a graded scale, as the 'reheating' (Cowan & Chen, 2009) of what we see into what we conceptualise may be a fluent process. For instance, increasing the amount of visible boundaries in a spatial array did not change the amount of activation in the hippocampal area in the brain, but the conjuring up of these boundaries in spatial imagery, i.e. in a mental representation of what was seen, did show the expected activation with increasing amounts of spatial boundaries (Bird et al., 2010). Long-term memory for array boundaries seems to be functional in animals, infants, and children alike (Lew, 2011). For instance, when 3- to 4-year-old children had to re-orient themselves in different spatial arrays and searched for an object, they were more successful when explicit spatial boundaries, either drawn or slightly elevated like a rim, delimited an area (Lee & Spelke, 2011).

While adults rely on boundary information in spatial memory, children use both landmarks and boundaries (Bullens et al., 2010; Lew, 2011). Adults were most accurate in coding more geometric *angular* design information, while children used topological *distance* as a spatial cue, which showed that they centred their attention on objects and their spatial relations to each other (Bullens et al., 2010). The precise memory of the geometric angular orientation of a single bar continuously improved in 7- to 13-year-olds' visual memory (Burnett Heyes et al., 2012, 2016).

In Chapter 5 on drawing, it was described that also children's own spontaneous explicit structuring of space increases. Initially, there is a topological accumulation of objects in empty implicit space followed by horizontal spatial axes where objects can be aligned. Finally, an integration of horizontal with vertical spatial axes results in areas that represent spatial fields. That is, only when drawing a spatial field, explicit Euclidian spatial concepts would emerge in the conventional sense. Thus, it was investigated whether this development of the graphic space concept would also matter when objects and locations are memory items that are presented in different kinds of ready-made spatial arrays.

In a first object-and-place memory task, a topological and a metrical array were compared (Lange-Küttner, 2010b) see Figure 7.6. The topological array consisted of a frame with animal landmarks at each corner denoting left and right, as well as up and down positions in the grid (see Figure 7.6. left). The metrical array was a grid where each individual place was visible (see Figure 7.6. right), whereas this was not the case in the intuitive and implicit landmarked array. However, the grid is a developmentally ambiguous array because young children would not copy a grid as a crossed spatial axes system, but draw each place of the grid individually and accumulate them into a grid like bricks in a wall (Metzger, 2006; Vinter & Marot, 2007).

The sequence of the arrays was controlled. The object and place memory task itself consisted of a randomised sequence of object shapes emerging and disappearing in their fixed locations on the screen, and either objects' shapes or

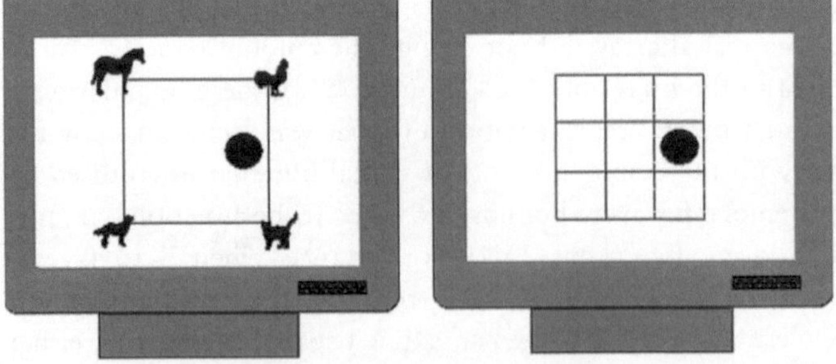

FIGURE 7.6 Topological and Metrical Spatial Array (Lange-Küttner, 2010b). *Note*: Left: Landmarked Frame, Right: Grid

objects' places needed to be remembered. The study clearly showed that object memory was better developed than place memory in 4- and 5-year-old children. The 5-year-olds remembered object shapes also faster than places. But this had changed in 7- and 10-year-old children, who remembered places as well as object shapes. In fact, 10-year-old children showed already the same memory accuracy as adults, and, like adults, they also remembered places faster than object shapes. This confirmed the *Spatial Model* (see Figure 3.4) that assumes that there is a priority of object shapes in young children who can show adult-like memory for specific objects accompanied by neural object memory consolidation (Sommer et al., 2021).

Furthermore, experience of explicit place boundaries of the grid had a facilitative effect particularly for place memory. However, this occurred independently of age as all children appeared to benefit from the explicit spatial structure of the grid with every single place clearly marked. It must be noted that the grid as such was not easier than the landmarked frame for spatial memory accuracy; instead, the grid had only an impact as a priming effect. Surprisingly, such an *array priming effect* showed that experiencing the grid with the explicitly denoted places in the first session would facilitate place memory in the second session with the empty frame. The explicit place boundaries in the grid array subsequently improved place memory in the landmarked array by about 10%. An array priming effect was also found within one session when using a real three-dimensional test box for spatial memory (Hund & Plumert, 2002). In short, grids with their explicit denotation of places can lead to positive *spatial priming* in children. Positive priming consists of the facilitation of behaviour through prior exposure to and experience of single events (Posner & Raichle, 1997). Priming does not require awareness, as the facilitation effect relies on implicitly stored perceptual knowledge from long-term memory.

Importantly, the spatial array priming effect in accuracy was statistically completely eliminated and absorbed by the variance of the spatial binding strategy in the CRT. This showed a trade-off between a 'self-made' spatial encoding strategy in drawing and perceptual priming with a 'ready-made' spatial array structure. The result demonstrated a strong intra-individual link within children between passive priming effects of boundary perception and the active drawing of explicit boundaries.

In another study, three arrays were compared and none of them had landmarks in order to more cleanly test the effect of spatial boundaries (Lange-Küttner, 2013); see Figure 7.7. In the left array, there were no spatial boundaries; in the centre, the boundaries framed an area, and in the right array, each individual place was framed by the grid. In order to avoid *spatial array priming*, the three different presentation arrays were used in a between-subjects design, that is, children took part in only one session. The three experimental groups consisted of two age groups each, 6- to 7-year-olds and 8- to 9-year-olds.

As in the studies before, in each array, five objects' shapes or places had to be remembered and distinguished from four distracters. The 'empty space' array

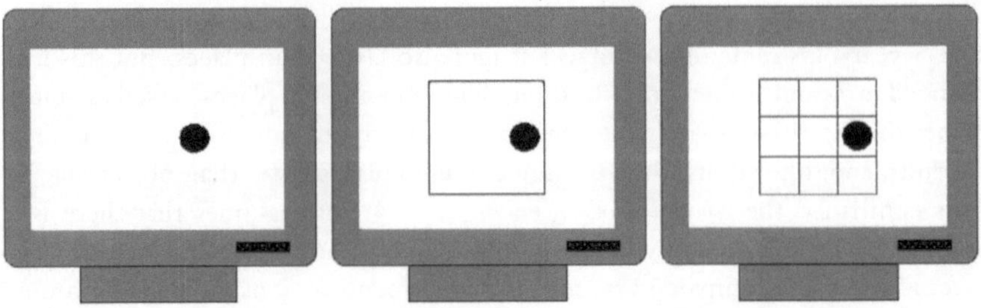

FIGURE 7.7 Empty Space, Frame and Metrical Spatial Array (Lange-Küttner, 2013).
Note: Left: Empty Array; Centre: Frame; Right: Grid

without explicit spatial boundaries was the most challenging compared to the frame and the grid to remember places, independently of age, and this was the also case when analysing microgenetic changes per experimental block; see Figure 7.8. Thus, array boundaries facilitated place memory and this stayed the same with age.

In short, the conclusion is that explicit spatial boundaries help to remember objects' places. Another finding was that the variability in children's memory responses depended on spatial binding as per CRT. Children who were encoding object-place units showed very irregular responses during the experiment. From a strategy perspective, one could call this a piecemeal strategy as only small local units were processed. In contrast, children who were attributing common region to pairs of matching objects in the CRT showed a systematic response pattern; see Figure 7.9.

The grid did not show a particular response pattern, most likely because the explicit place units in the grid did not bias responses either way. However, responses of common region coders in the empty space and in the frame groups showed very regular memory response patterns. While in empty space, the level of object memory was maintained during the experimental blocks, place memory was lower and deteriorated during the task until children's memory for locations was zero. In contrast, in the frame, a very rare occurrence happened as place memory turned out to be higher than object memory and stayed high during the experimental blocks, but object memory gradually caught up. Thus, empty space and the frame had opposite effects on object and place memory. The two arrays – 'unlimited' empty space and a delimited area in the frame – also allowed for performance changes in different ways. While in empty space, place memory deteriorated, in the frame, place memory was high and object memory improved. Thus, here we find that the fewer degrees of freedom of a constrained and delimited space helped children to remember locations.

The frame was the simplest array with spatial boundaries that delimited an area, without any landmarks or other spatial cues. In fact, the frame was the common region of all shapes that appeared and disappeared on the screen. It

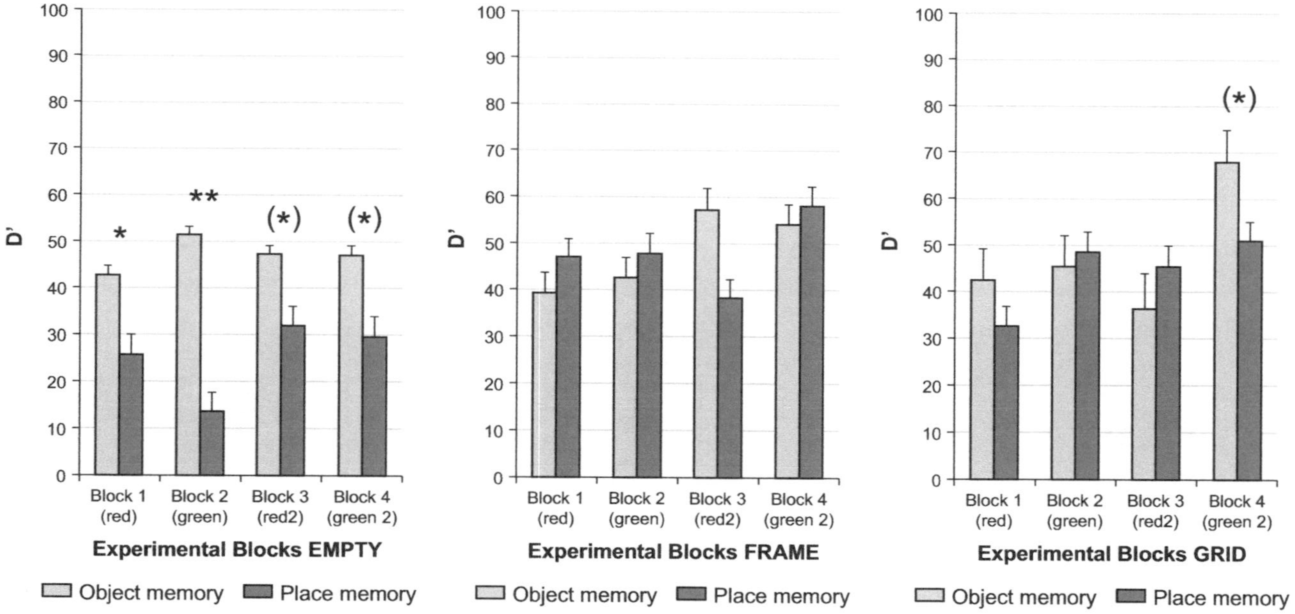

FIGURE 7.8 Object and Place Memory in Empty Space, Frame and Grid (Lange-Küttner, 2013)

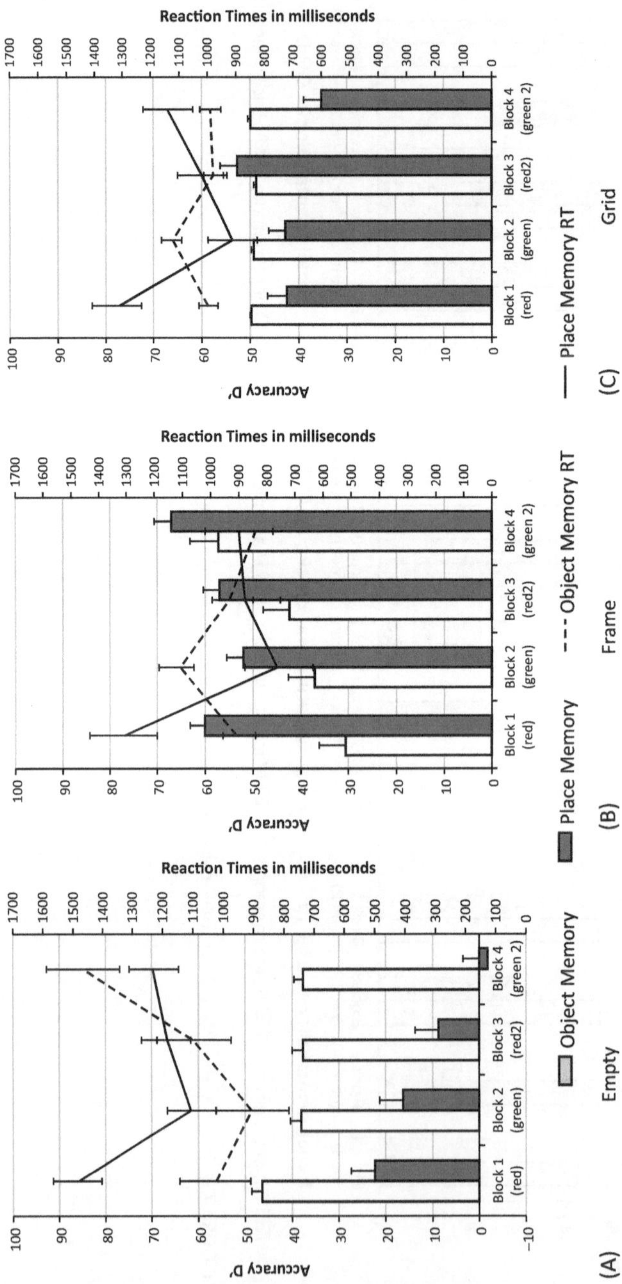

FIGURE 7.9 Direct Visual Mapping of Common Region in Memory (Lange-Küttner, 2013)

can thus be assumed that there occurred some direct *visual mapping* between the boundaries of the common region that children created in the CRT drawing task and the framed common region in the array of the memory task. The CRT was always given before the computerised memory task, and thus one could also hypothesise that the CRT was producing a visual priming effect. There were no age differences, so *visual mapping* stays the same in development.

In both the CRT and the frame, spatial boundaries simply encompassed object shapes. The frame was the only condition where place memory was better than object memory from the very beginning. There was no improvement of place memory via learning and practice; the simple constraint of a delimited area reduced the degrees of freedom where objects' shapes could appear and places would be occupied. This was sufficient to uplift place memory and reverse the object priority. One could take the reversal of the object priority in the frame as the most compelling proof for a *Spatial Freedom Theory* that increasing spatial constraints by reducing degrees of freedom with spatial boundaries creates a fine-grained mental map where places can be more successfully located and identified. Kosslyn (1996) described the visual field as a scanner with high resolution in the centre and lower resolution in the periphery. In Chapter 5 on drawing, it was described that ready-made delimited areas would also trigger drawings of smaller sized figures and more sophisticated overviews (Lange-Küttner, 2009a). However, while children spontaneously first create areas around age 9 (Lange-Küttner, 1997), the ready-made delimited areas in drawings and memory had an impact at any age (Lange-Küttner, 2009a).

7.1.5 Retrieval of Objects and Places

The visual memory paradigm was further tested by varying the retrieval array rather than testing encoding (Lange-Küttner et al., 2023), as was mentioned before. Retrieval is the last phase in memory experiments consisting of presentation-delay-retrieval. Retrieval is seen as an important phase in memory because of the facilitating effect that consistency between presentation and retrieval can have, called the *encoding-specificity effect* (Dietze et al., 2011; Godden & Baddeley, 1975; Goldston & Richman, 1985; Tulving & Thomson, 1973). For instance, Edgin et al. (2014) showed that a scene-scene test and an object-object test were easier than a scene-object test at all ages.

Memory was tested in three different retrieval arrays and one control condition. In this study, the focus was on place memory only (see Figure 7.4). In a new experimental design, the places in the presentation had individual *place-specific* colours, but the placeholders were uniform black stars, all with the same colour and shape. In this way, the visibility of objects and places was reversed, with places being vibrant and colourful, but shapes being dull and uniform. The result was a topographic multi-coloured map. On the one hand, children find it easy to conceptualise an array when the shape of part and whole is identical (Lange-Küttner, 2000). Especially younger children do not conceptualise a grid, but an aggregate of individual places (Lange-Küttner, 2009a; Metzger, 2006; Stiles & Tada, 1996). On the other hand, developmental theories about children's ability to use maps vary as either conceptual knowledge (Liben & Myers, 2007) or real-life experience (Davies & Uttal, 2007) is seen as a pre-requisite. However, both approaches agree that variability of topographic memory is large, as some young children can be at ceiling and some adults at floor level. Already 2½-year-old infants can read maps with abstract symbols that have no resemblance to the actual object in the room (Winkler-Rhoades et al., 2013). But 4- to 7-year-olds still struggle when the symbols are similar (Blades & Spencer, 1987): Place memory deteriorated when the usual single unique objects were changed to identical placeholders, from 100% to 2% accuracy in 4-year-olds and to 35.3% in 7-year-olds. Using a simpler circular array, the same effect of uniform placeholders was found in 4-year-olds' place memory (Lee et al., 2006).

As described before, the retrieval arrays varied according to how much information they would present; see Figure 7.4, Lange-Küttner et al. (2023). In all the previous experiments, only a star was used as a placeholder in a blank grid during the test, so this experiment was a new design to compare various retrieval arrays where places were perceptually enhanced.

Piaget (1969, p. 356) assumed that children would need to relegate figurative thinking to an illustrative factor rather than evaluate their perception as an indispensable source of knowledge. He assumed that the concept of Euclidian space requires the subjugation of figurative thinking as objects become just points in mathematical space determined by vectors. Hence, one retrieval array showed all colourful places and the placeholder moved from one place to another. The second retrieval array showed each place alone in a random order and with a placeholder. The third retrieval array showed only one colourful place at a time. Thus, the information in the retrieval arrays varied from rich to sparse. A control array used the usual object shapes in the same colours as the places. The hypothesis was that, especially the younger children of a sample of 5- to 10-year-olds would rely more on the placeholder and benefit from the figural richness of object shapes in the control condition.

Interestingly, the richest specified retrieval array that had also been the presentation array returned an *encoding specificity effect* (Godden & Baddeley, 1975) as locations were better remembered than single places without context. The placeholder helped especially the younger children to remember places even if just a single place was shown at a time in the retrieval array. But the most astonishing effect was that the control condition yielded the best memory in children, as shapes added an individual contour to the colour and delivered more distinct landmark-like cues to locations. Thus, the conclusion here must be that, contrary to the hypothesis of Piaget, rich perceptual spatial information works better for place memory than sparse geometric specifications, and this stays the same independently of age.

Moreover, another unexpected perceptual effect occurred as reaction times did not become faster with age. Instead, children were dwelling longer, the richer the visual content. Reaction times were fastest when they were looking at individually coloured places (and objects in the control condition), slower if a placeholder was added to a coloured place, and longest when the retrieval array resembled the presentation array with multi-coloured places. Thus, perceptual affordances of arrays can have a strong impact on 5- to 10-year-old children's place memory independently of their gains with age in capacity or speed.

In summary, the plain geometrical coloured places were remembered the least well. Places were better remembered when the placeholder was added. Thus, even though the uniform placeholder did not hold any additional informational value about the location in comparison to the empty single individually coloured place, there was a gain in memory function. Place memory was still more accurate when the spatial context of the entire array was available. The coloured object shapes that offered varied contour information in addition to just individual colour yielded even more accurate memory for location.

Confirming the importance of the placeholder for younger children, it turned out that 5- to 6-year-olds showed a more unified response towards figurative placeholders in their reaction times: Both the places with placeholders and the unique coloured object shapes of the control condition showed similar reaction times, while this was not the case in older children.

7.2 Concepts and Hebbian Learning in Object and Place Memory

As a rule of thumb, the difference between Piagetian conceptual and Hebbian learning is that the former is based on immediate insight – where parts fall into place given that the principle is understood – while the latter works via association, repetition, and conditioning. One could also say that top-down learning corresponds to Piagetian concepts, while bottom-up learning can be related to Hebbian learning. Accordingly, two types of spatial learning exist, one fast yet lasting, as in spatial priming and visual mapping, the other one slow and laborious: While holistic snapshot-like learning in the sub-cortical hippocampus occurs fast and is enduring even from the experience of a single presentation (McClelland et al., 1995), learning of associations between stimuli in the neocortex occurs comparably more slowly (O'Reilly & Rudy, 2000, 2001; Yonelinas et al., 2001).

A danger of conceptual learning is that concepts may become rigid and incompatible with the actual input; hence, there is research on how spatial memory can become flexible (Deák & Wiseheart, 2015; DeMaster et al., 2016). In contrast, a danger of association learning is that Hebbian learning may actually strengthen inappropriate associations if, for instance, an over-inclusive prototype was generated during learning (McClelland, 2001).

There is also the issue of repetitive responses in children themselves. While repetition as a form of rehearsal is beneficial to memory, repetition is not always productive in children. Until about age 12, children lose out in details in repetitive productive drawing tasks (Lange-Küttner et al., 2014), just like adults lose detail when they extract the gist of a narrative in their episodic memories (Bartlett, 1932).

A distinction is made between perseveration and perseverance (Kirkham & Diamond, 2003). Perseverance is the sustained attention that children need when solving repetitive tasks (White et al., 2017). Perseveration often occurs in children with attentional problems (George et al., 2005; Wilding, 2003; Wilding & Burke, 2006; Wilding et al., 2001). Perseveration in visual tasks consists of repetitive responses by revisiting places that had already been visited once before, leading to inefficient place memory (Danziger et al., 1998; Klein, 1988; Posner et al., 1985). Older children are becoming gradually aware of its undesirability and develop an anti-repetition bias (Witt & Vinter, 2011). The anti-repetition bias is termed inhibition of return (IoR), and the aim is to avoid attentional loops in order to stay efficient (Castel et al., 2003; Connelly & Hasher, 1993; Hartley & Kieley, 1995).

Perseveration can occur at any age. It can occur under high cognitive load both in children and in adults (Longstaffe et al., 2014; MacPherson et al., 2003). Also the A-not-B error constitutes a perseverative response because instead of turning attention towards the new hiding location, infants search again in the previous place (see Chapter 3). Adults show perseveration under time constraints (Briand et al., 2000; Howard et al., 1999). While perseveration can make place identification slow, inefficient, and inaccurate, the *repetition of the task presentation itself* leads to better memory. Thus, while repetition by the participant is usually a sign of a weakness, it seems that straightforward stimulus repetition is an important learning factor. It is suggested that *repetitions*, rather than *enduring presentations*, work like a visual memory trace refresher (Camos & Barrouillet, 2011; Logie & Della Sala, 1999); a mechanism that also may be active in rehearsal (Jarrold & Tam, 2011). From studies on the value of stimulus onset and offset, it appears that the *repeated stimulus onset* is more important than the stimulus offset (Luo et al., 2010; Pratt & Hirshhorn, 2003; Riggio et al., 1998; Samuel & Weiner, 2001). This makes sense as the stimulus offset would denote duration and not repetition.

A comparison of two arrays (see section 7.1.4) also included a comparison of object and place memory in 6- to 9-year-old children and adults (Lange-Küttner, 2010a). When learning during the experiment was analysed per experimental block, surprisingly, the young adults were starting off in their first block at about the same level as children in their last block, with better object shape than place memory, see Figure 7.10. But the adults constantly increased their place memory during the experiment until shape and place memory no longer differed. In contrast, children started off at a low level and then only improved their shape, but not their place memory. This priority of object shape over place was independent of their acceleration of reaction times during the experiment as children increased their speed more than adults did (but children were still much slower overall). It was also independent of the type of spatial array, that is, frame

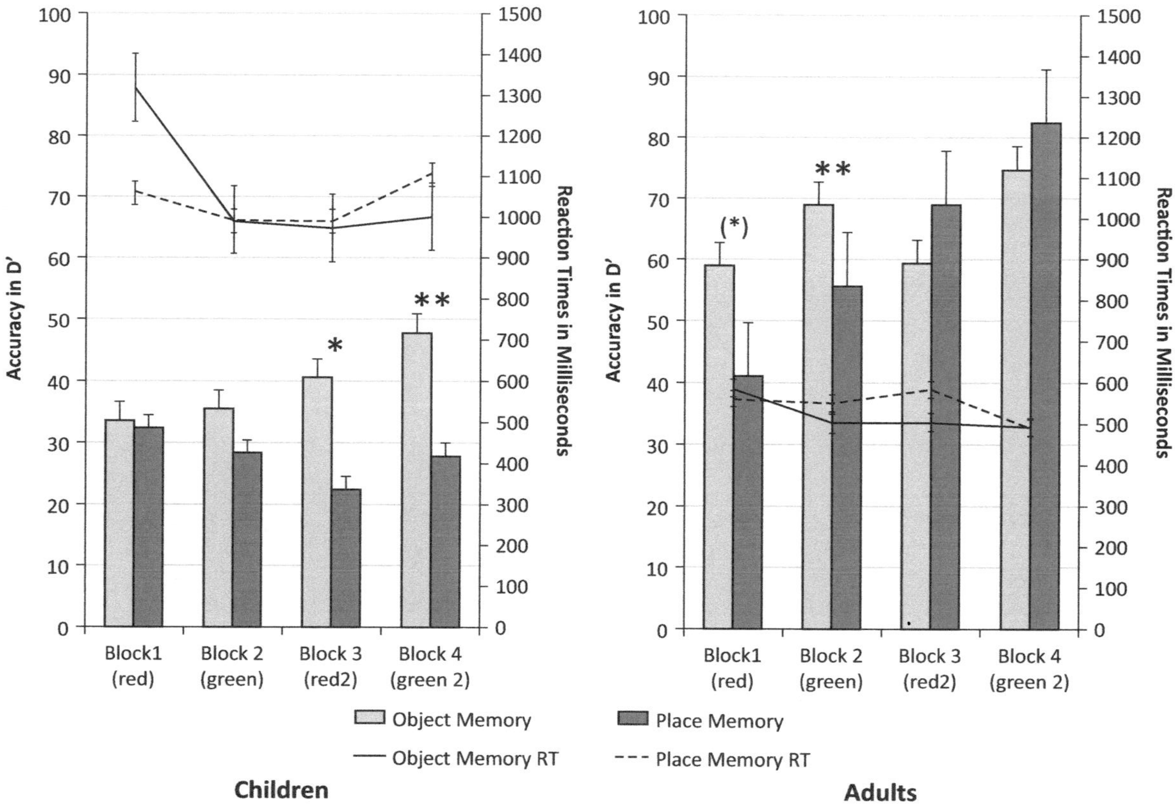

FIGURE 7.10 Object Shape Priority in Spatial Memory of Children and Adults (Lange-Küttner, 2010a)

or grid. Thus, while practice established better object than place memory in children, it abolished the object shape over place priority in adults as they doubled the accuracy of their memory for location.

The results confirm the *Spatial Model* (see Figure 3.4) where initially, figurative objects are more salient than their places and overshadow them. The object priority may have social origins as young children can find just one object very exciting, hold it very close, and do not monitor where other objects are in an array (Smith et al., 2011). Like in emotion regulation in a social context (Carlson & Wang, 2007; Ochsner et al., 2002), in individual visuo-perceptual experience, saliency of objects can also be regulated. The excitement that objects can elicit is still present in adults: Heart-beat evoked brain responses predict visual detection (Park et al., 2014) and paying attention to shapes enhances their perceived contrast and visibility (Liu et al., 2009). However, such salience of objects can distract from realising where objects actually are (Ansorge et al., 2013).

Piaget was heavily criticised by leading US intellectuals like Noam Chomsky and Jerry Fodor (Piatelli-Palmarini, 1980). In a well-documented conference, Chomsky said that more cognitive power could only be achieved by beliefs that would be modified by experience and not by conceptual change. One could explain this argument with the fact that Chomsky was a linguist, while Piaget studied the development of non-verbal cognitive development such as geometry, space, and mathematics. Piaget and Inhelder would interview children, but they would analyse the content of their responses and not the linguistic structure of their utterances. The philosopher Fodor stretched Chomsky's argument even further beyond the psychological concept of a belief (which became further investigated in Theory of Mind and Bayesian belief research, see Lange-Küttner et al., 2021) and said:

> We simply have no idea of what it would be like to get from a conceptually impoverished to a conceptually richer system by anything like a concept of learning. Thus there is an important sense in which the nativist hypothesis is the only one in the field, and the situation has been put exactly backwards over the last 300 years. The only intelligible theory of enrichment of conceptual resources is that it is a function of maturation, and there simply isn't any theory of how learning can affect concepts.
>
> *(Piatelli-Palmarini, 1980, p. 149)*

To this, Piaget answered that if cognitive structure were determined by a genetic code, there would be no human inventor who had the power to create a new idea. Three years later, Fodor (1983) published a book that was influential for the emerging brain imaging research. He claimed that cognitive structure consisted of modules that would be informationally encapsulated, basically functioning like a microchip in a computer. A microchip is a piece of hardware that, of course would not change its form, but software like neural networks can change their data processing. Another three years later, Karmiloff-Smith (1992) took up

Fodor's challenge with a representational redescription (RR) model where early concepts are reformatted into a more mature code (see Chapter 2). The transition from object-place to objects-region binding in the CRT would represent such a reformatting of a spatial code for visual input.

The important aspect here is Piaget's defence that conceptual development is necessary for novelty and innovation even though spatial conceptual development is rather protracted (Newcombe & Huttenlocher, 2003). Hence, an object and place memory experiment was run that compares how children deal with constantly novel sets of objects in new places, compared with always the same objects in always the same places (Lange-Küttner & Küttner, 2015), see Figure 7.11.

The philosophers Horkheimer and Adorno (2002) called mere repetition 'The comeback of always-the-same' ['Die Wiederkehr des Immergleichen'] that ensures nature's continuity. One would expect that the novelty condition could be more interesting and challenging for children, while the repetitive condition may be boring and mindless. However, the sequence of presentation and test was randomised, so it was not easy for children to spot that sets were repeated. Children in the repetition condition showed better recognition memory (66.0%) than children in the novelty condition (42.5%). Especially 7-year-old children found novel memory sets twice as hard as repeated sets (repetition 62.9%; novel 30.9%), while in 9-year-olds this was no longer the case (repetition 54.1%; novel 69.0%), which gave some support to the novelty hypothesis.

The microgenetic analysis of the data yielded very important results for the selective improvement of object and place memory. Figure 7.12 shows that in both conditions, memory for objects' shapes was better than for their places. While in the repeated condition, better object than place memory remained highly significant in all blocks (see Figure 7.12 right), in the novelty condition, the gap had closed at a very low level (see Figure 7.12 left). However, in the

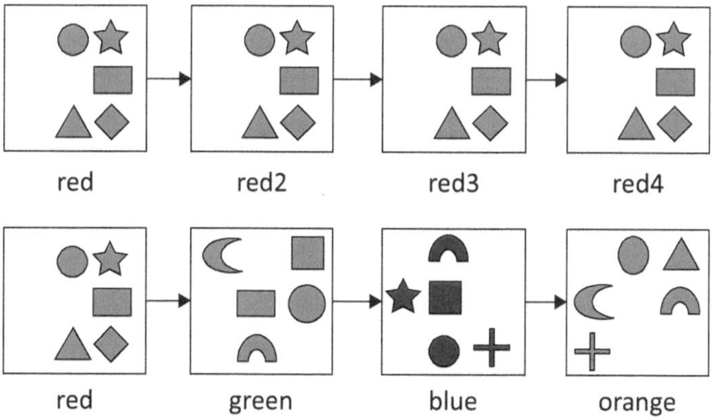

FIGURE 7.11 Stimulus Sets for Testing Novelty and Repetition in Object and Place Memory (Lange-Küttner & Küttner, 2015)

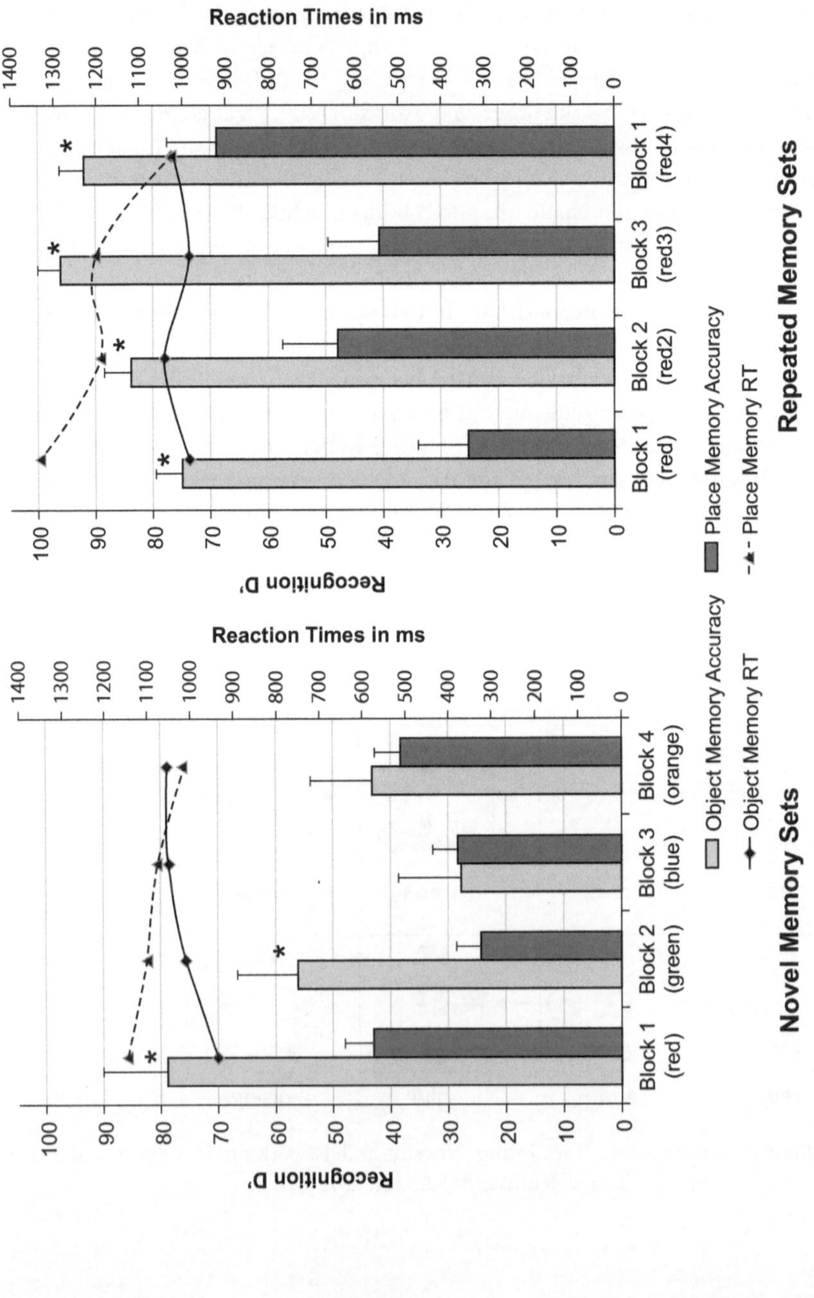

FIGURE 7.12 Object Shape Priority in Children's Spatial Memory of Novel vs. Repeated Memory Sets (Lange-Küttner & Küttner, 2015)

mere repetition condition, both object and place memory improved, while in the novelty condition, both object and place memory deteriorated in the first half of the experiment but then somewhat improved together in the second half of the experiment. The result clearly shows that repetition has a particularly beneficial effect on place memory. This may not be surprising for memory researchers, as most studies will show that rehearsal and practice enhance memory, but for developmental psychologists who do research on spatial concepts (Uttal et al., 2022), insight is the more precious learning compared to rote learning. Nevertheless, one could argue that during the repetition, the actual configuration of the places is discovered (Uttal & Chiong, 2004) as a meta-analysis showed that repetition and training turned out to be one of the most important factors in children's spatial cognition (Uttal et al., 2013).

An astonishing *equilibration regulation mechanism* was found in children's response times. Response times for place memory were initially slower but accelerated in both conditions, while latencies for object memory were initially fast but became somewhat longer in the course of the experiment until both had equilibrated and converged. The gap in reaction times closed earlier in the novelty than in the repetition condition. Thus, there was a down-regulation in dwelling on place memory and an up-regulation considering objects' shapes before responding. It was thus concluded that new shapes were allocated more attention to prevent pro-active interference from previous trials. Novelty was not conducive to enhanced memory but merely multiplied the memory load, as there were four different sets of shapes and places in four different configurations in comparison to just one in the mere repetition condition. Proactive-interference (PI) is a longstanding research topic investigated in cognitive psychology. It occurs when memory for the items of the previous block interferes with memory for the items in the current block and leads to memory deterioration (Underwood, 1945). The degree of pro-active interference depends on the amount of items that are recalled and the length of the delay before retrieval (Keppel & Underwood, 1962). It is possible to show resistance against PI by blocking out intrusive thoughts (Friedman & Miyake, 2004). Thus, as the ability for inhibition increases in development, the extent of PI decreases (Kail, 2002). Here, children had somewhat recovered from PI in the last set of novel items.

In the current context, and most importantly for the hypothesis of conceptual versus repetition learning, is the question of whether the conceptual change of spatial binding from object-place to objects-regions had a different impact on performance in the two conditions. Bohbot et al. (2012) describe that children use spatial strategies, while adults mostly use response strategies based on repetition, reward, and stress but fail to build novel spatial relationships. And indeed – only mentioned in the Discussion of the original paper – the Common Region Test (CRT) played no role in the mere repetition condition, but showed an impact on the reaction times in the novelty condition: Children who encoded object-place bindings had longer latencies for shape than for place, children who had an unsystematic approach had equally long latencies, and children who encoded objects-region bindings had longer place than shape latencies. Thus, in the novelty condition, explicit binding showed the expected conceptual influence where children with object-place binding in the CRT dwelled longer on shapes, and children with objects-region binding took longer to decide on places.

In contrast, in the mere repetitive condition, place latencies were always longer than shape latencies. Thus, when place memory accuracy actually increased, children's spatial concepts mattered the least. Instead, the absence of novel shapes and the deterministic nature of targets and distracters enabled place learning. Thus, while Fodor and Chomsky's predictions were correct in the current context insofar as repetition learning was not dependent on conceptual change, Piaget and Inhelder were correct that conceptual change and novelty are related and bias information processing into a direction of the dominating focus of attention.

Micro- and Macrogenetic Memory Improvements

Children's visual memory tremendously benefits from repetition (Lange-Küttner & Küttner, 2015). Repetition helps children and adolescents even when their performance suffers because of stochastic feedback (Lange-Küttner et al., 2012, 2021). Both shape and place memory benefit from repetition even if the repetition is non-obvious for children because of randomised sequential presentation. The gain of memory accuracy with age between 7 and 9 years was 14.6%, with an effect size of .19. In contrast, gain by repetition versus novelty was 23.5%, with an effect size of .39. Thus, children improved their spatial memory more during repetition in one hour than in two years of development. This result adds to the recent successes with computerised training (Holmes, Gathercole & Dunning, 2009; Jaeggi et al., 2011; Klingberg et al., 2002, 2005; Logie, 2012; Uttal et al., 2013). Repetition can even recover the object concept in patients with Alzheimer's (Bechari-Martin & Lange-Küttner, 2022).

A meta-analysis of 188 research studies showed that mere repeated practice of the same task proved to be the better method to increase spatial learning compared to training on several different spatial tasks, with nearly double the effect size (Uttal et al., 2013). The term *repetition priming* describes that the speed of processing increases as a power function of the number of exposures to a specific stimulus (Logan, 1990), while at the same time neural activity is decreased (Grill-Spector et al., 2006).

An interesting question is whether the same objects that were repeatedly seen in different places would be easier to memorise (Pinto et al., 2010). There is a visual memory task paradigm where the spatial configuration changes as part of the task: Visual memory is involved when identifying objects' shapes and locations after they have moved around (Allen et al., 2006). This task was called *multiple identity tracking (MIT)* when the objects were visible during the movement and masked before retrieval (Pylyshyn, 2004), or *multiple object tracking (MOT)* when objects were masked during the movement (Pylyshyn, 2004; Pylyshyn & Storm, 1988). In such a task, Pinto et al. (2010) required adult participants to answer a what-is-where question. For instance, they were asked 'where is the zebra?' and were awarded a location hit if there was any animal at a target and not a distracter location, and they scored an object hit if it was also the correct animal. In this way, the likelihood to score a hit for locations was higher than for objects. However, while the object score was lower, the gain was larger. Nevertheless, also in adults, in repeated blocks both the location and the object score increased. This repetition effect occurred with colourful drawn animals as well as with geometric coloured shapes. However, in a masked movement condition, the repetition effect did not occur as it was dependent on the perceptual input of the visible movement of objects. Pinto *et al.* suggested that repetition improves performance because it facilitates maintenance of target identities and updating of object-place binding.

Thus, as a resumé one could say that, yes, conceptual change is important and relevant when dealing with novelty, but there is no immediate gain. In contrast, a rather impressive yield of a one-hour experimental session of mere repetition was found. Children in the repetition condition showed better memory than those in the novelty condition with changing memory sets, and this did not vary with age. However, as when training mental rotation, it is an open question whether this item-based learning in children transfers to other tasks, for instance, to an object and place memory task with a larger set size in a larger grid, or to another kind of visual task such as a visual search task. The transfer seems only possible in young adults, most likely because of their fast baseline mental speed (Wright et al., 2008). In any case, though, item-based learning nevertheless is an important mechanism, and in my lab it was found to even work to the benefit of patients with Alzheimer's who have particular trouble with spatial cognition (Bechari-Martin & Lange-Küttner, 2022): Training with object-in-scenes improved spatial memory and contributed to restore a cohesive graphic object template.

7.3 Scene Memory

Scene memory is probably the most compelling example to test whether we process images in the mind, or not, and if yes, in which way. Scene memory is very robust also in long-term memory. A scene of an event is closest to the overall input that the eyes can see without effortful focused attention. Rather than the neocortical what-and-where system that focusses on objects and spatial context, for processing of scenes the subcortical area of the hippocampus and its portal the para-hippocampus are connected with the posterior neocortical visual areas that in turn process complete images in a raw and unselected format (Chadwick et al., 2013).

The visual input processing in the hippocampus is also important for episodic memory in the neocortex (DeMaster & Ghetti, 2013; Ghetti & Bunge, 2012). However, other sub-cortical areas of the limbic system are also important, as children's brains more often use the caudate nucleus, which belongs to the sub-cortical basal ganglia involved in motor regulation and pathway finding rather than episodic memory and cognitive maps stored in the hippocampus (West et al., 2021). In a virtual reality task, 83% of 8-year-old children used a spatial strategy, building relationships between landmarks, and only 17% used a response strategy that is based on associative learning and involved in the formation of habits (Blanchette et al., 2020). When a scenic background and its landmarks had disappeared from the screen, spatial learners made more errors than response learners, but they also showed more effort (learning to criterion) as indicated by higher levels of the stress hormone cortisol. There was no correlation with stress in response learners. Thus, again, a response strategy allowed for better spatial memory and it was unrelated to stress.

7.3.1 The Structure of a Scene

That images of scenes can contain objects, containers, areas, pathways, and so on makes them complex and more challenging to work with than the structured arrays that were described so far. Initial efforts to categorise scenes consisted of labelling them by hand, but this laborious exercise soon frustrated researchers. Instead, neural networks were invented that sorted categories, initially according to intermediate verbal labels (Fei-Fei & Perona, 2005) such as 'kitchen', 'forest', 'street' etc.

The examples in the study of Fei-Fei and Perona (2005) (see Figure 7.13) show the frequencies for categorised scenes and images of their 'textons' which visualise the contrast distribution. Like in a statistical factor analysis, one needs to label the communalities. It is suggested here that the network sorted the scenes most frequently according to how the light was distributed, e.g. whether there was a ray of light (20), a spot of light (19), or light came from above (21) sometimes outlining a horizon line. Scenes that were difficult for the network to categorise

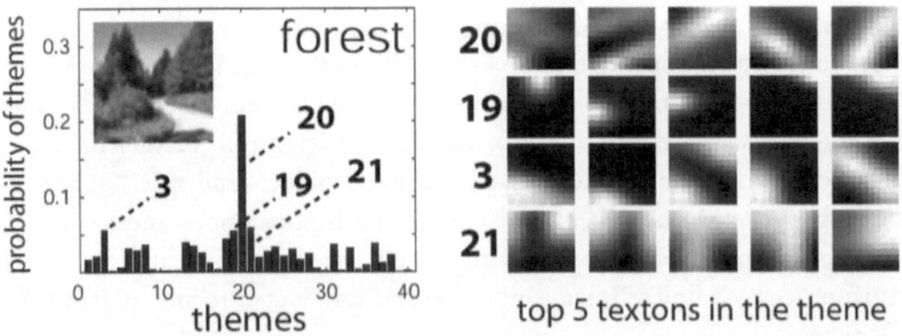

FIGURE 7.13 The Structure of a Scene (Fei-Fei & Perona, 2005, Figure 8)

were dimly lit indoor rooms. Another study used various types of image derivations (Lescroart & Gallant, 2019) that conceptualised such differences in luminance, or the x, y, and z coordinates of 3D objects' orientation in space. The best prediction for scene structure was a Gabor model that again captured large scenic luminance contrasts in visual brain V areas in the form of a spatial axis, and only to some degree the 3D objects in the brain areas processing places in the para-hippocampus and the occipital lobe. Thus, a scene is mainly defined by its overall structure and only to some extent by selective attention towards object-place bindings. That the overall structure of an image is important is not as self-evident as it sounds, because only some years ago it was argued that 'the (...) idea that the function of perception is to reconstruct the entire visual scene in the brain' is discredited (Hayhoe, 2009, p. 125).

Some studies investigate scene memory by testing object changes and object memory in scenes (Konkle et al., 2010; Stansbury et al., 2013), while others aim to test scene memory with regards to its spatial structure (Choo & Walther, 2016; Kravitz et al., 2011). Kravitz et al. found that for encoding in the para-hippocampal brain area, spatial rather than semantic factors defined the structure of scenes. For instance, it did not matter whether natural landscapes or urban built environments were classified as long as both showed a horizontal spatial axis, that is, a horizon or a skyline. Semantic categories for content were more relevant at the cognitive rather than the neurophysiological level (King et al., 2019). Nevertheless, image searches of five typical Oxford landmarks in millions of scenes appeared to work best with vocabulary (tags) as a first pass and visual descriptors derived from delimited regions in vector space (Philbin et al., 2007). Sources of error were the features' position and shape, missing and mismatched features, and occlusion.

Thus, here we find an interesting parallel to children's drawings as horizontal spatial axes drawings emerge as the first explicit Euclidean graphic construction after the early depictions of objects in implicit, empty space (see Chapter 5). The question of whether visually realistic scenes can be triggered in children's drawings was tested with a negative space technique by asking them to draw the empty space around objects (Lange-Küttner & Vinueza Chavez, 2022). It turned out that children could successfully follow instructions from age 9 onwards and produced a cohesive scene featuring a contour resembling a horizon line.

7.3.2 The Development of Scene Memory

Human infants' long-term memory for displays is easily disrupted when two or more novel objects are added (Rovee-Collier, 1993; Rovee-Collier et al., 2001). Only in 3-year-old children, experience with a small-scale spatial array in a first session improved memory in a large-scale spatial array in a second session (Marzolf & DeLoache, 1994), both after a day and after a week (DeLoache et al., 2004).

For older children, one could see Piaget and Inhelder's Three Mountains Task (Piaget & Inhelder, 1956) as the earliest attempt to test scene perception in children. Swiss children were seated in front of an array of three differently coloured mountains which resembled their local environment. They were then given four images and asked which one of them would represent their own view and which would represent views of others seated around the array. It turned out that until about seven years of age, children showed perseveration to the image that represented their own view. This task has been replicated several times (Gunia et al., 2021; Lange-Küttner, 2009b; Newcombe, 2019).

Especially Flavell's (1977) version of visual perspective-taking (VPT) is still in use to explore whether there are psychological factors that enable children to take others' perspective. The first question is what is visible and what is occluded for others (level 1 VPT), and the second question is prompting the understanding that others might see the same things but differently depending on their viewpoint (level 2 VPT). Level 1 VPT is mastered from age two onwards, while level 2 VPT takes some more years until children are about 4 years old (Moll & Tomasello, 2006). Different from scene memory, perspective-taking does not recruit the hippocampus but instead requires executive attention that is processed in the neocortex. Level 2 VPT shows shared variance with mental rotation and theory-of-mind tasks where children need to recognise that a person can be ignorant of events happening in her absence even though oneself and others know about the change (Gunia et al., 2021). Perspective-taking has also been tested in children with autism; see Chapter 9.

One of the earliest studies about place versus scene memory investigated whether spatial memory could be of an episodic flashback nature (Gaffan et al., 2004). One method of visual scene analysis is to test whether it is recognised that objects are in an inappropriate context, for instance, a car in a kitchen. Children remembered objects in visual scenes in the same way independently of whether they had to remember object changes in real visual scenes or in photographs (Dirks & Neisser, 1977; Newcombe et al., 1977). The easiest task was to remember items that were added to a scene. It was more difficult to recognise if objects had changed places, or if items were removed altogether from the scene (Dirks & Neisser, 1977; L. M. Horowitz et al., 1969; Lampel, 1973). While overall scene memory improved with age, the effects of such object manipulations in the scene stayed the same. Nevertheless, scene memory seems to be a more practically relevant way of remembering than standard memory scores, for instance, in a cross-cultural comparison with US children, 9-year-old Guatemalan children would perform worse on those but equally well on scene memory (Rogoff & Waddell, 1982).

Ofen et al. (2007) showed 8- to 12-year-old children, 13- to 17-year-old adolescents, and young adults 500 indoor and outdoor scenes in a recognition memory experiment with FMRI scanning during the presentation. All were right-handed and they responded with two fingers of only the right hand to decide what kind of scene they were seeing. They were not asked for objects in the scene. Scanning only took place during the presentation but not during the test. The highest activated regions in the brain were the right precuneus, the bilateral para-hippocampus, and the visual area in the right superior occipital gyrus, see Figure 7.14. However, these brain regions did not change with age. Instead, the bilateral inferior frontal gyrus showed increased activation with age. As scanning took place only during presentation, the activations were not related to retrieval but to encoding the scenes. Thus, it is likely that the increasingly better discrimination of the type of scene memory may have been due to the enhanced activation of the frontal lobe, but the actual scene viewing depended on a combined activation of the occipital and subcortical hippocampal systems.

For comparison, visual search activated areas in the occipital lobes in combination with the frontal and the parietal lobes (Kamienkowski et al., 2012). Thus, it could be concluded that scene memory has a different quality than visual search, which is devoid of a memory component (T. S. Horowitz & Wolfe, 1998). While certainly object configurations can be found in visual scenes (L. M. Horowitz et al., 1969), a crucial difference is that when searching in visual scenes, highly similar distracters do not have to be kept in check as in conjunction search, which yields serial search and individual differences (Lange-Küttner &

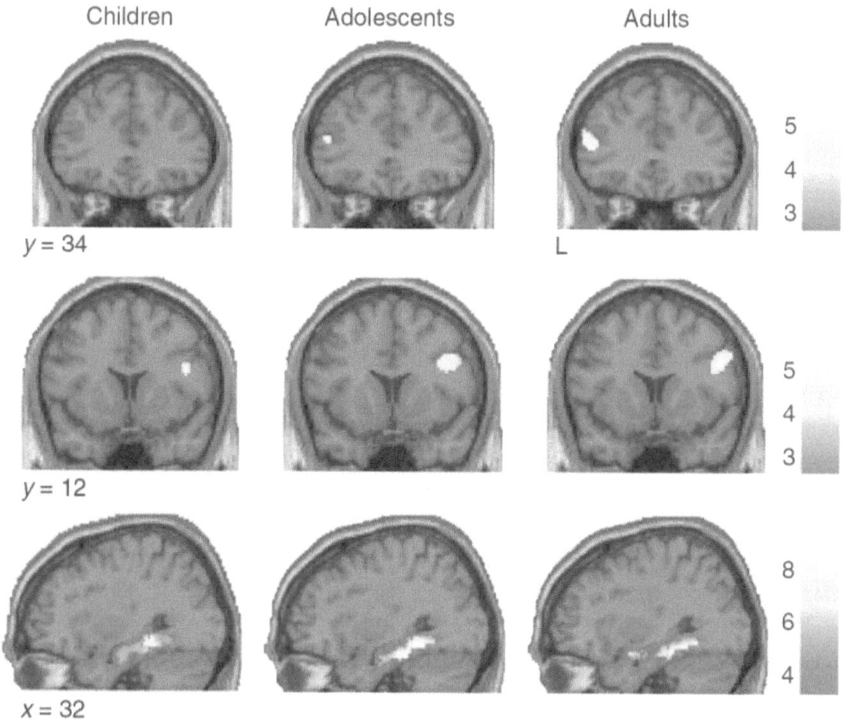

FIGURE 7.14 Neural Substrates in Children's Scene Memory (Ofen et al., 2007)

Puiu, 2021): In a kitchen scene, a nearby knife has no similarity with the tomato that would need to be sliced by it (Le-Hoa Võ & Wolfe, 2015).

7.4 Conclusions

This chapter on visual memory development shows that the principles of the early neural network simulations of spatial memory have lost nothing of their topicality and timeliness (McClelland et al., 1995; O'Reilly & Rudy, 2000, 2001). There clearly are brain substrates in children and adults that link hippocampal and occipital areas, permitting immediate and gestalt-like scene memory, while the neocortical what-and-where system in the frontal-temporal-parietal areas network allows for slower, associative learning of features, overviews and combinations of these, as well as pattern completions. There are also after images and mirror brain activations that last into delay periods before visual memory tests. Relatively speaking, for visual memory, in children the hippocampal limbic system is earlier active than the neocortical system. We also find that behavioural evidence can be different from brain activations, especially when decision-making is involved.

In visual memory, this decision-making has not been explored with verbal interviews with children, but with a Common Region Test that assesses whether children allocate one place to one object, or whether they allocate a region to matching objects. It has been stated here that the CRT is a prime example of a developmental redescription of a representational concept of objects in space. The early object-place unit has also been found in research with adults where concepts such as 'object-files' and 'one-place predicate' have been used to name this phenomenon. However, in children's visual memory, the object-place unit generates piecemeal learning and prevents learning of objects' places. Instead, objects-region bindings generate larger units that can be memorised and are more flexible as objects can dynamically change places. Nevertheless, while snapshot visual memory has boundaries that are constrained by head movements within the limits of the visual field, common region sets perceptual and conceptual boundaries and constraints that benefit visual memory. These constraints narrow down the area and increase the probability that objects and events have taken place there and thus optimise accuracy of visual memory. For this reason, in addition to the *Spatial Model* theory that assumes that saturation of object representations is necessary before attention can be directed to their places, a *Spatial Freedom* theory sees systematically set constraints to space as essential, as it creates a fine-grained cognitive map. This will become important again in the next chapters on developmental problems.

There are specific aspects to visual memory that differ from verbal memory development. While span measures almost always also involve names and numbers of objects that can be rehearsed, visual memory does not. In fact, verbal memory can get in the way. Instead, visual memory relies on visual mapping which involves similarities and projections. For this very reason, perceptual effects weigh heavily into children's visual memory. The consequence is that often age differences cannot be found for such perceptual effects. Infancy research has now shown for three decades that already infants can show sophisticated perceptual discriminations. The fact that perceptual effects are still important in visual memory of school children comes as a surprise to developmental psychologists who think that concepts and learning and mnemonic techniques would be the main motor for memory development.

References

Allen, R., McGeorge, P., Pearson, D. G., & Milne, A. (2006). Multiple-target tracking: A role for working memory? *The Quarterly Journal of Experimental Psychology, 59*(6), 1101–1116. http://doi.org/10.1080/02724980543000097

Allport, G. W. (1928). The eidetic image and the after-image. *The American Journal of Psychology, 40*(3), 418–425. http://doi.org/10.2307/1414458

Ansorge, U., Priess, H.-W., & Kerzel, D. (2013). Effects of relevant and irrelevant color singletons on inhibition of return and attentional capture. *Attention, Perception, & Psychophysics, 75*(8), 1687–1702. https://doi.org/10.3758/s13414-013-0521-2

Atkinson, J., & Braddick, O. (2003). Neurobiological models of normal and abnormal visual development. In M. De Haan & M. H. Johnson (Eds.), *The cognitive neuroscience of development* (pp. 63–82). Psychology Press.

Baddeley, A. D. (2000). The episodic buffer: A new component of working memory? *Trends in Cognitive Sciences, 4*(11), 417–423. https://doi.org/10.1016/S1364-6613(00)01538-2

Baddeley, A. D., & Hitch, G. (1974). Working memory. In G. H. Bower (Ed.), *Psychology of learning and motivation* (Vol. 8, pp. 47–89). Academic Press.

Bainbridge, W. A., Hall, E. H., & Baker, C. I. (2019). Drawings of real-world scenes during free recall reveal detailed object and spatial information in memory. *Nature Communications, 10*(1), 5. https://doi.org/10.1038/s41467-018-07830-6

Bainbridge, W. A., Kwok, W. Y., & Baker, C. I. (2021). Disrupted object-scene semantics boost scene recall but diminish object recall in drawings from memory. *Memory & Cognition, 49*(8), 1568–1582. https://doi.org/10.3758/s13421-021-01180-3

Barlow, C. M., Jolley, R. P., & Hallam, J. L. (2011). Drawings as memory aids: Optimising the drawing method to facilitate young children's recall. *Applied Cognitive Psychology, 25*(3), 480–487. https://doi.org/10.1002/acp.1716

Barrouillet, P., & Camos, V. (2012). As time goes by: Temporal constraints in working memory. *Current Directions in Psychological Science, 21*(6), 413–419. https://doi.org/10.1177/0963721412459513

Barrouillet, P., Gavens, N., Vergauwe, E., Gaillard, V., & Camos, V. (2009). Working memory span development: A time-based resource-sharing model account. *Developmental Psychology, 45*(2), 477–490. https://doi.org/10.1037/a0014615

Bartlett, F. C. (1932). *Remembering. A study in experimental and social psychology.* Cambridge University Press.

Bates, K. E., & Farran, E. K. (2021). Mental imagery and visual working memory abilities appear to be unrelated in childhood: Evidence for individual differences in strategy use. *Cognitive Development, 60*, 101120. https://doi.org/10.1016/j.cogdev.2021.101120

Bechari-Martin, H. S., & Lange-Küttner, C. (2022). Object-based practice effects recover the graphic object concept in Alzheimer's dementia. *Psychology of Aesthetics, Creativity, and the Arts.* Advance Online Publication. https://doi.org/10.1037/aca0000452

Benear, S. L., Horwath, E. A., Cowan, E., Camacho, M. C., Ngo, C. T., Newcombe, N. S., Olson, I. R., Perlman, S. B., & Murty, V. P. (2022). Children show adult-like hippocampal pattern similarity for familiar but not novel events. *Brain Research, 1791*, 1–11. https://doi.org/10.1016/j.brainres.2022.147991

Bird, C. M., Capponi, C., King, J. A., Doeller, C. F., & Burgess, N. (2010). Establishing the boundaries: The hippocampal contribution to imagining scenes. *The Journal of Neuroscience, 30*(35), 11688–11695. https://doi.org/10.1523/jneurosci.0723-10.2010

Bjorklund, D. F., Miller, P. H., Coyle, T. R., & Slawinski, J. L. (1997). Instructing children to use memory strategies: Evidence of utilization deficiencies in memory training studies. *Developmental Review, 17*(4), 411–441. https://doi.org/10.1006/drev.1997.0440

Blades, M., & Spencer, C. (1987). Young children's strategies when using maps with landmarks. *Journal of Environmental Psychology*, 7(3), 201–217. https://doi.org/10.1016/S0272-4944(87)80030-0

Blanchette, C.-A., Kurdi, V., Fouquet, C., Schachar, R., Boivin, M., Hastings, P., Robaey, P., West, G. L., & Bohbot, V. D. (2020). Opposing effects of cortisol on learning and memory in children using spatial versus response-dependent navigation strategies. *Neurobiology of Learning and Memory, 169*, 107172. https://doi.org/10.1016/j.nlm.2020.107172

Bohbot, V. D., McKenzie, S., Konishi, K., Fouquet, C., Kurdi, V., Schachar, R., Boivin, M., & Robaey, P. (2012). Virtual navigation strategies from childhood to senescence: Evidence for changes across the life Span. *Frontiers in Aging Neuroscience, 4*. https://doi.org/10.3389/fnagi.2012.00028

Briand, K. A., Larrison, A. L., & Sereno, A. B. (2000). Inhibition of return in manual and saccadic response systems. *Perception & Psychophysics, 62*(8), 1512–1524. https://doi.org/10.3758/BF03212152

Brooke, C. (2003). *The age of the cloister: The story of monastic life in the middle ages*. HiddenSpring. https://books.google.de/books?id=jy4LWze_kZoC

Bruck, M., Melnyk, L., & Ceci, S. J. (2000). Draw it again Sam: The effect of drawing on children's suggestibility and source monitoring ability. *Journal of Experimental Child Psychology*, 77, 169–196. https://doi.org/10.1006/jecp.1999.2560

Brückner, A. (1956). Der stereoskopische Effekt im Nachbild [The stereoscopic effect in the after-image]. *Ophthalmologica, 132*(1), 57–59. http://doi.org/10.1159/000302917

Bullens, J., Nardini, M., Doeller, C. F., Braddick, O., Postma, A., & Burgess, N. (2010). The role of landmarks and boundaries in the development of spatial memory. *Developmental Science, 13*(1), 170–180. https://doi.org/10.1111/j.1467-7687.2009.00870.x

Burnett Heyes, S., Zokaei, N., & Husain, M. (2016). Longitudinal development of visual working memory precision in childhood and early adolescence. *Cognitive Development, 39*, 36–44. https://doi.org/10.1016/j.cogdev.2016.03.004

Burnett Heyes, S., Zokaei, N., van der Staaij, I., Bays, P. M., & Husain, M. (2012). Development of visual working memory precision in childhood. *Developmental Science, 15*(4), 528–539. https://doi.org/10.1111/j.1467-7687.2012.01148.x

Camos, V., & Barrouillet, P. (2011). Factors of working memory development: The time-based resource-sharing approach. In P. Barrouillet & V. Gaillard (Eds.), *Cognitive development and working memory: A dialogue between Neo-Piagetian theories and cognitive approaches* (pp. 151–176). Psychology Press.

Carlson, S. M., & Wang, T. S. (2007). Inhibitory control and emotion regulation in preschool children. *Cognitive Development, 22*(4), 489–510. https://doi.org/10.1016/j.cogdev.2007.08.002

Carr, M., Steiner, H. H., Kyser, B., & Biddlecomb, B. (2008). A comparison of predictors of early emerging gender differences in mathematics competency. *Learning and Individual Differences, 18*(1), 61–75. https://doi.org/10.1016/j.lindif.2007.04.005

Castel, A. D., Chasteen, A. L., Scialfa, C. T., & Pratt, J. (2003). Adult age differences in the time course of inhibition of return. *The Journals of Gerontology: Series B: Psychological Sciences and Social Sciences, 58B*(5), P256–P259. https://doi.org/10.1093/geronb/58.5.P256

Chadwick, M. J., Mullally, S. L., & Maguire, E. A. (2013). The hippocampus extrapolates beyond the view in scenes: An fMRI study of boundary extension. *Cortex, 49*(8), 2067–2079. https://doi.org/10.1016/j.cortex.2012.11.010

Choo, H., & Walther, D. B. (2016). Contour junctions underlie neural representations of scene categories in high-level human visual cortex. *NeuroImage, 135*, 32–44. https://doi.org/10.1016/j.neuroimage.2016.04.021

Connelly, S. L., & Hasher, L. (1993). Aging and the inhibition of spatial location. *Journal of Experimental Psychology: Human Perception and Performance, 19*(6), 1238–1250. https://doi.org/10.1037/0096-1523.19.6.1238

Cowan, N. (2010). The magical mystery four: How is working memory capacity limited, and why? *Current Directions in Psychological Science, 19*(1), 51–57. https://doi.org/10.1177/0963721409359277

Cowan, N. (2022). Working memory development in childhood. In M. L. Courage & N. Cowan (Eds.), *The development of memory in infancy and childhood* (3rd ed., pp. 234–298). Routledge.

Cowan, N., & Chen, Z. (2009). How chunks form in long-term memory and affect short-term memory limits. In A. Thorn & M. Page (Eds.), *Interactions between short-term and long-term memory in the verbal domain* (pp. 86–101). Psychology Press.

Cowan, N., Morey, C. C., AuBuchon, A. M., Zwilling, C. E., Gilchrist, A. L., & Saults, J. S. (2011). New insights into an old problem: Distinguishing storage from processing in the development of working memory. In M. L. Courage & N. Cowan (Eds.), *Cognitive development and working memory: A dialogue between Neo-Piagetian theories and cognitive approaches* (3rd ed., pp. 127–150). Taylor & Francis.

Cowan, N., Saults, J. S., & Clark, K. M. (2015). Exploring age differences in visual working memory capacity: Is there a contribution of memory for configuration? *Journal of Experimental Child Psychology, 135*, 72–85. https://doi.org/10.1016/j.jecp.2015.03.002

Daniels, A. H. (1895). The memory after-image and attention. *The American Journal of Psychology, 6*(4), 558–564. https://doi.org/10.2307/1411192

Danziger, S., Kingstone, A., & Snyder, J. J. (1998). Inhibition of return to successively stimulated locations in a sequential visual search paradigm. *Journal of Experimental Psychology: Human Perception and Performance, 24*(5), 1467–1475. https://doi.org/10.1037/0096-1523.24.5.1467

Davies, C., & Uttal, D. H. (2007). Map use and the development of spatial cognition. In J. M. Plumert & J. P. Spencer (Eds.), *The emerging spatial mind* (pp. 219–247). Oxford University Press.

Deák, G. O., & Wiseheart, M. (2015). Cognitive flexibility in young children: General or task-specific capacity? *Journal of Experimental Child Psychology, 138*, 31–53. http://doi.org/10.1016/j.jecp.2015.04.003

Dehaene, S., Izard, V., Pica, P., & Spelke, E. S. (2006). Core knowledge of geometry in an Amazonian indigine group. *Science, 311*, 381–384. https://10.1126/science.1121739

Dellatolas, G., Braga, L. W., Souza, L. D. N., Filho, G. N., Queiroz, E., & Deloche, G. (2003). Cognitive consequences of early phase of literacy. *Journal of the International Neuropsychological Society, 9*(5), 771–782. https://doi.org/10.1017/S1355617703950107

DeLoache, J. S., Simcock, G., & Marzolf, D. P. (2004). Transfer by very young children in the symbolic retrieval task. *Child Development, 75*, 1708–1718. https://doi.org/10.1111/j.1467-8624.2004.00811.x

DeMaster, D., Coughlin, C., & Ghetti, S. (2016). Retrieval flexibility and reinstatement in the developing hippocampus. *Hippocampus, 26*(4), 492–501. https://doi.org/10.1002/hipo.22538

DeMaster, D., & Ghetti, S. (2013). Developmental differences in hippocampal and cortical contributions to episodic retrieval. *Cortex: A Journal Devoted to the Study of the Nervous System and Behavior, 49*(6), 1482–1493. https://doi.org/10.1016/j.cortex.2012.08.004

Dietze, P. M., Sharman, S. J., Powell, M. B., & Thomson, D. M. (2011). Context reinstatement effects in children's cued recall of strongly and weakly associated word pairs. *The Australian Educational and Developmental Psychologist, 28*(2), 91–100. https://doi.org/10.1375/aedp.28.2.91

Dirks, J., & Neisser, U. (1977). Memory for objects in real scenes: The development of recognition and recall. *Journal of Experimental Child Psychology, 23*(2), 315–328. https://doi.org/10.1016/0022-0965(77)90108-4

Dubravac, M., Roebers, C. M., & Meier, B. (2022). Age-related qualitative differences in post-error cognitive control adjustments. *British Journal of Developmental Psychology, 40*(2), 287–305. https://doi.org/10.1111/bjdp.12403

Edgin, J. O., Spanò, G., Kawa, K., & Nadel, L. (2014). Remembering things without context: Development matters. *Child Development*, 1491–1502. https://doi.org/10.1111/cdev.12232

Fechner, G. T. (1860). *Elemente der Psychophysik: 2. Band [Elements of psychophysics Vol. 2]*. Breitkopf & Härtel.

Fei-Fei, L., & Perona, P. (2005, 20–25 June 2005). A Bayesian hierarchical model for learning natural scene categories. IEEE Computer Society Conference on Computer Vision and Pattern Recognition (CVPR'05).

Flavell, J. H. (1977). The development of knowledge about visual perception. *Nebraska Symposium on Motivation, 25*, 43–76.

Fodor, J. A. (1983). *The modularity of mind: An essay on faculty psychology*. MIT Press.

Friedman, N. P., & Miyake, A. (2004). The relations among inhibition and interference control functions: A latent-variable analysis. *Journal of Experimental Psychology: General, 133*(1), 101–135. https://doi.org/10.1037/0096-3445.133.1.101

Gaffan, D., Healey, A. N., & Eacott, M. J. (2004). Objects and positions in visual sciences: Effects of perirhinal and postrhinal cortex lesions in the rat. *Behavioral Neuroscience, 118*(5), 992–1010. https://doi.org/10.1037/0735-7044.118.5.992

Geltner, G. (2008). *The medieval prison: A social history*. Princeton University Press.

George, M., Dobler, V., Nicholls, E., & Manly, T. (2005). Spatial awareness, alertness, and ADHD: The re-emergence of unilateral neglect with time-on-task. *Brain and Cognition, 57*(3), 264–275. https://doi.org/10.1016/j.bandc.2004.09.003

Ghetti, S., & Bunge, S. A. (2012). Neural changes underlying the development of episodic memory during middle childhood. *Developmental Cognitive Neuroscience, 2*(4), 381–395. https://doi.org/10.1016/j.dcn.2012.05.002

Godden, D. R., & Baddeley, A. D. (1975). Context-dependent memory in two natural environments: On land and underwater. *British Journal of psychology, 66*(3), 325–331. https://doi.org/10.1111/j.2044-8295.1975.tb01468.x

Goh, J. O., Chee, M. W., Tan, J. C., Venkatraman, V., Hebrank, A., Leshikar, E. D., Jenkins, L., Sutton, B. P., Gutchess, A. H., & Park, D. C. (2007). Age and culture modulate object processing and object-scene binding in the ventral visual area. *Cognitive, Affective, & Behavioral Neuroscience*, *7*, 44–52. https://doi.org/10.3758/CABN.7.1.44

Goldston, D. B., & Richman, C. L. (1985). Imagery, encoding specificity, and prose recall in 6-year-old children. *Journal of Experimental Child Psychology*, *40*(3), 395–405. https://doi.org/10.1016/0022-0965(85)90073-6

Grill-Spector, K., Henson, R., & Martin, A. (2006). Repetition and the brain: Neural models of stimulus-specific effects. *Trends in Cognitive Sciences*, *10*(1), 14–23. https://doi.org/10.1016/j.tics.2005.11.006

Guilbert, A., Perguilhem, S., & Guiraud-Vinatea, H. (2020). Visual search strategies in children: A reflection of working memory processes? *Journal of Clinical and Experimental Neuropsychology*, *42*(10), 975–981. https://doi.org/10.1080/13803395.2020.1830033

Guiso, L., Monte, F., Sapienza, P., & Zingales, L. (2008). Culture, gender and math. *Science*, *320*, 1164–1165. https://doi.org/10.1126/science.1154094

Gunia, A., Moraresku, S., & Vlček, K. (2021). Brain mechanisms of visuospatial perspective-taking in relation to object mental rotation and the theory of mind. *Behavioural Brain Research*, *407*, 113247. https://doi.org/10.1016/j.bbr.2021.113247

Halpern, D. F. (2000). *Sex differences in cognitive abilities* (3rd ed.). Erlbaum.

Hardman, K. O., & Cowan, N. (2015). Remembering complex objects in visual working memory: Do capacity limits restrict objects or features? *Journal of Experimental Psychology: Learning, Memory, and Cognition*, *41*(2), 325–347. https://doi.org/10.1037/xlm0000031

Hartley, A. A., & Kieley, J. M. (1995). Adult age differences in the inhibition of return of visual attention. *Psychology and Aging*, *10*(4), 670–683. https://doi.org/10.1037/0882-7974.10.4.670

Hawes, Z., LeFevre, J. A., Xu, C., & Bruce, C. D. (2015). Mental rotation with tangible three-dimensional objects: A new measure sensitive to developmental differences in 4- to 8-year-old children. *Mind, Brain, and Education*, *9*(1), 10–18. https://doi.org/10.1111/mbe.12051

Hayhoe, M. M. (2009). Visual memory in motor planning and action. In J. R. Brockmole (Ed.), *The visual world in memory* (pp. 117–139). Psychology Press.

Hitch, G. J., Halliday, S., Schaafstal, A. M., & Schraagen, J. M. (1988). Visual working memory in young children. *Memory & Cognition*, *16*(2), 120–132. https://doi.org/10.3758/BF03213479

Holmes, J., Gathercole, S. E., & Dunning, D. L. (2009). Adaptive training leads to sustained enhancement of poor working memory in children. *Developmental Science*, *12*(4), F9–F15. https://doi.org/10.1111/j.1467-7687.2009.00848.x

Horkheimer, M., & Adorno, T. (2002). *Dialectic of enlightenment*. Stanford University Press.

Horowitz, L. M., Lampel, A. K., & Takanishi, R. N. (1969). The child's memory for unitized scenes. *Journal of Experimental Child Psychology*, *8*(2), 375–388. http://doi.org/10.1016/0022-0965(69)90110-6

Horowitz, T. S., & Wolfe, J. M. (1998). Visual search has no memory. *Nature*, *394*(6693), 575–577. https://doi.org/10.1038/29068

Howard, L. A., Lupiáñez, J., & Tipper, S. P. (1999). Inhibition of return in a selective reaching task: An investigation of reference frames. *Journal of General Psychology*, *126*(4), 421–442. https://doi.org/10.1080/00221309909595374

Hund, A. M., & Plumert, J. M. (2002). Delay-induced bias in children's memory for location. *Child Development, 73*, 829–840. https://doi.org/10.1111/1467-8624.00441

Hund, A. M., & Plumert, J. M. (2005). The stability and flexibility of spatial categories. *Cognitive Psychology*, 1–44. https://doi.org/10.1016/j.cogpsych.2004.05.002

Jaeggi, S. M., Buschkuehl, M., Jonides, J., & Shah, P. (2011). Short- and long-term benefits of cognitive training. *Proceedings of the National Academy of Sciences of the United States, 108*(25), 10081–10086. https://doi.org/10.1073/pnas.1103228108

Jarrold, C., & Tam, H. (2011). Rehearsal and the development of working memory. In P. Barrouillet & V. Gaillard (Eds.), *Cognitive development and working memory: A dialogue between Neo-Piagetian theories and cognitive approaches* (pp. 177–200). Psychology Press.

Kail, R. V. (1986). The impact of extended practice on rate of mental rotation. *Journal of Experimental Child Psychology, 42*(3), 378–391. https://doi.org/10.1016/0022-0965(86)90032-9

Kail, R. V. (2002). Developmental change in proactive interference. *Child Development, 73*(6), 1703–1714. https://doi.org/10.1111/1467-8624.00500

Kail, R. V., & Ferrer, E. (2007). Processing speed in childhood and adolescence: Longitudinal models for examining developmental change. *Child Development, 78*(6), 1760–1770. https://doi.org/10.1111/j.1467-8624.2007.01088.x

Kail, R. V., & Miller, C. A. (2006). Developmental change in processing speed: Domain specificity and stability during childhood and adolescence. *Journal of Cognition and Development*, 7(1), 119–137. http://doi.org/10.1207/s15327647jcd0701_6

Kail, R. V., & Park, Y. S. (1990). Impact of practice on speed of mental rotation. *Journal of Experimental Child Psychology, 49*(2), 227–244. https://doi.org/10.1016/0022-0965(90)90056-E

Kamienkowski, J. E., Ison, M. J., Quiroga, R. Q., & Sigman, M. (2012). Fixation-related potentials in visual search: A combined EEG and eye tracking study. *Journal of Vision, 12*(7), ArtID 4. https://doi.org/10.1167/12.7.4

Karmiloff-Smith, A. (1992). *Beyond modularity*. MIT Press.

Keppel, G., & Underwood, B. J. (1962). Proactive inhibition in short-term retention of single items. *Journal of Verbal Learning and Verbal Behavior, 1*(3), 153–161. https://doi.org/10.1016/S0022-5371(62)80023-1

Kimura, D. (1999). *Sex and cognition*. MIT Press.

King, M. L., Groen, I. I. A., Steel, A., Kravitz, D. J., & Baker, C. I. (2019). Similarity judgments and cortical visual responses reflect different properties of object and scene categories in naturalistic images. *NeuroImage, 197*, 368–382. https://doi.org/10.1016/j.neuroimage.2019.04.079

Kirkham, N. Z., & Diamond, A. (2003). Sorting between theories of perseveration: Performance in conflict tasks requires memory, attention and inhibition. *Developmental Science, 6*(5), 474–476. https://doi.org/10.1111/1467-7687.00303

Klauer, K. C., & Zhao, Z. (2004). Double dissociations in visual and spatial short-term memory. *Journal of Experimental Psychology: General, 133*(3), 355–381. https://doi.org/10.1037/0096-3445.133.3.355

Klein, R. (1988). Inhibitory tagging system facilitates visual search. *Nature, 334*(6181), 430–431. https://doi.org/10.1038/334430a0

Klingberg, T., Fernell, E., Olesen, P. J., Johnson, M., Gustafsson, P., Dahlström, K., Gillberg, C. G., Forssberg, H., & Westerberg, H. (2005). Computerized training of working memory in children with ADHD - A randomized, controlled trial. *Journal of the American Academy of Child & Adolescent Psychiatry, 44*(2), 177–186. https://doi.org/10.1097/00004583-200502000-00010

Klingberg, T., Forssberg, H., & Westerberg, H. (2002). Training of working memory in children with ADHD. *Journal of Clinical and Experimental Neuropsychology, 24*(6), 781–791. https://doi.org/10.1076/jcen.24.6.781.8395

Konkle, T., Brady, T. F., Alvarez, G. A., & Oliva, A. (2010). Scene memory is more detailed than you think: The role of categories in visual long-term memory. *Psychological Science, 21*(11), 1551–1556. https://doi.org/10.1177/0956797610385359

Kosslyn, S. M. (1996). *Image and brain: The resolution of the imagery debate.* The MIT Press.

Kosslyn, S. M., Margolis, J. A., Barrett, A. M., Goldknopf, E. J., & Daly, P. F. (1990). Age differences in imagery abilities. *Child Development, 61*(4), 995–1010. https://doi.org/10.1111/j.1467-8624.1990.tb02837.x

Kravitz, D. J., Peng, C. S., & Baker, C. I. (2011). Real-World scene representations in high-level visual cortex: It's the spaces more than the places. *The Journal of Neuroscience, 31*(20), 7322–7333. https://doi.org/10.1523/jneurosci.4588-10.2011

Lampel, A. K. (1973). The child's memory for actional, locational, and serial scenes. *Journal of Experimental Child Psychology, 15*(2), 266–277. http://doi.org/10.1016/0022-0965(73)90148-3

Lange-Küttner, C. (1997). Development of size modification of human figure drawings in spatial axes systems of varying complexity. *Journal of Experimental Child Psychology, 66*, 264–278. https://doi.org/10.1006/jecp.1997.2386

Lange-Küttner, C. (2000). The role of object violations in the development of visual analysis. *Perceptual and Motor Skills, 90*, 3–24. https://doi.org/10.2466/pms.2000.90.1.3

Lange-Küttner, C. (2009a). Habitual size and projective size: The logic of spatial systems in children's drawings. *Developmental Psychology, 45*(4), 913–927. https://doi.org/10.1037/a0016133

Lange-Küttner, C. (2009b). Viewing and attention in children. *Acta Paediatrica, 98*(10), 1553–1555. https://doi.org/10.1111/j.1651-2227.2009.01422.x

Lange-Küttner, C. (2010a). Gender-specific developmental pathways for boys and girls: The Wertheimer common-region-test can predict spatial memory. *European Journal of Developmental Science, 4*(1), 46–66. https://doi.org/10.3233/DEV-2010-4104

Lange-Küttner, C. (2010b). Ready-made and self-made facilitation effects of arrays: Priming and conceptualization in children's visual memory. *Swiss Journal of Psychology, 69*(4), 189–200. https://doi.org/10.1024/1421-0185/a000023

Lange-Küttner, C. (2012). The importance of reaction times for developmental science: What a difference milliseconds make. *International Journal of Developmental Science, 6*, 51–55. https://doi.org/10.3233/DEV-2012-11089

Lange-Küttner, C. (2013). Array effects, spatial concepts, or information processing speed: What is the crucial variable for place learning? *Swiss Journal of Psychology, 72*(4), 197–217. https://doi.org/10.1024/1421-0185/a000113

Lange-Küttner, C. (2021). Common region test (CRT). A drawing test for assessment of the development of spatial organization in children. APA PsycTESTS control number 9999-79011-000.

Lange-Küttner, C., Averbeck, B. B., Hentschel, M., & Baumbach, J. (2021). Intelligence matters for stochastic feedback processing during sequence learning in adolescents and young adults. *Intelligence, 86*, article 101542. https://doi.org/10.1016/j.intell.2021.101542

Lange-Küttner, C., Averbeck, B. B., Hirsch, S. V., Wießner, I., & Lamba, N. (2012). Sequence learning under uncertainty in children: Self-reflection vs. self-assertion. *Frontiers in Psychology, 3*, open access article 127. https://doi.org/10.3389/fpsyg.2012.00127

Lange-Küttner, C., Collins, C., Ahmed, R. K., & Fisher, L. E. (2023). Rich and sparse figurative information in children's memory for colorful places. *Developmental Psychology*, *59*(2), 256–271. https://doi.org/10.1037/dev0001483

Lange-Küttner, C., & Friederici, A. D. (2000). Modularity of object and place memory in children. *Brain and Cognition*, *43*(1), 302–305. https://doi.org/10.1006/brcg.1999.1135

Lange-Küttner, C., & Green, H. (2007). What is the age of mental rotation? In *Proceedings of the 6th IEEE international conference on development and learning* (pp. 259–263). IEEE Press.

Lange-Küttner, C., & Küttner, E. (2015). How to learn places without spatial concepts: Does the what-and-where reaction time system in children regulate learning during stimulus repetition? *Brain and Cognition*, *97*, 59–73. https://doi.org/10.1016/j.bandc.2015.04.008

Lange-Küttner, C., Küttner, E., & Chromekova, M. (2014). Deterioration and recovery of DAP IQ scores in the repeated assessment of the Naglieri Draw-A-Person (DAP) test in 6- to 12-year-old children. *Psychological Assessment*, *26*, 297–306. https://doi.org/10.1037/a0034581

Lange-Küttner, C., & Martin, S. (1999). Reversed effects of familiarity and novelty in visual and auditory working memory for words. *Brain and Cognition*, *40*(1 (part 4)), 159–162. https://doi.org/10.1006/brcg.1998.1024

Lange-Küttner, C., & Puiu, A.-A. (2021). Perceptual load and sex-specific personality traits: The impact of the Big Five personality dimensions and the autism quotient on visual search. *Experimental Psychology*, *68*, 149–164. https://doi.org/10.1027/1618-3169/a000520

Lange-Küttner, C., & Vinueza Chavez, X. (2022). The space paradox in graphic representation. *Frontiers in Psychology*, *13*, article 968918. https://doi.org/10.3389/fpsyg.2022.968918

Le-Hoa Võ, M., & Wolfe, J. M. (2015). The role of memory for visual search in scenes. *Annals of the New York Academy of Sciences*, *1339*(1), 72–81. https://doi.org/10.1111/nyas.12667

Lee, S. A., Shusterman, A., & Spelke, E. S. (2006). Reorientation and landmark-guided search by young children: Evidence for two systems. *Psychological Science*, *17*(7), 577–582. https://doi.org/10.1111/j.1467-9280.2006.01747.x

Lee, S. A., & Spelke, E. S. (2011). Young children reorient by computing layout geometry, not by matching images of the environment. *Psychonomic Bulletin & Review*, *18*(1), 192–198. https://doi.org/10.3758/s13423-010-0035-z

Lescroart, M. D., & Gallant, J. L. (2019). Human scene-selective areas represent 3D configurations of surfaces. *Neuron*, *101*(1), 178–192.e177. https://doi.org/10.1016/j.neuron.2018.11.004

Levine, S. C., Vasilyeva, M., Lourenco, S. F., Newcombe, N. S., & Huttenlocher, J. (2005). Socioeconomic status modifies the sex difference in spatial skill. *Psychological Science*, *16*(11), 841–845. https://doi.org/10.1111/j.1467-9280.2005.01623.x

Lew, A. (2011). Looking beyond the boundaries: Time to put landmarks back on the cognitive map ? *Psychological Bulletin*, *137*(3), 484–507. https://doi.org/10.1037/a0022315

Liben, L. S. (1981). Copying and reproducing pictures in relation to subjects' operative levels. *Developmental Psychology*, *17*(3), 357–365. https://doi.org/10.1037/0012-1649.17.3.357

Liben, L. S., & Myers, L.J., (2007). Developmental changes in children's understanding of maps: What, when and how? In J. M. Plumert & J. P. Spencer (Eds.), *The emerging spatial mind* (pp. 193–218). Oxford University Press.

Liu, T., Abrams, J., & Carrasco, M. (2009). Voluntary attention enhances contrast appearance. *Psychological Science, 20*(3), 354–362. https://doi.org/10.1111/j.1467-9280.2009.02300.x

Logan, G. D. (1990). Repetition priming and automaticity: Common underlying mechanisms? *Cognitive Psychology, 22*(1), 1–35. https://doi.org/10.1016/0010-0285(90)90002-L

Logie, R. H. (2012). Cognitive training: Strategies and the multicomponent cognitive system. *Journal of Applied Research in Memory and Cognition, 1*(3), 206–207. https://doi.org/10.1016/j.jarmac.2012.07.006

Logie, R. H., & Della Sala, S. (1999). Repetita (non) iuvant. In S. D. Sala (Ed.), *Mind myths: Exploring popular assumptions about the mind and brain.* (pp. 125–137). Wiley.

Logie, R. H., & Pearson, D. G. (1997). The inner eye and the inner scribe of visuo-spatial working memory: Evidence from developmental fractionation. *European Journal of Cognitive Psychology, 9*(3), 241–257. https://doi.org/10.1080/713752559

Longstaffe, K. A., Hood, B. M., & Gilchrist, I. D. (2014). The influence of cognitive load on spatial search performance. *Attention, Perception, & Psychophysics, 76*(1), 49–63. https://doi.org/10.3758/s13414-013-0575-1

Luo, C., Lupiáñez, J., Fu, X., & Weng, X. (2010). Spatial stroop and spatial orienting: The role of onset versus offset cues. *Psychological Research, 74*(3), 277–290. https://doi.org/10.1007/s00426-009-0253-z

Luria, R., Balaban, H., Awh, E., & Vogel, E. K. (2016). The contralateral delay activity as a neural measure of visual working memory. *Neuroscience & Biobehavioral Reviews, 62*, 100–108. https://doi.org/10.1016/j.neubiorev.2016.01.003

Lütke, N., & Lange-Küttner, C. (2021). The magical number four in children's mental rotation of cube aggregates. *Developmental Psychology, 57*, 211–226. https://doi.org/10.1037/dev0001139

MacPherson, A. C., Klein, R. M., & Moore, C. (2003). Inhibition of return in children and adolescents. *Journal of Experimental Child Psychology, 85*(4), 337–351. https://doi.org/10.1016/S0022-0965(03)00104-8

Manly, T., Cornish, K., Grant, C., Dobler, V., & Hollis, C. (2005). Examining the relationship between rightward visuo-spatial bias and poor attention within the normal child population using a brief screening task. *Journal of Child Psychology and Psychiatry, 46*(12), 1337–1344. https://doi.org/10.1111/j.1469-7610.2005.01432.x

Marzolf, D. P., & DeLoache, J. S. (1994). Transfer in young children's understanding of spatial relations. *Child Development, 64*, 1–15. https://doi.org/10.1111/j.1467-8624.1994.tb00730.x

McClelland, J. L. (2001). Failures to learn and their remediation: A Hebbian account. In J. L. McClelland & R. R. Siegler (Eds.), *Mechanisms of cognitive development: Behavioral and neural perspectives* (pp. 97–121). Psychology Press.

McClelland, J. L., McNaughton, B. L., & O'Reilly, R. C. (1995). Why there are complementary learning systems in the hippocampus and neocortex: Insights from the successes and failures of connectionist models of learning and memory. *Psychological Review, 102*(3), 419–457. https://doi.org/10.1037/0033-295X.102.3.419

Mecklinger, A., & Meinshausen, R.-M. (1998). Recognition memory for object form and object location: An event-related potential study. *Memory & Cognition, 26*(5), 1068–1088. https://doi.org/10.3758/BF03201184

Mecklinger, A., & Müller, N. (1996). Dissociations in the processing of "what" and "where" information in working memory: An event-related potential analysis. *Journal of Cognitive Neuroscience*, *8*(5), 453–473. https://doi.org/10.1162/jocn.1996.8.5.453

Mecklinger, A., & Pfeifer, E. (1996). Event-related potentials reveal topographical and temporal distinct neuronal activation patterns for spatial and object working memory. *Cognitive Brain Research*, *4*, 211–224. https://doi.org/10.1016/S0926-6410(96)00034-1

Merrill, E. C., Yang, Y., Roskos, B., & Steele, S. (2016). Sex differences in using spatial and verbal abilities influence route learning performance in a virtual environment: A comparison of 6- to 12-Year old boys and girls. *Frontiers in Psychology*, *7*, article 258. https://doi.org/10.3389/fpsyg.2016.00258

Metzger, W. (2006). *Laws of seeing*. MIT Press.

Moll, H., & Tomasello, M. (2006). Level 1 perspective-taking at 24 months of age. *British Journal of Developmental Psychology*, *24*(3), 603–613. https://doi.org/10.1348/026151005X55370

Newcombe, N. S. (2019). Navigation and the developing brain. *Journal of Experimental Biology*, *222*(Supplement 1), article jeb186460. https://doi.org/10.1242/jeb.186460

Newcombe, N. S., & Huttenlocher, J. (2003). *Making space: The development of spatial representation and reasoning*. MIT Press.

Newcombe, N. S., Rogoff, B., & Kagan, J. (1977). Developmental changes in recognition memory for pictures of objects and scenes. *Developmental Psychology*, *13*, 337–341. https://doi.org/10.1037/0012-1649.13.4.337

O'Reilly, R. C., & Rudy, J. W. (2000). Computational principles of learning in the neocortex and hippocampus. *Hippocampus*, *10*, 389–397. https://doi.org/10.1002/1098-1063(2000)10:4<389::AID-HIPO5>3.0.CO;2-P

O'Reilly, R. C., & Rudy, J. W. (2001). Conjunctive representations in learning and memory: Principles of cortical and hippocampal function. *Psychological Review*, *108*(2), 311–345. https://doi.org/10.1037/0033-295X.108.2.311

Ochsner, K. N., Bunge, S. A., Gross, J. J., & Gabrieli, J. D. E. (2002). Rethinking feelings: An fMRI study of the cognitive regulation of emotion. *Journal of Cognitive Neuroscience*, *14*(8), 1215–1229. https://doi.org/10.1162/089892902760807212

Ofen, N., Kao, Y.-C., Sokol-Hessner, P., Kim, H., Whitfield-Gabrieli, S., & Gabrieli, J. D. E. (2007). Development of the declarative memory system in the human brain. *Nature Neuroscience*, *10*(9), 1198–1205. https://doi.org/10.1038/nn1950

Olson, D. R. (1996). *Cognitive development: The child's acquisition of diagonality*. Erlbaum. (1970).

Orlian, E. K., & Rose, S. A. (1997). Speed vs. thoroughness in infant visual information processing. *Infant Behavior & Development*, *20*(3), 371–381. https://doi.org/10.1016/s0163-6383(97)90008-4

Owen Blakemore, J. E., Berenbaum, S. A., & Liben, L. S. (2009). *Gender development*. Psychology Press.

Pannevis, M. (1947). Über den Helligkeitsverlauf positiver Nachbilder [On the course of light in positive after-images]. *Ophthalmologica*, *113*(5), 280–289. http://doi.org/10.1159/000300430

Park, H.-D., Correia, S., Ducorps, A., & Tallon-Baudry, C. (2014). Spontaneous fluctuations in neural responses to heartbeats predict visual detection. *Nature Neuroscience*, *17*(4), 612–618. https://doi.org/10.1038/nn.3671

Pathman, T., Samson, Z., Dugas, K., Cabeza, R., & Bauer, P. J. (2011). A "snapshot" of declarative memory: Differing developmental trajectories in episodic and autobiographical memory. *Memory*, *19*(8), 825–835. https://doi.org/10.1080/09658211.2011.613839

Peters, L., & De Smedt, B. (2018). Arithmetic in the developing brain: A review of brain imaging studies. *Developmental Cognitive Neuroscience*, *30*, 265–279. https://doi.org/10.1016/j.dcn.2017.05.002

Philbin, J., Chum, O., Isard, M., Sivic, J., & Zisserman, A. (2007, June 17–22). Object retrieval with large vocabularies and fast spatial matching. *IEEE conference on computer vision and pattern recognition*.

Piaget, J. (1969). *The mechanisms of perception*. Routledge & Kegan Paul.

Piaget, J., & Inhelder, B. (1956). *The child's conception of space*. Routledge & Kegan Paul.

Piaget, J., & Inhelder, B. (1968/2015). *Memory and intelligence*. Psychology Press.

Piatelli-Palmarini, M. (Ed.). (1980). *Language and learning: The Debate between Jean Piaget and Noam Chomsky*. Harvard University Press/Routledge and Kegan Paul.

Pickering, S. J., Gathercole, S. E., Hall, M., & Lloyd, S. A. (2001). Development of memory for pattern and path: Further evidence for the fractionation of visuo-spatial memory. *The Quarterly Journal of Experimental Psychology Section A*, *54*(2), 397–420. https://doi.org/10.1080/713755973

Pinto, Y., Howe, P. D. L., Cohen, M. A., & Horowitz, T. S. (2010). The more often you see an object, the easier it becomes to track it. *Journal of Vision*, *10*(10). https://doi.org/10.1167/10.10.4

Portrat, S., Barrouillet, P., & Camos, V. (2008). Time-related decay or interference-based forgetting in working memory? *Journal of Experimental Psychology: Learning, Memory, and Cognition*, *34*(6), 1561–1564. https://doi.org/10.1037/a0013356

Posner, M. I., Rafal, R. D., Choate, L. S., & Vaughan, J. (1985). Inhibition of return: Neural basis and function. *Cognitive Neuropsychology*, *2*(3), 211–228. https://doi.org/10.1080/02643298508252866

Posner, M. I., & Raichle, M. E. (1997). *Images of mind*. Scientific American Library.

Pratt, J., & Hirshhorn, M. (2003). Examining the time course of facilitation and inhibition with simultaneous onset and offset cues. *Psychological Research*, *67*(4), 261–265. https://doi.org/10.1007/s00426-003-0130-0

Pylyshyn, Z. W. (2001). Is the imagery debate over? If so, what was it about? In E. Dupoux (Ed.), *Language, brain, and cognitive development: Essays in honor of Jacques Mehler* (pp. 59–83). The MIT Press.

Pylyshyn, Z. W. (2004). Some puzzling findings in multiple object tracking: I. Tracking without keeping track of object identities. *Visual Cognition*, *11*(7), 801–822. https://doi.org/10.1080/13506280344000518

Pylyshyn, Z. W. (2007). *Things and places*. MIT Press.

Pylyshyn, Z. W., & Storm, R. W. (1988). Tracking multiple independent targets: Evidence for a parallel tracking mechanism. *Spatial Vision*, *3*(3), 179–197. https://doi.org/10.1163/156856888X00122

Rao, S. C., Rainer, G., & Miller, E. K. (1997). Integration of what and where in the primate prefrontal cortex. *Science*, *276*(5313), 821–824. https://doi.org/10.1126/science.276.5313.821

Richardson, C., Anderson, M., Reid, C. L., & Fox, A. M. (2011). Neural indicators of error processing and intraindividual variability in reaction time in 7 and 9 year-olds. *Developmental Psychobiology*, *53*(3), 256–265. https://doi.org/10.1002/dev.20518

Riggio, L., Bello, A., & Umiltà, C. (1998). Inhibitory and facilitatory effects of cue onset and offset. *Psychological Research*, *61*(2), 107–118. https://doi.org/10.1007/s004260050017

Robertson, I. H., Hogg, K., & McMillan, T. M. (1998). Rehabilitation of unilateral neglect: Improving function by contralesional limb activation. *Neuropsychological Rehabilitation*, *8*(1), 19–29. https://doi.org/10.1080/713755556

Rogoff, B., & Waddell, K. J. (1982). Memory for information organized in a scene by children from two cultures. *Child Development*, *53*(5), 1224–1228. https://doi.org/10.2307/1129009

Rose, S. A., Jankowski, J. J., & Feldman, J. F. (2002). Speed of processing and face recognition at 7 and 12 months. *Infancy*, *3*(4), 435–455. https://doi.org/10.1207/s15327078in0304_02

Rovee-Collier, C. K. (1993). The capacity for long-term memory in infancy. *Current Directions in Psychological Science*, *2*, 130–135. https://doi.org/10.1111/1467-8721.ep10772618

Rovee-Collier, C. K., Hayne, H., & Colombo, M. (2001). *The development of implicit and explicit memory*. Benjamins.

Samuel, A. G., & Weiner, S. (2001). Attentional consequences of object appearance and disappearance. *Journal of Experimental Psychology: Human Perception and Performance*, *27*(6), 1433–1451. https://doi.org/10.1037/0096-1523.27.6.1433

Schneider, W. (1986). The role of conceptual knowledge and metamemory in the development of organizational processes in memory. *Journal of Experimental Child Psychology*, *42*(2), 218–236. https://doi.org/10.1016/0022-0965(86)90024-X

Schumann-Hengsteler, R., Strobl, M., & Zoelch, C. (2004). Temporal memory for locations: On the coding of spatiotemporal information in children and adults. In G. L. Allen (Ed.), *Human spatial memory. Remembering where* (pp. 101–124). Erlbaum.

Shiffrin, R. M., & Atkinson, R. C. (1969). Storage and retrieval processes in long-term memory. *Psychological Review*, *76*, 179–193. https://doi.org/10.1037/h0027277

Shimi, A., & Scerif, G. (2017). Towards an integrative model of visual short-term memory maintenance: Evidence from the effects of attentional control, load, decay, and their interactions in childhood. *Cognition*, *169*, 61–83. https://doi.org/10.1016/j.cognition.2017.08.005

Siegler, R. S., & Crowley, K. (1991). The microgenetic method: A direct means for studying cognitive development. *American Psychologist*, *46*, 606–620. https://doi.org/10.1037/0003-066X.46.6.606

Silverman, I., Choi, J., & Peters, M. (2007). The hunter-gatherer theory of sex differences in spatial abilities: Data from 40 countries. *Archives of Sexual Behavior*, *36*(2), 261–268. https://doi.org/10.1007/s10508-006-9168-6

Smith, L. B., Yu, C., & Pereira, A. F. (2011). Not your mother's view: The dynamics of toddler visual experience. *Developmental Science*, *14*(1), 9–17. https://doi.org/10.1111/j.1467-7687.2009.00947.x

Sommer, V. R., Mount, L., Weigelt, S., Werkle-Bergner, M., & Sander, M. C. (2021). Memory specificity is linked to repetition effects in event-related potentials across the lifespan. *Developmental Cognitive Neuroscience*, *48*. https://doi.org/10.1016/j.dcn.2021.100926

Spelke, E. S. (2005). Sex differences in intrinsic aptitude for mathematics and science: A critical review. *American Psychologist*, *60*, 950–958. https://doi.org/10.1037/0003-066X.60.9.950

Spencer, J. P., & Hund, A. M. (2003). Developmental continuity in the processes that underlie spatial recall. *Cognitive Psychology*, *47*(4), 432–480. https://doi.org/10.1016/S0010-0285(03)00099-9

Stansbury, D. E., Naselaris, T., & Gallant, J. L. (2013). Natural scene statistics account for the representation of scene categories in human visual cortex. *Neuron*, *79*(5), 1025–1034. https://doi.org/10.1016/j.neuron.2013.06.034

Stiles, J., & Tada, W. L. (1996). Developmental change in children's analysis of spatial patterns. *Developmental Psychology, 32*(5), 951. https://doi.org/10.1037/0012-1649.32.5.951

Suárez-Pellicioni, M., Prado, J., & Booth, J. R. (2023). Neurocognitive mechanisms underlying multiplication and subtraction performance in adults and skill development in children: a scoping review. *Current Opinion in Behavioral Sciences, 48*, article 101228. https://doi.org/10.1016/j.cobeha.2022.101228

Towse, J. N., & Hitch, G. J. (1995). Is there a relationship between task demand and storage space in tests of working memory capacity? *The Quarterly Journal of Experimental Psychology Section A, 48*(1), 108–124. https://doi.org/10.1080/14640749508401379

Towse, J. N., Hitch, G. J., & Hutton, U. (2002). On the nature of the relationship between processing activity and item retention in children. *Journal of Experimental Child Psychology, 82*(2), 156–184. https://doi.org/10.1016/S0022-0965(02)00003-6

Treisman, A. (2006). Object tokens, binding and visual memory. In H. D. Zimmer, A. Mecklinger, & U. Lindenberger (Eds.), *Handbook of binding and memory* (pp. 315–338). Oxford University Press.

Treisman, A., & Zhang, W. (2006). Location and binding in visual working memory. *Memory and Cognition, 34*, 1704–1719. https://doi.org/10.3758/BF03195932

Tresch, M. C., Sinnamon, H. M., & Seamon, J. G. (1993). Double dissociation of spatial object visual memory: Evidence from selective interference in intact human subjects. *Neuropsychologica, 31*(3), 211–219. https://doi.org/10.1016/0028-3932(93)90085-E

Tse, P., Kohler, P., & Reavis, E. (2010). Attention modulates perceptual rivalry within after-images. *Journal of Vision, 10*(7), 194–194. https://doi.org/10.1167/10.7.194

Tulving, E., & Thomson, D. M. (1973). Encoding specificity and retrieval processes in episodic memory. *Psychological Review, 80*(5), 352–373. https://doi.org/10.1037/h0020071

Tyler, N., Miles, H. L., Karadag, B., & Rogers, G. (2019). An updated picture of the mental health needs of male and female prisoners in the UK: Prevalence, comorbidity, and gender differences. *Social Psychiatry and Psychiatric Epidemiology, 54*(9), 1143–1152. https://doi.org/10.1007/s00127-019-01690-1

Underwood, B. J. (1945). The effect of successive interpolations on retroactive and proactive inhibition. *Psychological Monographs, 59*(3), i-33. https://doi.org/10.1037/h0093547

Uttal, D. H., & Chiong, C. (2004). Seeing space in more than one way: Children's use of higher order patterns in spatial memory and cognition. In G. L. Allen (Ed.), *Human spatial memory: Remembering where* (pp. 125–142). Lawrence Erlbaum Associates Publishers.

Uttal, D. H., Meadow, N. G., Tipton, E., Hand, L. L., Alden, A. R., Warren, C., & Newcombe, N. S. (2013). The malleability of spatial skills: A meta-analysis of training studies. *Psychological Bulletin, 139*(2), 352–402. https://doi.org/10.1037/a0028446

Uttal, D. H., Sotelo, J., & Shah, P. (2022). Development of working memory and spatial representation: How are they related? In M. L. Courage & N. Cowan (Eds.), *The development of memory in infancy and childhood* (3rd ed.). Taylor and Francis.

van Koppen, M. V. (2018). Criminal career dimensions of juvenile- and adult-onset offenders. *Journal of Developmental and Life-Course Criminology, 4*(1), 92–119. https://doi.org/10.1007/s40865-017-0074-5

Vergauwe, E., & Cowan, N. (2015). Working memory units are all in your head: Factors that influence whether features or objects are the favored units. *Journal of Experimental Psychology: Learning, Memory, and Cognition, 41*(5), 1404–1416. https://doi.org/10.1037/xlm0000108

Vinter, A., & Marot, V. (2007). The development of context sensitivity in children's graphic copying strategies. *Developmental Psychology*, *43*(1), 94–110. https://doi.org/10.1037/0012-1649.43.1.94

West, G. L., Kurdi, V., Fouquet, C., Schachar, R., Boivin, M., Hastings, P., Robaey, P., & Bohbot, V. D. (2021). Differential stress response to psychological and physical stressors in children using spatial versus response-dependent navigation strategies. *Comprehensive Psychoneuroendocrinology*, *6*, 100043. https://doi.org/10.1016/j.cpnec.2021.100043

White, R. E., Prager, E. O., Schaefer, C., Kross, E., Duckworth, A. L., & Carlson, S. M. (2017). The "Batman effect": Improving perseverance in young children. *Child Development*, *88*(5), 1563–1571. https://doi.org/10.1111/cdev.12695

Wilding, J. M. (2003). Attentional difficulties in children: Weakness in executive function or problems in coping with difficult tasks? *British Journal of Psychology*, *94*(4), 427–436. https://doi.org/10.1348/000712603322503015

Wilding, J. M., & Burke, K. (2006). Attentional differences between groups of preschool children differentiated by teacher ratings of attention and hyperactivity. *British Journal of Developmental Psychology*, *24*(2), 283–291. https://doi.org/10.1348/026151005X36029

Wilding, J. M., Munir, F., & Cornish, K. (2001). The nature of attentional differences between groups of children differentiated by teacher ratings of attention and hyperactivity. *British Journal of Psychology*, *92*(2), 357–371. https://doi.org/10.1348/000712601162239

Winkler-Rhoades, N., Carey, S. C., & Spelke, E. S. (2013). Two-year-old children interpret abstract, purely geometric maps. *Developmental Science*, *16*(3), 365–376. https://doi.org/10.1111/desc.12038

Witt, A., & Vinter, A. (2011). Learning implicitly to produce avoided behaviours. *The Quarterly Journal of Experimental Psychology*, *64*(6), 1173–1186. https://doi.org/10.1080/17470218.2010.543283

Wright, R., Thompson, W. L., Ganis, G., Newcombe, N. S., & Kosslyn, S. M. (2008). Training generalized spatial skills. *Psychonomic Bulletin & Review*, *15*(4), 763–771. https://doi.org/10.3758/PBR.15.4.763

Yonelinas, A. P., Hopfinger, J. B., Buonocore, M. H., Kroll, N. E. A., & Baynes, K. (2001). Hippocampal, parahippocampal and occipital-temporal contributions to associative and item recognition memory: An fMRI study. *Neuroreport*, *12*(2), 359–363. https://doi.org/10.1097/00001756-200102120-00035

Zimmer, H. D., Mecklinger, A., & Lindenberger, U. (Eds.). (2006). *Handbook of binding and memory*. Oxford University Press.

PART 2

Visual and Motor Skills in Children with Developmental Problems

8

MOTOR AND VISUAL ABILITIES IN ATTENTION DEFICIT HYPERACTIVITY DISORDER (ADHD)

8.1 Cognitive Functions in Children with ADHD

Symptoms leading to a diagnosis of attention-deficit/hyperactivity disorder (ADHD) are inattention or motor restlessness that cannot be explained by oppositional behaviour, defiance, hostility or failure to understand instructions (American Psychiatric Association, 2013). Symptoms need to occur in more than one setting, that is, at school, at home or with friends, and they need to interfere with academic achievements. There are many direct effects of inattention and hyperactivity such as academic underachievement, criminal careers and more frequent accidents (Faraone et al., 2021). An often successful medication for ADHD is the stimulant methylphenidate that has an effect on the parietal cortex (Liotti et al., 2005) which controls spatial field perception. This medical effect would support the notion that in ADHD, development of spatial field perception (not in an ophthalmologic sense) (see Chapters 3, 5 and 6) may be delayed. We remember that spatial field perception beginning in infancy develops from relatively random and passive perception while being carried to action control around the body at arms' length as a diameter, followed by a more active spatial overview (see Chapter 1).

If children show noticeable ADHD symptoms, the question for developmental psychologists in general is whether they are the result of a developmental delay, or whether development occurred along atypical trajectories (Hulme & Snowling, 2013). Functional magnetic resonance imaging (FMRI) can help to identify the brain areas in children that are typically underactivated given a certain problem. An early neuropsychological account was that children with ADHD would show the typical symptoms of adult neuropsychological patients with frontal lobe damage (Marks et al., 2010), that is, poor impulse control and inattention.

DOI: 10.4324/9780429270604-10

However, in a Go/No-Go task requiring inhibition of pressing a button, male adolescents with childhood ADHD showed greater activation of several gyri in the frontal lobes indicating involvement of working memory, while typically developing children activated a neural network that consisted of the right temporal lobe (object perception), the bilateral cerebellum (automation) and the left hippocampus (verbal spatial long-term memory) (Schulz et al., 2004). Verbal long-term memory would be equivalent to event narratives. The Go-/No-go task consisted of pressing a button when seeing the letters A–E, but not when seeing the target X. The brain activations of boys with ADHD indicate that they try to perceptually keep track of the rare targets. They made more 'commission' errors, that is, they more often pressed a button than required. In contrast, the brain activations of the comparison group suggest that they appeared to activate a response script based on previously experienced tasks, for instance, computer games, while boys with ADHD were responding in the 'here and now'.

Responding in the 'here and now' as if there was no experience to draw on also showed in visual search tasks. Ten-year-old children with ADHD were searching as well as children in a control group when there was one target in a group of dissimilar distracters (see Chapter 6), but they were less successful in the serial search when the target and distracters shared some features (Mullane & Klein, 2008). This was particularly pronounced at the lowest level of complexity – perhaps responses were too fast – and at the highest level of complexity, most likely because this was too challenging. Children with ADHD also show moment-to-moment fluctuation both in their reaction times and in their eye movements, and this was particularly pronounced if a child also showed some co-morbid autistic traits (Seernani et al., 2021). Autistic traits in children are characterised by more passivity and less social initiative (Griffith et al., 1999).

Visual search times improve in adolescents with ADHD (Canu et al., 2022). Their brain substrate of the cerebellum that is responsible for repetition, practice and automation remained smaller, while differences with a control group in another brain region, the caudate nucleus, vanished in adolescence (Castellanos et al., 2002). The caudate nucleus processes correct action schemas and selects appropriate sub-goals based on an evaluation of action-outcomes (Grahn et al., 2008). This would indicate that adolescents with childhood ADHD can become able to progress from what was called sluggishness (McBurnett et al., 2001) to an action- and goal-orientated approach to tasks.

8.2 Fine and Gross Motor Skills in ADHD

It was hypothesised that because ADHD is often comorbid with Developmental Coordination Disorder (DCD) (see Chapter 10), brain abnormalities should be observed in the premotor prefrontal cortex as well as in the dorsal striatum and cerebellum (Castellanos et al., 2006). Surprisingly, Faraone et al. (2021) report a two- to three-fold higher incidence of obesity in ADHD, which makes movement more difficult. Systematic reviews showed that more than half of children with ADHD have difficulties with gross and fine motor skills (Kaiser et al., 2015) and benefit from relatively unspecific motor training (Neudecker et al., 2019; Ziereis & Jansen, 2015). Moreover, when comparing different non-pharmacological treatments such as neurofeedback, cognitive-behavioural therapy, cognitive training and physical exercises, it was physical exercise that was the type of treatment with the highest average effect size (Morris d = 0.93) (Lambez et al., 2020). Of the cognitive processes of attention, inhibition, flexibility and working memory, it was inhibition that showed the largest average effect size (Morris d = 0.68). These results clearly show a strong impact of gross motor development on ADHD.

A large meta-analysis of training studies to reduce hyperactivity and increase academic performance in ADHD did not yield significant effects (Cortese et al., 2015). Inattention could be reduced, though, and it seems that more is known about the different types of attention and their deficits than about a lack of prompt inhibition and the ability to stop.

Medication helps children with a combined ADHD and a DCD diagnosis to improve fine motor skills (Flapper et al., 2006). Flapper et al. showed that children with ADHD–DCD performed more poorly on the manual dexterity subtests, had a poorer quality of handwriting, and drew more rapidly and more fluently, but less accurately than controls in a graphomotor task. With stimulant medication, manual dexterity and quality of handwriting improved, and strokes in the graphomotor task became less fluent but were more accurate. Indeed, when children learn to write by hand, they need to slow down the movement of the hand holding the pen (Lange-Küttner, 1998). Cursive writing as well as drawing produces synchronisation between the parietal and central regions in the brain even in 12-year-olds and adults, while typewriting does not (Ose Askvik et al., 2020).

8.3 Spatial Categories in Children with ADHD

Neural networks function because they (spatially) categorise stimuli. For instance, a neural network can learn to transform a musical notation into the fine motor skills required to play a recorder by categorising the upper and lower holes that the fingers of the right vs. the left hand need to cover, and the pressing down vs. lifting up of the finger movement (Lange-Küttner & Finn, 2008). We have seen in Chapter 5 that in the Common Region Test (Lange-Küttner, 2006), dots were not grouped by four- and five-year-old children but instead each dot was associated with one place. However, following an often short transition period of unsystematic spatial binding, older children grouped pairs of dots within a common region according to the Gestalt principles of similarity and proximity as well as all together if there were no such features. In Chapter 7, the ability to group according to object features was found to be predictive for visual memory. How would spatial categorisation function in children who are not developing in a neurotypical way?

There are only few studies on drawing development in children with ADHD. They were adept in drawing familiar figural objects such as figures and houses (Booth et al., 2003). In the neuropsychological clock drawing test, they were less skilled in drawing the hands of a clock into the circle of numbers for the hours of the day (Ghanizadeh et al., 2013; Lipowska, 2012). A prospective study demonstrated that children with ADHD show deficits in executive function, design fluency, spatial organisation and visual memory (Robinson & Tripp, 2013). Thus, one could hypothesise that children with ADHD would be more likely to show an unsystematic approach to spatial categorisation. Because children with ADHD pay less attention to detail (Song & Hakoda, 2012), a global rather than a local bias and age-appropriate grouping could be expected in their Common Region Test (CRT) drawings.

A comparison of children with ADHD and those with autism spectrum disorder showed clear differences to neurotypically developing control children (Lange-Küttner & Kochhar, 2020). The overwhelming majority of 70% of the children with ADHD showed unsystematic spatial binding of objects. While in the typically developing children, the transition from object-place binding to objects-region binding was correlated with age, with $r = .41$ explaining close to half of the differences between children, in children with ADHD this was not significant. In fact, common region binding was so delayed that it only appeared in some 11-year-olds, while the youngest typically developing child already drew common region at seven years. However, also in the group of typically developing children of the same chronological age (but not of the same mental age who were on average about a year older), more than half were ignoring object features and unsystematically allocating common region.

Unsystematic binding was then further categorised; see Figure 8.1. Type I consisted of binding object-place and objects-region at the same time. As soon as there were one or more object-place bindings in the CRT that were 'under-inclusive' as matching pairs of objects were ignored, it was classified as Type I unsystematic binding. Type II consisted of only objects-region binding, but 'overinclusive' groupings were overriding the salient Gestalt stimulus properties. That is, (a) there was no object-place binding and (b) regions were conceptualised for objects that did not have features in common and/or (c) regions were allocated across rows. In short, both Types I and II are unsystematic spatial bindings, but one includes under-inclusive, while the other includes over-inclusive spatial groupings; see Figure 8.1.

When comparing these two types of unsystematic spatial binding in children with ADHD, there was a significant and clear majority of more than 70% of children showing Type II unsystematic spatial binding where they were drawing an overinclusive common region. However, in these unsystematic coders with ADHD, over-inclusive spatial binding was not different from the gender-matched control children also consisting of mainly boys. This was the case because in the neurotypical control sample, there was an age-constant proportion of unsystematic coders (Lange-Küttner & Kochhar, 2020, Figure 3).

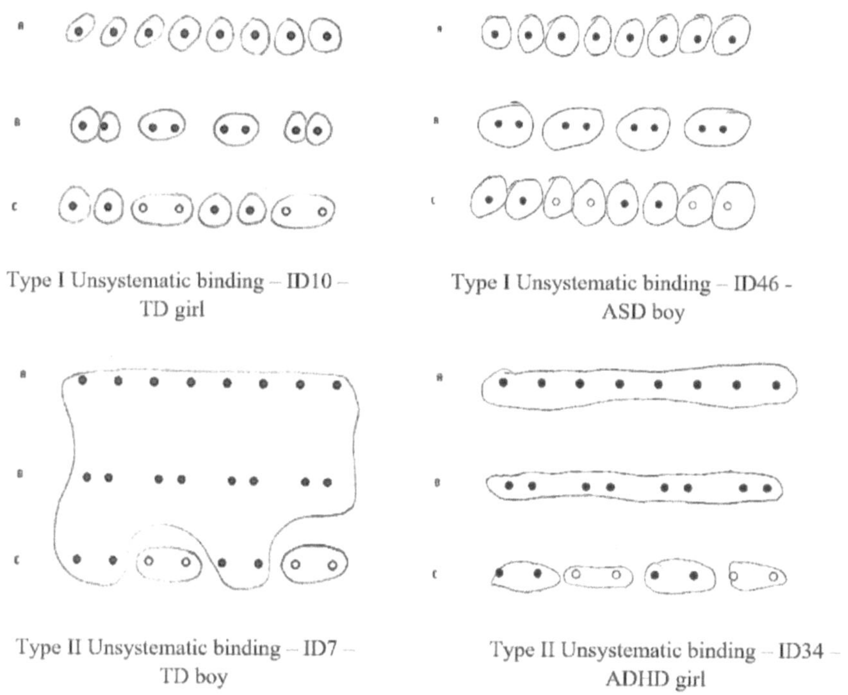

FIGURE 8.1 Types of Unsystematic Coding of Spatial Categories (Lange-Küttner & Kochhar, 2020)

This meant that unsystematic spatial binding was not a transitory phenomenon in this London (UK) sample of children as it had not disappeared even at age 16. There was, however, a trade-off between decreasing unsystematic binding and increasing common region coding from age 11.

In this study, there was a second drawing task assessed, namely the Bender Gestalt Test assessing Bender perception, Bender motor, Bender copying, and Bender recall scores. The CRT and Bender test scores were significantly correlated in typically developing children. In the control sample, the Bender motor score was the only factor actually predicting the developmental transition of the CRT score, but not unsystematic spatial binding. In contrast, the Bender motor score in children with ADHD was highly correlated with unsystematic spatial binding, explaining 76% of common variance. There was a clear split between those children with ADHD with low and those with high Bender motor scores, as only the latter showed the more mature Type II overinclusive CRT binding. Thus, while both children with and without ADHD showed over-inclusive spatial binding, only in those with ADHD were fine motor skills relevant for the global bias.

The question that remains is why most children with ADHD and many without ADHD would show a global bias. There is a bias-variance dilemma (Geman et al., 1992) where special items are identified and individually categorised, but if many individual items are appreciated in this way, processing is easily overburdened and becomes slow. Thus, grouping as many items as possible may be a bias towards faster generalisation where the relevance of 'superficial' features such as similarity in colour or proximity in spatial position are ignored as a criterion for classification. From a Neo-Piagetian developmental perspective, operational intelligence would override, control and direct Gestalt-like fast impressions (Field or F-factor) (Pascual-Leone, 1989; Piaget, 1969). However, categorical judgment and neat classification of input is at the heart of learning, whether in Piaget's concrete and formal-operational thought (Piaget, 1969), or in neural networks (e.g. Elman et al., 1996). If specific object features are ignored, categorisation could be based on a random embrace-all mental disposition.

8.4 Conclusions

While there is clearly a lot more to say about ADHD and thousands of research studies exist, the current chapter focused on some psychological studies in the visuo-spatial and motor domain. Research on spatial categorisation in children with ADHD (Lange-Küttner & Kochhar, 2020) could confirm that a lack of fine motor skills would mediate cognitive performance (Ziereis & Jansen, 2015). However, first, existing data showing whether over-inclusive spatial categorisation also predicts their visual memory is not yet analysed, and second, there is a dire need to investigate their (1) perceived motor competencies and their (2) actual fitness, in addition to (3) fine motor skills (Bondi et al., 2022). Nevertheless, the ability to draw spatial boundaries for spatial regions potentially also facilitates parsing a spatial array with a high density of shapes into clearly delimited smaller regions. This was described as a major problem for children with ADHD who are less prone to restrict their visual attention to a limited spatial area (Shalev & Tsal, 2003). Such lack of visual focus speaks again to the constraints factor in the *Spatial Freedom Theory* but clearly needs more research.

References

American Psychiatric Association. (2013). *Diagnostic and statistical manual of mental disorders: DSM-5*. American Psychiatric Association.

Bondi, D., Robazza, C., Lange-Küttner, C., & Pietrangelo, T. (2022). Fine motor skills and motor control networking in developmental age. *American Journal of Human Biology, 34*(8), e23758. https://doi.org/10.1002/ajhb.23758

Booth, R., Charlton, R., Hughes, C., & Happé, F. (2003). Disentangling weak coherence and executive dysfunction: Planning drawing in autism and attention-deficit/hyperactivity disorder. *Philosophical transactions of the Royal Society of London. Series B, Biological sciences, 358*(1430), 387–392. http://ukpmc.ac.uk/abstract/MED/12639335

Canu, D., Ioannou, C., Müller, K., Martin, B., Fleischhaker, C., Biscaldi, M., Beauducel, A., Smyrnis, N., van Elst, L. T., & Klein, C. (2022). Visual search in neurodevelopmental disorders: Evidence towards a continuum of impairment. *European Child & Adolescent Psychiatry, 31*(8), 1–18. https://doi.org/10.1007/s00787-021-01756-z

Castellanos, F. X., Lee, P. P., Sharp, W., Jeffries, N. O., Greenstein, D. K., Clasen, L. S., Blumenthal, J. D., James, R. S., Ebens, C. L., Walter, J. M., Zijdenbos, A., Evans, A. C., Giedd, J. N., & Rapoport, J. L. (2002). Developmental trajectories of brain volume abnormalities in children and adolescents with attention-deficit/hyperactivity disorder. *JAMA, 288*(14), 1740–1748. https://doi.org/10.1001/jama.288.14.1740

Castellanos, F. X., Sonuga-Barke, E. J. S., Milham, M. P., & Tannock, R. (2006). Characterizing cognition in ADHD: Beyond executive dysfunction. *Trends in cognitive sciences, 10*(3), 117–123. https://doi.org/10.1016/j.tics.2006.01.011

Cortese, S., Ferrin, M., Brandeis, D., Buitelaar, J., Daley, D., Dittmann, R. W., Holtmann, M., Santosh, P., Stevenson, J., Stringaris, A., Zuddas, A., & Sonuga-Barke, E. J. S. (2015). Cognitive training for attention-deficit/yyperactivity disorder: Meta-analysis of clinical and neuropsychological outcomes from randomized controlled trials. *Journal of the American Academy of Child & Adolescent Psychiatry, 54*(3), 164–174. https://doi.org/10.1016/j.jaac.2014.12.010

Elman, J. L., Bates, E. A., Johnson, M. H., Karmiloff-Smith, A., Parisi, D., & Plunkett, K. (1996). *Rethinking innateness.* The MIT Press.

Faraone, S. V., Banaschewski, T., Coghill, D., Zheng, Y., Biederman, J., Bellgrove, M. A., Newcorn, J. H., Gignac, M., Al Saud, N. M., Manor, I., Rohde, L. A., Yang, L., Cortese, S., Almagor, D., Stein, M. A., Albatti, T. H., Aljoudi, H. F., Alqahtani, M. M. J., Asherson, P., … Wang, Y. (2021). The world federation of ADHD international consensus statement: 208 evidence-based conclusions about the disorder. *Neuroscience and Biobehavioral Reviews, 128*, 789–818. https://doi.org/10.1016/j.neubiorev.2021.01.022

Flapper, B. C. T., Houwen, S., & Schoemaker, M. M. (2006). Fine motor skills and effects of methylphenidate in children with attention-deficit–hyperactivity disorder and developmental coordination disorder. *Developmental Medicine and Child Neurology, 48*(3), 165–169. https://doi.org/10.1017/S0012162206000375

Geman, S., Bienenstock, E., & Doursat, R. (1992). Neural networks and the bias/variance dilemma. *Neural Computation, 4*(1), 1–58. https://doi.org/10.1162/neco.1992.4.1.1

Ghanizadeh, A., Safavi, S., & Berk, M. (2013). Clock face drawing test performance in children with ADHD. *Basic and Clinical Neuroscience, 4*(1), 50–56.

Grahn, J. A., Parkinson, J. A., & Owen, A. M. (2008). The cognitive functions of the caudate nucleus. *Progress in Neurobiology, 86*(3), 141–155. https://doi.org/10.1016/j.pneurobio.2008.09.004

Griffith, E. M., Pennington, B. F., Wehner, E. A., & Rogers, S. J. (1999). Executive functions in young children with autism. *Child Development, 70*(4), 817–832. 10.1111/1467-8624.00059

Hulme, C., & Snowling, M. J. (2013). *Developmental disorders of language learning and cognition.* Wiley-Blackwell.

Kaiser, M., Schoemaker, M., Albaret, J., & Geuze, R. (2015). What is the evidence of impaired motor skills and motor control among children with attention deficit hyperactivity disorder (ADHD)? Systematic review of the literature. *Research in Developmental Disabilities, 36*, 338–357. https://dx.doi.org/10.1016/j.ridd.2014.09.023

Lambez, B., Harwood-Gross, A., Golumbic, E. Z., & Rassovsky, Y. (2020). Non-pharmacological interventions for cognitive difficulties in ADHD: A systematic review and meta-analysis. *Journal of Psychiatric Research, 120*, 40–55. https://doi.org/10.1016/j.jpsychires.2019.10.007

Lange-Küttner, C. (1998). Pressure, velocity and time in speeded drawing of basic graphic pattern by young children. *Perceptual and Motor Skills, 86*, 1299–1310.

Lange-Küttner, C. (2006). Drawing boundaries: From individual to common region – the development of spatial region attribution in children. *British Journal of Developmental Psychology, 24*(2), 419–427. https://doi.org/10.1348/026151005X50753

Lange-Küttner, C., & Finn, C. (2008). Musical notation and fine motor skills when playing the soprano recorder: Making a neural network lift a finger. In M. Schlesinger, L. Berthouze, & C. Balkenius (Eds.), *Proceedings of the 8th international conference on epigenetic robotics: Modeling cognitive development in robotic systems* (Vol. 139). Lund University Cognitive Studies.

Lange-Küttner, C., & Kochhar, R. (2020). Fine motor skills and unsystematic spatial binding in the common region test: Under-inclusivity in autism spectrum disorder and over-inclusivity in attention-deficit hyperactivity disorder. *Journal of Motor Learning and Development, 8*(3), 544–568. https://doi.org/10.1123/jmld.2019-0033

Liotti, M., Pliszka, S. R., Perez, R., Kothmann, D., & Woldorff, M. G. (2005). Abnormal brain activity related to performance monitoring and error detection in children with ADHD. *Cortex, 41*(3), 377–388. https://doi.org/10.1016/S0010-9452(08)70274-0

Lipowska, M. (2012). Graphomotor functions in ADHD -motor or planning deficit? A microgenetic approach. *Acta Neuropsychologica, 10*(1), 69–80. https://dx.doi.org/10.5604/17307503.995089

Marks, D., Trampush, J., & Chacko, A. (2010). Attention deficit hyperactivity disorder in children and adolescents. In J. Donders & S. J. Hunter (Eds.), *Principles and practice of lifespan developmental neuropsychology*. Cambridge University Press.

McBurnett, K., Pfiffner, L. J., & Frick, P. J. (2001). Symptom properties as a function of ADHD Type: An argument for continued study of sluggish cognitive tempo. *Journal of Abnormal Child Psychology, 29*(3), 207–213. https://doi.org/10.1023/A:1010377530749

Mullane, J. C., & Klein, R. M. (2008). Visual search by children with and without ADHD. *Journal of Attention Disorders, 12*(1), 44–53. https://doi.org/10.1177/1087054707305116

Neudecker, C., Mewes, N., Reimers, A. K., & Woll, A. (2019). Exercise interventions in children and adolescents with ADHD: A systematic review. *Journal of Attention Disorders, 23*(4), 307–324. https://doi.org/10.1177/1087054715584053

Ose Askvik, E., Van der Weel, F. R., & Van der Meer, A. L. H. (2020). The importance of cursive handwriting over typewriting for learning in the classroom: A high-density EEG study of 12-year-old children and young adults. *Frontiers in Psychology, 11*, article 1810. https://doi.org/10.3389/fpsyg.2020.01810

Pascual-Leone, J. (1989). An organismic process model of Witkin's field-dependence-independence. In T. Globerson & T. Zelniker (Eds.), *Cognitive style and cognitive development* (pp. 36–70). Ablex.

Piaget, J. (1969). *The mechanisms of perception*. Routledge & Kegan Paul.

Robinson, T., & Tripp, G. (2013). Neuropsychological functioning in children with ADHD: Symptom persistence is linked to poorer performance on measures of executive and nonexecutive function. *Japanese Psychological Research, 55*(2), 154–167. https://doi.org/10.1111/jpr.12005

Schulz, K. P., Fan, J., Tang, C. Y., Newcorn, J. H., Buchsbaum, M. S., Cheung, A. M., & Halperin, J. M. (2004). Response inhibition in adolescents diagnosed with attention deficit hyperactivity disorder during childhood: An event-related fMRI study. *American Journal of Psychiatry, 161*(9), 1650–1657. https://doi.org/10.1176/appi.ajp.161.9.1650

Seernani, D., Damania, K., Ioannou, C., Penkalla, N., Hill, H., Foulsham, T., Kingstone, A., Anderson, N., Boccignone, G., Bender, S., Smyrnis, N., Biscaldi, M., Ebner-Priemer, U., & Klein, C. (2021). Visual search in ADHD, ASD and ASD + ADHD: Overlapping or dissociating disorders? *European Child & Adolescent Psychiatry, 30*(4), 549–562. https://dx.doi.org/10.1007/s00787-020-01535-2

Shalev, L., & Tsal, Y. (2003). The wide attentional window: A major deficit of children with attention difficulties. *Journal of Learning Disabilities, 36*(6), 517–527. https://doi.org/10.1177/00222194030360060301

Song, Y., & Hakoda, Y. (2012). The interference of local over global information processing in children with attention deficit hyperactivity disorder of the inattentive type. *Brain and Development, 34*(4), 308–317. https://doi.org/10.1016/j.braindev.2011.07.010

Ziereis, S., & Jansen, P. (2015). Effects of physical activity on executive function and motor performance in children with ADHD. *Research in Developmental Disabilities, 38*, 181–191. https://doi.org/10.1016/j.ridd.2014.12.005

9

MOTOR AND VISUAL ABILITIES IN AUTISM SPECTRUM DISORDER (ASD)

9.1 Cognitive Functions in Children with ASD

Childhood autism is no longer differentiated into different sub-groups of Asperger's disorder, pervasive developmental disorder, childhood disintegrative disorder and others, but instead such sub-groups are included in the diagnosis of Autism Spectrum Disorder (ASD) in the *Diagnostic and Statistical Manual of Mental Disorders* (DSM5) (Lai et al., 2013). The most important symptoms are problems in social communication and interaction as well as restricted and repetitive behaviours (Frazier et al., 2012). Childhood autism is on average diagnosed at around 6 years of age even if parents were already concerned when children were about 2 years old (Höfer et al., 2019). Atypical autism or Asperger's was diagnosed on average at 7 to 8 years of age, or even later.

Thus, screening and early diagnosis became an important research focus (Accardo, 2008). Early markers of autism are lack of pretend play (Jarrold, 2003), obsessive repetitive behaviours (McDougle et al., 2008, 2000) and resisting change in routines (Mink, & Mandelbaum, 2006). Moreover, a significant proportion of children with a risk to develop ASD fail to learn to learn to speak in sentences (syntactic structures) (Brynskov et al., 2017) and often give up on speaking altogether (regression, mutism) (Jones et al., 2011). But even when advanced language did develop, delayed syntax development reliably predicted a lack of theory of mind (Paynter & Peterson, 2010). Initially, autism was more often diagnosed in children with fathers in engineering professions than in those with fathers who worked as lawyers, doctors and journalists (Frith et al., 2003), with the former requiring more visual design and fewer verbal skills. Still, even nowadays, parents with autistic traits prefer to select technical toys which do not require as much dialogue as role-playing toys (Lange-Küttner et al., 2019). However, this was only the case if parents had a son rather than a daughter which

DOI: 10.4324/9780429270604-11

coincides with the fact that autism is more prevalent in boys than in girls (Baron-Cohen, 2002).

A language development breakdown in the second year of life may occur even if children with ASD in general show good voice processing (Boucher et al., 2000) and memory for sounds (Bordignon et al., 2015). Children with ASD can relate pictures to meaningful environmental sounds, but not to meaningful words (McCleery et al., 2010). Children with ASD develop a level of theory of mind similar to deaf children (Siegal & Surian, 2012), as they prefer not to listen to language (Kuhl et al., 2005; Paul et al., 2007). Already newborns prefer their mother's language (Moon et al., 1993). Hence, it is quite out of the ordinary that when given a choice between the mother's clear voice and her voice in noise-overlaid conversations like in an open plan office, 5-year-old children with autism preferred the noise-disrupted voice, while same-aged children with learning difficulties and typically developing children preferred to listen to their mother's voice (Klin, 1991). This disinterest was seen as a primary indicator of their social withdrawal.

There was a reduced activation of the insular cortex in children with ASD between 8 and 12 years when a partner in crime defected in the prisoner dilemma game (Edmiston et al., 2015). The insular cortex is an old, deep, multi-functional brain structure (Nieuwenhuys, 2012) that processes hunger, pain and fatigue, but also cognitive control processes (Wu et al., 2019) such as compassion, empathy, taste, perception, motor control, and self-awareness that together encompass nearly all the components of early interactions between mother and child.

Another brain structure that is often found to be relevant in ASD is the amygdala, which belongs to the limbic system and processes emotional arousal (Baron-Cohen et al., 2000). However, while some detected accelerated growth of the amygdala even when matched against overall brain volume (Nordahl et al., 2012), others found that the brain growth was not due to neural growth but because of glial cell proliferation (Aoki et al., 2012). These authors suggest an underactivated 'social brain' consisting of several small brain areas that contribute to ASD in children, but not the cerebellum. We remember that the cerebellum was an important underactivated brain structure in ADHD, so this may be one substrate that is functional in children with ASD and facilitates learning from practice. Still other researchers suggest that disrupted connectivity of the amygdala with frontal and temporal lobes explains ASD symptom severity (Shen et al., 2016).

9.2 Development of Spatial and Motor Abilities in ASD

There were no differences in the A-not-B task (see Chapter 3), when matched for mental age, between neurotypical 2-year-old toddlers and 3½-year-old children with ASD, or children with learning difficulties (Dawson et al., 2002). However, a prospective longitudinal study of toddlers at genetic risk of ASD, because they had a sibling with ASD, assessed infants at one and two years (St. John et al.,

2016). Differences between these groups in visual perception as well as fine and gross motor skills increased with age and also maternal education became more an important factor. The study showed that both infants with ASD and those who were at high risk of being diagnosed with ASD in the future showed no improvement in the amount of A-not-B errors, while those infants with the lowest risk showed increasingly more correct searches. Fine but not gross motor skills had an impact on correct reaches of at-risk children at 12 months, while the reverse was true at 24 months. This may reflect the increasing importance of children's increasing movement radius and sphere of action.

Another longitudinal study with children at risk because of siblings with ASD showed that poor motor skills as toddlers predicted ASD symptom severity at ages 5–7 years, independently of IQ (Leonard et al., 2014). The motor skills were so low that standardised scores could not be determined, but only raw scores were used. Unfortunately, in the Leonard et al. study, only aggregate poor and average motor performance scores were analysed even though both gross and fine motor raw scores were available. Gross and fine motor skills were highly correlated with $.57 < r_s < .69$. The authors suggest that less spatial exploration prevents social contacts and encounters, which in turn leads to reduced social skills as evidenced by lower face processing. Here, a lack of spatial freedom is held responsible for several shortcomings in ASD.

Another test that is frequently used with older children with ASD is the theory of mind (TOM) task (Baron-Cohen, 2000). The core component is the assessment of awareness of deception, but the task is of interest in this context because it also involves a change of object locations. TOM is testing a belief about what somebody may know about where a hidden object was relocated during their absence. This 'cheeky' relocation is already an appropriate task for 3- and 4-year-olds as they talk about thoughts and begin to engage in lies and trickery (Wellman, 2011). In a visual hiding-versus-search task, even in adults search and concealment varied depending on whether a friend or a foe was involved (Anderson et al., 2014).

The social dimension of TOM tasks plays an important role as it involves the knowledge that somebody *could* not know about the new actual location of a hidden object. There are two aspects to object search in children with ASD. On the one hand, they show very delayed development in such false belief tasks (Happé, 1995; Peterson et al., 2005). On the other hand, they are very good at block design (Happé, 1994), at the embedded figures test (Muth et al., 2014) and at visual search, especially in serial search where they detect the target much faster than controls (O'Riordan et al., 2001). They also show more parietal activation in their spatial field perception in interactive tidying-up sessions of blocks (Su et al., 2020). Children with ASD find it easier than typically developing controls to understand the hidden emotions of another child that was the target of abuse (Peterson et al., 2005) when compared to changing perspective, which was more difficult.

Functional MRI showed that the kind of neural networks involved in 13-year-olds' visual search appeared to be very similar, although network activation was stronger in teenagers with ASD (Keehn et al., 2013). However, when in the Keehn et al. study brain regions activated by visual search were compared against those by empty screens with just a fixation star of a similar duration, very clear differences between brain region activations of the two groups emerged, without any overlaps (Keehn et al., 2013, Figure 3A). It appeared that in such intervals between visual search arrays containing a target T and (rotated) Ts, typically developing teenagers were more likely to activate higher-order visual areas responsible for letter perception. In contrast, those with ASD were activating lower-order visual areas that map the visual percept plus the parietal cortex for spatial field perception. This suggests that they were not trying to encode the variety of Ts like the controls, but instead – in a neat split of target (e.g., friend) and distracters (e.g., foe) – controlled the spatially distributed distracters in the array, which is an important ability developing in middle childhood (Buchberger et al., 2023). The occipital and parietal regions remain core regions for the visual exploration network, while other regions become less active during development (Lidzba et al., 2013). Moreover, the activation of the lower visual processing brain region supports the view that persons with ASD use veridical mapping (Mottron et al., 2013) and are more sensitive to first-order rather than to second-order visual information (Simmons et al., 2009), an ability that can prevent them from succumbing to visual illusions (Happé, 1996; but see Ropar & Mitchell, 1999; Ropar & Mitchell, 2001).

A retrospective study of videos of early motor actions of children who were later diagnosed with ASD showed no differences to typically developing children in supine or prone posture, rolling, sitting, crawling, walking and movement abnormalities (Ozonoff et al., 2008). However, another well-controlled study showed significantly lower performance scores for fine and gross motor skills in infants with ASD,independently of whether they were at high risk of ASD by having an older sibling with ASD, or at low risk of ASD by having a typically developing older sibling and no family history of ASD (St. John et al., 2016). As reported above, spatial perseverative responses did not improve between 1 and 2 years (see Chapter 3).

A lack of fine motor skills in children with ASD has an impact at school age. For instance, they showed less smooth movements and significantly greater sizing variability and peak velocity when writing the words *eeee, eeel, eeem, elel* and *emem* on a graphic tablet (Grace et al., 2017). These non-words when handwritten contain loops for the *e*, and arcs for the *m*. Loops are movements that require children to slow down the speed of their pen in order to keep the circular movements of loops apart rather than drawing fast overlapping circles (Lange-Küttner, 1998). The children with ASD also showed less prowess in aiming and catching and were less well-balanced (Grace et al., 2017). Thus, a lack of motor skills continues to have an impact on children with ASD in middle childhood (Torres & Donnellan, 2015).

9.3 Spatial Categories in Children with ASD

In the previous chapter, it was reported that children with ADHD showed a global bias in the Common Region Test (CRT) (Lange-Küttner & Kochhar, 2020). This study also tested a group of children with ASD. It was hypothesised that children with ASD would show a local bias (Happé, 2001), that is, in the CRT, they would be more likely to focus on attributing a place to a single dot rather than an area to pairs of matching dots that were similar in appearance or located in each other's vicinity. Similarity and proximity are two of several Gestalt grouping principles that children with ASD are less likely to consider (Brosnan et al., 2004). Common region is seen as an even higher Gestalt principle as it explicitly overrules intuitive Gestalt organisations in implicit space (Palmer, 1992). Moreover, based on the systematising-empathising hypothesis of Baron-Cohen (2009) that holds that males in the autistic spectrum would be more systematic, we did not predict unsystematic spatial binding in the CRT in children with ASD.

While 4- to 5-year-old children systematically attribute one place to each individual dot in the CRT (Lange-Küttner, 2006), children with ASD do not systematically create object-place units. Instead, they showed more unsystematic spatial binding. Figure 8.1 in Chapter 8 showed the type of unsystematic coding of a boy (ID 46) with ASD who attributed a common region to proximally located dots but not to dots that were of a similar appearance. There were 74% of children with ASD who showed significantly more unsystematic spatial binding than either of both control groups of children matched for mental age (MA) or chronological age (CA), see Figure 9.1a.

When it was further analysed whether Type I (object-place and objects-region) or Type II (objects-region and overinclusive objects-region) would be the more frequent unsystematic response, almost all children with ASD (92.9%) showed Type I unsystematic binding with occasional object-place bindings, while this was rare in the control groups. Thus, the Type I unsystematic spatial binding with object-place units clearly indicates an unsystematic local bias in the CRT.

When children with ASD were allocating regions unsystematically, they would create some object-place units in their region allocation, while children with ADHD would allocate large regions to a greater number of dots than the matched Gestalt pairs. Type I of unsystematic coding showed under-inclusivity as Gestalt dots were not included in a common region, and this was more likely in children with ASD, while Type II of unsystematic coding was overinclusive as dots were included in the common region whose features did not match, see Figure 9.1b. Type I coding of children with ASD was significantly different to that of typically developing controls, while Type II coding of children with ADHD was not.

Fine motor skills in children with ASD were lowest, compared to both children with ADHD and typically developing children, but because they were near floor level, there was no correlation. Instead, children with ASD showed

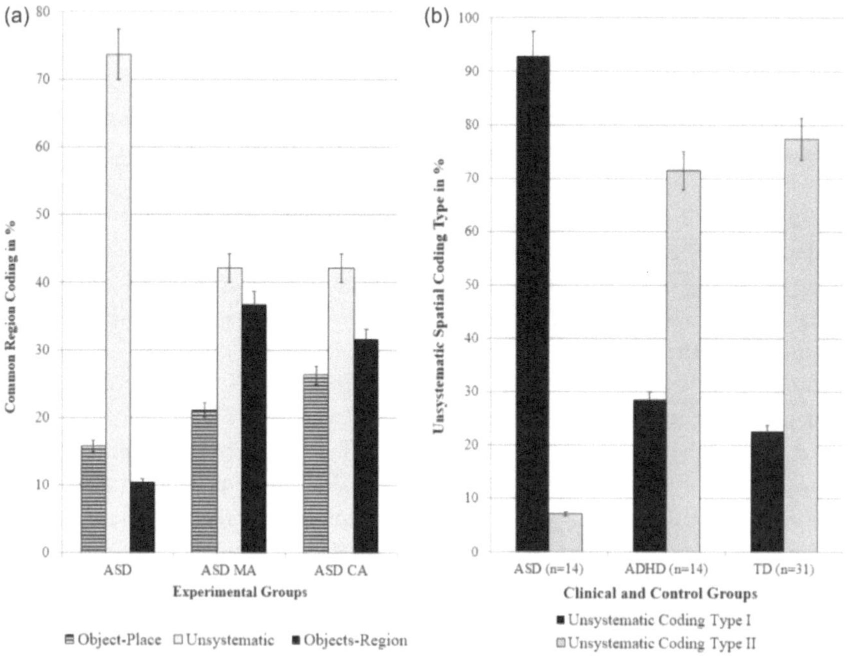

FIGURE 9.1 Unsystematic Common Region Allocation in Children with ASD (Lange-Küttner & Kochhar, 2020)

a significant correlation between their non-verbal spatial reasoning score in the Raven's Coloured Progressive Matrices Test and unsystematic spatial binding, $r = -.64$. In both children with ADHD, $r = -.01$, $p = .968$, and in typically developing children, $r = .09$, $p = .439$, this correlation was near-zero. Children with ASD had significantly lower average Raven scores than both MA and CA control groups, even though their verbal intelligence was equal.

Thus, at least for children, we find here a clear rejection of the hypothesis that in the autistic spectrum more systematic thinking would occur (Baron-Cohen et al., 2009). A very high percentage of two-thirds to three-quarters of children with ASD and ADHD were engaging in unsystematic spatial binding. The age range of these two groups with special needs was large, between 7 and 15 years. Hence, it can be concluded that behind the detail-focused style of children with ASD (Happé & Frith, 2006) lies some immature spatial coding that continues to create object-place units and does not use spatial grouping and binding in a consistent fashion. The new explanation here is that while the local bias usually refers to a detail that can be a visual feature that is directly visible without thinking about the place, to allocate a single object to one single place is creating an integrated individual spatial unit. Object-place units can be seen in level 2 of the *Spatial Field Model* in Figure 3.4 on the emergence of locations.

Moreover, another important aspect of the unsystematic common region binding of children with ASD is that other factors can intervene and interfere with consistent spatial coding, for instance, a lack of fine motor skills and logical spatial reasoning.

Children with ASD also do not show grouping strategies when encoding for memory (Williams et al., 2006). A well-controlled study shows that they have the most severe problems with spatial span and design memory, but there are also significant problems with picture memory, sentence memory and story memory. Moreover, the control groups showed three types of memory, visual, verbal and learning, with clear factor loadings of the nine subtests except spatial span (a 'Finger Windows' test that is similar to the Corsi Test) that did not load highly on any of the three factors. In the ASD group, there was one main factor with loadings of all sub-tests except for picture memory and story memory, which loaded on a second factor that could be labelled as episodic memory. Also other research with the Autism Diagnostic Observation Module (ADOS) monkey cartoon story test showed a significant problem in ASD with producing a cohesive narrative (Canfield et al., 2016). When Williams et al. forced a two-factor instead of the three-factor model on the control group data, the second factor had high loadings of sentence memory and letter memory, which would rather point to reading as a source of memory rather than picture stories. Thus, William et al.'s (2006) factorial structure analyses clearly show that visual memory is the medium for children with ASD, even if these memory scores were lower, while reading is the medium for the memory of the neurotypical control group.

9.4 Mapping vs. Stages: Early Visual Realism in Children with ASD

As described in Chapter 5, there is a clear-cut stage concept that has been described and replicated in almost all publications on drawing development. The first stage is incidental realism (fortuitous realism) where no realistic depiction is intended but post-hoc explanations provide a label (Freeman & Adi-Japha, 2008). The second stage is failed realism, where an intention to draw a recognisable object is present but the meaning of the graphic form is not identifiable. The third stage is intellectual realism when children selectively draw what they know about objects and efficiently use schemata to depict familiar, canonical object views (Davis, 1985). Finally, the fourth stage is visual realism where recognisable renditions are produced which agree with the optical impression and potentially can depict any view of an object (Lange-Küttner et al., 2002). The important point of visual realism is that 3D objects are mapped on a 2D drawing surface (Lange-Küttner & Reith, 1995; Reith & Dominin, 1997) and their schematic outline of a template is changed to a visually realistic contour (Reith, 1988; Willats, 1997). Learning to draw visually realistically takes several years until children are about 10 years old (Lange-Küttner et al., 2002). But when 7-year-olds were presented with real models that had perspective as a built-in design property thus appealing to their intellectual realism, children were mapping and sketching the converging diagonals in their drawings (Lange-Küttner, 2014) (see Chapter 5).

However, the universality of this stage concept was challenged by a rather slim book by Selfe (1977) about an autistic girl with the name of Nadia who could draw visually realistically like an adult artist at 3½ years of age and skipped all drawing stages, see Figure 9.2. Her mother was in hospital treatment and the grandmother caring for her only spoke Russian. It was during this time that Nadia produced her most impressive visually realistic drawings. Because her language ability had faltered, she received speech therapy. Thereafter, Nadia had lost her ability to sketch in a visually realistic fashion and began to draw 'age-appropriate' intellectually realistic pictures using typical templates to produce schematic drawings. She ended up permanently hospitalised in her adult life (Selfe, 2011). Such a fate is not inevitable, as other gifted children with autism became successful artists (Pring et al., 1997).

Is it a requirement that language takes a backseat when drawing visually realistically? A study with 5-, 8- and 11-year-old children as well as children with ASD and learning difficulties (LD) investigated intellectual and visually realistic picture choices (Ropar & Mitchell, 2001). Intellectual realism would show if children were selecting the colour yellow according to what they knew about

FIGURE 9.2 Visual Realism in 4-year-old Nadia's Drawing of a Horse (Selfe, 1977)

the object but not according to how the actual blue model banana looked like. Five-year-olds and children with ASD – but not children with LD – were more likely to choose the natural colour yellow when making a choice whether blue or yellow best matched a blue banana. This stereotypical choice was rarely made by 8- and 11-year-olds, who selected the arbitrary surface colour blue in the case of the blue banana. Blue was selected because it matched the image of the banana, not the identity of a banana as such (see also Robinson et al., 1994). To answer the question whether language takes a backseat in visual realism, in this study, one needs to compare the children with ASD and those with ASD but with intact language ability (Asperger). There was a gradually decreasing likelihood with increasing language ability (ASD 61%; ASD + Asperger 44%; Asperger 31%, 8- and 11-year-olds 17%) to prefer colour identity over the blue appearance. Thus, this study suggests that language ability actually supports visual realism.

Not all children with autism have the talent to draw visually realistic pictures at an early age (Charman & Baron-Cohen, 1993). The ability to recognise an object in visual noise in the Embedded Figures Test (EFT) (Witkin et al., 1971) and the arrangement of blocks to form a cohesive pattern were more predictive for visually realistic drawing than the diagnosis of ASD (Drake, 2013). Good identification of an embedded shape in the EFT also predicts talent (Chamberlain et al., 2013; Chamberlain & Wagemans, 2015), particularly in boys (Lange-Küttner & Ebersbach, 2013) as it involves contour detection in a visually messy, noisy context. Talent is indicated by an intense interest and an easy uptake of the production rules that must precede extensive practice (Winner & Drake, 2013). In gifted children who draw visually realistically, the local bias was associated with a tendency towards repetitive behaviours as assessed with the parent questionnaire Childhood Asperger Syndrome Test (CAST) (Drake et al., 2010). Adults drawing visually realistically with a local bias did not show autistic traits (Drake & Winner, 2011). In adults, savant expertise can become superior even in comparison to a professorial level (Pring & Hermelin, 2002). Thus, in adults, the autistic spectrum may be blurry, but in children, savant talents may come at a cost.

9.5 Conclusions

There is no medication for autistic symptoms as antipsychotic medications are not recommended and are often discontinued because of adverse side effects (Alfageh et al., 2019). Mood stabilisers and anti-depressants can be given for emotion regulation to prevent aggressive outbursts in situations that are not predictable (Anagnostou et al., 2007). However, because associative learning is intact and the cognitive mechanisms behind many of the ASD symptoms are now known, training may be a viable alternative to medication. For instance, although about a quarter of children with ASD did not complete a cognitive training, those who did improved in working memory, cognitive flexibility, attention and even in the behavioural ratings by their parents (Vries et al., 2015). Also, the where-system could be trained by requiring children with ASD to track a moving target on a computer screen with a digital pen, where children with ASD learnt as well as typically developing children albeit on a lower level (Sparaci et al., 2015). Finally, also language, literacy and social computerised trainings of children with ASD are quite successful, even though these successes sometimes do not transfer into more naturalistic environments (Wass & Porayska-Pomsta, 2014). Hence, it becomes clear that the research about the cognitive origins of ASD is beginning to bear fruit, as it is also helpful in therapeutic approaches.

References

Accardo, P. J. (2008). Autism spectrum disorders: A conceptualization. In B. K. Shapiro & P. J. Accardo (Eds.), *Autism frontiers: Clinical issues and innovations* (pp. 207–219). Paul H Brookes Publishing.

Alfageh, B. H., Wang, Z., Mongkhon, P., Besag, F. M. C., Alhawassi, T. M., Brauer, R., & Wong, I. C. K. (2019). Safety and tolerability of antipsychotic medication in individuals with autism spectrum disorder: A systematic review and meta-analysis. *Pediatric Drugs*, *21*(3), 153–167. https://doi.org/10.1007/s40272-019-00333-x

Anagnostou, E., Fisher, A. J., & Hollander, E. (2007). Treatment of autism with anticonvulsants and mood stabilizers. In E. Hollander & E. Anagnostou (Eds.), *Clinical manual for the treatment of autism* (pp. 81–97). American Psychiatric Publishing, Inc.

Anderson, G. M., Foulsham, T., Nasiopoulos, E., Chapman, C. S., & Kingstone, A. (2014). Hide and seek: The theory of mind of visual concealment and search. *Attention, Perception, & Psychophysics*, *76*(4), 907–913. https://doi.org/10.3758/s13414-014-0675-6

Aoki, Y., Kasai, K., & Yamasue, H. (2012). Age-related change in brain metabolite abnormalities in autism: A meta-analysis of proton magnetic resonance spectroscopy studies. *Translational Psychiatry*, *2*(1), article e69. https://doi.org/10.1038/tp.2011.65

Baron-Cohen, S. (2000). Theory of mind and autism: A review. *International Review of Research in Mental Retardation*, *23,* 169–184. https://doi.org/10.1016/S0074-7750(00)80010-5

Baron-Cohen, S. (2002). The extreme male brain theory of autism. *Trends in Cognitive Sciences*, *6*(6), 248–254. https://doi.org/10.1016/S1364-6613(02)01904-6

Baron-Cohen, S., Ashwin, E., Ashwin, C., Tavassoli, T., & Chakrabarti, B. (2009). Talent in autism: Hyper-systemizing, hyper-attention to detail and sensory hypersensitivity. *Philosophical Transactions of the Royal Society B: Biological Sciences*, *364*(1522), 1377–1383. https://doi.org/10.1098/rstb.2008.0337

Baron-Cohen, S., Ring, H. A., Bullmore, E. T., Wheelwright, S., Ashwin, C., & Williams, S. C. R. (2000). The amygdala theory of autism. *Neuroscience & Biobehavioral Reviews*, *24*(3), 355–364. https://doi.org/10.1016/S0149-7634(00)00011-7

Bordignon, S., Endres, R. G., Trentini, C. M., & Bosa, C. A. (2015). Memory in children and adolescents with autism spectrum disorder: A systematic literature review. *Psychology & Neuroscience*, *8*(2), 211–245. https://doi.og/10.1037/h0101059

Boucher, J., Lewis, V., & Collis, G. M. (2000). Voice processing abilities in children with autism, children with specific language impairments, and young typically developing children. *Journal of Child Psychology and Psychiatry*, *41*(7), 847–857. https://doi.og/10.1111/1469-7610.00672

Brosnan, M. J., Scott, F. J., Fox, S., & Pye, J. (2004). Gestalt processing in autism: Failure to process perceptual relationships and the implications for contextual understanding. *Journal of Child Psychology and Psychiatry, 45*(3), 459–469. https://doi.org/10.1111/j.1469-7610.2004.00237.x

Brynskov, C., Eigsti, I.-M., Jørgensen, M., Lemcke, S., Bohn, O.-S., & Krøjgaard, P. (2017). Syntax and morphology in Danish-Speaking children with autism spectrum disorder. *Journal of Autism and Developmental Disorders, 47*(2), 373–383. https://doi.org/10.1007/s10803-016-2962-7

Buchberger, E., Brandmaier, A. M., Lindenberger, U., Werkle-Bergner, M., & Ngo, C. (2023). The process structure of memory abilities in early and middle childhood (registered report). *PsyArXiv Preprints*. https://doi.org/10.31234/osf.io/p84a6

Canfield, A. R., Eigsti, I.-M., Marchena, A. d., & Fein, D. (2016). Story goodness in adolescents with Autism Spectrum Disorder (ASD) and in optimal outcomes from ASD. *Journal of Speech, Language, and Hearing Research, 59*(3), 533–545. https://doi.org/10.1044/2015_JSLHR-L-15-0022

Chamberlain, R., McManus, I. C., Riley, H., Rankin, Q., & Brunswick, N. (2013). Local processing enhancements associated with superior observational drawing are due to enhanced perceptual functioning, not weak central coherence. *The Quarterly Journal of Experimental Psychology, 66*(7), 1448–1466. https://doi.org/10.1080/17470218.2012.750678

Chamberlain, R., & Wagemans, J. (2015). Visual arts training is linked to flexible attention to local and global levels of visual stimuli. *Acta Psychologica, 161*, 185–197. https://doi.org/10.1016/j.actpsy.2015.08.012

Charman, T., & Baron-Cohen, S. (1993). Drawing development in autism: The intellectual to visual realism shift. *British Journal of Developmental Psychology, 11*(2), 171–185. https://doi.org/10.1111/j.2044-835X.1993.tb00596.x

Davis, A. (1985). Conflict between canonicality and array-specificity in young children's drawings. *British Journal of Developmental Psychology, 3*(4), 363–372. https://doi.org/10.1111/j.2044-835X.1985.tb00988.x

Dawson, G., Munson, J., Estes, A., Osterling, J., McPartland, J., Toth, K., Carver, L., & Abbott, R. (2002). Neurocognitive function and joint attention ability in young children with autism spectrum disorder versus developmental delay. *Child Development, 73*(2), 345–358. https://doi.org/10.1111/1467-8624.00411

Drake, J. E. (2013). Is superior local processing in the visuospatial domain a function of drawing talent rather than autism spectrum disorder? *Psychology of Aesthetics, Creativity, and the Arts*, 7(2), 203–209. https://doi.org/10.1037/a0030636

Drake, J. E., Redash, A., Coleman, K., Haimson, J., & Winner, E. (2010). 'Autistic' local processing bias also found in children gifted in realistic drawing. *Journal of Autism and Developmental Disorders, 40*(6), 762–773. https://doi.org/10.1007/s10803-009-0923-0

Drake, J. E., & Winner, E. (2011). Realistic drawing talent in typical adults is associated with the same kind of local processing bias found in individuals with ASD. *Journal of Autism and Developmental Disorders, 41*(9), 1192–1201. https://doi.org/10.1007/s10803-010-1143-3

Edmiston, E. K., Merkle, K., & Corbett, B. A. (2015). Neural and cortisol responses during play with human and computer partners in children with autism. *Social Cognitive and Affective Neuroscience, 10*(8), 1074–1083. https://doi.org/10.1093/scan/nsu159

Frazier, T. W., Youngstrom, E. A., Speer, L., Embacher, R., Law, P., Constantino, J., Findling, R. L., Hardan, A. Y., & Eng, C. (2012). Validation of proposed DSM-5 criteria for autism spectrum disorder. *Journal of the American Academy of Child & Adolescent Psychiatry, 51*(1), 28–40.e23. https://doi.org/10.1016/j.jaac.2011.09.021

Freeman, N. H., & Adi-Japha, E. (2008). Pictorial intention, action and interpretation. In C. Lange-Küttner & A. Vinter (Eds.), *Drawing and the non-verbal mind: A life-span perspective* (pp. 104–120). Cambridge University Press.

Frith, U., Hill, E. L., Hippler, K., & Klicpera, C. (2003). A retrospective analysis of the clinical case records of autistic psychopaths diagnosed by Hans Asperger and his team at the University Children's Hospital, Vienna. *Philosophical Transactions of the Royal Society of London. Series B: Biological Sciences, 358*(1430), 291–301. https://doi.org/10.1098/rstb.2002.1197

Grace, N., Enticott, P. G., Johnson, B. P., & Rinehart, N. J. (2017). Do handwriting difficulties correlate with core symptomology, motor proficiency and attentional behaviours? *Journal of Autism and Developmental Disorders, 47*(4), 1006–1017. https://doi.org/10.1007/s10803-016-3019-7

Happé, F. G. E. (1994). Wechsler IQ profile and theory of mind in autism: A research note. *Journal of Child Psychology and Psychiatry, 35*(8), 1461–1471. https://doi.org/10.1111/j.1469-7610.1994.tb01287.x

Happé, F. G. E. (1995). The role of age and verbal ability in the theory of mind task performance of subjects with autism. *Child Development, 66*(3), 843–855. https://doi.org/10.2307/1131954

Happé, F. G. E. (1996). Studying weak central coherence at low levels: Children with autism do not succumb to visual illusions: A research note. *Journal of Child Psychology and Psychiatry, 37*(7), 873–877. https://doi.org/10.1111/j.1469-7610.1996.tb01483.x

Happé, F. G. E. (2001). Social and nonsocial development in autism: Where are the links? In J. A. Burack, T. Charman, N. Yirmiya, & P. R. Zelazo (Eds.), *The development of autism: Perspectives from theory and research* (pp. 237–253). Lawrence Erlbaum Associates Publishers.

Happé, F. G. E., & Frith, U. (2006). The weak coherence account: Detail-focused cognitive style in autism spectrum disorders. *Journal of Autism and Developmental Disorders, 36*(1), 5–25. https://doi.org/10.1007/s10803-005-0039-0

Höfer, J., Hoffmann, F., Kamp-Becker, I., Poustka, L., Roessner, V., Stroth, S., Wolff, N., & Bachmann, C. J. (2019). Pathways to a diagnosis of autism spectrum disorder in Germany: A survey of parents. *Child and Adolescent Psychiatry and Mental Health, 13*(1), article 16. https://doi.org/10.1186/s13034-019-0276-1

Jarrold, C. (2003). A review of research into pretend play in autism. *Autism, 7*(4), 379–390. https://doi.org/10.1177/1362361303007004004

Jones, C. R. G., Pickles, A., Falcaro, M., Marsden, A. J. S., Happé, F., Scott, S. K., Sauter, D., Tregay, J., Phillips, R. J., Baird, G., Simonoff, E., & Charman, T. (2011). A multimodal approach to emotion recognition ability in autism spectrum disorders. *Journal of Child Psychology and Psychiatry, 52*(3), 275–285. https://doi.org/10.1111/j.1469-7610.2010.02328.x

Keehn, B., Shih, P., Brenner, L. A., Townsend, J., & Müller, R.-A. (2013). Functional connectivity for an "Island of sparing" in autism spectrum disorder: An fMRI study of visual search. *Human Brain Mapping, 34*(10), 2524–2537. https://doi.org/10.1002/hbm.22084

Klin, A. (1991). Young autistic children's listening preferences in regard to speech: A possible characterization of the symptom of social withdrawal. *Journal of Autism and Developmental Disorders, 21*(1), 29–42. https://doi.org/10.1007/BF02206995

Kuhl, P. K., Coffey-Corina, S., Padden, D., & Dawson, G. (2005). Links between social and linguistic processing of speech in preschool children with autism: Behavioral and electrophysiological measures. *Developmental Science, 8*(1), F1–F12. https://doi.org/10.1111/j.1467-7687.2004.00384.x

Lai, M.-C., Lombardo, M. V., Chakrabarti, B., & Baron-Cohen, S. (2013). Subgrouping the autism "spectrum": Reflections on DSM-5. *PLoS Biology, 11*(4), article e1001544. https://doi.org/10.1371/journal.pbio.1001544

Lange-Küttner, C. (1998). Pressure, velocity and time in speeded drawing of basic graphic patterns by young children. *Perceptual and Motor Skills, 86*(3, Pt 2), 1299–1310. https://doi.org/10.2466/pms.1998.86.3c.1299

Lange-Küttner, C. (2006). Drawing boundaries: From individual to common region--The development of spatial region attribution in children. *British Journal of Developmental Psychology, 24*(2), 419–427. https://doi.org/10.1348/026151005x50753

Lange-Küttner, C., & Ebersbach, M. (2013). Girls in detail, boys in shape: Gender differences when drawing cubes in depth. *British Journal of Psychology, 104*(3), 413–437. https://doi.org/10.1111/bjop.12010

Lange-Küttner, C. (2014). Do drawing stages really exist? Children's early mapping of perspective. *Psychology of Aesthetics, Creativity, and the Arts, 8*(2), 168–182. https://doi.org/10.1037/a0036199

Lange-Küttner, C., Kerzmann, A., & Heckhausen, J. (2002). The emergence of visually realistic contour in the drawing of the human figure. *British Journal of Developmental Psychology, 20*(3), 439–463. https://doi.org/10.1348/026151002320620415

Lange-Küttner, C., & Kochhar, R. (2020). Fine motor skills and unsystematic spatial binding in the common region test: Under-inclusivity in autism spectrum disorder and over-inclusivity in attention-deficit hyperactivity disorder. *Journal of Motor Learning and Development, 8*(3), 544–568. https://doi.org/10.1123/jmld.2019-0033

Lange-Küttner, C., Korte, M. A., & Stamouli, C. (2019). Parents' autistic personality traits and sex-biased family ratio determine the amount of technical toy choice. *Frontiers in Psychology, 10*, article 2101. https://doi.org/10.3389/fpsyg.2019.02101

Lange-Küttner, C., & Reith, E. (1995). The transformation of figurative thought: Implications of Piaget and Inhelder's developmental theory for children's drawings. In C. Lange-Küttner & G. V. Thomas (Eds.), *Drawing and looking* (pp. 75–92). Harvester Wheatsheaf/Pearson.

Lange-Küttner, C., Kerzmann, A., & Heckhausen, J. (2002). The emergence of visually realistic contour in the drawing of the human figure. *British Journal of Developmental Psychology, 20*(3), 439–463. https://doi.org/10.1348/026151002320620415

Leonard, H. C., Bedford, R., Charman, T., Elsabbagh, M., Johnson, M. H., Hill, E. L., Baron-Cohen, S., Bolton, P., Chandler, S., Garwood, H., Holmboe, K., & Hudry, K. (2014). Motor development in children at risk of autism: A follow-up study of infant siblings. *Autism, 18*(3), 281–291. https://doi.org/10.1177/1362361312470037

Lidzba, K., Ebner, K., Hauser, T. K., & Wilke, M. (2013). Complex visual search in children and adolescents: Effects of age and performance on fMRI activation. *PLOS ONE, 8*(12), article e85168. https://doi.org/10.1371/journal.pone.0085168

McCleery, J. P., Ceponiene, R., Burner, K. M., Townsend, J., Kinnear, M., & Schreibman, L. (2010). Neural correlates of verbal and nonverbal semantic integration in children with autism spectrum disorders. *Journal of Child Psychology and Psychiatry, 51*(3), 277–286. https://doi.org/10.1111/j.1469-7610.2009.02157.x

McDougle, C. J., Hulvershorn, L. A., Erickson, C. A., Stigler, K. A., & Posey, D. J. (2008). Autistic syndromes. In J. S. Abramowitz, D. McKay, & S. Taylor (Eds.), *Clinical handbook of obsessive-compulsive disorder and related problems* (pp. 238–256). Johns Hopkins University Press.

McDougle, C. J., Kresch, L. E., & Posey, D. J. (2000). Repetitive thoughts and behavior in pervasive developmental disorders: Treatment with serotonin reuptake inhibitors. *Journal of Autism and Developmental Disorders, 30*(5), 427–435. https://doi.org/10.1023/a:1005551523657

Mink, J. W., & Mandelbaum, D. E. (2006). Stereotypies and repetitive behaviors: Clinical assessment and brain basis. In R. Tuchman & I. Rapin (Eds.), *Autism: A neurological disorder of early brain development* (pp. 68–78). Mac Keith Press.

Moon, C., Cooper, R. P., & Fifer, W. P. (1993). Two-day-olds prefer their native language. *Infant Behavior & Development, 16*(4), 495–500. https://doi.org/10.1016/0163-6383(93)80007-U

Mottron, L., Bouvet, L., Bonnel, A., Samson, F., Burack, J. A., Dawson, M., & Heaton, P. (2013). Veridical mapping in the development of exceptional autistic abilities. *Neuroscience & Biobehavioral Reviews, 37*(2), 209–228. https://doi.org/10.1016/j.neubiorev.2012.11.016

Muth, A., Hönekopp, J., & Falter, C. M. (2014). Visuo-spatial performance in Autism: A meta-analysis. *Journal of Autism and Developmental Disorders, 44*(12), 3245–3263. https://doi.org/10.1007/s10803-014-2188-5

Nieuwenhuys, R. (2012). The insular cortex: A review. In M. A. Hofman & D. Falk (Eds.), *Progress in brain research* (Vol. 195, pp. 123–163). Elsevier.

Nordahl, C. W., Scholz, R., Yang, X., Buonocore, M. H., Simon, T., Rogers, S., & Amaral, D. G. (2012). Increased rate of amygdala growth in children aged 2 to 4 years with autism spectrum disorders: A longitudinal study. *Archives of General Psychiatry, 69*(1), 53–61. https://doi.org/10.1001/archgenpsychiatry.2011.145

O'Riordan, M. A., Plaisted, K. C., Driver, J., & Baron-Cohen, S. (2001). Superior visual search in autism. *Journal of Experimental Psychology: Human Perception and Performance, 27*(3), 719–730. https://doi.org/10.1037/0096-1523.27.3.719

Ozonoff, S., Young, G. S., Goldring, S., Greiss-Hess, L., Herrera, A. M., Steele, J., Macari, S., Hepburn, S., & Rogers, S. J. (2008). Gross motor development, movement abnormalities, and early identification of autism. *Journal of Autism and Developmental Disorders, 38*(4), 644–656. https://doi.org/10.1007/s10803-007-0430-0

Palmer, S. E. (1992). Common region: A new principle of perceptual grouping. *Cognitive Psychology, 24*(3), 436–447. https://doi.org/10.1016/0010-0285(92)90014-S

Paul, R., Chawarska, K., Fowler, C., Cicchetti, D., & Volkmar, F. (2007). "Listen my children and you shall hear": Auditory preferences in toddlers with autism spectrum disorders. *Journal of Speech, Language, and Hearing Research, 50*(5), 1350–1364. https://doi.org/10.1044/1092-4388(2007/094)

Paynter, J., & Peterson, C. (2010). Language and ToM development in autism versus Asperger syndrome: Contrasting influences of syntactic versus lexical/semantic maturity. *Research in Autism Spectrum Disorders, 4*(3), 377–385. https://doi.org/10.1016/j.rasd.2009.10.005

Peterson, C. C., Wellman, H. M., & Liu, D. (2005). Steps in theory-of-mind development for children with deafness or autism. *Child Development, 76*(2), 502–517. https://doi.org/10.1111/j.1467-8624.2005.00859.x

Pring, L., & Hermelin, B. (2002). Numbers and letters: Exploring an autistic savant's unpractised ability. *Neurocase, 8*(4), 330–337. https://doi.org/10.1076/neur.8.3.330.16193

Pring, L., Hermelin, B., Buhler, M., & Walker, I. (1997). Native savant talent and acquired skill. *Autism, 1*(2), 199–214. https://doi.org/10.1177/1362361397012006

Reith, E. (1988). The development of use of contour lines in children's drawings of figurative and non-figurative three-dimensional models. *Archives de Psychologie, 56*(217), 83–103.

Reith, E., & Dominin, D. (1997). The development of children's ability to attend to the visual projection of objects. *British Journal of Developmental Psychology, 15*(2), 177–196. https://doi.org/10.1111/j.2044-835X.1997.tb00733.x

Robinson, E. J., Nye, R., & Thomas, G. V. (1994). Children's conceptions of the relationship between pictures and their referents. *Cognitive Development, 9*(2), 165–191. https://doi.org/10.1016/0885-2014(94)90002-7

Ropar, D., & Mitchell, P. (1999). Are individuals with autism and Asperger's syndrome susceptible to visual illusions? *Journal of Child Psychology and Psychiatry, 40*(8), 1283–1293. https://doi.org/10.1111/1469-7610.00544

Ropar, D., & Mitchell, P. (2001). Susceptibility to illusions and performance on visuospatial tasks in individuals with autism. *Journal of Child Psychology and Psychiatry, 42*(4), 539–549. https://doi.org/10.1111/1469-7610.00748

Selfe, L. (1977). *Nadia - A case of extraordinary drawing ability in an autistic child.* Academic Press.

Selfe, L. (2011). *Nadia revisited: A longitudinal study of an autistic savant.* Psychology Press.

Shen, M. D., Li, D. D., Keown, C. L., Lee, A., Johnson, R. T., Angkustsiri, K., Rogers, S. J., Müller, R.-A., Amaral, D. G., & Nordahl, C. W. (2016). Functional connectivity of the amygdala is disrupted in preschool-aged children with autism spectrum disorder. *Journal of the American Academy of Child & Adolescent Psychiatry, 55*(9), 817–824. https://doi.org/10.1016/j.jaac.2016.05.020

Siegal, M., & Surian, L. (2012). *Access to language and cognitive development.* Oxford University Press.

Simmons, D. R., Robertson, A. E., McKay, L. S., Toal, E., McAleer, P., & Pollick, F. E. (2009). Vision in autism spectrum disorders. *Vision Research, 49*(22), 2705–2739. https://doi.org/10.1016/j.visres.2009.08.005

Sparaci, L., Formica, D., Lasorsa, F. R., Mazzone, L., Valeri, G., & Vicari, S. (2015). Untrivial pursuit: Measuring motor procedures learning in children with autism. *Autism Research, 8*(4), 398–411. https://doi.org/10.1002/aur.1455

St. John, T., Estes, A. M., Dager, S. R., Kostopoulos, P., Wolff, J. J., Pandey, J., Elison, J. T., Paterson, S. J., Schultz, R. T., Botteron, K., Hazlett, H., & Piven, J. (2016). Emerging executive functioning and motor development in infants at high and low risk for autism spectrum disorder. *Frontiers in Psychology,* 7, article 1016. https://doi.org/10.3389/fpsyg.2016.01016

Su, W.-C., Culotta, M., Mueller, J., Tsuzuki, D., Pelphrey, K., & Bhat, A. (2020). Differences in cortical activation patterns during action observation, action execution, and interpersonal synchrony between children with or without autism spectrum disorder (ASD): An fNIRS pilot study. *PLOS ONE, 15*(10), ArtID e0240301. https://dx.doi.org/10.1371/journal.pone.0240301

Torres, E. B., & Donnellan, A. M. (2015). Editorial for research topic "Autism: The movement perspective". *Frontiers in Integrative Neuroscience, 9.* https://doi.org/10.3389/fnint.2015.00012

Vries, M., Prins, P. J. M., Schmand, B. A., & Geurts, H. M. (2015). Working memory and cognitive flexibility-training for children with an autism spectrum disorder: A randomized controlled trial. *Journal of Child Psychology and Psychiatry, 56*(5), 566–576. https://doi.org/10.1111/jcpp.12324

Wass, S. V., & Porayska-Pomsta, K. (2014). The uses of cognitive training technologies in the treatment of autism spectrum disorders. *Autism, 18*(8), 851–871. https://doi.org/10.1177/1362361313499827

Wellman, H. M. (2011). Developing a theory of mind. In U. Goswami (Ed.), *The Wiley-Blackwell handbook of childhood cognitive development* (2nd ed., pp. 258–284). Wiley-Blackwell.

Willats, J. (1997). *Art and representation: New principles in the analysis of pictures*. Princeton University Press.

Williams, D. L., Goldstein, G., & Minshew, N. J. (2006). The profile of memory function in children with autism. *Neuropsychology, 20*(1), 21–29. https://doi.org/10.1037/0894-4105.20.1.21

Winner, E., & Drake, J. E. (2013). The rage to master: The decisive role of talent in the visual arts. In S. B. Kaufman & S. B. Kaufman (Eds.), *The complexity of greatness: Beyond talent or practice.* (pp. 333–365). Oxford University Press.

Witkin, H. A., Oltman, P. K., Raskin, E., & Karp, S. A. (1971). *Manual for embedded figures test, children's embedded figures test, and group embedded figures test*. Consulting Psychologists Press.

Wu, T., Wang, X., Wu, Q., Spagna, A., Yang, J., Yuan, C., Wu, Y., Gao, Z., Hof, P. R., & Fan, J. (2019). Anterior insular cortex is a bottleneck of cognitive control. *NeuroImage, 195*, 490–504. https://doi.org/10.1016/j.neuroimage.2019.02.042

10

MOTOR AND VISUAL ABILITIES IN DEVELOPMENTAL COORDINATION DISORDER (DCD)

10.1 Diagnosis of Children with DCD

Dyspraxia and developmental coordination disorder (DCD) are the most often diagnosed motor disorders when special needs assessments are made (Gibbs et al. 2007). However, they are both aspects of ataxia, translated from the Greek meaning 'without order' (Lawerman et al., 2020). Ataxia can be hereditary (Milne et al., 2023). Ataxia originates from disturbed, mainly subcortical neural functioning, namely in the basal ganglia, the cerebellum, the thalamus and in the sensory afferents. Especially the cerebellum has been held responsible for motor coordination since the 19th century, and the neural networks within this brain substrate are seen as important for motor learning (Strata, 2009) (cerebellar hypothesis). Ataxia can, for instance, cause overshoot of movements, impaired gait and posture, intention tremor, oculomotor dysfunction and speech abnormalities. The latter is called oral apraxia, which causes difficulties of language articulation, especially in the slow speech of Broca's, but not in Wernicke's aphasia (De Renzi et al., 1966). Typical difficulties occur in drawing and writing, everyday activities such as dressing and shoelace tying, as well as sports activities (Schoemaker et al., 2013). The Beery drawing test (Beery, 2004; Doney et al., 2016) can be evaluated by expert judgment (Bieber et al., 2016) or by computer algorithm (Tabatabaey-Mashadi et al., 2015). However, there are many tests available to diagnose DCD (Bieber et al., 2016). Different from the Beery Visual Motor Integration Test (BVMI), the M-ABC test provides age norms for manual dexterity, aiming and catching, as well as balance, and thus it is often used for a diagnosis of DCD. Unfortunately, in research studies, the cut-off point for a diagnosis of DCD, for instance when using the Movement Assessment Battery for Children (MABC-2) (Brown & Lalor, 2009), can range from the lower 5th

DOI: 10.4324/9780429270604-12

to the lower 20th percentile (Adams et al., 2014) which can make results more difficult to compare.

Problems in visual-motor integration (VMI) in children can be caused by prenatal alcohol exposure (PAE) (Johnston et al., 2019). Moderate deficits in VMI due to PAE can be endemic in remote and/or disadvantaged communities where children also underperform academically (Doney et al., 2016). Pre-term birth and low birth weight can also be a cause of DCD, with symptoms still occurring in school-age children (Edwards et al., 2011). Sex differences in the incidence of DCD are not reported (e.g. Doney et al., 2016), unlike in ADHD and ASD (see Chapters 8 and 9). However, large-scale longitudinal research of teenagers with multiple waves of assessment between 10 and 12 years of age showed that boys with DCD engage more in free play activities so that the gap with typically developing peers diminishes, while in girls with DCD it increases (Cairney et al., 2010). This should be noted because children with DCD are typically excluded from sports lessons in school (O'Dea et al., 2021). Extra physical activity does improve almost all abilities in children and adolescents with DCD: Dynamic and static balance, running, jumping, walking, pacing, object reception and passing, eye-hand coordination, reaction time, agility, endurance, but also strengthening of the muscles and improved bone strength (Zaragas et al., 2023).

DCD is often co-morbid with other developmental challenges. In a rare differential diagnostic study, 7- to 13-year-old children with ADHD and ASD and typically developing control children were compared on several tests (De Francesco et al., 2023), a DCD questionnaire (DCDQ), the MABC2, the sensori-motor subtests of NEPSY-II, and a kinematic analysis of a reach-to-drop task. Principal component analysis of the tests revealed (a) a Caregiver Report factor, (b) an object interception and balance factor, (c) a motor imitation factor, (d) a fine motor skills factor, (e) a velocity and acceleration factor, (f) a timing of two movements factor and (g) a wrist control factor. The caregiver report and the motor imitation factor predicted the autism diagnosis with 87.2% accuracy. The caregiver report and the fine motor skills factor correctly predicted 73.5% of the ADHD diagnoses. It is very likely that the caregiver report captured the social dimension of the diagnoses. Such results make it clear that motor skills are an important dimension to consider also in children with other diagnoses than DCD.

Dysgraphia is a relatively recent diagnosis that concerns only fine motor skills and VMI for children who find it difficult to draw and write (O'Hare & Brown, 1989a, 1989b). Drawing is a precursor to handwriting (Lange-Küttner, 1998; Tabatabaey-Mashadi et al., 2015), but the onset of writing also changes many drawing parameters (Lange-Küttner, 2008). Possible problems in handwriting are the relative size of component strokes in letters, an incorrect number of strokes (missing or additional strokes) or an incorrect orientation or curvature of these strokes. On the word and sentence level, problems are inter-letter spacing (too far apart or superimposed) and a failure to write along a straight line

(Biotteau et al., 2019). Beginning writers are best supported by detailed instructions about the stroke sequence (Berninger et al., 1997).

Motor imagery training can override entrenched habits because it provides a model of the end-state-comfort (Bhoyroo et al., 2019; Steenbergen et al., 2020) (see Chapter 4). A sword-task showed that children with DCD planned less for end-state comfort, but this was specific to the object, and did not occur when grasping a bar (Adams et al., 2016). There is evidence that some words can also imply high body–object interaction: The words tool, drum or rope imply more motor imagery and are thus more easily accessible for 5-year-old kindergarten children in a manual pointing response than words that have no such connotations, for instance, words like cloud, cliff or dorm (Suggate & Stoeger, 2017).

The incidence of dysgraphia seems to spontaneously decline in the primary school years (Overvelde & Hulstijn, 2011). Sensori-motor based VMI training did not yield improvements in speed and accuracy of handwriting in 6- to 8-year-old primary school beginners (Chang & Yu, 2014): A computer-assisted training programme where children copied the word from a computer screen onto paper was pitched against the more often used VMI training (visual and haptic perception). Children who trained on the computer for six weeks daily for 45 minutes needed significantly fewer pauses between writing the next word, could write faster, and applied more pressure than controls. In contrast, those who had received VMI training fared worse than the control group with no intervention – even if VMI training is the most often used remediation method for dysgraphia (Chang & Yu, 2014). From this study it can be concluded that writing engages a supervised neural network that ideally has a perfect model available against which one's deviations can be controlled. It is well known from drawing research that mapping a model yields better results than drawing from memory (Chen & Cook, 1984): Line drawing models yielded better results in 6- to 8-year-olds than photographs and real 3D models (see Chapter 5).

10.2 Fine and Gross Motor Skills in Children with DCD

Traditionally, fine and gross motor skills are seen as separate clusters of abilities (Bondi et al., 2022). For DCD, however, a more general motor functioning deficit is suggested by a study that systematically compared fine and gross motor skills (Schott et al., 2016). A trail-making task was given to 7- to 10-year-old children with and without DCD in two conditions: In one condition, they were making trails between circles with arrows indicating direction, or between numbers, or between a combination of numbers and letters on paper. In a second condition, they were walking the trails in a lab. Sequencing, shifting and extended search patterns were measured. Interestingly, the slopes showed that the kind of object that denoted a location in the trail-making tasks was important, similar to feature and conjunction visual search tasks (see Chapter 6). Task difficulty gradually increased: It was easiest when only circles with arrows were to be connected, more difficult when distinct numbered locations were to be connected, and most difficult when locations denoted by numbers and letters were to be alternately connected. In short, both groups of children, drawing or walking, took more time, the more specific the points were that needed to be connected. This confirms again that the object itself can carry a rich informational load while the representation of locations as such is sparse (Lange-Küttner et al., 2023) (see Chapter 7). Children with DCD were slower, but otherwise the same kind of task effects were found as in typically developing children; see Figure 10.1. There were three times as many children with DCD (17.6% vs. 5.1%) who were overweight; they exercised less and were less likely to be a member of

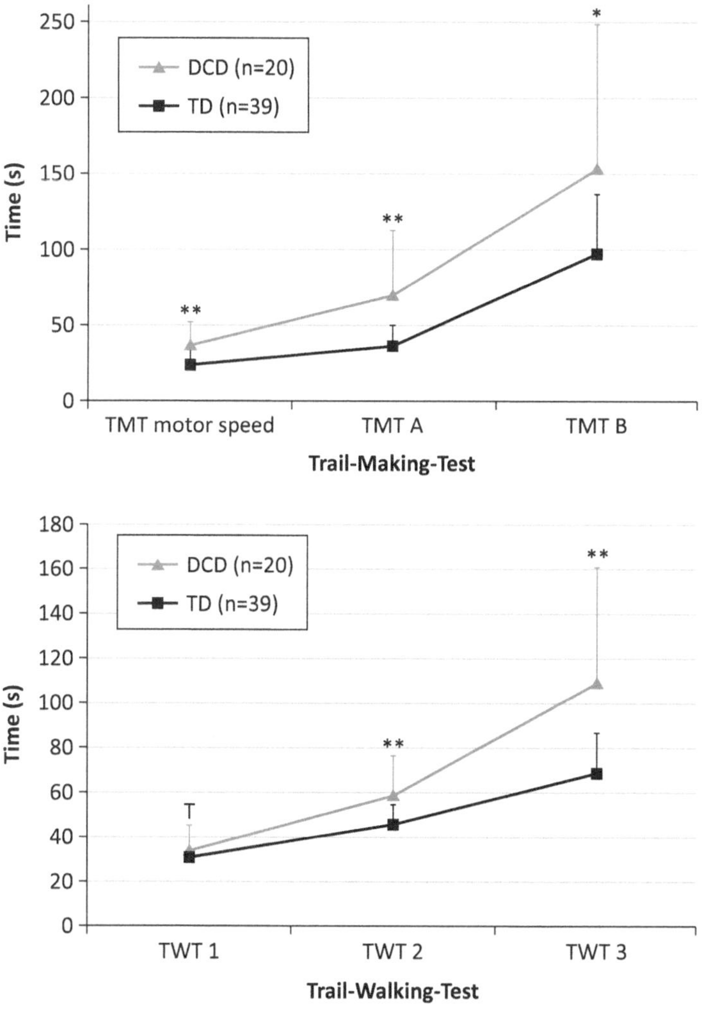

FIGURE 10.1 Increase of Trail-Making Time in Conjunction Search (Drawing/Walking) (Schott et al., 2016)

a sports club. However, there was no difference in the kind of slope and thus task difficulty whether children were creating the trail on paper (fine motor skills) when body weight would not matter, or walking the trail (gross motor skills) when body weight could have mattered.

The question then arises whether children with DCD were slow in spatial *perception* (Bonifacci, 2004). This question was tested with two groups of 11-year-old teenagers with and without DCD (Tsai et al., 2012). In a matching-to-sample task, they had to identify whether two halves of a spatial array presented simultaneously without a delay, or in a sequence after a delay of three or six seconds, were matching. It was very clear that the two groups showed comparable visual perception, that is, they were able to combine the two half arrays into one array and judge whether the full array was the same or different when no delay was involved. However, after a delay, the teenagers with DCD showed slower reaction times and lower accuracy. A lower P3 amplitude in the parietal cortex could be observed in the 11-year-olds with DCD during responses after delays. This unequivocally showed that spatial memory was impaired. However, because only event-related potentials were used for assessment, subcortical processes could not be assessed and the cerebellar activation could not be measured. It would also be interesting to know about a hippocampal contribution, as spatial memory was affected.

That spatial perception is not impaired was also shown in a study that investigated attention disengagement in 7- to 8-year-old children with DCD and a 3- to 8-year-old comparison group (Wilmut et al., 2007). They were sitting in a booth with snowmen arranged in a half-circle on either side of the child, each with a light underneath. When a light was switched on, the child was supposed to either just look at the lit-up snowman, or to hit the snowman with a small plastic hammer. Eye and motor movements were measured with a Vicon motion capture system. There was no difference in eye movements between the groups, except that the 3-year-olds were slower to initiate looking. However, when disengagement of attention from a central fixation point and reaching out were analysed, the 7- to 8-year-olds with DCD significantly differed from the typically developing children of the same age, but their performance was indistinguishable from that of 3- and 4-year-old children. This strongly suggests a developmental delay in visual attention and reaching but not in visual perception. What was specific to children with DCD in this study was that they made nearly twice as many errors compared to any of the other age groups when the central green light remained on display at the onset of one of the red peripheral lights (signal overlap) while hitting a snowman (Wilmut et al., 2007). This increased error rate showed a large effect of visual distractibility during action that was not a developmental delay and thus would not be likely to disappear with age. However, for now it seems that an interference theory of motor learning is less in favour than an error-correction network (inverse motor learning) in addition to a feedforward learning network (Wolpert et al., 1998). However, another suggestion was that an early estimate of the motor output is used as a predictor during a reach in a feedforward neural network (Smith predictor model) because error corrections would not be timely enough to be considered (Miall & Wolpert, 1996).

10.3 Motor Learning in Children with DCD

We will see that indeed timeliness is one major problem in motor learning. While the above studies used many trials, for instance, Schott et al. (2016) overall tested 45 to 75 locations, Tsai et al. (2012) used three consecutive blocks of 108 trials each, and Wilmut et al. (2007) tested 48 trials, motor learning over the repeated trials was not analysed. A more differentiated version of the cerebellar hypotheses of DCD could assume that motor learning in DCD does not occur in repeated trials, hence the motor sequence does not become automatised and thus stays vulnerable to interference. In a study of Wilson et al. (2003) who analysed implicit spatial array learning in children with and without DCD, the motor learning hypothesis could not be confirmed. There were five blocks each with 100 trials. The array consisted of four lined-up squares. A star was to be mapped on the four squares with the keyboard keys for D, F, G and H. Blocks one to four consisted of repeating sequences of positions, but the fifth block was in a random sequence. Neither the 8- to 12-year-old children with DCD nor their comparison peers were aware of the repetition. Thus, no conscious prediction could be used and if the children improved, this was due to implicit motor learning. Only few errors (less than 5%) were made by either group. The reaction times showed that children with DCD were slower but showed the same learning slope by also accelerating their reaction times during the repeated trials and showing increased latencies when the sequence was random in the fifth block, see Figure 10.2. This

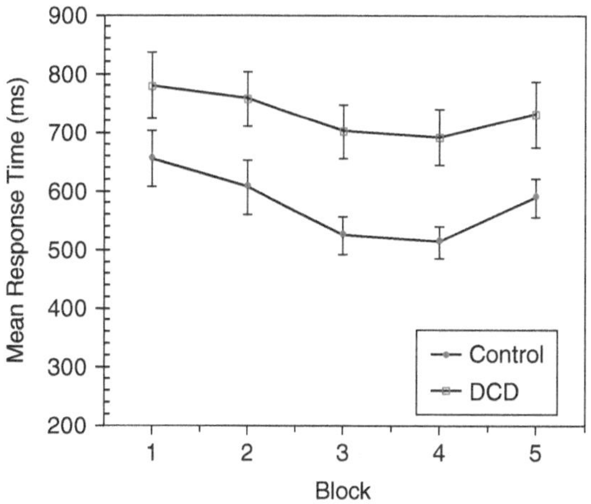

FIGURE 10.2 Motor Learning in Children with DCD (Wilson et al., 2003)

clearly showed that children with DCD can automatise their responses just like typically developing children, who were reported by their parents to engage about three times more in moving about than the DCD group (Wilson et al., 2003).

If the ability to predict events would also determine motor control, the insertion of some uncertainty should lead to deterioration of such button presses. In fact, the ability to cope with uncertainty in sequences of four left-and-right button presses is not well developed even at age 11 (Hentschel et al., 2022; Lange-Küttner et al., 2012). An increased error rate by nearly two-thirds compromised an ability that was already mastered at ceiling when only 15% of a randomly false visual red-green feedback signal was given. The ability to evaluate a false feedback signal improves well into adolescence (Lange-Küttner et al., 2021). Regrettably, no study of children with DCD is currently available using this task. However, there were two factors that ameliorated the performance deterioration. The first factor was a high non-verbal reasoning score (Hentschel et al., 2022; Lange-Küttner et al., 2021) and the second factor was an auditory verbal explanation received after each false feedback (Hentschel et al., 2023).

A false auditory signal during motor activity during a stepping training was used with 13- to 14-year-old adolescents with and without DCD (Al-Yahya et al., 2023). The signal was an auditory Stroop where the words 'high' and 'low' were said with low and high pitch, respectively. In a dual-task paradigm, the teenagers had to respond to the pitch but not the word while stepping. It turned out that both groups benefited from a 7-week training, both with respect to mobility as well as coping with the ambiguous signal. However, the brain responses were different, which showed particularly at a follow-up test three months later. While the fit group had improved in the dual task and showed relatively stronger brain activations in the left ventrolateral prefrontal (LVPFC) cortex, the DCD group showed relatively stronger activations in the right ventrolateral prefrontal (RVPFC) cortex, with overall activation the same. The two halves of the prefrontal cortex process different information: The LVPFC deals with the semantic, conceptual dimensions (Badre & Wagner, 2007), while the RVPFC attends to the necessity of behavioural inhibition (Levy & Wagner, 2011). Figure 10.3 illustrates the contribution of the VPFC to the what-and-where system in the brain (from Sakagami & Pan, 2007, p. 231). The VPFC receives information from the posterior brain in a topographic map and controls and selects the input into the motor cortices (Hagler & Sereno, 2006).

That children with DCD appear to prioritise holistic inhibition rather than semantic analysis of distracters could perhaps explain their often-found reduced speed in motor learning (Piek et al., 2007; Prunty et al., 2013; Wilson et al., 2003). It could also be the case that unanalysed distracting language input may arrive in the vestibular system that is located just behind the ear canal (Day & Fitzpatrick, 2005) and thus could positively or negatively affect the internal state of balance and posture. In fact, the more rarely diagnosed developmental dyspraxia in children not only implies early motor deficits in drawing, but involves

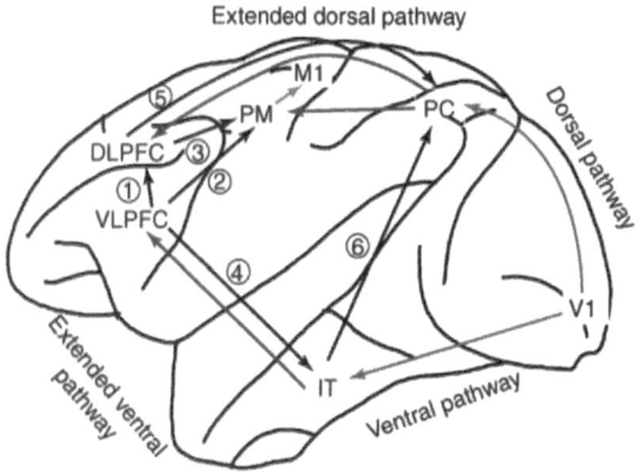

FIGURE 10.3 Binding of the Motor Cortex into the What-and-Where System (from Sakagami & Pan, 2007, p. 231). *Note*: PC = parietal cortex, PM = premotor cortex (PM), DLPFC = dorsolateral prefrontal cortex, VLPFC = ventrolateral pathway, IT = inferotemporal cortex, V1 = primary visual cortex.

speech and language problems more often than in children with dyslexia where problems were found to be limited to phonology (Waber et al., 2021).

10.4 Conclusions

Developmental coordination disorder was in former times labelled clumsiness. This was a fairly global label without much consideration of the different components of motor control and the factors that would impact and cause the lack of coordination (Hulme & Lord, 1986). Much research since these early times has shown that especially the planning of motor tasks and the speed of motor execution is responsible for problems in DCD. However, speeded movement tasks with children are usually only carried out in sports athletics. It is known that video games can accelerate reaction times in children, so would they also work as a training for children and teenagers with DCD? Children with DCD were said to be unable to select a game and claimed that lack of time, illness, technical difficulties and boredom would prevent them from improving their condition (Howie et al., 2017; Howie et al., 2016). Moreover, children nevertheless perceived their physical skills to be improved after 16 weeks of training with active video games, even though this could not be measured by the tests (Straker et al., 2015). A recent review only found research articles of apparently low research quality and no studies using virtual reality equipment (Mentiplay et al., 2019). Nevertheless, a very recent study revealed that Wii-Fit and Xbox Kinect improved motor performance by 35% in the comparison children and by 76% in children with DCD (Jelsma, Cavalcante Neto, et al., 2023). Both accuracy and response times were significantly improved and transferred to non-trained tasks

(Jelsma et al., 2023). Thus, this is ongoing research, but it seems that there is some optimism allowed that also in DCD, training and practice can make a difference.

References

Adams, I. L., Ferguson, G. D., Lust, J. M., Steenbergen, B., & Smits-Engelsman, B. C. (2016). Action planning and position sense in children with developmental coordination disorder. *Human Movement Science, 46*, 196–208. https://doi.org/10.1016/j.humov.2016.01.006

Adams, I. L., Lust, J. M., Wilson, P. H., & Steenbergen, B. (2014). Compromised motor control in children with DCD: A deficit in the internal model?—A systematic review. *Neuroscience & Biobehavioral Reviews, 47*, 225–244. https://doi.org/10.1016/j.neubiorev.2014.08.011

Al-Yahya, E., Esser, P., Weedon, B. D., Joshi, S., Liu, Y. C., Springett, D. N., Salvan, P., Meaney, A., Collett, J., Inacio, M., Delextrat, A., Kemp, S., Ward, T., Izadi, H., Johansen-Berg, H., Ayaz, H., & Dawes, H. (2023). Motor learning in developmental coordination disorder: Behavioral and neuroimaging study. *Frontiers in Neuroscience, 17*, article 1187790. https://doi.org/10.3389/fnins.2023.1187790

Badre, D., & Wagner, A. D. (2007). Left ventrolateral prefrontal cortex and the cognitive control of memory. *Neuropsychologia, 45*(13), 2883–2901. https://doi.org/10.1016/j.neuropsychologia.2007.06.015

Beery, K. E. (2004). *Beery VMI: The Beery-Buktenica developmental test of visual-motor integration*. Pearson.

Berninger, V. W., Vaughan, K. B., Abbott, R. D., Abbott, S. P., Rogan, L. W., Brooks, A., Reed, E., & Graham, S. (1997). Treatment of handwriting problems in beginning writers: Transfer from handwriting to composition. *Journal of Educational Psychology, 89*(4), 652–666. https://doi.org/10.1037/0022-0663.89.4.652

Bhoyroo, R., Hands, B., Wilmut, K., Hyde, C., & Wigley, A. (2019). Motor planning with and without motor imagery in children with developmental coordination disorder. *Acta Psychologica, 199*, article 102902. https://doi.org/10.1016/j.actpsy.2019.102902

Bieber, E., Smits-Engelsman, B. C. M., Sgandurra, G., Cioni, G., Feys, H., Guzzetta, A., & Klingels, K. (2016). Manual function outcome measures in children with developmental coordination disorder (DCD): Systematic review. *Research in Developmental Disabilities, 55*, 114–131. https://doi.org/10.1016/j.ridd.2016.03.009

Biotteau, M., Danna, J., Baudou, É., Puyjarinet, F., Velay, J. L., Albaret, J. M., & Chaix, Y. (2019). Developmental coordination disorder and dysgraphia: Signs and symptoms, diagnosis, and rehabilitation. *Neuropsychiatric Disease and Treatment, 15*, 1873–1885. https://doi.org/10.2147/ndt.S120514

Bondi, D., Robazza, C., Lange-Küttner, C., & Pietrangelo, T. (2022). Fine motor skills and motor control networking in developmental age. *American Journal of Human Biology, 34*(8), article e23758. https://doi.org/10.1002/ajhb.23758

Bonifacci, P. (2004). Children with low motor ability have lower visual-motor integration ability but unaffected perceptual skills. *Human Movement Science, 23*(2), 157–168. https://doi.org/10.1016/j.humov.2004.08.002

Brown, T., & Lalor, A. (2009). The movement assessment battery for children—Second edition (MABC-2): A review and critique. *Physical & Occupational Therapy in Pediatrics, 29*(1), 86–103. https://doi.org/10.1080/01942630802574908

Cairney, J., Hay, J. A., Veldhuizen, S., Missiuna, C., & Faught, B. E. (2010). Developmental coordination disorder, sex, and activity deficit over time: A longitudinal analysis of participation trajectories in children with and without coordination difficulties. *Developmental Medicine & Child Neurology, 52*(3), e67–72. https://doi.org/10.1111/j.1469-8749.2009.03520.x

Chang, S. H., & Yu, N. Y. (2014). The effect of computer-assisted therapeutic practice for children with handwriting deficit: A comparison with the effect of the traditional sensorimotor approach. *Resarch in Developmental Disabilities, 35*(7), 1648–1657. https://doi.org/10.1016/j.ridd.2014.03.024

Chen, M. J., & Cook, M. (1984). Representational drawings of solid objects by young children. *Perception, 13*(4), 377–385. https://doi.org/10.1068/p130377

Day, B. L., & Fitzpatrick, R. C. (2005). The vestibular system. *Current Biology, 15*(15), R583–R586. https://doi.org/10.1016/j.cub.2005.07.053

De Francesco, S., Morello, L., Fioravanti, M., Cassaro, C., Grazioli, S., Busti Ceccarelli, S., Nobile, M., Molteni, M., & Crippa, A. (2023). A multimodal approach can identify specific motor profiles in autism and attention-deficit/hyperactivity disorder. *Autism Research, 16*(8), 1550–1560. https://doi.org/10.1002/aur.2989

De Renzi, E., Pieczuro, A., & Vignolo, L. (1966). Oral apraxia and aphasia. *Cortex: A Journal Devoted to the Study of the Nervous System and Behavior, 2*(1), 50–73. https://doi.org/10.1016/S0010-9452%2866%2980028-X

Doney, R., Lucas, B. R., Watkins, R. E., Tsang, T. W., Sauer, K., Howat, P., Latimer, J., Fitzpatrick, J. P., Oscar, J., Carter, M., & Elliott, E. J. (2016). Visual-motor integration, visual perception, and fine motor coordination in a population of children with high levels of fetal alcohol spectrum disorder. *Research in Developmental Disabilities, 55*, 346–357. https://doi.org/10.1016/j.ridd.2016.05.009

Edwards, J., Berube, M., Erlandson, K., Haug, S., Johnstone, H., Meagher, M., Sarkodee-Adoo, S., & Zwicker, J. G. (2011). Developmental coordination disorder in school-aged children born very preterm and/or at very low birth weight: A systematic review. *Journal of Developmental & Behavioral Pediatrics, 32*(9), 678–687. https://doi.org/10.1097/DBP.0b013e31822a396a

Gibbs, J., Appleton, J., & Appleton, R. (2007). Dyspraxia or developmental coordination disorder? Unravelling the enigma. *Archives of Disease in Childhood, 96*(6), 534–539. http://dx.doi.org/10.1136/adc.2005.088054

Hagler, D. J., & Sereno, M. I. (2006). Spatial maps in frontal and prefrontal cortex. *Neuroimage, 29*(2), 567–577. https://doi.org/10.1016/j.neuroimage.2005.08.058

Hentschel, M., Averbeck, B. B., & Lange-Küttner, C. (2022). The role of IQ and social skills in coping with uncertainty in 7- to 11-year-old children. *Zeitschrift fur Entwicklungspsychologie und Padagogische Psychologie, 54*(3), 105–123. https://doi.org/10.1026/0049-8637/a000256

Hentschel, M., Averbeck, B. B., & Lange-Küttner, C. (2023). The difference an explanation makes: Verbal debrief effects when children cope with uncertainty. *Cognitive Development, 66*, article 101317. https://doi.org/10.1016/j.cogdev.2023.101317

Howie, E. K., Campbell, A. C., Abbott, R. A., & Straker, L. M. (2017). Understanding why an active video game intervention did not improve motor skill and physical activity in children with developmental coordination disorder: A quantity or quality issue? *Research in Developmental Disabilities, 60*(2), 1–12. https://doi.org/10.1016/j.ridd.2016.10.013

Howie, E. K., Campbell, A. C., & Straker, L. M. (2016). An active video game intervention does not improve physical activity and sedentary time of children at-risk for developmental coordination disorder: A crossover randomized trial. *Child: Care, Health and Development*, *42*(2), 253–260. https://doi.org/10.1111/cch.12305

Hulme, C., & Lord, R. (1986). Clumsy children—A review of recent research. *Child: Care, Health and Development*, *12*(4), 257–269. https://doi.org/10.1111/j.1365-2214.1986.tb00505.x

Jelsma, L. D., Cavalcante Neto, J. L., Smits-Engelsman, B., Targino Gomes Draghi, T., Araújo Rohr, L., & Tudella, E. (2023). Type of active video-games training does not impact the effect on balance and agility in children with and without developmental coordination disorder: A randomized comparator-controlled trial. *Applied Neuropsychology: Child*, *12*(1), 64–73. https://doi.org/10.1080/21622965.2022.2030740

Jelsma, L. D., Targino Gomes Draghi, T., Cavalcante Neto, J., & Smits-Engelsman, B. (2023). Improved attentional abilities after playing five weeks of active video games in children with and without developmental coordination disorder. *Applied Neuropsychology: Child*, 1–9. https://doi.org/10.1080/21622965.2023.2190024

Johnston, D., Branton, E., Rasmuson, L., Schell, S., Gross, D. P., & Pritchard-Wiart, L. (2019). Accuracy of motor assessment in the diagnosis of fetal alcohol spectrum disorder. *BMC Pediatrics*, *19*(1), article 171. https://doi.org/10.1186/s12887-019-1542-3

Lange-Küttner, C. (1998). Pressure, velocity and time in speeded drawing of basic graphic patterns by young children. *Perceptual and Motor Skills*, *86*(3, Pt 2), 1299–1310. https://doi.org/10.2466/pms.1998.86.3c.1299

Lange-Küttner, C. (2008). Size and contour as crucial parameters in children drawing images. In H.-M. Trautner & C. Milbrath (Eds.), *Children's understanding and production of pictures, drawings, and art: Theoretical and empirical approaches* (pp. 89–106). Hogrefe & Huber Publishers US.

Lange-Küttner, C., Averbeck, B. B., Hentschel, M., & Baumbach, J. (2021). Intelligence matters for stochastic feedback processing during sequence learning in adolescents and young adults. *Intelligence*, *86*, article 101542. https://doi.org/10.1016/j.intell.2021.101542

Lange-Küttner, C., Averbeck, B. B., Hirsch, S. V., Wiesner, I., & Lamba, N. (2012). Sequence learning under uncertainty in children: Self-reflection vs. self-assertion. *Frontiers in Psychology*, *3*, article 127. https://doi.org/10.3389/fpsyg.2012.00127

Lange-Küttner, C., Collins, C. L., Ahmed, R. K., & Fisher, L. E. (2023). Rich and sparse figurative information in children's memory for colorful places. *Developmental Psychology*, *59*(2), 256–271. https://doi.org/10.1037/dev0001483

Lawerman, T. F., Brandsma, R., Maurits, N. M., Martinez-Manzanera, O., Verschuuren-Bemelmans, C. C., Lunsing, R. J., Brouwer, O. F., Kremer, H. P., & Sival, D. A. (2020). Paediatric motor phenotypes in early-onset ataxia, developmental coordination disorder, and central hypotonia. *Developmental Medicine & Child Neurology*, *62*(1), 75–82. https://doi.org/10.1111/dmcn.14355

Levy, B. J., & Wagner, A. D. (2011). Cognitive control and right ventrolateral prefrontal cortex: Reflexive reorienting, motor inhibition, and action updating. *Annals of the New York Academy of Sciences*, *1224*(1), 40–62. https://doi.org/10.1111/j.1749-6632.2011.05958.x

Mentiplay, B. F., FitzGerald, T. L., Clark, R. A., Bower, K. J., Denehy, L., & Spittle, A. J. (2019). Do video game interventions improve motor outcomes in children with developmental coordination disorder? A systematic review using the ICF framework. *BMC Pediatrics*, *19*(1), 22. https://doi.org/10.1186/s12887-018-1381-7

Miall, R. C., & Wolpert, D. M. (1996). Forward models for physiological motor control. *Neural Networks, 9*(8), 1265–1279. https://doi.org/10.1016/S0893-6080(96)00035-4

Milne, S. C., Roberts, M., Ross, H. L., Robinson, A., Grove, K., Modderman, G., Williams, S., Chua, J., Grootendorst, A. C., Massey, L., Szmulewicz, D. J., Delatycki, M. B., & Corben, L. A. (2023). Interrater reliability of the scale for the assessment and rating of ataxia, Berg Balance Scale, and functional independence measure motor domain in individuals with hereditary cerebellar ataxia. *Archives of Physical Medicine and Rehabilitation*. https://doi.org/10.1016/j.apmr.2023.05.003

O'Dea, Á., Stanley, M., Coote, S., & Robinson, K. (2021). Children and young people's experiences of living with developmental coordination disorder/dyspraxia: A systematic review and meta-ethnography of qualitative research. *PLoS One, 16*(3), article e0245738. https://doi.org/10.1371/journal.pone.0245738

O'Hare, A. E., & Brown, J. K. (1989a). Childhood dysgraphia. Part 1. An illustrated clinical classification. *Child: Care, Health and Development, 15*(2), 79–104. https://doi.org/10.1111/j.1365-2214.1989.tb00606.x

O'Hare, A. E., & Brown, J. K. (1989b). Childhood dysgraphia. Part 2. A study of hand function. *Child: Care, Health and Development, 15*(3), 151–166. https://doi.org/10.1111/j.1365-2214.1989.tb00612.x

Overvelde, A., & Hulstijn, W. (2011). Handwriting development in grade 2 and grade 3 primary school children with normal, at risk, or dysgraphic characteristics. *Research in Developmental Disabilities, 32*(2), 540–548. https://doi.org/10.1016/j.ridd.2010.12.027

Piek, J. P., Dyck, M. J., Francis, M., & Conwell, A. (2007). Working memory, processing speed, and set-shifting in children with developmental coordination disorder and attention-deficit-hyperactivity disorder. *Developmental Medicine & Child Neurology, 49*(9), 678–683. https://doi.org/10.1111/j.1469-8749.2007.00678.x

Prunty, M. M., Barnett, A. L., Wilmut, K., & Plumb, M. S. (2013). Handwriting speed in children with developmental coordination disorder: Are they really slower? *Research in Developmental Disabilities, 34*(9), 2927–2936. https://doi.org/10.1016/j.ridd.2013.06.005

Sakagami, M., & Pan, X. (2007). Functional role of the ventrolateral prefrontal cortex in decision making. *Current Opinion in Neurobiology, 17*(2), 228–233. https://doi.org/10.1016/j.conb.2007.02.008

Schoemaker, M. M., Lingam, R., Jongmans, M. J., van Heuvelen, M. J., & Emond, A. (2013). Is severity of motor coordination difficulties related to co-morbidity in children at risk for developmental coordination disorder? *Research in Developmental Disabilities, 34*(10), 3084–3091. https://doi.org/10.1016/j.ridd.2013.06.028

Schott, N., El-Rajab, I., & Klotzbier, T. (2016). Cognitive-motor interference during fine and gross motor tasks in children with developmental coordination disorder (DCD). *Research in Developmental Disabilities, 57*, 136–148. https://doi.org/10.1016/j.ridd.2016.07.003

Steenbergen, B., Krajenbrink, H., Lust, J., & Wilson, P. (2020). Motor imagery and action observation for predictive control in developmental coordination disorder. *Developmental Medicine & Child Neurology, 62*(12), 1352–1355. https://doi.org/10.1111/dmcn.14612

Straker, L., Howie, E., Smith, A., Jensen, L., Piek, J., & Campbell, A. (2015). A crossover randomised and controlled trial of the impact of active video games on motor coordination and perceptions of physical ability in children at risk of developmental coordination disorder. *Human Movement Science, 42*, 146–160. https://doi.org/10.1016/j.humov.2015.04.011

Strata, P. (2009). David Marr's theory of cerebellar learning: 40 years later. *Journal of Physiology, 587*(Pt 23), 5519–5520. https://doi.org/10.1113/jphysiol.2009.180307

Suggate, S., & Stoeger, H. (2017). Fine motor skills enhance lexical processing of embodied vocabulary: A test of the nimble-hands, nimble-minds hypothesis. *Quarterly Journal of Experimental Psychology, 70*(10), 2169–2187. https://doi.org/10.1080/17470218.2016.1227344

Tabatabaey-Mashadi, N., Sudirman, R., Khalid, P. I., & Lange-Küttner, C. (2015). Automated syntax analyses of drawing two tangent patterns in children with low and average handwriting ability. *Perceptual and Motor Skills, 120*(3), 865–894. https://doi.org/10.2466/24.10.PMS.120v15x1

Tsai, C. L., Chang, Y. K., Hung, T. M., Tseng, Y. T., & Chen, T. C. (2012). The neurophysiological performance of visuospatial working memory in children with developmental coordination disorder. *Developmental Medicine & Child Neurology, 54*(12), 1114–1120. https://doi.org/10.1111/j.1469-8749.2012.04408.x

Waber, D. P., Boiselle, E. C., Yakut, A. D., Peek, C. P., Strand, K. E., & Bernstein, J. H. (2021). Developmental Dyspraxia in children with learning disorders: Four-year experience in a referred sample. *Journal of Child Neurology, 36*(3), 210–221. https://doi.org/10.1177/0883073820966913

Wilmut, K., Brown, J. H., & Wann, J. P. (2007). Attention disengagement in children with developmental coordination disorder. *Disability & Rehabilitation, 29*(1), 47–55. https://doi.org/10.1080/09638280600947765

Wilson, P. H., Maruff, P., & Lum, J. (2003). Procedural learning in children with developmental coordination disorder. *Human Movement Science, 22*(4–5), 515–526. https://doi.org/10.1016/j.humov.2003.09.007

Wolpert, D. M., Miall, R. C., & Kawato, M. (1998). Internal models in the cerebellum. *Trends in Cognitive Sciences, 2*(9), 338–347. https://doi.org/10.1016/S1364-6613(98)01221-2

Zaragas, H., Fragkomichelaki, O., Geitona, M., Sofologi, M., Papantoniou, G., Sarris, D., Pliogou, V., Charmpatsis, C., & Papadimitropoulou, P. (2023). The effects of physical activity in children and adolescents with developmental coordination disorder. *Neurology International, 15*(3), 804–820. https://doi.org/10.3390/neurolint15030051

INDEX

3D 73, 79–80, 82, 109, 151, 186, 198

Abbott 59
Abrahamson 23
Accardo 180
Adams 197–198
Adi-Japha 83, 186
Adolph 21, 33; & Robinson 47, 58
Adorno 145
Alesi 111
Alfageh 188
Allen 86, 148
Allport 122
Alp 74
Al-Yahya 202
Amso 33, 106
Amsterdam 7
Anagnostou 188
Anderson 182
Andersson 82
Angell 65
A-not-B error 32–33, 36–38, 42–44, 48–49, 142
A-not-B task 9, 31, 33–34, 36–37, 39–40, 42, 44–46, 48–50, 73, 181
Ansorge 144
Anton-Erxleben 106
Aoki 181
Arce 106
Arden 81
Arnheim 73
array priming effect 135
Association-Dissociation-Association (ADA) 37
ataxia 196
attention deficit hyperactivity disorder (ADHD) 76, 125, 171–176, 181, 184–185, 197
Atkinson 38, 119, 125
attention network test 100
autism spectrum disorder (ASD) 73, 76, 87, 180–189, 197

Baddeley 25–26, 119, 139–140
Badre 202
Baillargeon 32, 33
Bainbridge 129
Baltes 44
Barlow 129
Baron-Cohen 73, 181–182, 184–185, 188
Barrouillet 122–123, 142
Bartlett 59, 87, 142
Bartsch 42
Bates 128
Battaglia-Mayer 38
Baylis 77
Beery 85, 196
Beery Visual Motor Integration Test (BVMI) 85
Beilei 85
Bell 40, 41
Bender 72, 175
Benear 119
Berger 45, 49
Berninger 198
Bhoyroo 198
Bieber 196
Biederman 81

binding 37–38, 42, 44, 66, 75–76, 129–130, 132–133, 135–136, 145, 147–149, 173–175, 184–185; object-place 37–38, 42–43, 50, 66, 75–76, 129–130, 132, 136, 145, 147–149, 151, 154, 174, 184–185; objects-region 66, 75–76, 129–130, 145, 148, 174, 184
Biotteau 198
Bird 133
Bjork 48–49
Bjorklund 122
Blades: & Spencer 140
Blanchette 150
block construction 84
Boere-Boonekamp 59
Bohbot 147
Bondi 64, 176, 198
Bonifacci 200
Bonoti 83
Booth 174
Bordignon 181
Boucher 181
boundaries 4, 11, 36, 65–66, 75–77, 109, 133–136, 139, 154, 176
Braddick 38, 125
Braswell 85
Bremner, A. & Bryant 44
Bremner, J. G. 4–6, 8, 32, 38, 44, 58; & Batten 81; & Bryant 44; & Dunn 33; & Moore 79
Brenneman 84
Briand 142
Broadbent 100
Brooke 133
Brooks 23
Brosnan 184
Brown 196–197
Bruck 129
Brückner 122
Bryant 44
Brynskov 180
Buchberger 183
Bullens 134
Bunge 150
Burack 107
Burgess 11, 37
Burk 72
Burkitt 80
Burnett Heyes 134
Butterbaugh 64
Butterfield 64–65
Butterworth 40–41; & Ingram 82

Caetano 65
Cairney 197
Caminiti 38
Camos 87, 122, 142
Campbell 83
Canfield 186
Cantrell 35
Canu 172
Caramazza 22
Carlson & Wang 144
Carpenter 101
Carr 128
Carrasco & Anton-Erxleben 106
Carruth 63
Castel 111, 142
Castellanos 172
Cavalcante Neto 203
Chadwick 149
Chamberlain 188
Chang 198
Chaplais 21
Charman 73, 188
Chen 82, 198
Chomsky 144, 148
Choo 151
Christidou 109
chunking 6, 25
Cieraad 59
Clark 72
classification 46
Clohessy 9
cognitive load 25, 108–109, 112, 142
Colombo 39
common region 50, 66, 75–76, 78, 129, 132, 136, 139, 154, 173–175, 184, 186
Common Region Test (CRT) 129, 147, 154, 173, 174, 184; CRT 75–77, 107, 129–130, 132–133, 135–136, 139, 145, 147–148, 154, 174–175, 184
Connelly 142
contrast 4, 25, 32, 38, 40–41, 43–44, 46, 64, 80, 84, 106, 123, 125, 136, 141–142, 144, 148–149, 150, 172, 175, 183, 198; luminance 122, 151; speech 21, 46, 187, 196, 203
Cook 198
Corter 33, 49
Cortese 173
Costall 72, 78
Cowan 5, 100, 120–121, 130; & Chen 133; & Hardman 120; & Vergauwe 120
Cox 77, 80–81; & Chapman 77
Crawford 45
Cronin 87
Crook 82
Cross 42
Csikszentmihalyi 7

Csink 33
Cuevas 41
Cummings 48–49
Cunnane 45
curvature 101–102, 107, 197

D Prime 121
Dalrymple 8
Daniels 122
Danziger 142
DAP test 87; DAP-IQ 87
Darby 109, 111
Davis 81, 186
Dawson 46, 181
Day 202
De Francesco 197
De Renzi 196
De Smedt 125
Deák 141
DeBolt 101
Dehaene 132
Dellal 65
Della Salla 142
Dellatolas 120
DeLoache 83, 151
DeMaster 141, 150
Dembo 12
Deregowski 79
Descartes 22
Desmottes 83
developmental coordination disorder (DCD) 172–173, 196–200, 201–203
Diamond 34–36, 38–39, 43, 46, 142
Dietze 139
Dillon 74
discrimination 46, 111, 153
distances 7, 11, 35, 49
Doney 196–197
Donnellan 183
Donnelly 106
Drake 73, 87, 188
Draschkow 108
drawing models 73, 78, 81, 198
Driver 44, 77
Dubravak 125
Duncan 76
Dunning 148
Dziurawiec 79

Ebersbach & Hagedorn 86, 89
Edgin 139
Edmiston 181
Edwards 79, 197
Elman 25, 176
Embedded Figures Test 106, 188
embodied cognition 4, 23
Eng 72
Enns 112
Enoch 101
equilibration regulation mechanism 147
Eriksen 77
Erickson 101
Erzinclioglu 83
exercise 64–65, 83, 150, 173
exploration 58
Eysenck & Keane 100

Faber 64
Fagard 48, 64
Fagen 8, 33; & Ohr 33
Falco 65
familiarity 41, 46, 89, 119
Faraone 171–172
Farran 128
Fechner 122
Fei-Fei 150
Fein 73
field theory 4, 11, 12, 35
Fiske 38
Fitzpatrick 202
Flapper 173
Flavell 152
Fodor 144–145, 148
Forsyth 45
Fournier 63
Francesco 197
Frazier 180
free movement 59
Freeman 20, 73–74, 81–83, 186; & Berti 82; & Janikoun 109
Friedman 147
Frith 180, 185
Fry 108
Fugate 23

Gabor model 151
Gaffan 152
Gallant 151
Gathercole 25, 148
Gelade 102–103
Geltner 132
Geman 176
George 142
Gerardi-Caulton 101
Gerhardstein 109
Gerstadt 18, 82
Gesell 3, 21
Gestalt 8, 61, 72, 75, 107, 130, 173–176, 184
G-factor 5

Ghanizadeh 174
Ghetti 150
Gibbs 196
Gibson 33, 61, 101–102, 104; & Jonas 102; & Walk 33
Gil-Gomez de Liano 108
Gimenez-Egido 65
Go-/No-go task 172
Gobet 23
Godden 139–140
Goh 132
Goldinger 22
Goldston 139
Goodenough 20, 72, 81
Goodnow 81; & Friedman 81; & Harris 81
Goswami 25
Grace 183
Grahn 172
Gray 100
Griffith 172
Grill-Spector 148
grouping 6, 25, 75, 107, 111, 129, 174, 176, 184–186
Guilbert 106, 130
Guiso 132
Gunia 152

Hafner 58
Hagen 77, 87
Hagler 202
Hakoda 174
Hale 108
Halpern 132
Happé 182–185
Harlow 46
Harris 43
Hartley 142
Hasher 142
Hawes 129
Hayhoe 151
Hayne 8, 81
Heller 57
Helsen 110
Hendricks 57
Hentschel 202
Hermelin 188
hierarchically competing systems 43, 47
Hieu 45
Hinchcliffe 61
Hirshhorn 142
Hirshman 33
Hitch 119–120, 125
Höfer 180
holistic 80–82, 141, 202
Holman 82
Holmes 148
horizon 80, 150, 151
Horkheimer 145
Horowitz L. M., 152–153
Horowitz T. S., 153
Howard 142
Howie 203
Hulme 171, 203
Hulstijn 198
Humphreys 44
Hund 125, 129, 135; & Spencer 125
Huttenlocher 145

Imuta 81
individual differences 34, 81, 125
Inhelder 72, 110, 118, 133, 144, 148, 152
interference 65, 121, 125–129, 133, 147, 200–201
intellectual realism 78, 186, 187
Ishihara 64
item-specific learning 122
Ittelson 78
Izard 7

Jaeggi 148
Jaensch 79
Jansen & Ziereis 173, 176
Jarrold 107, 180; & Tam 24, 142
Jelsma 203
Jensen 82
Johnson 3, 106
Johnson-Laird 3
Johnston 197
Jolley 83
Jones 18, 82, 180
Jung 64

Kail 24, 102, 119, 122, 125, 147; & Ferrer 125; & Miller 122; & Park 24, 119, 122
Kaiser 173
Kamienkowski 106, 153
Karmiloff-Smith 5, 24, 82, 86, 89, 144
Keehn 183
Kellogg 83
Kemler 80
Keppel 147
Kerschensteiner 72
Kieley 142
Kimura 132
King 151
Kirkham 36, 142
Klauer & Zhao 126
Kleberg 101
Klein 142, 172

Klin 181
Klingberg 148
Knauff 3, 12, 13
Koch 106
Konkle 118, 151
Koppitz 72
Kosslyn 74, 122, 128, 139
Krakowski 107
Kravitz 151
Kretch 49
Kuhl 181
Küttner 60, 81, 87, 108, 145–146, 148, 185

Lai 180
Lalor 196
Lamb 5
Lambez 173
Lampel 152
Lange-Küttner 6, 9, 13, 21–23, 25–26, 36, 40–48, 50, 61–62, 72–88, 101, 104–105, 107–111, 119, 122, 123–140, 142–146, 148–149, 151–153, 173–176, 180, 183–184, 186–188, 197, 199, 202; & Bechari-Martin 83, 119, 148–149; & Beringer 23; & Bosco 109, 111; & Chromekova 81, 87; & Crichton 6, 9, 21–22, 43, 48; & Ebersbach 81–82, 188; & Finn 25, 173; & Friederici 126; & Green 82, 125; & Kochhar 174–176, 184–185; & Krappmann 25–26; & Lütke 62, 105, 129; & Martin 119; & Puiu 101, 104; & Reith 73, 80, 110, 186; & Vinueza Chavez 79–80, 82, 151
Larson & Guggenheimer 65
Lavie 7
Lawerman 196
learning mechanism 46
Lee 140
Le-Hoa Võ 154
Leonard 182
Lescroart 151
Levine 132
Levy 202
Lew 40, 133–134
Lewin 11–12, 35, 43
Lewis 6, 77, 80
Li, A.-S. 103, 106
Li, J. 111
Liben 118, 140; & Myers 140
Lidzba 183
Light 75; & MacIntosh 75
Lin 85
Lindenberger 44, 85
Lindgren 23–24
Liotti 171
Lipina 45
Lipowska 174
Liu 144
Lobaugh 104–105
Lockman 64
Logan 13, 44, 76, 148
Logie 129, 142, 148
Lohaus 59
Longobardi 74
Longstaffe 142
Looft 109
Lord 203
Lövdén 85
Löwenfeld 74
Luchins 87
Luo 142
Luquet 72–73
Luria 121–122

Macfarlane 21
Mackintosh 41
Mackworth 101
MacNeill 39
MacPherson 142
Mandelbaum 180
Manly 126
mapping 25, 80, 118, 139, 141, 154, 183, 198
Marcovitch 33, 42–43, 47
Mareschal 38, 46
Marks 171
Martzog 84–85
Marzolf 151
Maurer 6, 85
McBride-Chang 84
McBurnett 172
McCleery 181
McClelland 141, 154
McDougle 180
McKague 25
McLeod 4
McMullen 106
mechanization of intelligence *see* mental set
Mecklinger & Meinshausen 126; & Müller 126; & Pfeifer 126
mental rotation 24, 84, 105, 122, 125, 128–129, 149, 152
mental set 87–88;
mental speed 4, 5, 24, 108, 149
Mentiplay 203
Merrill 108, 121; & Conners 111
meta-knowledge 83
Metzger 134, 140
Meulenbroek 82

Milbrath 87
Milne 196
Mink 180
Mishkin 37
Mitchell 183, 187
Mitchelmore 81
Miyake 147
modality 9, 25–27, 100, 119, 121
Moll 152
Moller & Bogels 33; & Majdandzic 33
Montangero 84
Moon 181
Moore 74, 81
Morra 16–20, 73–75, 81; & Panesi 18–20, 74–75, 83
motor memory 8, 43; motor response memory 43
Mottron 183
Mounoud 85
Movement Assessment Battery for Children (MABC-2) 196
Mullane 172
multiple object tracking 148–149
Munakata 45–47; & Shinskey 32–33, 47
Murre 38
Muth 182

Naglieri 81, 87; & Ronning 81
Nakamura 59
Narizuka 65
Navon 107
Neisser 101; & Dirks 152
Neudecker 173
neural activity 148
Nevill 110
Neville 65
Newcombe 145, 152
Newell 65
Nieuwenhuys 181
Nobre & Stokes 100; & Shimi 123
Nordahl 181
Nurmi 82
Nybakken 65

O'Dea 197
Oberer 64
object concept 4–5, 31, 89
object perception 172
object permanence 31–32, 37, 43–44
obstacles 10–11, 36, 49
Ochsner 144
Ofen 152–153
Ogilvie 110
Ogino 89
O'Hare 197
Olson 133
O'Reilly & Rudy 141, 154
O'Riordan 182
Orlian 123
Ose Askvik 173
Oseretzky 57
Ossmy 63–64
Oudejans 110
Oudgenoeg-Paz 59, 61
Overvelde 198
Owen Blakemore 132
Ozonoff 183

Palmer 75, 184
Palmis 84
Pan 202–203
Pannevis 122
Park 144
Pascual-Leone 16–18, 176; & Case 17; & Goodman 16
Pathman 118
Patterson 83
Paul 181
Paynter 180
Pearson 129
Peers 65
Perona 150
perseveration 36, 142
Peters 125
Peterson 180, 182
Philbin 151
Piaget 3–11, 16, 18, 21, 23, 31–36, 47–48, 58, 72, 80, 85, 110, 118, 133, 140, 144–145, 148, 152, 176
Piatelli-Palmarini 144
Picard 86, 89
Pickering 120, 125
Piek 202
Pierce 60
Pinto 148–149
place 9, 13, 22, 31–32, 36–38, 40–41, 43–44, 46–48, 59, 75–76, 109–112, 126, 128–130, 132, 134–136, 139–142, 144–145, 147–149, 152–154, 173, 184–185
playpen 58–61
Plumert 129, 135
Plunkett 25
Poincaré 5
Polk 65
Pomaranski 11
Popick 46–47
Porayska-Pomsta 189
Porter 57
Portrat 123
Posner 31, 100, 135, 142; & Raichle 31, 135

practice 5, 27, 41–42, 46, 48, 59, 83, 87, 139, 144, 147–148, 181, 188, 203
Pratt 142
Priewasser 111
priming 103, 135, 139, 141, 148
Pring 187–188
proactive-interference 147
Prunty 202
Pylyshyn 128, 130, 149; & Storm 149

Quaglia 80

Rachwani 58
Rader 33
Rao 125
Ratuski 61
Raven 105–106, 185
realism: failed 34, 73, 186; fortuitous 73, 186; incidental 10, 73, 186; intellectual 48, 57, 64, 73, 78, 81, 186, 187; visual 73, 80, 186–188
Redder 6
refreshing 87; attentional 87; mental 87
Reith & Dominin 80, 186
repetition 4, 18, 24, 41, 43, 45, 87–88, 141–142, 145, 147–149, 172, 201; anti-repetition bias 142; attentional loops 142; inhibition of return 9, 142; micro- and macrogenetic memory improvements 148
representational redescription (RR) 5, 145
Rescorla 21
Richards 33
Richardson 125
Richman 139
Riggio 142
Riggs 83
Robertson 126
Robinson 174, 188
Rochat 3
Roebers & Maurer 6, 85
Rogoff 152
Ropar 183, 187
Rose, D. H. 88
Rose, S. A. 123
Rosenbaum, D. A. 61, 64
Rosenbaum, J. 60
Rosengren 85
Ross 83
rote learning 25, 118, 147
Rothbart 100–101
Rovee-Collier 8, 104, 151; & Borovsky 8; & Dufault 8; & Gerhardstein 104, 109
Rovegno 65
Rückriegel 85
Rueda 101
Ruffman & Ahmed 34
Rutishauser 106

Sailer & Homner 111
Sakagami 202–203
Samuel 142
Sarafino 59
Scarborough 62
scene 22, 80, 89, 104, 118, 139, 149, 151–154
Scerif 123
Schillaci 58
Schmidt 64–65
Schneider 130
Schoemaker 196
Schott 198, 199, 201
Schulz 172
Schumann-Hengsteler 125
Seccareccia-DeClerico 65
Seernani 172
selective optimisation with compensation 44
self 5–8, 36, 60, 65, 103, 108, 135, 151, 181; just-me 7; knowing oneself 7; not-me 7; part-of-me 7
Selfe 73, 187
Sereno 202
set size 35, 103, 107–108, 112, 121–122, 149
Shalev 176
Shen 181
Shiffrin 119
Shimi 123
Siegal & Surian 181
Siegel 57
Siegler 42; & Crowley 4
Silverman 132
Simmons 183
Simpson 20
simulation 18, 46, 47
Singer 57
size 11, 78; habitual 9, 63, 78
Smith 4, 21, 40, 43, 57, 144, 201
Snowling 171
Soepnel 57
Sommer 135
Song 174
space 5–11, 13, 23–24, 31–32, 34, 36–37, 44, 59–60, 72–73, 75–80, 82, 85, 89, 110, 129–130, 133–136, 140, 144, 151, 154, 184; Euclidian 134, 140; negative 80; objective 5, 8–10, 31, 34–38; practical 4–6, 9–10, 31, 35–36, 48;

subjective 5–6, 8–10, 31–32, 34, 36; topological 11, 35, 134
space concept 10, 23, 31, 72, 133–134
Sparaci 189
spatial array 41, 133, 135, 142, 151, 176, 200, 201
spatial axes 77–79, 82, 133–134, 151
spatial boundaries 66, 133, 135
spatial conflict 100, 101
spatial constraints 59
spatial encoding 4, 133, 135; allocentric 3–4, 11, 36–37; egocentric 3, 6, 11, 32, 36–37; object-based 76; object-centred 43; object-place 75, 185; space-based 13, 44, 76, 79, 130; space-centred 43
spatial field 3, 5–6, 9, 11–13, 21–22, 31, 35–38, 40–43, 46, 48, 58, 61, 65, 106–107, 110, 125, 129, 134, 171, 182–183; zones 11–12, 35–36
Spatial Field Model 38–39, 185
Spatial Freedom Theory 130, 132, 139, 154
Spatial Model 135, 144, 154
speed of processing 148
Spelke 32, 132–133; & Lee 133, 140
Spence & Wu 111, 181
Spencer 125
St. John 181, 183
Stansbury 151
Starch 72
Steenbergen 198
Stetsenko 73
Stiles & Tada 140
Stoeger 198
Straker 203
stranger anxiety 46
Strata 196
Su 182
Suárez-Pellicioni 125
Suggate 198
Sully 72
Sutton 88

Tabatabaey-Mashadi 82, 85–86, 196–197
Targino Gomes Draghi 203
Tarrasch 109
Taylor 106
Tham 8
Thelen 4, 21, 44; & Fisher 21
Theory of Constructive Operators 16
theory of mind 180–182
Thomas, B. A. 45
Thomas, G. V. 72–73; & Silk 81
Thomson 139
Tofler 64
Tomasello 152
Toomela 84
Torres 183
Towse 119, 125
trade-off 46
transfer 24, 27, 40–42, 122, 149, 189
Trautner 84
Treisman 13, 38, 44, 100, 102–103; & Zhang 130
Tresch 126
Trick 112
Tripp 174
Tryphon 84
Tsai 200, 201
Tsal 176
Tse 84, 122
Tulving 139
Tyler 132

Underwood 147
Ungerleider 37
Uttal 80, 130, 140, 147–148; & Chiong 130, 147; & Davies 140

Valenza 9
van der Linden-Kuiper 59
van Koppen 132
Van Sommers 73, 87
Van Swieten 64
vectors 12, 140
Vilar 65
Vinter 72–73, 84–86, 89, 107, 134, 142; & Chartrel 84; & Marot 134
visual field 6, 21–22, 40–41, 48, 75, 139, 154
visual memory 10, 66, 75, 77, 108, 118, 120–122, 125, 129, 133–134, 139, 142, 148, 154–155, 173–174, 176, 186
visual priority map 106
visual working memory 32, 119, 121
Volkelt 72
Vries 188

Waber 203
Waddell 152
Wagemans 188
Wagner 202
Walker 79
Wallin 57
Walther 151
Wass 189
Watanabe 89
Weiner 142
Wellman 42, 182
Wenger 85
Werchan 33

Wertheimer 75
West 150
Westendorp 64
what-and-where system: what-system 38, 126, 129; where-system 38, 125–126, 128–129, 188
White 6, 142
Wickens 43, 102
Wilding 50, 142; & Burke 142
Willats 72, 81, 83, 186
Willatts 45
Willcock 81
William 186
Williams 65–66, 186
Wilmut 200–201
Wilson 22, 201–202
Winkler-Rhoades 140
Winner 73, 87, 188
Winnicott 7
Wisconsin Card Sorting Test (WCST) 89
Wiseheart 141
Witkin 188
Wolfe 101, 104, 153–154
Wolpert 200–201; & Miall 201
Woods 106
working memory 83
Wright 149
Wu 181

Yang 108
Yeh 77
Yonas 101, 102, 104
Yonelinas 141
Yu 198

Zaragas 197
Zelazo 42, 43, 47
Zhang 130
Ziegler 25
Zimmer 130
Zmyj 34
Zupan 107